Energy Economics

Energy Economics

Science, Policy, and Economic Applications

Thomas R. Sadler

LEXINGTON BOOKS
Lanham • Boulder • New York • London

Published by Lexington Books
An imprint of The Rowman & Littlefield Publishing Group, Inc.
4501 Forbes Boulevard, Suite 200, Lanham, Maryland 20706
www.rowman.com

6 Tinworth Street, London SE11 5AL, United Kingdom

British Library Cataloguing in Publication Information Available

Library of Congress Control Number: 2019954883
ISBN 978-1-4985-8658-0 (cloth)
ISBN 978-1-4985-8660-3 (pbk.)
ISBN 978-1-4985-8659-7 (electronic)

Contents

List of Figures, Tables, and Examples

FIGURES

TABLES

EXAMPLES

Acknowledgments

In writing this book, I've benefitted from the help, guidance, and encouragement of many people. First, I'd like to thank my colleagues in the Department of Economics and Decision Sciences at Western Illinois University. They encouraged me to present this material in department seminars and asked questions throughout the writing process. Second, I'd like to thank my editor at Lexington Books, Joseph Parry, who was interested in the book idea during our first meeting and offered guidance in the months that followed. Third, I'd like to thank the readers. I hope this book offers a fair treatment of the evolving field of energy economics. Finally, I'd like to thank my family—Holly, Maya, and Mathew—who are my love and inspiration. This book and all of my work is for you.

Part 1

FUNDAMENTALS OF ENERGY ECONOMICS

Chapter 1

Introduction to Energy Economics

A NEW ENERGY LANDSCAPE

Since the beginning of this century, energy markets have experienced tremendous change. The reasons are both new market realities and unforeseen events. Surging more than 80 percent in ten years, for example, oil production in the United States exceeded 10 million barrels per day in November 2017. The previous record was 9.63 million in 1970. Evolving technologies augmented by rising prices transformed the country's petroleum outlook. Today, producers operate efficiently and precisely in designing and operating their wells. Amid steady demand, companies in the United States are exporting oil, a possibility unthinkable when the surge began.

But natural gas has strengthened the energy position of the United States even more than oil. In 2017, for the first time in sixty years, the country became a net exporter of natural gas. The global market for natural gas provides a resource that is cleaner—as measured by carbon content—than oil. Advanced methods of extraction will keep natural gas on the world's energy forefront.

Meanwhile, for the first time, *renewable energy resources*—those that maintain indefinite flows—account for a majority of the world's new electricity-generating capacity. In 2015, more than half of the $286 billion invested worldwide in solar, wind, and other renewables occurred in emerging markets such as Brazil, China, and India (United Nations Environmental Program, 2016). From 2009 to 2015, the average cost of generating electricity decreased by 61 percent for solar panels and 14 percent for land-based wind turbines. These trends mean developers of solar and wind farms will eventually offer electricity for less than the average per unit price of electricity generated by all sources.

Even natural disasters played a role. On March 11, 2011, at 2:46 in the afternoon, Japan time, 17 miles below the ocean's surface, pressure between tectonic plates created an upward force that set off one of the most powerful earthquakes ever recorded. Fifty minutes later, a tsunami unleashed by the earthquake pounded the Japanese coast, resulting in damage to buildings, infrastructure, and the power system. As waves crashed and buildings fell, 80,000 people evacuated, but 20,000 drowned. One-hundred-and-seventy miles north of Tokyo, three active nuclear reactors at the Fukushima Daiichi Nuclear Power Station on the island's edge suffered meltdowns. The tsunami knocked out the power and then flooding disabled the backup generators, which were in place to maintain the cooling system. After the natural disaster compromised the integrity of the nuclear facilities, explosions and fires cracked the containment vessel in at least one reactor, leading to the release of radioactive gases. The hot nuclear reactors were deprived of the cooling water required to keep them under control. In the following days, explosions damaged the plant, radiation was released, and a meltdown of nuclear rods occurred. This nuclear disaster, the worst in twenty-five years, incited a global response: Germany, for example, vowed to close all of its nuclear power plants.

These market realities and unforeseen events demonstrate the importance of the field of energy economics. Energy not only powers the global economy but also facilitates our daily lives. We need safe and reliable energy systems to heat and cool our homes and buildings, fuel our transportation systems, and satisfy our demand for electricity. In the future, the provision of clean energy will be crucial to help balance the world's needs for both economic growth and environmental quality.

This book explains energy systems from an economics perspective. Specifically, the book uses the tools of economics to analyze the development of modern energy systems, the world's reliance on fossil fuels, and the components of a transition to cleaner energy resources. But as the book's title makes clear, the book also considers the science underlying important energy issues, especially with respect to nuclear energy and the climate crisis. In addition, a chapter on energy policy makes clear how properly crafted incentives provide a framework for a clean energy future.

Throughout the book, an economic analysis of the environmental implications of our energy choices occurs. For example, the air pollution in many metropolitan areas that results from fossil fuel consumption is getting worse, especially in large cities such as Zingtai—an extremely polluted city in China—Delhi, Jakarta, and many others. At the global level, climate change, which results from our current energy consumption patterns, threatens to permanently alter weather systems, ocean levels, and patterns of human settlement. These problems are made more acute by global population growth. An increase in the demand for energy will continue for decades. Without changes to our fossil fuel consumption patterns, the increase in demand for energy will exacerbate environmental problems.

These realities demonstrate the importance of an economic analysis of primary energy sources, energy supply and demand, and energy systems. The book's thesis is that energy matters are fundamental to our way of life. Yet, when it comes to energy economics, many people do not have a working vocabulary. So in addition to providing an academic treatment of the field of energy economics, this book fills that void.

GLOBAL TRENDS

The global economy relies on fossil fuels. Fossil fuels are combustible organic materials, such as coal, oil, and natural gas, derived from the remains of former plant life. A variety of technologies extract and produce fossil fuels and other energy resources, convert them into usable forms, and deliver the product to end users. The interconnectedness between energy sectors such as transportation, power generation, and manufacturing highlights the need to understand global trends in population, changes in gross domestic product (GDP), energy sources, electricity production, and carbon emissions—an important byproduct of the burning of fossil fuels.

The United Nations Population Fund picked October 31, 2011, as the best estimate of the day when global population reached 7 billion. It's a coincidence that this was Halloween in the United States. But it took humanity a long time to reach the milestone. Ten thousand years ago, 5 million people lived on the planet. Two thousand years ago, the world's population reached 200 million. In the seventeenth century, global population more than doubled to 500 million people. But the next doubling took less than two centuries, from 1650 to 1800. At this time, Thomas Malthus (1798) famously published *An Essay on the Principle of Population*, warning of the grave dangers of over-population. In 1960, the world reached 3 billion. By the end of 1999, world population was 6 billion. The United Nation's forecast for 2050 is almost 10 billion. Individuals born at the beginning of this century, therefore, may expect global population to rise more than 50 percent during their lifetimes.

The key to understanding the population trend is the specific nature of change. During the first half of this century, four global megatrends will develop (Goldstone, 2010):

- Population growth in developing countries
- Smaller demographic weight of developed countries

- Aging pains in the developed world
- Urbanization

Of the additional 2 to 3 billion people that will consume energy resources by the middle of this century, more than 90 percent will be born in developing countries. The United Nations Population Division reports that out of a world population of 7.7 billion in 2019, 60 percent reside in Asia (4.5 billion) and 16 percent in Africa (1.2 billion). Throughout this century, these two continents will experience the highest absolute levels of population growth.

At the beginning of the twentieth century, the combined populations of the United States, Canada, and Europe accounted for 21 percent of the world's inhabitants, producing more than 32 percent of the world's GDP (Goldstone, 2010). Living conditions in these areas reflected the most modern social, political, and economic systems. But after World War I, as healthcare systems improved, people in other parts of the world, including Africa, Asia, and Latin America, experienced longer lifespans.

Today, the combined populations of the United States, Canada, and Europe account for 17 percent of the world's inhabitants and 47 percent of the world's GDP. By 2050, these percentages are expected to decline. Moving forward, most of the world's economic growth will occur outside of the United States, Canada, and Europe.

The economic powerhouses of the United States and the European Union, plus China, Canada, Japan, and South Korea, are becoming older societies. According to Goldstone (2010), in 2050, 40 percent of Japanese and South Koreans and 30 percent of the people living in the United States, Canada, China, and Europe will be older than sixty. In these countries, labor force participation will decline. In many cases, less than two workers will exist for every non-working citizen.

In 2008, the world reached a milestone: for the first time in history, half the world's population lived in urban areas. In historical context, the trend of *urbanization*—an increasing percentage of the population living in cities and suburbs—is amazing. As of 1950, less than 30 percent of the world's people lived in urban areas. By 2050, according to projections of the United Nations Population Division, 70 percent of the world's population will live in urban areas. For the next few decades, almost all of the world's population growth will occur in cities.

What are the energy implications of these population megatrends? The most important implications relate to both population growth in developing countries and urbanization. The reason is that, during the process of economic development, countries consume higher levels of resource inputs, including energy. At the same time, higher levels of urbanization decrease the demand for energy resources. The relative impact of these two effects depends on economic development, income distribution, and the consumption of energy.

Economies in developing countries with small levels of capital stock—machines, equipment, and factories—initially achieve higher levels of economic growth, increasing both their capital stock and demand for energy. But as these economies increase the provision of service industries, both technological and production changes occur. Technological change leads to greater efficiency in energy resources. This effect tempers rising demand for energy. With the mix of output, developing economies shift from agriculture to industry and then to services and lighter manufacturing. Over time, this process decreases energy use per unit of output.

Urbanization decreases energy consumption per capita, but leads to modernization, migration, and structural transformation. Population density increases. Buildings and transportation systems acquire more efficient energy profiles. Eventually, as cities modernize, they update power plants, transmission lines, and systems of energy distribution.

But the impact of urbanization on energy consumption is not homogeneous. It depends on a country's level of development. In an article published in the journal *Ecological Economics*, Poumanyvong and Kaneko (2010) provide the reason: in low income countries, the process of urbanization leads to the reduction of energy consumption as residents substitute modern fuels and methods for traditional practices. In middle- and high-income countries, urbanization increases the use of energy resources, because of an increase in the demand for goods and services.

These trends demonstrate that urbanization in developing countries may partially offset the increase in demand for energy resources that occurs with population growth. What are the energy policy implications? Energy policy must attempt to balance the needs for job creation, consumption of more energy resources, and environmental protection. When both population and economic growth increase air and water pollution, cities experience undesirable health outcomes. Beijing in China is a case in point with its high levels of air pollution and lung-related illnesses.

Energy policy may reduce polluting emissions, conserve energy, and increase energy efficiency. But job creation may serve as a country's highest priority. Therefore, efficiency upgrades to power stations, the incorporation of large-scale and cleaner urban mass transit systems, and full-scale investment in alternative energy sources such as hydropower, geothermal, solar, and wind may mitigate harmful environmental consequences and create economic opportunities.

A NEW AGE OF GLOBALIZATION

The production of output requires energy inputs. The relationship between economic production and energy reveals an important reality: since the mid-1800s, the consumption of every major energy source has increased at nearly the rate of global economic growth. Throughout the twentieth century, the global economy was fueled by the burning of oil for trains and vehicles and the burning of coal for factories and power plants.

Fossil fuels meet 80 percent of global energy demand (IEA, 2017a). But the environmental risks associated with additional oil exploration are high. The 2010 BP oil spill and the controversy of extracting tar sands in Canada serve as important examples. Geopolitical challenges such as instability and revolution in the Middle East will continue to attract the world's attention, because of the variability of the supply of oil from the region.

According to John S. Avery (2007) of the University of Copenhagen, the current fossil fuel era will continue for more than a century. But that's a lot of time to pollute the planet. Assuming current production rates for fossil fuels, the world will continue to supply coal, oil, and natural gas for decades. The discovery of new oil wells, natural gas deposits, and coal seams will continue, especially in the Arctic Ocean, central Asia, and the South China Sea. In the South China Sea, 60 billion barrels of petroleum reserves have been identified with tens of billions yet to be discovered.

At the same time, fossil fuel consumption continues to rise. Advances are occurring in the current era of *globalization*, which refers to the widening and deepening interconnections between the world's people through all forms of exchange. As transplanetary processes both strengthen the world's networks of exchange and enhance the flow of goods, services, technology, information, capital, and migration; energy is becoming an even more important global resource. Consider three examples. By 2008, in Beijing, 1,000 new cars were added to the roads each day (Fan, 2008). As reported in *Time*, more than 6 billion people in the world have access to cell phones (Wang, 2013). Nokia, the world's largest manufacturer of cell phones, operates plants in Finland, Brazil, Romania, China, Hungary, India, Mexico, and South Korea, and sells its products in over 150 countries.

Why is energy so important for the networks of globalization? Supply chains such as Nokia's require efficient systems of distribution. This, in turn, necessitates inexpensive fossil fuels. Currently, for transportation, oil is the fuel of choice. Freight transportation accounts for 35 percent of all transport energy use worldwide. With freight transportation, oil is used almost exclusively, because the system's infrastructure is set up to consume oil. If the supply of oil decreases, transportation costs rise. As transportation costs rise, the comparative advantage of global supply chains erode. Supply-side energy shocks alter the pattern of international trade. Companies like Nokia then re-evaluate their global supply chains.

ENERGY AND THE CLIMATE CRISIS

Energy economists study energy resources, not only because the resources impact economic growth, but the pattern of energy consumption helps determine the impact on the environment. In particular, countries must balance the goals of energy stability and environmental quality. The problem is that fossil fuel consumption leads to the emission of *greenhouse gases* (GHG), which are gases in the atmosphere that both absorb solar radiation and cause the greenhouse effect.

Higher levels of GHG from factories, vehicles, and power plants increase their atmospheric concentrations, measured in parts per million (ppm). In 2014, carbon dioxide, the most prevalent greenhouse gas, passed 400 ppm, higher than any level in the last 800,000 years. It continues to rise every year. The problem with this trend is that higher atmospheric concentrations of GHG increase average global temperatures. Some climate scientists now argue that global temperature could increase by as much as 3°C by the end of this century, relative to preindustrial levels. This outcome would lead to more severe storms, changes in agricultural patterns, rising ocean levels, and human displacement.

While the world must address the climate crisis, the energy resources that cause the problem—fossil fuels—remain relatively inexpensive in historical perspective. Policies that move the global economy away from reliance on fossil fuels are often viewed as beneficial from a climate perspective, but expensive from an economic perspective. In response, many energy economists and policy makers have adopted the position that countries must implement energy policies such as carbon taxation, energy conservation, and renewable mandates, all addressed in this book.

RENEWABLE AND NONRENEWABLE ENERGY RESOURCES

The global supply of energy includes both renewable and nonrenewable energy resources. Renewable resources naturally replenish on a human time scale. Nonrenewables, in contrast, are not replaced by natural means at the levels of current consumption. Even though fossil fuels—oil, coal, and natural gas—regenerate over the course of millions of years, they are considered nonrenewable: humans may deplete them in a few centuries. With the increase in supply of renewable energy resources and the decrease in cost of providing them in the marketplace, electricity sectors around the world will eventually use fewer nonrenewable resources. The economic and environmental benefits of such a shift are clear: slowing the release of GHG, increasing energy security, and stimulating the green economy. But the transition may be slow. As Amy Jaffe (2011) of the James A. Baker III Institute for Public Policy at Rice University writes:

> The scale of renewable energy today . . . is still extremely limited when put into the context of total world use of fossil fuels. In 2007, the world used the equivalent of 113,900 terawatt hours of fossil energy to fuel economic activity, human mobility and global telecommunications, among other activities. Replacing those terawatt hours with non-fossil energy would be the equivalent of constructing an extra 6,020 nuclear plants across the globe, or 14 times the number of nuclear power plants in the world today. In renewable energy terms, it is 133 times the amount of solar, wind and geothermal energy currently in use on the planet.

NONRENEWABLE ENERGY RESOURCES

The consumption of nonrenewables—including coal, natural gas, oil, and uranium for nuclear power—could eventually lead to depletion, but, according to Bardi (2013), a number of factors characterize global markets:

- Stable world oil production. Some areas are in decline, such as the North Sea. Other areas, especially North America, continue to grow.
- Increasing coal production.
- Increasing natural gas production from underground sources with low permeability.
- A lack of growth in nuclear energy production.

Oil

Oil companies undertake expansive processes of oil extraction and distribution in areas such as the United States, Canada, Russia, Venezuela, and the Arctic rim. Industrialization in developing countries, particularly China and India, will require more oil. In the United States, more than 800 motor vehicles exist per 1,000 people, but in China, the number is less than 100. In India, it is less than fifty. As per capita income levels increase in these countries, the automobile market will grow. In 2019, the world supplied more than 100 million barrels of oil per day.

Coal

For electricity generation, coal serves as the world's most important fuel. But compared to oil and natural gas, coal possesses the highest carbon content per unit. At the present rate of consumption, coal reserves will last two centuries.

But more coal will be converted into liquid fuel. According to Avery (2007), two-thirds of the world's recoverable coal reserves exist in four countries: United States (27%), Russia (17%), China (13%), and India (10%). But in China and India, the rates of extraction and consumption of coal are expected to rise. Despite a higher level of environmental awareness, global coal consumption is expected to increase.

Natural Gas

Natural gas, a combustible fossil fuel, is extracted from underground reservoirs. Initially thought to be a waste product in oil fields at the beginning of the twentieth century, natural gas now heats homes and serves as a source of energy for power plants. The market for natural gas exhibits a large volume of proven reserves. However, the process of *hydraulic fracturing*, or fracking, now common in the industry, creates environmental problems. This method involves the use of a high-pressure water mixture that releases gas inside of rocks. In areas such northern Pennsylvania, central Texas, Arkansas, and Louisiana, fracking increases the yield of existing reservoirs. While many landowners object to the presence of drilling rigs, pipes, and water-storage ponds, they receive royalties. But additional environmental concerns involve the contamination of both underground and surface water supplies from the spilling of hydraulic fluid. Despite these concerns, natural gas continues to serve as an important source of energy.

Nuclear Power

Public concern over the 2011 nuclear disaster in Japan notwithstanding, in thirty-one countries, more than 400 nuclear power plants generate 10 percent of the world's electricity. During the 1960s, nuclear power was viewed as an inexhaustible source of low-cost electricity. Today, concerns about safety, cost, and the environment have divided energy analysts. On the plus side, nuclear power generates electricity without greenhouse gas emissions. But the cost of construction of a new nuclear power plant exceeds $10 billion. In addition, nuclear waste remains radioactive for tens of thousands of years. (Compared to coal mining, however, many fewer people have died in the nuclear power industry.) Until global perceptions of safety and security change, it is unlikely the world will build many more nuclear power plants. But with the existing stock of plants, nuclear energy will continue to constitute an important part of the global energy supply.

Nonrenewable Energy Resources and Electricity Generation

Electricity is not a source of primary energy from nature. It is produced. To generate electricity, power plants use resources such as coal, natural gas, and

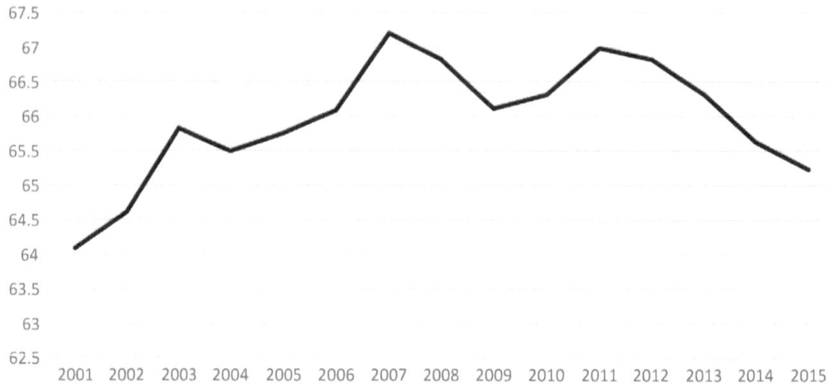

Figure 1.1 Percentage of Global Electricity Production from Oil, Gas, and Coal Sources. *Source*: Author using data from The World Bank, https://data.worldbank.org/indicator/EG.ELC.FOSL.ZS.

nuclear power to heat water and produce steam. The steam turns turbines that power electric generators, transforming kinetic energy into electricity. To put these traditional energy sources in perspective, consider their share in world electricity production in 2015, according to IEA (2017a):

- Coal (39%)
- Natural gas (23%)
- Hydropower (16%)
- Nuclear power (11%)
- Solar, wind, geothermal, tides (5%)
- Oil (4%)
- Biofuels (2%)

If global electricity systems relied more on renewables and nuclear energy, fossil fuels would exhibit a declining share in electricity generation. In 2001, the percentage of global electricity production from oil, gas, and coal was 64. By 2015, the percentage rose to 65.2, but appears to be declining (figure 1.1).

RENEWABLE ENERGY RESOURCES

Renewable energy resources also generate electricity. In Denmark and Spain, for example, the generation of electricity from wind is cheaper than coal-fired plants. If this trend spreads, wind power could serve as a substitute for coal. But this transition would occur if electricity were a *homogenous economic good* with little or no differentiation in output or price. If electricity were a homogenous good, one megawatt-hour of electricity generated by wind turbines would be identical to one megawatt-hour generated by coal-fired plants. The two resources would be pure substitutes. The output would be compared in a pure cost basis. However, with respect to price, electricity is still a *heterogeneous economic good.* With wind power, electricity prices differ because of wind variability and intermittency. Wind energy cannot be stored; unless batteries are used, wind cannot be harnessed to meet the demand for electricity.

With respect to the composition of wind and coal inputs, electricity prices are formed differently in these two markets. Because of this reality, the marketplace favors energy resources that provide stable and reliable sources of electricity, which currently means fossil fuels and nuclear energy. But as renewable energy resources such as wind, solar, bioenergy, hydropower, and geothermal become more integrated in electricity systems, this preference for stability with fossil fuels and nuclear energy will change. Consumers want a steady supply of electricity, but usually do not consider the energy resource used to generate the electricity. Most consumers look at monthly utility bills. But they may analyze the details only when the monthly cost changes.

Several factors affect the price of electricity, including the choice of fuel, the age of the power plant, the efficiency of transmission, regulations, the type of customer (residential, transportation, commercial, industrial), the season, and location. For example, the price of electricity is usually highest in the summer, as more expensive generation is necessary to meet the demand for air conditioning. In addition, certain states, such as Hawaii, experience a relatively high average price of electricity, because power plants there generate electricity with fuel oil, an expensive choice. The State of Idaho, in contrast, experiences relatively low average prices for electricity, because of the availability of low-cost hydroelectric power. The United Nations Environmental Program (2016) provides perspective for global renewable energy markets:

- Renewable energy excluding large hydropower plants constitutes more than half of new power generating capacity
- The annual contribution to global electricity generation from renewable energy sources continues to increase
- Renewable energy attracts more investment than new gas- and coal-fired power plants

From an environmental perspective, these trends are laudable. But average power plant operating costs for renewable energy sources exceed the costs from nonrenewables, with the exception of hydropower. From the perspective of moving to a clean energy economy, a major challenge involves decreasing the unit cost of electricity from these sources.

Bioenergy

Bioenergy is derived from biological resources. It is used for vehicle fuel, electricity, and heat. A typical process involves crops such as sugar cane, corn, or switchgrass. Because these feedstocks derive energy from the sun using the process of photosynthesis, the final product is considered renewable. In countries such as Brazil and the United States, combustion-engine vehicles are built to operate with an ethanol blend. However, even though ethanol and biodiesel are becoming more prevalent at filling stations and many vehicles have engines that run on these fuel mixes, both economic and environmental concerns exist. Industrial farming produces ethanol, requiring a large amount of cultivated land. The fermentation/distillation process requires fossil energy, which leads to carbon emissions. The industrial crops that are used to generate bioenergy are not used for food production. A decrease in supply of food crops puts upward pressure on price.

Geothermal

Geothermal processes harness heat from the earth to create energy. Geothermal processes serve as both cost-effective and reliable sources of energy. Not only is the energy found below the Earth's crust in molten rock called magma, the amount of heat within a few thousand meters of the surface contains more energy than the world's entire supply of remaining natural gas and oil. Tapping the potential of this renewable source of energy, however, depends on the economics of production and distribution. For geothermal power plants, capacity depends on technology, the size of the plant, and the cost of generating electricity. But at the micro level, ground-source pumps tap geothermal energy to heat and cool homes and buildings. On a global scale, millions of ground-source pumps exist, with installations occurring at the rate of tens of thousands of new pumps annually. Because geothermal energy is both cost-effective and provides baseload electricity generation at low marginal cost, investments in exploration technology, power conversion, and demonstration projects are growing.

Hydropower

Historically important as a source of energy, hydropower technologies capture the kinetic energy of moving water to turn a turbine, which generates electricity. In terms of renewable energy, hydropower is the world's largest and least-expensive source. Recent projects such as the Bakun Dam in Malaysia, the Narmada project in India, and the Three Gorges Dam in China have received global attention both for their energy-generating capacity and their impact on the environment. On a global scale, hydropower has long played an important role in the development of economies. After the invention of the wooden waterwheel, many regions in Europe and Asia relied on hydropower 2,000 years ago. Today, advanced hydropower systems make the technology more efficient and cost-effective. As long as water flows, dams produce electricity at stable rates, do not generate carbon emissions, and contribute to a region's supply of energy. Future challenges include the costs of new dam projects, human displacement, and changes in the ecology of rivers.

Solar Power

The Sun's solar radiation may be used to generate electricity. *Photovoltaic (PV) devices* convert sunlight directly into electricity. Recent advances in the production of PV panels have led to higher efficiencies and the installation of lightweight and weather-resistant solar systems on buildings and houses. *Solar thermal power plants* concentrate solar energy to heat water, which powers generators and produces electricity. Although small in number, compared to coal-fired power plants, solar thermal plants, along with PV panels, do not produce greenhouse gases. But limitations exist. Intermittent sunlight arrives on the Earth's surface. Insufficient storage capacity exists for times when the sun is not shining. For PV devices, a large surface area is necessary to collect sunlight at a useful rate. Solar thermal power plants far from population centers require investment in power lines.

Wind Power

For centuries, humans have relied on wind power. Thousands of years ago, wind energy propelled boats along the Nile River and elsewhere. In China, wind-powered pumps secured water. In the Middle East, wind-powered blades were used to grind grains. Today, wind turbines harness the kinetic energy of wind to produce power. Although wind power provides less than 1 percent of global energy, the demand continues to grow. The market is characterized by advances in blade technology, the connection of wind turbines to regional power grids, and public/private partnerships for technological advance. However, during times of low natural gas and coal prices, governing authorities may choose to "protect" consumer interests by choosing energy options that guarantee the lowest end-use price for consumers of electricity. This reality has meant choosing fossil fuels. Like solar energy, the growth of wind power depends on both the price of fossil fuels and the ability of firms to allocate resources toward wind technology. Currently, wind power has achieved significant gains onshore in countries such as Portugal, Spain, Ireland, Germany and the United States, and offshore in the United Kingdom, Denmark, and the Netherlands.

Large-Scale Deployment of Renewables for Electricity Generation

Because global electricity generation relies on fossil fuels and nuclear power, a greater use of renewables offers three benefits. From an economics perspective, less dependence on fossil fuel imports decreases the exposure of economies to international price fluctuations, resource constraints, and political instability. From an energy perspective, a greater production of renewables helps to diversify the energy supply. From an environmental perspective, renewables offer a method to reduce GHG emissions.

Given these advantages, the way forward is to support renewables, so they contribute more than their current share in electricity generation. Mature technologies include hydropower, biofuels, and geothermal. According to IEA (2018), these resources generate almost 20 percent of the world's electricity, with hydro accounting for the greatest share of 16 percent. These technologies are already competitive with fossil fuels and nuclear power, provided the renewable power sources are connected to electricity grids. The challenge is to expand these technologies, given their up-front costs. The emerging technologies of wind, solar, and tides generate about 4 percent of the world's electricity. These technologies require cost reductions that come with expanding markets.

In decentralized energy markets, consumers, producers, and investors should, in theory, face the full costs of their decisions, including the environmental costs of their actions. But this standard is not met. One reason is a lack of accountability for the negative impacts of fossil fuel consumption. The pollution damage and climate impacts of fossil fuels are not internalized in price. Producers bring more to the market than is optimal. In this context, consumers pay less for fossil fuels than they should. Another reason is the prevalence of subsidies for fossil fuels. A final reason is that a function of an electricity sector is to establish a stable supply. As a result, the market favors centralized power plants, conventional technologies, and traditional energy sources such as fossil fuels and nuclear power.

These barriers serve as reasons for the strategic deployment of renewables. To transition to a clean energy economy, large-scale investment must occur. Energy policies must deliver financial support to specific projects, such as wind farms in the United States or solar farms in the Middle East. Public and private partnerships must serve as the main drivers for longer term developments in renewable technologies markets. Storage capabilities must advance to the point where renewables serve as cost-effective options for electricity generation.

Energy and Sustainability

Sustainability—a term widely used in community, government, nongovernment, academic, and corporate settings—means the priority of maintaining planetary resources to meet both current needs and the needs of future generations. We must not deplete our resource base today and leave insufficient resources for the future.

In this context, adequate supplies of energy help determine the degree of economic development. Energy is important for housing, food production, transportation, heating, cooling, manufacturing, water purification, and waste disposal. Over time, the growth of these processes, and therefore improvements in living standards, will rely on reliable and enduring energy systems. The problem is that the choice of specific energy resources may not satisfy the dimensions of sustainable energy systems: security of energy supply, environmental quality, and economic vitality.

This reality is a problem because a number of critical connections between energy and other processes exist. One example is the connection between energy and water. To pump, transport, distribute, treat, and heat water for residential, commercial, and industrial use, energy is consumed. Another example is energy and food. Energy is required for the application of fertilizer at the beginning of the food chain, the disposal of industrial food by-products at the end, and all of the steps in between. In a static framework, this multiplicity of linkages complicates a proper evaluation of energy resources. But in the dynamic world in which we live, an increase in the demand for energy leads to multiple implications for energy security, environmental quality, and economic performance.

In this book, questions concerning sustainability—specific to the topic of energy—will inform our discussion of fossil fuels, nuclear power, and renewables. With individual sources of energy, such as oil, nuclear power, and wind, we will evaluate the security of supply, baseload power, environmental impacts, atmospheric consequences, human health, and economic performance. We will address a number of questions. Concerning energy security, will resource flows provide a long run supply? With power systems, baseload power means the ability to satisfy the minimum level of electricity demand. Do specific energy resources provide baseload power? With environmental quality, are the ecologically damaging by-products of our energy choices decreasing? With respect to climate change, do our energy choices increase greenhouse gases in the atmosphere? With health, are the damaging by-products of our energy choices being reduced? With economic performance, do our energy choices enhance economic activity?

In parts two and three in this book, we will evaluate individual forms of energy in terms of costs, benefits, and these sustainability criteria (table 1.1). When analyzing energy resources, we will find that an important challenge is to balance the tradeoffs of competing goals. Some energy resources satisfy a number of the sustainability criteria, but others do not.

The aim of this book is to explore the components of energy markets and systems, address the realities of policy and climate change, and evaluate individual energy resources, both traditional and alternative. Along with costs and benefits, the sustainability questions will help us determine that some forms of energy are more suitable for the grand challenge of energy transition than others.

Table 1.1 Sustainability Criteria

Sustainability Category	*Criterion*	*Question*	*Indicator*
Security of energy supply	Energy supply	Is the energy resource available long term?	Proven reserves or resource flows
Security of energy supply	Baseload power	Does the choice of energy satisfy baseload-generating capacity?	Existing and forecasted generating capacity
Environmental quality	Environmental impacts	Are ecologically incompatible by-products of the energy choice continuously reduced, eliminated, or recycled?	Pollution into the air, water, and earth
Environmental quality	Atmospheric consequences	Does the choice of energy stress the atmosphere?	Concentration of greenhouse gas emissions
Environmental quality	Human health	Are by-products of the energy choice incompatible to human health continuously reduced, eliminated, or recycled?	Mortality
Economic vitality	Economic performance	Is the choice of energy compatible to an open and participatory economic process that focuses on long-term performance?	Output and employment

Source: Author.

THE GRAND CHALLENGE OF ENERGY TRANSITION

Taken together, these factors—the choice between renewable and nonrenewable energy resources, rising population in developing countries, increasing energy supply and demand, and a greater reliance on electricity grids to power growing levels of urbanization—demonstrate our current energy landscape. It is difficult, however, to establish a greater energy challenge than the transition to a clean energy system. This transition requires the substitution of renewables for their nonrenewable counterparts.

Consider how energy transition occurs. Energy systems experience "phases" with respect to innovation, adoption, and diffusion of new technologies, products, and services. In an important article on energy transition, Benjamin Sovacool (2016)—Director of the Danish Center for Energy Technology and Professor of Social Sciences at Aarhus University—argues that four phases occur:

- An extended period of time of experimentation and learning with new technologies
- Scaling up at the unit level with design improvements and economies of scale
- Scaling up at the industry level
- Standardization at the industry level, globalization of technologies, products, and services, and diffusion of successful design from core to periphery markets

Each of these phases takes time, but is crucial for energy transition. Ultimately, in the year 2050 and beyond, the strength of both the global economy and the climate system will depend on energy transition, including the speed of technical innovation, how quickly substitution to renewables takes place, and the diffusion of clean energy products and services. Whether or not one believes these components of energy transition will occur by the middle of this century leads to competing visions of the future.

VISIONS OF THE FUTURE

Pessimistic Vision of the Future

The "mainstream" vision views energy transition as a protracted process, taking multiple decades or centuries. Energy system inertia exists because of long investment cycles and the diffusion of new techniques. Inertia is ingrained in energy systems, including machines, structures, and investments;

business interests favor existing techniques; and industry and political concerns connect to particular forms of fuel and processes.

The mainstream view acknowledges that transformative change must occur at every level of the energy system, including technologies, legal and political regulations, economies of scale, price signals, and social attitudes. Innovation phases for new technologies could take a century, while diffusion could take an additional fifty years. Some examples support this view. In the United States, from the exploratory stages in the 1860s, crude oil took fifty years to capture 10 percent of the market and thirty more years to reach 25 percent. Coal needed more than 100 years to capture 5 percent of energy consumption. Starting in the mid-1960s, nuclear electricity took almost forty years to reach a 20 percent share. This pessimistic vision also acknowledges the following trend: on a global scale, the consumption of fossil fuels continues to rise.

With a growing global population, the potential slow pace of energy transition, and current dependence on fossil fuels, the pessimistic vision of the future forecasts a slow transition to a clean energy system. In an essay which makes a case to fight global warming, Friedmann (2011) argues that "neither conservation nor alternative energy sources are currently viable answers." The problem with renewable power, according to Friedmann (2011), is that the technology has not evolved fast enough. Moreover, electric grids are ill-equipped to handle the amount of renewables necessary to power the global economy.

Climate change complicates the picture. In 2018, more than 37 billion tons of carbon emissions entered the atmosphere, an increase in 10 billion tons in fifteen years. Over the course of this century, the world's average temperature is forecasted to increase. With ice melting around the world, ocean levels will rise, perhaps even more than the worst-case scenario posited by the United Nations. Severe weather patterns could alter the agricultural landscape, pressuring farmers worldwide to change their production methods and growing patterns. Human displacement from resource scarcity could weaken the social safety nets of countries around the world, exacerbating trends already underway in the European Union and the United States. Given these possibilities, the world's commitment to the pursuit of a clean energy future could lack the funds and resources necessary to accomplish the goal of a rapid and secure transition.

Optimistic Vision of the Future

An alternative, optimistic vision of the future also exists. In an article in *Scientific American*, Jacobson and Delucchi (2009) write that water, wind, and solar (WWS) technologies could provide the entire world with power.

Because energy systems that rely on fossil fuels lead to pollution, climate change, and other undesirable environmental outcomes, Jacobson and Delucchi make the case for large-scale changes. Here's their plan: technologies that exist today, but on a much larger scale, could use WWS to supply electric power for heating and transportation. Electric systems could replace fossil fuel heating for ovens and stoves. Battery and fuel-cell vehicles could replace fossil fuel transportation. Fuel cells could power industry and airplanes. Millions of new non-rooftop photovoltaics, concentrated solar plants, and wind turbines would occupy a small percentage of the world's land. The building of this energy system would take time, but shifting to sustainable sources of energy would reduce the environmental impacts.

How feasible is the plan? Could the world eliminate its reliance on fossil fuels and nuclear power by 2030 (as Jacobson and Delucchi propose) or even by 2050 (a more realistic timeframe)? To answer these questions, consider that a new energy system must meet rising demand. The power that flows from the system must be affordable. Energy transformation must be politically feasible. As population grows, industrialization occurs, and urbanization transforms societies in developing countries such as China, India, Brazil, Indonesia, Nigeria, South Africa, and Malaysia, but a new energy infrastructure that relies on renewable sources must have little downtime. According to Jacobson and Delucchi (2009), downtime for modern wind turbines, when they are not turning in the wind, is less than 2 percent on land and 5 percent at sea. Solar systems are less than 2 percent, but don't generate power at night. When distributed on a widespread basis, both provide stable sources of power. Countries could address the intermittency of wind and solar by a balance of sources. Connecting power sources across a country's landscape could compensate for a short-term reduction of power at an individual plant. Because the sun would compensate for a lack of wind, and windy weather often exists during storms when the sun doesn't shine, combining wind, solar, geothermal, and tidal could meet rising energy demand.

Writing in *The Electricity Journal*, Benjamin Sovacool and Charmaine Watts (2009) provide further context. In the long term, not only are renewable power systems technically feasible, but they currently provide baseload power, reduce the variability of solar and wind with smart planning, and operate as reliably as traditional systems. Considering the capital costs of conventional and renewable power plants, wind, hydroelectric, and geothermal are among the most cost-effective. In terms of the expense of building, fueling, operating, and maintaining a power plant, marginal costs favor renewable power sources. Even though the problem of energy storage for renewables remains, additional benefits include more stable fuel prices, fewer greenhouse gas emissions, less water use, and higher levels of efficiency.

Which Vision Is More Likely?

To determine which vision is more likely, consider the following realities. First, in developing countries, the establishment of power plants that burn fossil fuels is meeting much of the rising demand for energy. Second, while technological advance continues to reduce the costs of renewables, transferring this technology and updating electricity grids remain challenging processes. Third, because fossil fuel companies influence political systems, public policy that encourages renewables is often difficult to enact. As a result, in 2050, the world will still likely rely on fossil fuels and nuclear power. But it is probable that a much higher percentage of energy will be derived from solar, wind, wave, and geothermal sources. The reason is that, while historical transitions took a great deal of time, our knowledge and rate of technological advance may expedite a more rapid future energy transition. In addition, previous transitions may have been circumstantial, but our future transition may be a political or social priority, given the growing problem of climate change. After reading this book, the reader may wish to return to this section to establish a well-informed vision of the future. Sovacool (2016) leaves us with hope:

> Perhaps future energy transitions, because they can draw on synergistic advances in multiple domains at once—cutting across multiplicity of energy services, materials science, computing, combustion dynamics, gasification, nanotechnology, biological and genetic engineering, 3D printing and the industrial internet—can truly be accelerated in ways that past transitions have (generally) not been, despite the fact that it may be scarcity or concerns about climate change, rather than abundance or price, driving them.

ORGANIZATION OF THE BOOK

This book is organized in three parts. The first part on the fundamentals of energy economics addresses global energy systems, efficiency, and conservation (chapter 2), power and electricity (chapter 3), fuels, buildings, industry, and transportation (chapter 4), energy policy (chapter 5), and energy supply, demand, and markets (chapter 6). The second part on traditional energy resources includes oil (chapter 7), coal (chapter 8), natural gas (chapter 9), and nuclear energy (chapter 10). The third part discusses a way forward with renewable energy (chapter 11), energy and the climate crisis (chapter 12), and energy security (chapter 13). Chapter 14 concludes. For instructors interested in specific examples of traditional energy sources or renewables, it is possible to read chapters from parts two and three in a different order without losing momentum.

SUMMARY

Since the beginning of this century, global energy markets have experienced tremendous change. Global population, GDP, fossil fuel consumption, renewable energy, electricity production, and carbon emissions continue to rise. Globalization, the interconnections of the world's peoples through all forms of exchange, will ensure a growing demand for energy resources far into the future. The environmental implications of the world's energy mix such as climate change emphasize why a global transition to a safe, reliable, and clean energy system is important. An energy transition will entail a greater reliance on clean energy sources such as wind, geothermal, and solar power but must include technological advancement in energy system capacity, storage, and distribution. Whether one adopts an optimistic or pessimistic vision of the future depends on how fast one envisions the world making these changes.

TERMS

Bioenergy
Fossil fuels
Globalization
Greenhouse gases
Heterogeneous economic goods
Homogeneous economic goods
Hydraulic fracturing
Nonrenewable energy resources
Photovoltaic devices
Renewable energy resources
Solar thermal power plants
Sustainability
Urbanization

QUESTIONS

1. Explain the current trends for global population, GDP, energy sources, electricity production, and carbon emissions. What factors are causing the trends?
2. Explain the process of globalization as it relates to energy consumption. Because of more integrated networks of globalization, including production and exchange, are specific regions of the world likely to increase their consumption of fossil fuels more than others?

3. Explain why fossil fuel consumption increases atmospheric concentrations of greenhouse gases. If global temperature continues to rise, explain the potential long-term outcomes in terms of energy, the environment, agriculture, transportation, and human displacement.
4. Define renewable energy resources. List and discuss examples. In countries such as Denmark and Germany, why are renewable energy resources prevalent?
5. Define nonrenewable energy resources. Over the course of the last 100 years, in the developed world, why have oil, coal, and natural gas served as the most prominent sources of energy? In your answer, consider the supply-side factors of extraction and distribution.
6. Should the world start planning today for the eventual depletion of fossil fuels? What should the process of transition from a high fossil fuel economy to an economy that relies more heavily on alternative sources of energy entail?
7. What does energy transition entail? What phases are necessary for energy transition to occur? What are examples of slow transitions? What are examples of rapid transitions? For context and many useful examples, read the article by Sovacool (2016) in the Bibliography.
8. Do you believe in the optimistic or pessimistic vision of our energy future? To establish an informed position, read the papers by Sovacool (2016), Friedmann (2010), Sovacool and Watts (2009), and others from journals such as *Energy Economics*, *Energy Research & Social Science*, and *Energy Policy*.

Chapter 2

Energy Systems, Efficiency, and Conservation

SAVING ENERGY

The networks that link energy supply to the users who demand energy output are important for economies. But these networks lead to specific problems, such as pollution and climate change. Energy efficiency has long been an important element in the debate over the best method to address these problems. Many policy makers and proponents of energy efficiency argue that using more energy-efficient products, enhancing the efficiency of energy processes, and reducing the demand for primary energy resources serve as cost-effective methods of addressing these challenges. This chapter discusses these important topics, arguing that, while energy transition to more renewable energy resources serves as a viable long-term prospect, in the short term greater energy efficiency serves as an important goal. The chapter begins by discussing energy systems and sectors. The chapter then establishes a model of the energy conversion chain. Next, the chapter addresses energy efficiency and conservation. The chapter concludes with a discussion of the environmental implications of energy consumption.

ENERGY SYSTEMS AND SECTORS

The *Quadrennial Technology Review* of the U.S. Department of Energy (2015a, 2015b) describes an *energy system* as an interrelated network of energy sources and storage with transmission and distribution to the places where energy is needed. An *energy sector* serves a specific purpose within the

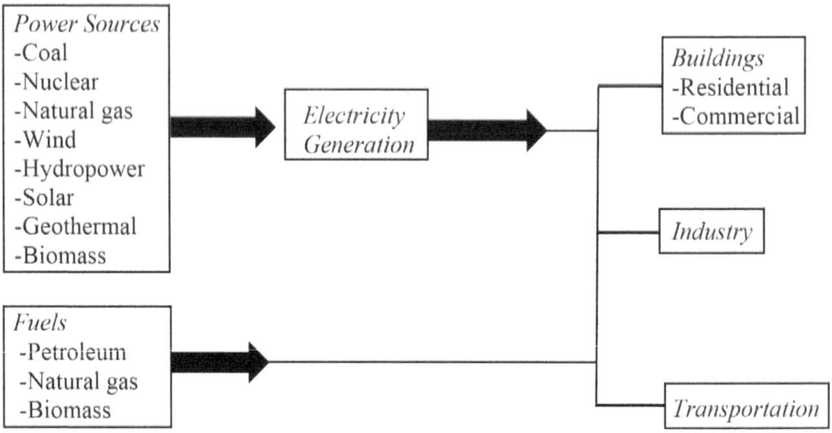

Figure 2.1 Model of the Energy System. *Source*: Author using information from U.S. Department of Energy (2015a, 2015b).

energy system—power source, the electric grid, and energy demand: fuels, buildings (residential and commercial), manufacturing, and transportation (figure 2.1). According to the U.S. Department of Energy (2015b), in the United States, more than 80 percent of the country's energy infrastructure is owned by the private sector. Examples include supplying fuels to the transportation industry, fuels for electricity production, and electricity to businesses and households.

Here, it is important to understand the difference between energy and power. Energy is the capacity to do work. Different forms of energy exist, such as thermal energy, which is the energy that comes from heat. Thermal energy is measured in British Thermal Units (Btu) or joules. One Btu is the amount of heat that increases 1 pound of water by 1 ° Fahrenheit. A Btu is the amount of heat produced from the burning of one match. In terms of conversion, 1 Btu = 1,055 joules. But 1 joule is the equivalent of 1 watt of power radiated for 1 second.

In this context, power is the rate at which energy is transmitted, or work is done. For the purpose of measurement, a watt is a measurement of power. A watt describes, for example, the rate at which electricity is used at a specific moment. At any moment, a 40-watt light bulb draws 40 watts. In 1 hour, it uses 40 watt-hours of electricity. But a typical electricity bill uses kilowatt-hours. One kilowatt equals 1,000 watts. Using electricity at a rate of 1,000 watts provides 1 kilowatt-hour of consumption.

To provide context for chapters 3 and 4, which address individual energy sectors, figure 2.2 shows U.S. primary energy consumption by source and sector. The sources of energy—fossil fuels, nuclear power, and renewables—are used for the transportation, industrial, buildings, and electricity sectors.

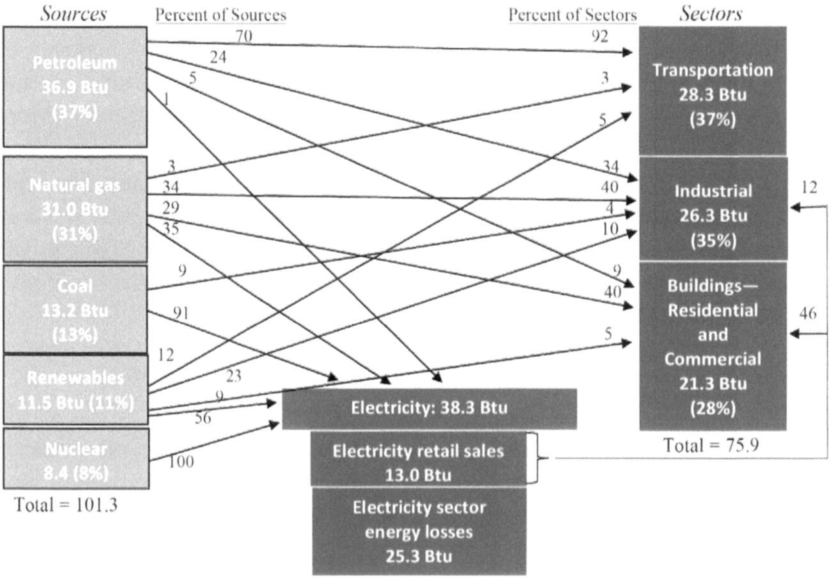

Figure 2.2 U.S. Primary Energy Consumption, 2018. *Source*: Author using data from the U.S. Energy Information Administration, https://www.eia.gov/totalenergy/data/monthly/pdf/flow/css_2018_energy.pdf.

ENERGY CONVERSION CHAIN

Every time we use energy to fuel our vehicles or heat our homes, we convert one form of energy into another. In other words, we turn energy into useful work. For example, when we drive cars, the engine converts the chemical energy in gasoline into mechanical work, which powers the wheels. When we heat our homes, we use the chemical energy available in natural gas or fuel oil, converting it into thermal energy by burning it in a furnace. These are two examples of the *energy conversion chain*, which demonstrates how sources of primary energy are converted into final end-use form. The chain is useful to analyze the fuel, building, industrial, and transportation sectors. When we use fuel to power buildings, manufacturing plants, and vehicles, the complete energy conversion chain is at work. To understand the framework, associated inefficiencies, and policies that address fuel choices, we need to address each stage of the energy conversion chain: energy sources, refining, energy carriers, storage, end-use conversion, and energy demand.

Energy Sources

The energy conversion chain starts with three *primary energy sources*: fossil fuels, renewable energy, and nuclear power. Whenever we use an energy-consuming device, such as cell phone charger, laptop, or vehicle, we may trace the energy chain back to these primary sources. The majority of energy used to generate electricity stems from fossil fuels, mainly coal and natural gas, although nuclear power is also an important contributor. More than three-fourths of all U.S. electricity and more than 40 percent of all energy consumption flow to commercial and residential buildings for heating, cooling, lighting, and other uses. For industry, electricity provides and powers lighting, machinery, and space conditioning. Petroleum powers our transportation system, with natural gas and renewables proving a small percentage of the total consumption.

Energy Refining

Before fuels power our vehicles, *energy refining* occurs. An oil refinery, for example, transforms petroleum into gasoline, liquefied petroleum gas, jet fuel, or diesel fuel. With biomass refining, the production of ethanol from sugar-based feedstocks or starch involves wet milling or dry milling, processes that target the initial treatment of the grain. Ethanol is refined out of plant matter; in this process, fossil fuel energy is used to distill every molecule of water out of the process. As a result, new technologies are looking to reduce the requirement by capturing methane from landfills, low heat fermentation, and biomass gasification. Vegetable oils, fats, and greases serve as sources of biodiesel, and biodiesel is a commercially proven fuel technology. Natural gas is purified by removing contaminants, including hydrogen sulfide and water. The refining of natural gas leads to hydrogen, methanol, and natural gas liquids.

Hydrogen has been touted as a future clean energy source; however, hydrogen is locked up in water, hydrocarbons, and organic matter. Therefore, processing must first extract hydrogen from these compounds in the form of steam reforming or electrolysis. Renewable sources such as solar may also be used to produce hydrogen in processes called thermolysis and photolysis.

Energy Carriers

The result of processing or refining is the production of a secondary form of energy, an *energy carrier*. Four main energy carriers may be converted into mechanical work or heat: refined petroleum products, refined biomass, refined natural gas, and electricity. With electricity, power plants use fossil fuels or nuclear energy to heat water running through a boiler to generate steam. The pressure of the steam on a turbine blade rotates a shaft, which produces electricity. For reasons of cost-effectiveness and convenience, energy carriers are transformed, some from solids to liquids and others from liquids to gases. Energy carriers today reach consumers through distribution grids in the form of electricity, gas, and liquid forms (oil products in transportation).

Storage

In its conversion from primary energy to energy carrier, energy is often not ready for end-use conversion. As a result, it is often stored. This is important in the case of transportation, as storage is necessary to avoid the impracticality of a continuous supply of gasoline to the fuel tanks of vehicles. In this case, the energy carrier is stored in many places, including in large tanks at refineries, tanker trucks, filling stations, and the fuel tanks of vehicles. Benefits of liquid fuels include a high storability factor and energy density.

Natural gas may also be used as an alternative transportation fuel. Two forms of natural gas are used in vehicles: liquefied natural gas (LNG) and compressed natural gas (CNG). The LNG is natural gas in its liquid form. To obtain this substance, natural gas is purified and cooled to −260°F to turn it into a liquid. What's left is largely methane with a few traces of hydrocarbons. To maintain cold temperatures, the LNG is stored in insulated pressure vessels inside trucks. With CNG, natural gas is compressed to less than 1 percent of its volume and stored onboard vehicles within cylinders such as trucks, transit buses, school buses, and some light-duty cars, vans, and pickup trucks.

With electricity, most is produced and delivered according to market demand. It moves from energy carrier to end-use conversion, skipping storage altogether. Over long distances, electricity moves through power lines. For fixed applications in buildings, factories, and homes, storage is not a requirement. The storage of electricity in batteries, however, occurs in limited examples in the electricity sector. In a few power stations, batteries store electricity during daylight hours when solar panels flood the grid with power. The batteries release electricity in the evening. In residential and commercial sectors, lead acid, lithium-ion, and flow batteries all provide the opportunity to store electricity until consumers need it. This storage capability is advantageous because it is cost-effective, provides greater flexibility, and provides the opportunity for more clean energy. With small devices, such as cell phones and laptops, batteries are effective options, although the capacity of small-scale batteries to store power is limited but growing.

In October 2015, when a geyser of gas spewed from the ground in Southern California, many lives were upended. Thousands of people had to move to temporary housing and motels. Schools relocated to different sites. The leak from the Aliso Canyon gas storage facility sprayed methane into the atmosphere, a greenhouse gas. Energy officials closed the facility until it found the cause of the leak and demonstrated that the facility was safe to open again.

The Southern California Gas Company had a problem. Not only were citizens in the area weary of recurring catastrophes, the gas leak and resulting shut down knocked out an important source of fuel for regional power plants. In response, energy regulators turned to a different option. Instead of relying on gas, they turned to batteries (Cardwell and Krauss, 2017).

The plan was bold. Batteries store electricity during daylight hours when the solar panels in the area flood the grid with power. The power is then released when demand peaks, often in early evening when people return from work. The idea is that the batteries both provide power on-demand and store it for future use.

Nationwide, power plants have been studying the potential of using more battery storage. But some power companies in Southern California have surged ahead with this process. The idea of using battery storage on a large scale would transform the industry. Power providers would be able to rely on solar and wind power on a much wider scale. The problem is that batteries pose their own risks, including explosion or fire, if the technology is not properly maintained. In Southern California, three energy storage sites serve the electric grid. These sites include thousands of lithium-ion batteries, the same type in laptops, smart phones, and other digital devices, but on a much larger scale. At one particular site, the Gas & Electric operations center, 30 miles north of San Diego, 19,000 battery modules are wired together. Each the size of a drawer, the batteries provide a backup source in case of fuel shortages. Long used in consumer products, power tools, and transportation, lithium batteries are new technology for the electricity grid. Because lithium entails the capacity to absorb more energy than other metals, they offer greater potential for resilience and life span (Cardwell and Krauss, 2017).

The installation site is strategic. On the regional electric grid, the batteries are installed where solar and wind arrays and the wires from power plants connect in the network to local power lines. At this point, the batteries may reduce the pressure in the network during peak hours. They absorb low-cost energy from the sun during the day and release it back into the grid in the evening when the demand for power is high and the sun sets. When the batteries were installed, enough capacity existed to provide power to 20,000 homes for 4 hours. If this convergence of technology succeeds, it will provide a model to integrate other power sources. Greater use of renewables and batteries provides additional balance in the system. If they work, solar generators will become more like traditional plants, providing baseload power (Cardwell and Krauss, 2017).

End-use Conversion

Energy refers to the capacity for doing work. But energy in storage is still not ready for direct application for specific energy needs. The process of *energy conversion* is necessary: the transformation of energy from one form to another. In theory, many forms of energy may be transformed into work. In the case of combustion, chemical energy in the molecules of fuels, when burned, are freed to produce heat energy. The heat energy is subsequently converted into mechanical energy to run the engine. In other words, the engine burns a fuel and an oxidizer. The products of combustion act directly on rotor or piston surfaces.

Direct energy conversion devices—solar cells, thermoelectric generators, fuel cells, and electric batteries—all had their origins in the 1800s. They use electrons for work applications. To take one example, fuel cells produce an electrical current that does work outside the cells. Specifically, a chemical process converts hydrogen-rich fuel into electricity. Hydrogen molecules split into protons and electrons. The electrons pass through a circuit, generating heat and electric current. Applications include the illumination of a city or light bulb or powering an electric motor. While the benefits of fuel cells include scalability, durability, and high levels of efficiency, they are currently cost-prohibitive and not widespread in the marketplace.

Energy Demand

The energy conversion chain exists to satisfy the demand for energy. We demand energy for buildings, industry, and transportation. As energy needs increase, the demand for energy from fossil fuels, nuclear power, and renewables rises. It's important to keep in mind, however, that the amount of energy available as energy sources is not the amount that exists at the end of the chain. During energy conversion, a loss of usable energy occurs in the form of waste heat. In addition, emissions flow from the process. The next two sections consider these inefficiencies.

Efficiency Losses

The First Law of Thermodynamics states that, in an isolated system, energy may not be created or destroyed. The law means that energy is always conserved; however, energy may be transformed. As a result, some aspects of energy may become unavailable in the energy conversion chain. The unavailable or "wasted" energy normally exists as low-temperature heat. Even though it is still a form of energy, it is not technically available. In the case of vehicles, energy is lost at different stages. Some usable energy is lost during the processing stage as crude oil is refined into gasoline. During the end-use conversion stage, more energy is lost.

When comparing the performance of different approaches to satisfy energy needs, such as fossil fuels or renewables to generate electricity or fossil fuels or electric charges to power vehicles, it is useful to estimate energy losses.

An efficiency value may quantify this loss. It is common for more than 50 percent of primary energy to become unavailable or lost during the energy conversion chain, so the efficiency calculation helps to both understand this loss and determine how to improve the process.

To calculate the efficiency value (E_V) for a specific energy conversion scenario, divide the usable energy produced at the end of the chain (E_P) by the total energy available at the beginning of the chain (E_A): $E_V = E_P \div E_A$. Robert L. Evans (2007) of the University of British Columbia provides informative calculations for E_V. In his book, *Fueling Our Future*, he explains that, the efficiency of conversion of crude oil into gasoline at the refinery is normally 85 percent. As a numerical example, if we start with 100 kilojoules (kJ) of primary energy in the form of crude oil, 85 kJ of energy in gasoline is left. Furthermore, the 85 kJ is then transformed into 17 kJ of useful work at the wheels. In other words, when the engine in the vehicle burns the gasoline to generate mechanical power, 20 percent of useful work is generated. In this example, the E_V of the energy conversion chain is 17 percent (17 kJ of useful work results from 100 kJ of primary energy). Eighty-three percent of the primary energy winds up being unavailable during the energy conversion chain. Waste heat, the unavailable energy, flows into the ambient air from hot exhaust gases and from engine cooling water by the radiator.

For a comparison between the performances of different energy resources or between policies to encourage different energy outcomes, calculations of efficiency losses provide a method of evaluation. For example, the performance of the entire energy conversion chain may be evaluated with a particular energy resource, such as oil from primary source to end-use application. With 100 percent energy input available in a steam power station, energy may be lost in the boiler (27% loss), condenser (15% loss), piping network (9% loss), and turbine (4% loss). With all efficiency losses, the power station may have energy efficiency of 35 percent. In fact, with electricity generation, it is common for over half the energy in gas and about two-thirds of the energy in coal to be lost as waste heat. No device or process is 100 percent efficient, but more technologically advanced systems attempt to minimize efficiency losses.

Emissions

An important feature of the energy conversion chain is the emissions that result from the processing and final end-use stages. When energy processing occurs and crude oil is refined into gasoline, for example, carbon emissions, unburned hydrocarbon gases, nitrogen oxides, and carbon monoxide are released into the atmosphere. During the end-use stage, when we drive our vehicles, these gases are released. As another example, the reaction of nitrogen oxides and unburned hydrocarbons in the presence of sunlight leads to smog. To alleviate the smog problem, some countries and cities implement stringent emission regulations on power stations and vehicles.

Energy Efficiency

There is an important difference between economic efficiency and energy efficiency. *Economic efficiency* refers to the optimal use of scarce resources. The economic approach teaches us that we should make choices to the point where marginal cost equals marginal benefit. Before the optimal point, choosing additional units creates net gains; after the optimal point, choosing additional units creates net losses. But *energy efficiency* is different. It refers to the amount of output produced per unit of energy consumption: energy efficiency = output ÷ energy consumption. For example, the energy efficiency of an air conditioner is the amount of heat removed from the air per kilowatt hour of electricity. An increase in energy efficiency, therefore, means more energy services produced from each unit of energy used.

In this context, *energy services* are "functions performed using energy which are means to obtain or facilitate desired end services or states" (Fell, 2017). In other words, energy efficiency facilitates a greater provision of products or energy services. Energy services are the services provided by energy, the benefits to consumers, and what is demanded by and delivered to people. A first category includes cooking, lighting, cooling, water heating, and refrigeration. These are things that energy does for people: converting energy performs the activity of cooking, lighting, or cooling, etc. Another category is associated with end products, such as hot water or heat. These are forms of output that energy facilitates. A third category, such as electricity, appliances, or television, appears as a means of energy carriers (electricity) or conversion, such as appliances and television (Fell, 2017).

At the aggregate level, to measure energy efficiency, we may calculate the ratio of GDP to total energy consumption. Assessing how this value changes over time provides a method to evaluate the *energy productivity* of a country. In the United States, for example, energy productivity per unit of GDP rose 2.4 times between 1949 and 2009 (Allcott and Greenstone, 2012). Changes in energy productivity originate at the sectoral level with the following variables playing important roles: income per capita, urbanization rate, investment, energy prices, and energy imports.

Energy economists are interested in energy-efficient policies and programs that are also economically efficient. In these situations, energy-efficient investments pay for themselves. But this is not always the case. Since its inception in 1976, for example, the United States Weatherization Assistance Program has provided $5,130 on average to more than 7 million low income households for weatherization and other home improvements, including furnace replacements and insulation. While the program reduces monthly energy consumption (and increases energy efficiency), the present value of future monetary benefits do not exceed upfront costs. According to Fowlie et al. (2018), the program is not economically efficient. As another example, to reduce a ton of carbon dioxide emissions, a number of policies and programs are available, but they come with different costs. Some, such as installing LED lighting in commercial buildings or residential water heaters, lead to cost savings. But other programs do not. The point is that not all energy-efficient options are cost-effective (McKinsey & Company, 2009).

THE BENEFITS OF ENERGY EFFICIENCY

Because of the release of the Intergovernmental Panel on Climate Change's 2018 report—which warns of potentially dire effects of higher global temperatures—interest is growing rapidly in finding solutions for the climate crisis. The climate crisis is exacerbated by the combustion of fossil fuels and the resulting releases of greenhouse gas emissions. But many countries are reluctant to introduce national policy responses, such as carbon taxes. As a result, the focus is on decentralized commitments to emission reduction. Energy efficiency is an example. Compared to carbon taxes, energy efficiency has more political support. Energy efficiency increases energy productivity of the economy while reducing energy costs.

Energy efficiency may deliver a substantial amount of value through multiple benefits: some impacts may deliver up to 2.5 times the value of a decrease in energy demand (IEA, 2014a). From the perspectives of both the public and the private sectors, efforts to identify these benefits will stimulate energy efficiency and increase the allocation of resources for the effort. A spillover effect from one benefit may contribute to greater benefits in other areas, such as when lower levels of greenhouse gas emissions improve health effects. According to IEA (2014a), the benefits of energy efficiency include:

- Energy savings
- Fewer greenhouse gas emissions
- Energy security
- Industrial productivity
- Health and well-being
- Employment
- Less pollution
- Resource management
- Higher asset values

THE ADOPTION OF ENERGY-EFFICIENT TECHNOLOGY

Four steps characterize the process of adopting energy-efficiency technology: invention, innovation, diffusion, and product use. Invention involves establishing a new idea, process, or device. Innovation occurs when the new idea, process, or device is brought to the market and offered for sale. Diffusion reflects the purchase of the product by individuals and firms. The use of efficient products reduces energy demand. Higher energy prices reduce energy utilization, but increase the invention, innovation, and diffusion of energy-efficient technology. In the four-step process, the rate of application of more energy-efficient device patents such as solar panels, heat pumps, and fuel cells is correlated with higher energy prices. Energy-efficient technologies reduce both the environmental damages and the financial costs of energy consumption.

But the adoption of energy-efficient technology depends on future expectations. For firms, the choice of achieving greater energy efficiency today is a function of upfront capital costs and the present value of lower future operating costs. Upfront capital costs equal the difference between the costs of purchase and installation of more energy-efficient technology and the costs of purchase and installation of technology that provides the same services but with more energy. Future operating costs are a function of the equipment's expected lifetime, energy efficiency of the technology, energy charges and fees, and future energy prices. Therefore, initial costs are known but future savings may vary according to future operating costs (Gillingham et al., 2009).

In an economic perspective, we may think of optimal private behavior and social behavior. Optimal private behavior entails the choice of energy efficiency that minimizes the present value of private costs. But optimal behavior also entails the minimization of social costs. Because of the uncertainty of future outcomes, it is difficult to identify optimal behavior in either case.

For households, the value of energy efficiency takes different forms. The cost of more energy-efficient products, for example, must be weighed against future savings. For households, what encourages investment in energy efficiency? Higher energy prices increase the demand for more energy-efficient water heaters, air conditioners, and vehicles. But the responsiveness of households to higher energy prices depends on price elasticity of energy demand. In contrast, higher adoption costs decrease the demand for more energy-efficient products. Interestingly, choices for energy efficiency are more sensitive to product cost than the expected price of energy. For the same economic incentive, therefore, subsidies for energy-efficient products may be more effective than energy taxes on resource use (Jaffe et al., 2004).

THE ENERGY EFFICIENCY GAP AND POLICY RESPONSES

From society's perspective, energy-efficient technologies are not adopted at levels that seem justified. A number of private and social inefficiencies create an energy efficiency gap between the cost-minimizing level of energy efficiency and the actual level. The energy efficiency gap has been used to identify previous efficiency gains and future investment opportunities. According to the IEA (2018), efficiency improvements during this century prevent more than 10 percent additional energy consumed annually and 10 percent more greenhouse gas emissions.

But the energy efficiency gap demonstrates that a dollar of energy savings is undervalued. The IEA (2018) reports potential for further gains. According to the IEA's calculations, the gap increases on an annual basis. But if energy efficiency opportunities are adopted, the global economy would continue to grow and only a marginal increase in primary energy demand would occur. In this scenario, investments in energy efficiency would create value over time.

According to Gillingham et al. (2018), three reasons exist for the energy efficiency gap. First, the emissions that result from energy use harm human health, reduce environmental quality, and accelerate climate change. These externalities contribute to a social energy efficiency gap: the private market does not lead to the socially optimum level of energy efficiency. Second, at the level of the household, inattention, myopia, cognitive limitations, systematically biased beliefs, and loss aversion may limit the adoption of energy-efficient products. These behavioral barriers contribute to a private energy efficiency gap. Third, imperfect information causes producers and consumers to undervalue opportunities for investment in energy efficiency. A lack of information on the financial savings from energy-efficient equipment or an inability to discount future benefits may reduce the demand for the equipment.

To analyze the energy efficiency gap, consider the factors that influence the adoption of energy-efficient technology. As Gerarden et al. (2015) explain in an article on energy efficiency, new adopters of energy-saving technology seek to minimize: $K(E) + O(E, P_E)\ x\ D(r, T) + C$, where the cost of purchasing equipment $K(E)$ is a function of annual energy use (E); operating costs over time equal annual operating cost $O(E, P_E)$ multiplied by a discount factor $D(r, T)$, P_E is energy price, r is a discount factor, and T is the time horizon, while C is other costs including behavioral barriers.

If externalities from energy use (E) constitute the only market failure, economic theory suggests that optimal policy implementation in a first best framework would ensure that marginal external cost is added to the price of energy. This would decrease the consumption of fossil fuels, encourage more energy-efficient choices, and reduce carbon emissions. These policies may be categorized as incentives and financing. Carbon taxes or cap-and-trade policies serve as first-best options. Second-best alternatives have higher potential welfare costs, including subsidies for energy-efficient products, product standards for energy efficiency, and financial incentives—such as rebates, tax deductions, and tax credits (Allcott and Greenstone, 2012).

But in the presence of behavioral barriers and information inefficiencies, additional policy is necessary. With behavioral barriers and other costs (C), consumers may be inattentive to P_E, r, or T. For example, with T (time horizon), the typical service life of household appliances is 8–12 years; for automobiles, 10–20 years; for industrial equipment, 10–70 years; and for residential buildings, 60–100 years. Monetary savings from the adoption of energy-efficient technology, therefore, accrues over time but may be difficult to estimate upfront (Jaffe et al., 2004). Behavioral policies, also called "nudges," are low-cost interventions that encourage optimal choices.

With investment inefficiencies, adopters consider both the cost of purchasing equipment (K) and the operating costs (O). Because innovation entails upfront costs for the adopters but future benefits for both the adopters and the competitors, firms may spend less than the optimal amount on energy efficient K. They may not realize the cost savings from energy efficient O. Households may undervalue the future benefits of more energy-efficient appliances, relative to upfront costs.

Information, education, and financial incentives increase awareness about the net benefits of energy efficiency. They encourage end users to act in their own best interest, thus addressing behavioral barriers and investment inefficiencies. Examples include home energy reports, product labeling, home energy audits and assessments, product standards, awareness campaigns, building codes for new construction, and subsidizing technological advance (Gillingham et al., 2018).

POLICY DESIGN AND IMPLEMENTATION

Consider the context for both energy efficiency policy design and implementation. The evaluation of energy efficiency policies and programs entails an assessment of the change in energy demand. To date, changes in greenhouse gas emissions and reductions in energy demand have been evaluated systematically. But additional research is necessary to evaluate the environmental, macroeconomic, and social benefits of energy efficiency. The reason is that improvements in energy efficiency may first decrease energy service costs and then increase energy consumption. This rebound effect, a negative and unintended outcome, exists in the context of the multiple benefits framework.

Lower energy consumption is a goal, but a number of other goals exist, including increasing prosperity, environmental sustainability, social development, economic development, and energy security. The negative outcome of the rebound effect, to the extent that it exists, must be weighed against other benefits.

Targeted policies and programs must therefore address the multiple benefits of energy efficiency, geography, the mix of energy resources, and the stage of economic development. The reason is that, depending on its economic circumstances, a country may prioritize both a decrease in energy demand and cost savings for consumers. These factors impact the specific approach necessary to achieve the goals. But other countries may prioritize these goals, an increase in productivity in industrial sectors, and equitable outcomes. The identification of goals influences how effectively energy-efficient improvements occur.

An example offers perspective. With traditional regulation, utilities report to a regulatory authority with respect to load forecasts and the resources necessary to meet the future demand for electricity or natural gas. But options in meeting changes in the marketplace are sometimes limited to the supply side, such as the provision of more power. By establishing *integrated resource planning*, a utility reports both its resource forecast and load for a given period of time. It then incorporates a least-cost resource mix with both demand- and supply-side options. Because energy efficiency serves as a low-cost resource, the implementation of integrated resource planning often results in the implementation of energy-efficient choices. These choices reduce the need for additional options and reduce total costs for utilities.

A case study offers further perspective. In Finland, the development of building-related energy efficiency policy includes the goals of halting the growth in energy consumption, improving the existing building stock, and creating zero carbon new buildings. The policy mix includes different types of instruments: regulatory, information, voluntary, and economic (energy taxation, research and development, and subsidies for building innovations such as more energy-efficient ventilation systems, insulation, and heat pumps). Overall, Finland implements a stable policy, which improves energy efficiency (Kern et al., 2017).

In practical terms, many policies and programs exist simultaneously, such as in Finland. As a result, “complementary policy instruments are required to create a structural market for energy saving, while evaluations of policy instruments should take into account that several different measures are usually required for an effective policy mix” (Kern et al., 2017). These policy mixes must be flexible, coherent, able to evolve, reinforcing, and coordinating among multiple policy aims. They must establish specific objectives such as energy efficiency and emission reduction. They must also establish mechanisms that will achieve the objectives. McKinsey & Company (2009) explain that a comprehensive strategy should:

- Recognize energy efficiency as an important energy resource
- Launch an integrated portfolio of policies and programs
- Identify methods to provide upfront funding
- Forge greater alignment among household, business, and government stakeholders
- Foster development of next-generation energy-efficient technologies

In addition, tailoring the mix of energy efficiency policies and programs to individual countries supports goals and objectives; builds a broad range of support; creates collaboration across sectors; and encourages countries to address more complex issues, such as the appropriate responses to climate change.

IMPEDIMENTS TO ENERGY EFFICIENCY

If energy efficiency is important, what impediments exist? In an article on the United States, Sovacool (2009) answers the question. The first, a market impediment, leads to barriers to greater energy efficiency. The reasons are information failure, low returns on investment, and predatory market power. The second impediment, political and regulatory obstacles, leads to barriers to greater energy efficiency because of flawed expectations, varying state standards, underfunded research and development, and problematic bureaucracy. The third impediment, cultural and behavioral restraints, leads to barriers with respect to public apathy and misunderstanding, predispositions to excess energy consumption, and psychological resistance. The fourth impediment, aesthetic and environmental challenges, leads to barriers such as environmental costs, objections to new technologies, and distrust of government.

In this framework, coordinated and comprehensive policies are necessary to overcome the impediments. Examples include the elimination of subsidies for fossil fuels, the creation of accurate electricity prices, the establishment of renewable energy mandates, and the provision of information to the public. "No single-policy mechanism is a panacea, and until comprehensive policy changes are implemented . . . energy efficiency will never realize (its) full potential" (Sovacool, 2009). These and other policies should not work in isolation, but complement each other to achieve greater energy efficiency. Monetarily, the savings from greater energy efficiency could partially or fully offset the costs of policy implementation.

ENERGY INTENSITY

This discussion of energy efficiency raises an important question. How energy efficient is the economy? We have learned that the United States consumes a large quantity of energy for power, buildings, industry, and transportation. This consumption pattern is by conduct and choice. But our houses are, on average, twice as large as those in Asia or Europe. Average household utility bills demonstrate the increase in energy demand in the winter for heat and in summer for cooling. But from a different perspective, the rate of energy consumption in the United States has decreased. Technologically, our refrigerators use half the electricity they did in 1980. Our dryers, furnaces, hot water heaters, and industrial processes do more work using less energy when compared to the previous generation. Per square foot, our homes are as energy efficient as those in Europe. The residential buildings in New York City are more energy efficient than many around the world.

How do we know these trends? The answer is a statistic called *energy intensity* (EI), which measures the amount of energy needed to produce one unit of Gross Domestic Product (GDP): *EI = Total energy consumption ÷ GDP*. Lower levels of EI imply higher levels of efficiency (fewer Btus to generate the same level of output) and vice versa. Empirically, global EI has declined since 1980 despite an increase in output and energy use. This decrease is the result of improvements in industrial technologies and changes in the structural composition of the global economy. Countries operate less energy-intensive industrial divisions.

For two reasons, EI calculations are useful. First, high EI values signal a greater need for policies and programs that enhance energy efficiency. Businesses may use technological means to reduce the amount of energy consumed for the production of goods or services. Households may adopt more innovative and advanced aspects of the modern world to gain utility (satisfaction) in terms of air conditioners, heating systems, transportation, and communication.

Second, high income countries generally possess lower energy intensities than lower income countries. In many energy-intensive industries such as steel, business has been offshored to developing countries. But for high income countries, energy efficiency measures for the production system and lifestyle may differ. These countries possess relatively low levels of EI for industry (compared to low income countries) but higher EI for household lifestyles, which includes vehicles and appliances. Lower income countries have the opposite: energy-intensive production systems and non-energy-intensive lifestyles.

The EI calculations account for important factors such as the evolution of economies (how changes in income impact energy efficiency), the process of industrialization, and demographic trends (such as urbanization). According to Sadorsky (2013), in developing countries, income has a negative impact on EI. That is, increases in income reduce EI. But the process of industrialization has a positive impact on EI: higher levels of industrialization increase EI in the short and long runs. With urbanization, the results are mixed. Urbanization may increase production and city traffic. It may alter consumption patterns. It may increase the demand for infrastructure such as buildings and power plants. Therefore, growing cities may increase the demand for energy-intensive materials and products. But they may also adopt innovative strategies to reduce energy consumption with LEED buildings, high-mileage vehicles, and economies of scale.

ENERGY CONSERVATION

Energy conservation—a reduction in the total amount of energy consumed—is achieved by using either fewer energy services or energy more efficiently. For two reasons, these aspects of energy conservation are important. First, rebound effects in the short run, as previously mentioned, may increase the demand for energy when energy-efficient outcomes reduce the marginal cost of energy services. Second, long run changes in the demand for energy services depend on the energy efficiency of products, equipment, and technology.

Energy conservation requires repeated consumer attention and effort. It does not exist as a one-time occurrence. For example, as part of a routine, we may choose to walk or bike instead of drive a vehicle. But when we drive, we may also choose a vehicle with higher fuel efficiency, measured in miles per gallon. With respect to the energy conversion chain, conservation normally occurs at the final stage of energy needs, when individuals and businesses alter their behavior in the transportation, industrial, commercial, or residential sectors.

Barriers to Energy Conservation

In an article on the promotion of household energy conservation, Steg (2008) argues that three barriers limit energy conservation: insufficient knowledge, upfront costs, and a lack of feasible alternatives. Habitual behaviors such as unplugging charging devices or turning off lights require reminders. Consumers may not observe the negative externalities associated with their electricity consumption, such as air pollution or adverse health consequences. As a result, communities may promote energy conservation by facilitating behavioral changes. Examples include monitoring electricity consumption, promoting the adoption of energy-efficient appliances, increasing knowledge of the benefits of conservation, and increasing awareness of climate change.

One area of focus in the residential sector, new home technologies and energy management systems, shows great promise. In fact, one of the European Union's 10 priority action items in its Strategic Energy Technology Plan, established in 2007 and revised in 2015, is to "create technologies and services for smart homes" (Wilson et al., 2017). Smart homes help homeowners meet goals for energy control and management.

Smart homes possess a number of technological advances. They are equipped with connection capabilities, sensors, monitors, interfaces, home automation, and modern appliances, which may communicate with each other, connect with off-site controls, and provide methods to maximize conservation efforts. Controllable devices and appliances include windows, lighting, washing machines, coffee makers, alarms, heating and cooling systems, garage doors, and others. Smart fans, activated by human activities, humidity, and temperature, improve thermal comforts. Monitors and sensors detect motion, light, humidity, and temperature. Controls and management devices include smartphones, PCs, laptops, and tablets. Smart metering is a process that monitors the consumption of energy and communicates the information to the utility. Smart meters connect technologies, appliances, and devices, putting households in position to conserve energy. Wireless and networked technologies use standardized communication protocols. By providing greater levels of monitoring and connection, smart home technologies also improve lifestyles, safety, and security. When fully connected to both smart phones and grids, smart homes may maximize energy conservation efforts (Wilson et al., 2017).

Another area, the provision of information, is also promising. More salient information influences decisions about conservation. In a much-cited article on social norms and energy conservation, Allcott (2011) evaluated a series of programs that sent home energy feedback reports to residential utility customers. The reports contained two pieces of information: household energy consumption data and comparisons between energy use of the household and that of neighbors. The article found that the program reduced energy consumption: "non-price interventions can substantially and cost effectively change consumer behavior" (Allcott, 2011).

A potential problem is that households may reduce electricity consumption after receiving a report, but return to their initial behavior over time. The key in maintaining the desired behavior, therefore, is to continually provide reports and build "capital stock" or consumption habits with respect to energy behavior. Reports that both build capital stock and account for the time element may improve behavioral responses (Allcott and Rogers, 2014). Finally, if the reports also focus on the health and environmental impacts of electricity use, persistent energy savings may result (Asensio and Delmas, 2016).

But four interventions offered in tandem—social comparisons, commitment devices, goal setting, and labeling—may encourage an even greater level of conservation (Andor and Fels, 2018). Social comparison, as described above, provides information that contrasts household energy consumption with the behavior of neighbors. Commitment encourages households to follow their preferences for conservation, even in the presence of short-term costs. Goal setting, even if non-binding, may reduce residential electricity consumption. Labeling affixed to products informs consumers about the energy consequences of their purchases.

Interventions for Energy Conservation

Because energy conservation requires a change in behavior, conservation efforts are challenging for both consumers and policy makers. For consumers, a choice of greater conservation may be cost-effective over the long term; however, even when the benefits of energy conservation outweigh upfront costs, individuals may deviate from optimal decisions. In other words, when faced with the possibility of choosing energy conservation, suboptimal choices may result.

For policy makers, nudging individuals in the direction of conservation requires a comprehensive effort. The reasons are numerous. According to Frederiks et al. (2015), individuals often choose to maintain the status quo. For example, even when alternatives yield better results, people often resist change. In addition, people often settle for what is good enough, but not optimal. They often choose the most familiar option. People may follow the behavior of others and conform to social norms. Even more, many people are loss averse, valuing upfront costs higher than long-term benefits. Finally, people may value opportunities (such as the money saved from conservation efforts) less if the opportunities occur in the future.

Given these insights from behavioral economics, how may policy makers nudge consumers toward energy conservation? Again, turning to Frederiks et al. (2015), policy makers should target consumer behaviors that are adjustable, including the purchase of efficient household appliances or more fuel-efficient vehicles. To avoid information overload, policy makers should present consumer tips in a limited choice context. To address the problem of upfront costs, policy makers should emphasize that conservation reduces or minimizes costs over the long term. To make consumers feel they are contributing to the public good, energy conservation should be framed as socially desirable. To increase fairness, reliability, and consistency, information on the benefits of conservation should come from highly credible sources, such as public service commissions.

ENERGY AND THE ENVIRONMENT

An important lesson from the energy conversion chain at the beginning of the chapter is the link between energy and the environment. Some polluting emissions occur in the processing stage; however, most emissions are released during the final end-use stage. In the final stage, engines turn chemical energy into useful work. But the combustion of gasoline leads to polluting emissions: carbon dioxide, carbon monoxide, hydrocarbon gases, and nitrogen oxide. An urban environmental problem results from this process: smog. Smog occurs when sunlight reacts with nitrogen oxides and at least one volatile organic compound. Smog is unhealthy for humans. Another environmental problem impacts the atmosphere, humans, and the environment: increasing concentrations of greenhouse gases such as carbon dioxide. Higher concentrations of greenhouse gases accelerate the greenhouse effect. The greenhouse effect leads to higher average global temperatures, more volatile storms in wet areas, longer droughts in dry areas, and other impacts that alter the world's climate patterns.

But some positive environmental trends have resulted from our energy choices. Since 1990, ambient concentrations of carbon monoxide, lead, nitrogen dioxide, certain particulate matter, and sulfur dioxide have decreased. During the same period, both economic growth and vehicle travel miles increased. In addition, since the beginning of this century, air quality has improved in most urban areas in the United States. These results are driven by state and federal regulations on stationary and mobile sources. As another example, in the United States, electricity generation from coal-fired power stations continues to decline. But in recent years, electricity-related sulfur dioxide emissions have fallen even faster. The implication is that, in many states, sulfur dioxide concentrations are reaching much healthier levels. In addition, electricity generation at utility scale facilities in the United States from renewable sources, including wind, solar, photovoltaic and thermal, wood, landfill gas, municipal solid waste, other waste biomass, and hydro continues to increase. Even though the percentage of electricity from renewables is a small part of the total, the increase leads to healthier environmental impacts. Finally, in the United States, carbon dioxide emissions from energy consumption are declining or stabilizing by source: coal and petroleum. This trend reflects greater energy efficiency and conservation, plus an increase in the use of renewables in electricity generation.

SUMMARY

Energy systems consist of different sectors. The energy conversion chain demonstrates how primary energy sources are converted into final energy needs. With respect to energy efficiency and conservation, producers and consumers are not always rational utility maximizers. The reasons are many, but one reason is that producers and consumers may not identify net gains from greater levels of efficiency and conservation if costs accrue in the present but benefits accrue over time. Another reason is that monetary gains from greater levels of efficiency and conservation may yield temporary and inconsistent effects. If producers and consumers use mental shortcuts to manage complexities, incentives that emphasize financial rewards (cost-effectiveness) and non-pecuniary rewards such as praise, social approval, and recognition may serve as effective methods to increase both energy efficiency and conservation.

CONCEPTS

Economic efficiency
Energy carrier
Energy conversion chain
Energy conversion devices
Energy efficiency gap
Energy efficiency
Energy conservation
Energy intensity
Energy productivity
Energy refining
Energy services
Integrated resource planning
Primary energy sources
Rebound effect

QUESTIONS

1. Describe each stage of the energy conversion chain. Read the article by Evans (2008), cited in the Bibliography. The article demonstrates the energy conversion chain for both fuel cell vehicles and battery electric vehicles. What are the benefits and costs of each process? For fuel cells

and batteries, what efficiency losses result during stages of the energy conversion chain?

2. Explain the difference between economic efficiency and energy efficiency. How is it possible that an energy policy or program may be energy efficient but not economically efficient or vice versa? What is an example? For context, read the report by McKinsey & Company (2009) and the article by Fowlie et al. (2018) listed in the Bibliography.
3. Countries may have specific goals in addition to energy efficiency, such as equitable impacts, increases in productivity, and cost savings. How do a country's goals help determine the appropriate mix of energy efficiency policies and programs?
4. For a particular country, gather data on energy consumption and GDP. For the last ten years, calculate both energy efficiency and EI. How have they changed? What are the reasons?
5. The U.S. Energy Information Administration (https://www.eia.gov/state/rankings/) provides data on total energy consumption per capita for states. What states are at the top of the list? What states are at the bottom? What are the reasons for these placements?
6. The *Electric Power Annual* of the U.S. Energy Information Administration, available online, provides information and statistics from the electricity sector. Using the latest data, what are the recent trends for next generation and fuel consumption for fossil fuels, nuclear, and renewables? How have average prices per kilowatt hour changed in recent years in the residential, commercial, industrial, and transportation sectors? Graph these data and identify trends.
7. Suppose a policy standard that requires energy efficiency technology lowers the marginal cost of energy provision, but creates a rebound effect, energy consumption increases. Under what conditions, if any, would you advocate such a policy?
8. The American Council for an Energy-Efficient Economy (https://aceee.org/state-policy/scorecard) provides an energy efficiency scorecard for states. Which rank at the top? Which are at the bottom? What are the reasons? How have the rankings changed?
9. Research hydrogen as an energy carrier. In the case of transportation, is hydrogen currently cost-effective? What economic and technological barriers limit the use of hydrogen? What policies or economic changes would increase the production and consumption of hydrogen?

Chapter 3

Energy Sectors, Part I

Power and Electricity

POWER OUTAGE

On Thursday, August 14, 2003, shortly after 2:00 p.m. Eastern Daylight Time, some overgrown trees in northern Ohio brushed against a high-voltage power line. Heat created by high electricity current running through the line had softened it. The tree problem should have sounded an alarm at the control room of the First Energy Corporation in Ohio. But the alarm system failed. The lack of warning left operators unaware of the necessity of redistributing power in transmission lines throughout the regional system. During the next hour and a half, three other lines bowed into trees. They switched off. Extra burden in the system then fell on other power lines. Overloaded, they cut off a little after 4:00 p.m., creating a deluge of failures in northeastern United States and southeastern Canada. The biggest blackout in the history of North America began, with 50 million people eventually without power for two days and an estimated $6 billion cost. Communications, transportation, waste-water treatment, and 9-1-1 services went down several times (Minkel, 2008).

The blackout of 2003 exposed many flaws in the nation's electric grid. Faulty computer software, uninformed system operators, and neglected transmission lines all played a part. When the overgrown trees sagged into power lines, system operators could have compensated for the problem, but software they used to monitor the grid didn't help: before going to lunch, a technician turned it off. Because the problem was not addressed immediately, distributed currency overloaded other power lines in the system. One by one, they shut themselves down. But in some areas, power was restored within a few hours. In others, it took two days.

In response, the National Energy Power Act of 2005 was designed to prevent another widespread blackout. It holds utilities and producers to tougher guidelines, encourages the production of renewable energy, provides tax breaks for energy conservation, and increases the amount of biofuel that must be mixed with gasoline sold in the United States. Since the Act was implemented, no major blackouts have occurred in the United States, although smaller ones continue to disrupt economic activity in different parts of the country. This chapter addresses these and other related issues, focusing on the economics of power and the electric grid. By developing a model of power and the electric grid, the next section begins a discussion of the energy system.

POWER AND THE ELECTRIC GRID

Power and the electricity grid serve as engines for the economy. But effective electricity networks rely on stable sources of power. Cities, buildings, manufacturing plants, and households rely on a cost-effective flow of electricity. To address the importance of power and electricity to economies, consider the fallout from power failures, those not considered major disruptions like the blackout of 2003. Eaton's *Blackout Tracker Annual Report*, an online compilation of data and analysis of blackouts in the United States, reports some fascinating findings. During 2015, in the United States, for example, 3,571 power outages occurred, affecting 13.2 million people. This is slightly less than the total for 2014. Electrical power outages cost the economy more than $150 billion annually. For businesses, the irretrievable loss of revenue, which may occur in a matter of minutes, can be disastrous. The reason is that power interruptions are a leading cause of business continuity insurance losses. For power outages, an upswing in the number and severity of extreme weather events, a lack of investment in the U.S. electrical grid, and the aging of the country's transmission grid and power plants serve as primary causes. What is clear from the report is that a strong economy requires a stable flow of electricity.

In the United States, coal, natural gas, and nuclear energy serve as the three largest sources of power, generating almost 90 percent of the total (table 3.1). Hydro and wind contribute the next largest amount, with biomass, solar, and geothermal contributing the rest.

Since 2005, in the United States, *energy resource capacity*—the maximum amount of electricity that a generating unit can produce—increased for renewables, but declined for coal. For renewables, public policies at both the state and the federal levels provide incentive for greater wind and solar generation. Most states have *renewable portfolio standards*: mandates that

Table 3.1 Electric Power Capacity and Production, 2014

Source of power	*Generation capacity 2014 (Gigawatts)*	*Power production 2014 (Terawatts)*	*Power production, % of the total*
Coal	300.4	1,586	39.2
Natural gas	430.3	1,122	27.8
Nuclear	99.2	795	19.7
Hydropower	79.2	258	6.3
Wind	66	182	4.5
Biomass	13.4	64	1.6
Solar	9.3	18.3	0.4
Geothermal	2.6	17	0.4

Source: Author using data from U.S. DOE (2015b), Table 4.1.

increase the production of energy from renewable sources. More than two-thirds of states have goals for deployment of renewables in the electricity mix. Tax incentives at the federal level, including the production tax credit (since 1992) and the investment tax credit (since 2006), facilitate the growth of renewable industries.

The transportation of energy resources to electricity-generating plants requires an extensive distribution network. For coal, the most important source of power in the United States, power stations annually consume more than 700 million tons. Trains transport nearly 70 percent of the total. Barges and trucks constitute two other important methods. The specific form of transportation for energy resources is a function of transportation cost, including supply source options, the availability of transport mode, and route length. If the cost of shipping by rail increases, power companies look to other forms of transportation. At the Black Thunder Coal Mine in the Powder river Basin in Wyoming, the largest coal mine in the country, miners extract coal by power shovels and then load the coal onto haul trucks. The trucks take the coal a short distance, where it is loaded onto trains. At the Black Thunder Mine, enough coal is extracted daily to fill twenty-five trains, each more than a mile long. More than thirty states receive coal from Wyoming, with power plants in cities as far away as Kansas City and Chicago on the supply chain.

Other sources of energy present different challenges. With natural gas, the process of exploration identifies gas deposits and reservoir size. The process of extraction depends on the nature of the formation to be drilled, characteristics of subsurface geology, and the deposit's depth and size. After extraction, the energy resource is processed at the wellhead into pipeline quality and then transported to power plants. If it is not used immediately, natural gas may be stored at a power station.

Nuclear power stations smash subatomic particles (neutrons) into atoms of uranium. In this process, more neutrons are released, which then smash into other atoms, releasing energy. The energy boils water, produces steam, spins turbines, and generates electricity. While the fission of an atom of uranium produces 10 million times the energy produced by the combustion of coal, the distribution of electricity from nuclear power stations employs traditional networks of distribution in electricity grids.

In solar plants, sun-tracking mirrors reflect solar energy onto a receiver, which collects the sun's heat and increases the temperature of synthetic oil, circulating through a piping system. This system heats water, produces steam, and generates electricity in conventional steam turbines. Wind power is similar. Wind turns blades on the turbine, which spin a shaft connected to a generator. The generator then makes electricity. With hydro power, the energy of falling or fast running water from a waterfall or dam flows through a turbine, spins it, and activates a generator that produces electricity. In each of these cases, electricity flows through the local grid and connects to the energy system.

The goal of an electric sector is to provide affordable, flexible, reliable, resilient, and secure power. But the system must also possess the ability to respond both to changing demand and system disruptions. Current communication and control systems are transitioning to digital technology, where millions of control points inform the system of changes in supply and demand. Advanced technologies monitor the flow of electricity and enable a two-way flow of information between producers and consumers.

MARKET CONSIDERATIONS

Changes in both demand- and supply-side technologies are impacting the electric grid. A greater use of variable and distributed resources—such as electronic converters and consumer devices—is changing the nature of the demand side of the market. A shift from large generators to light-weight, gas-fired turbines, a greater use of renewables, and the employment of more digital communications in control systems are altering the supply side. But as energy consumption increases, the power system requires greater flexibility in meeting growing demand. Because many parts of the system are outdated, such as limited control points and old transmission lines, fundamental changes to the system must occur. The changes will attempt to increase reliability, decrease cost, and implement technological advances in all aspects of the electric grid, including generation, distribution, and consumption. Because the electric grid powers the economy, every aspect of industry and commerce depends on stable and affordable electric power. Communities, homes, businesses, and factories are integrating automated systems and digital technologies into their activities and production processes. However, in

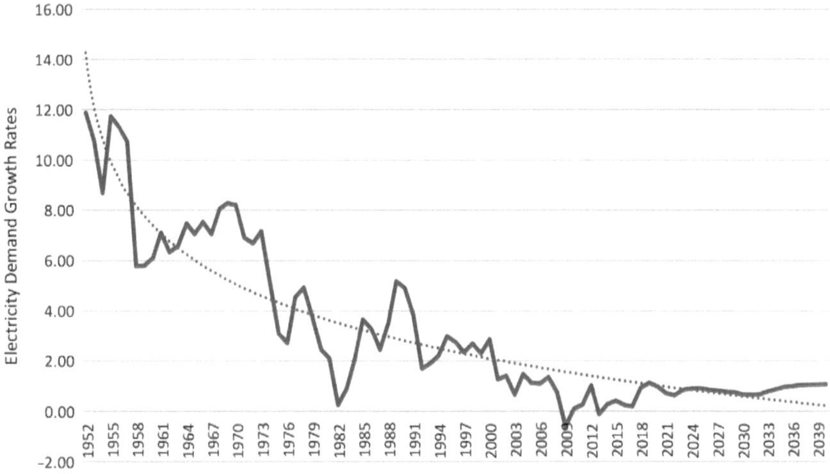

Figure 3.1 Annual Electricity Demand in the United States 1952–2015 Actual Data, 2016–2040 Forecasted Data. *Source*: Author using data from the U.S. Energy Information Administration, https://www.eia.gov/forecasts/aeo/MT_electric.cfm.

the United States, annual electricity demand growth rates have decreased on average, because of the transition to a service economy and energy-efficient improvements (figure 3.1).

From the 1920s to the 1970s, the U.S. electric grid grew with bigger power plants and more transmission wires. The problem during this time was technical stagnation. While the power grid grew, efficiency waned. With rising costs to consumers in the 1970s and early 1980s, change was underway. The movement of power plants and their polluting emissions to the outskirts of cities meant more than 10 percent of the power was lost during transmission. Power plants in cities had often reused steam to heat nearby buildings, eliminating the need for separate heating systems. In remote locations, however, waste heat vents into the air. One solution in the 1970s was the spread of new technology, smaller and mass-produced turbines powered with natural gas. For these plants, which were cleaner than coal plants, pollution was not as big of a problem. A new path forward entailed a more decentralized and efficient industrial approach.

In the 1980s, change came in the form of deregulation, not industrial organization. Experience with deregulation demonstrated more innovative services and lower prices to consumers, especially in industries such as airlines and telephone companies. The deregulation that introduced competition in the coal industry began with leadership from Ronald Reagan in the United States and Margaret Thatcher in the United Kingdom, who championed markets and less government influence. The process of deregulation in both countries introduced more privatization and competition, which was already taking place in the natural gas industry.

The coal industry, however, was slow to change, due to entrenched political power and a steady consumer price. Instead of large-scale deregulation, electricity restructuring occurred. Regional transmission organizations and independent system operators facilitated competitive bidding among generators. They maintained a flow of electricity from coal-fired plants. Some government intervention prevailed, especially with respect to price.

THE TRADITIONAL ELECTRIC GRID

In a traditional electric grid, electricity flows from power stations through transmission lines to transmission substations through distribution lines to customers. An information infrastructure operates the grid by monitoring and coordinating the production and delivery of electricity. Of the 97 quads (quadrillion British thermal units) of energy used in the United States in 2014, the energy system transformed 38 quads into 3,900 terawatt-hours of electricity (U.S. DOE, 2015b). In the United States, an infrastructure of more than 19,000 power stations, 642,000 miles of high-voltage lines, 55,000 transmission substations, and 6.3 million miles of distribution lines provides electricity to 145 million customers (U.S. DOE, 2015b).

In traditional power stations, a fuel source heats water running through a boiler, which generates steam. The steam is piped into a turbine. The pressure of the steam against turbine blades turns a shaft, which produces electricity. Cool water from a nearby source is pumped through tubes to a condenser, converting the steam back into water. To repeat the process, water from the steam returns to the boiler and the cooling water returns to its source.

BASE LOAD, PEAK LOAD, AND INTERMEDIATE LOAD POWER

The demand for electricity varies during the day and night. To meet these variations, power stations supply base load, intermediate load, and peak load power (figure 3.2). A *base load* level of electricity is available at all times. A weighted global average indicates that around 60 percent of generating capacity is base load. Although countries differ with respect to base load generation, certain patterns exist. Sweden relies on both hydropower and nuclear power to establish base load power. The United States, Denmark, and Australia use coal. In Norway, hydropower serves as the main source of energy for base load production.

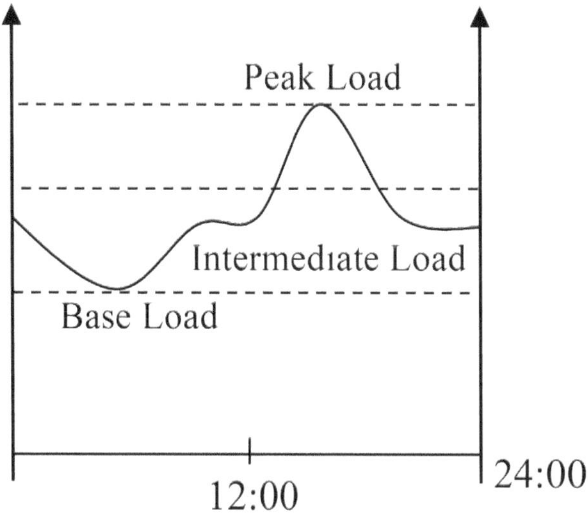

Figure 3.2 Electricity Load Requirements. *Source*: Author using information from Banks (2007).

Electric grids, however, cannot rely exclusively on base load power. Specifically, base load stations cannot handle p*eak load*, the maximum load that exists a small percentage of the time. Peak load power stations are designed to supply power for short periods, often fueled by natural gas (such as in the United States), when demand is high during extreme weather conditions. In between is *intermediate load*. Intermediate load stations, running during the day and in the evening, fill the gap between base and peak load power, usually with coal or natural gas.

The deployment of electricity in these three situations depends on market conditions, weather, geology, and historical trends. Tradeoffs occur. If too many peak load plants exist, costs are high, but generating capacity is reliable. Conversely, base load plants are cost-effective, but do not guarantee capacity during peak demand, such as extreme heat conditions in the summer.

The interconnected transmission system which facilitates the movement of electricity is a country's *transmission network*. After power stations generate electricity, the power is sent through transmission lines. To maintain a safe distance from human and economic activity, they are generally placed on tall structures. These lines or sets of wires (conductors) are high voltage and carry electricity over long distances to transmission substations. Transmission substations reduce the electric energy down to a lower voltage. They then make high-volume deliveries over short distances. Two types of transmission substations exist. Traditional substations operate a short distance from homes, buildings, farms, and schools. But because they need higher voltage to run large machinery, industrial substations operate near industrial plants. Distribution lines—flowing from substations to customers—offer the final stage of delivery of electricity. Distribution lines are lower in voltage than transmission lines. They carry medium voltage power to distribution transformers on the customer's premises. The United States possesses over 5 million miles of distribution lines, completing the link from power stations to final customers.

THE PORTFOLIO PROBLEM OF POWER TECHNOLOGY

This section discusses the criteria for the evaluation of power technology, including electric requirements, siting characteristics, and environmental outcomes. Each criterion possesses specific characteristics. Electric requirements include:

- Affordability
- Flexibility
- Reliability
- Resilience
- Security

Siting characteristics include:

- Local resources
- Traditional pollutants
- Transmission connection
- Water availability

Environmental outcomes include:

- Greenhouse gas footprint
- Land use
- Waste management
- Water impacts

The consideration of criteria for selecting power technology is a portfolio problem. For instance, optimal siting characteristics increase the efficiency of transportation; however, the burning of fossil fuels increases environmental degradation. A greater use of renewables reduces greenhouse gas emissions, but requires investment in transmission connection. Nuclear energy provides power without greenhouse gas emissions, but it generates nuclear waste. Another potential tradeoff is that an efficient siting location may compromise the security of a nuclear power station.

The decision to adopt specific technology is made at the local level with state and federal oversight. The factors that determine both the adoption of energy resources and the location of power stations are regional characteristics, transportation networks, customer demand, pollution, and the availability of water. Communities open in previous decades to nuclear power generation, for example, chose to locate plants nearby. For these plants, a lack of carbon emissions and efficient transmission connections made them appealing. The tradeoff, however, is high capital costs of construction and hazardous waste disposal. For fossil fuel power stations, the location on a river, lake, or other feasible site allows transportation of coal by barge or train. The tradeoffs for the use of coal include carbon emissions and water impacts. Clean power technologies possess different attributes with respect to the evaluation criteria. The most efficient choices maximize net benefits with respect to the evaluation criteria.

Responding to market developments, consumer demand, and regulatory oversight, the private sector generally decides which technologies to deploy. In the United States, the federal government oversees the process with policy and regulation. For an efficient electric grid, energy policy may emphasize environmental outcomes, subsidize technologies, or accentuate siting characteristics. Policy may also help to increase system reliability, affordability, security, flexibility, and resilience. But power generation technologies must integrate with the overall energy system, allow for interdependencies, and interface with global energy choices.

BIOPOWER

Biopower plants in the United States are typically fired with wood and agricultural residues, municipal solid waste, and sewage sludge. But for biopower to serve as a reliable contributor to the electricity sector, biopower must adopt domestically sourced biomass, provide low-cost power when the cost of biomass is competitive with other clean power sources, and obtain biomass from managed plantations (U.S. DOE, 2015b).

GEOTHERMAL POWER

Geothermal power technology uses the Earth's internal heat as a source of energy. Specific locations with a high level of heat flow make them suitable for power generation. Iceland, for example, powers almost 90 percent of its homes with geothermal energy. The United States is one of the largest producers. Regionally significant in the western part of the country, geothermal provides more than 4 percent of total system power in California, but less than 1 percent in Hawaii, Nevada, Oregon, and Utah. Geothermal power stations use hydrothermal resources that possess both water (hydro) and heat (thermal). In *dry steam plants*, steam from geothermal reservoirs is pumped into power stations to turn generator turbines. In *flash steam plants*, high-pressure hot water from deep inside the Earth is converted into steam, which turns generator turbines. In *binary cycle power plants,* heat from geothermal hot water is transferred to another liquid, which transforms to steam and turns generator turbines.

According to U.S. DOE (2015b), two major technological challenges exist for geothermal technology: the development of subsurface engineering technologies necessary for additional deployment and the reduction of risk associated with subsurface exploration. In these cases, advances in subsurface characterization, exploration technologies, fracture networks, and observational methods improve drilling success rates and reduce high upfront costs. These technological challenges are related to the challenges for other technologies that rely on subsurface exploration. Therefore, opportunities for cross-sector collaboration exist.

Geothermal power technologies possess three important benefits: they require minimal land use, produce low carbon baseload electricity (low greenhouse gas footprint), and are not intermittent power sources like solar or wind. But in order to increase the viability of geothermal and increase the scale of power generation, power companies must discover new sites, identify suitable heat resources, and translate the resources into power reserves. The problem for expansion is that the majority of readily identifiable geothermal systems has been or is currently being developed. In addition, because of the requirement of tapping into geothermal heat sources, the limitation of geothermal plant siting requires an emphasis on transmission lines. The installation of these lines may be expensive and necessitate the acquisition of installation permits.

HYDROPOWER

For over a century in the United States, hydropower technology has provided a consistent source of power. Since 1950, it has contributed on average 10 percent of cumulative power generation annually, but almost 50 percent of renewable power generation. Market challenges stem from the development and management of water resources. Metrics that establish the sustainability of hydropower development are not well-defined (U.S. DOE, 2015b). Because hydropower has historically been site-specific, little standardization of design exists. The problem is that standardization encourages the reduction of cost and uncertainty. In addition, water resources possess competing uses, including recreation, navigation, drinking supply, and species protection, which impact the operational decisions of hydropower. Production challenges result from a lack of investment in aging infrastructure and increasing environmental constraints. But large hydropower turbine generator technologies are cost-effective. Peak conversion efficiencies are high. In the United States and other parts of the world, hydropower potential exists with small-scale opportunities. Environmental performance of turbines continues to rise as blade enhancements reduce injuries to fish and turbine flow passages increase the water quality of releases. Over time, because hydropower will remain important for the generation of electricity, innovations must address the trade-offs between environmental outcomes and electric requirements. Water availability and impacts are high, but the technology has been affordable, reliable, and secure.

MARINE AND HYDROKINETIC POWER

Marine and hydrokinetic technology (MHKT) converts the energy of tides, waves, and ocean currents into electricity. In the United States, more than 50 percent of the population lives within 50 miles of the coast. For these residents, MHKT could contribute renewable energy sources to base load power. Particularly relevant for states with relatively higher electricity rates, including Alaska, Hawaii, Connecticut, Rhode Island, and Massachusetts, MHKT possesses a resource potential between 538 and 757 terawatt hours of generation per year, a substantial amount of electricity (U.S. DOE, 2015b).

Although the particular technology varies slightly by the source of energy, MHKT channels the power of moving water. One technology, *wave energy converters*, converts wave power into electricity. Another technology, *rotating devices*, takes a variety of forms, but generally captures water flowing through a rotor. The faster the current, the greater the level of energy generation.

The MHKT represents a powerful and largely untapped clean energy resource: hydrokinetic energy is predictable. Scientists predict wave patterns for days in advance and tides for centuries in advance. Even though ocean currents and waves are variable, they may provide continuous power. This is different than wind or solar. The MHKT also avoids greenhouse gas emissions and other air pollutants.

Full development of this form of technology could satisfy more than 10 percent of U.S. demand for electricity. Because this form of technology does not require a dam or water diversion, it avoids many negative environmental impacts of hydropower, including biological, chemical, and physical alterations. However, according to U.S. DOE (2015b), many challenges exist for commercial deployment. First, capital cost reductions and performance improvements must occur. Second, a lack of available full-scale, grid-connected test facilities exists. Third, a lack of information on monitoring costs and local environmental impacts are apparent. For these reason, MHKT is in the early stages of development. The technology is reliable and secure, but requires the availability of water and investment in transmission connection.

NUCLEAR POWER

In the United States, nuclear power provides almost 20 percent of the electricity. In 2019, ninety-eight reactors operated at sixty sites. The fuel cycle of nuclear reactors employs low-enriched uranium to generate heat. But in the United States, the entire fleet of reactors annually generates more than 2,000 metric tons of radioactive waste. Spent fuel rods reside in the reactor for four to six years before being removed and stored in pools of water. The radioactive waste is then air cooled above ground in welded stainless steel canisters in concrete casks. Eventually, a geologic repository will constitute the final resting place.

Of all the types of energy that are used to generate electricity, nuclear power is the only technology which accounts for all waste on site with the cost of disposal internalized in monthly utility bills; however, radioactive waste decays over time, so it has to be isolated and confined. The United States now has more than 70,000 metric tons of total nuclear waste scattered across seventy sites in thirty-nine states. The spent fuel will continue to emit harmful radiation for hundreds of thousands of years. The security outcome for this technology is important. Terrorist attacks or on-site accidents could crack the storing casks or drain the pools. The exposed waste could then catch fire and spread radioactive soot into the environment, water supply, and food chain. The longer the period of time it takes the country to identify a final, geological resting place, the longer the security risk remains. Therefore, in terms of the portfolio problem of power technology, nuclear power does not have a greenhouse gas footprint, generates reliable and affordable electricity, but has important security requirements and nuclear waste implications.

SOLAR POWER

In the United States, solar power generates about 2 percent of the country's electricity-generating capacity; however, solar capacity is increasing (U.S. DOE, 2015b). The reason is that hardware prices of solar panels have decreased. But, for solar power to become more competitive with other power sources, the *soft costs of solar energy* must also decline. Soft costs include the non-hardware costs of solar power. These costs are included in the overall price a customer pays for solar energy. Examples include the cost of connection, permit fees, sales taxes, transaction costs, profits for installers, costs of customer acquisition, labor for installation, and costs embedded in the supply chain.

Solar power is deployed on utility scales to contribute to peak load power. The stations turn traditional turbine engines and generate electricity during the day; however, the thermal energy concentrated in the power station is stored and used to produce electricity at night. The challenges involved with the implementation of more solar technology include grid integration, reliability, hardware costs, life-cycle sustainability of solar panels, and energy storage. Large-scale solar farms are inhabiting more desert and other suitable areas, but grid connection remains a challenging proposition. To implement solar on a greater scale, however, they require the additional use of land. Due to zoning and other restrictions that may attempt to preserve open space for habitat preservation or the minimization of habitat fragmentation, finding suitable locations for large-scale solar farms is a challenge. Nevertheless, solar systems in California, Arizona, Nevada, Florida, and elsewhere provide an increasing amount of power.

WIND POWER

Wind power, an established power source, supplies more than 4 percent of electricity end-use demand in the United States. With access to transmission capacity, wind technology is cost competitive in specific locations, such as Nebraska, Kansas, Oklahoma, and Texas. But in the United States and around the world, a significant amount of offshore and land-based wind resource potential exists. With continued innovation in markets and technologies, higher integration of wind power into the electric grid will occur. One estimate reveals that, by 2050, wind technology could provide up to 35 percent of U.S. power requirements and high grid reliability (U.S. DOE, 2015b). With wind power, challenges and portfolio tradeoffs involve reliability, transmission, and environmental outcomes. Once wind turbines are in place, portfolio costs include reliability and resilience. The extent to which wind turbines provide power to the system and demonstrate resilience, therefore, the greater the contribution of this power source.

STATIONARY FUEL CELLS

Stationary fuel cells generate electricity with an electrochemical reaction, not fuel combustion. Differentiated by fuels, a variety of fuel cell types exist, including polymer electrolyte membrane, alkaline membrane, and direct methanol fuel cells. Stationary fuel cells provide backup, clean, efficient, and reliable power to businesses, homes, telecommunication networks, and others. Several companies adopt fuel cells for primary and backup power, including Microsoft, Honda, Google, Adobe, Target, and many others. Benefits of fuel cells include low emissions, flexibility in installation, on-site power generation, and a lack of efficiency losses that are associated with long-range grid transmission. Fuel cells also take up much less space than other sources of energy. For example, a 10-megawatt fuel cell requires an acre of land. To produce an equivalent amount of power, solar requires 10 acres, and wind requires 50.

In addition to providing micro-level backup power for homes and businesses, stationary fuel cells connect to the electricity grid through the nation's natural gas infrastructure; therefore, when grid power is not available, fuel cells generate resilient power to important facilities. During the Northeast blackout of 2003, for example, in which more than 14 million people in the New York City area lost power, a fuel cell plant at the New York City Police Department's Central Park Precinct kept power on. In fact, during the blackout, the station remained fully operational. With its stationary fuel cells generating uninterrupted power, the station provided additional firefighters, ambulances, paramedics, and dispatchers. During Hurricane Irene in 2011 and Superstorm Sandy in 2012, fuel cells provided emergency backup power to many telecommunications towers, schools, and businesses. Fuel cells that power office and electrical equipment, air conditioning, heating systems, and chargers for electric vehicles offer an important method to maintain system reliability and resilience.

Economic and technical challenges of stationary fuel cells include capital costs, contaminant removal, durability, and performance stability. Because they operate on-site, they are flexible and secure. They do not require transmission connection and minimize the use of land. Compared to power from coal and natural gas, they lead to fewer carbon emissions. Other benefits include nearly silent operation, high reliability, and low maintenance. But the reason stationary fuel cells are not more widespread is that high capital startup costs do not make them cost competitive. Nevertheless, in Connecticut, the Dominion Bridgeport Fuel Cell Plant, located in downtown Bridgeport, the largest fuel cell plant in the United States, began operating in 2013. It produces 15 megawatts of clean energy, enough to power 15,000 homes.

The technology of fuel cells is straightforward. When the fuel of choice, in this case natural gas, passes through the cells, an electrochemical reaction produces heat, water, and electricity. The process emits very small amounts of sulfur and nitrogen oxides. The largest fuel cell park, completed in South Korea in 2014, provides baseload electricity to the country's grid and heat for the district heating system. The use of fuel cells in South Korea is intended to enhance the resiliency of the electricity system as a whole while increasing environmental quality. To provide power from fuel cells at scale, additional research on materials, integrated fuel cell systems, and production methods is necessary.

POLICY AND REGULATION

By updating the electricity grid, policy makers address the challenges of transmission and distribution, environmental quality, security, and the need to attract private investment. At the same time, they consider market realities, including how and where the grid is managed, the need for technological advances, and evolving forces of supply and demand. At the federal level, policy efforts accelerate the deployment of energy-efficient applications through research, development, and technical assistance. State governments are implementing regulatory reforms, investments, and planning, often partnering with energy companies and utilities. Policy and regulation at all levels include public and private partnerships, financial incentives, emission reduction, demand-driving policies, grid integration, and the harmonization of policy and planning.

PUBLIC AND PRIVATE PARTNERSHIPS

Energy policies should improve the efficiency of the system, foster economic development, and mitigate financial risk. According to the U.S. DOE (2015b), because uncertain cost recovery and profit potential characterize forays into energy markets, principles of public- and private-sector partnerships, implemented in an energy system, may:

- Establish a clearly defined partnership
- Provide stable funding for research, development, demonstration, and deployment
- Commit a national energy plan and legislation to the promotion of clean technologies
- Provide a plan for cost recovery and profit potential for investors
- Maximize the benefits of upgrades in the power and electricity sectors
- Optimize the private sector's financing alternatives
- Align public and private goals for the sustainable and reliable provision of electricity

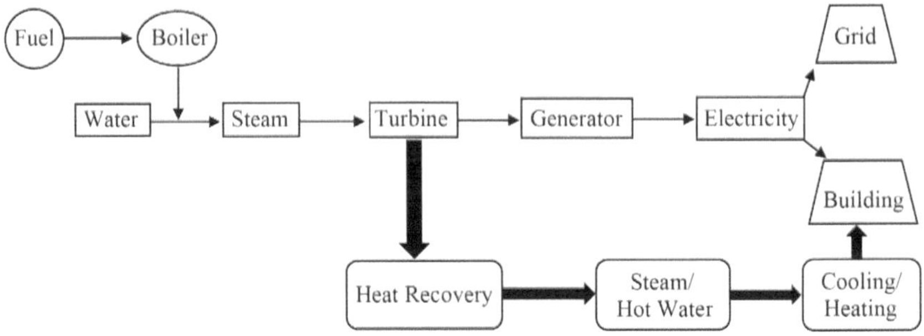

Figure 3.3 Combined Heat and Power Configuration. *Source*: Author using information from the U.S. Environmental Protection Agency.

An example of public and private cooperation, the U.S. Environmental Protection Agency's (EPA) Combined Heat and Power (CHP) Partnership, addresses the inefficiency of heat discharge from electricity generation. To reduce efficiency losses, the EPA works with CHP stakeholders—utilities, companies, equipment manufacturers, and financiers—to first capture the heat that would otherwise escape. Second, the process provides thermal energy—such as hot water or steam—and channels it into space heating, cooling, or industrial processes (figure 3.3). This technology is used in over 4,000 facilities nationwide, including manufacturers, municipal districts, universities, schools, residential neighborhoods, and commercial buildings.

FINANCIAL INCENTIVES

Policies at the national and state levels provide incentive to decrease the demand for fossil fuels and increase the supply of renewable energy. In the United States, petroleum products are taxed at the federal and state levels, including gasoline and diesel (for heavy trucks). As taxation increases the relative price of gasoline, some consumers switch to more fuel-efficient vehicles. In the United States, a federal investment tax credit supports the deployment of solar energy. This policy encourages production of solar panels in the private sector, increases utility, commercial, and residential scale installations, and reduces cost. For utilities, companies, and households, the existence of the solar investment tax credit increases market certainty.

Emission Reduction

The electricity sector emits about 40 percent of current and projected U.S. carbon emissions (RFF and NEPI, 2010). Public policies focus on the reduction of electricity-related emissions. Research in the field of economics demonstrates that national carbon tax and cap-and-trade policies offer the greatest potential to reduce carbon emissions at the lowest economic cost. When the price of fossil fuels and electric utility bills reflect the external cost of emission damage, households and businesses have the incentive to adopt energy-saving technologies, switch to lower-carbon fuel, or reduce the consumption of energy-intensive products.

In 2015, the EPA implemented a Clean Power Plan, the first *national standard* for power stations for the reduction of carbon emissions. The plan aims to reduce carbon emissions for existing power plants by 32 percent from 2005 levels by 2030. The plan establishes state-by-state targets for emission reduction, provides time and flexibility to achieve emission cuts, and encourages collaboration in finding the lowest cost reduction methods. While the plan acknowledges that fossil fuels will remain a fundamental source of energy in the United States, it intends to expand the capacity for low- and zero-emitting power sources.

Clean Energy

Twenty-nine U.S. states and the District of Columbia have *renewable energy (portfolio) standards*. They require utilities to sell a specific percentage of electricity from renewable sources. For example, in 2007, the state of Illinois established a standard that 25 percent of its electricity must come from renewable sources by 2025. (You may find state-level standards at the National Conference of State Legislatures' website, www.ncsl.org, in the section on "State Renewable Portfolio Standards and Goals.") Not only do renewable energy standards require the adoption of more renewable energy for the generation of electricity, but they advance the country's markets for solar, wind, and other renewable sources. The policies promote economic development, encourage the diversification of the energy mix, and reduce carbon emissions.

Grid Integration

State public utility commissions are responsible for the management of grid interconnection. *Grid interconnection* refers to a region of interconnected power stations. In the United States, the electric grid is serviced by three regional interconnections: the Eastern Interconnection, the Western Interconnection, and the Texas Interconnection. Each system includes networks of utility companies, power producers, distributors, and customers. The infrastructure of each system is established to accommodate many power sources, including fossil fuels, nuclear power, and renewables. With the expansion of renewable energy markets—especially wind power—transmission networks must increase their capacity to transmit energy from its sources to the locations where it is needed.

According to Kruger (2016), technological advances and market trends are providing new options for grid integration. The utilization of *distributed energy resources*—smaller power sources that help to meet energy demand—is increasing. Examples include renewable technologies, microgrids, and energy storage. In response to these technical and market changes, many states are updating their methods of regulatory oversight. For example, New York's Public Service Commission is proposing a utility-run platform that facilitates distributed energy with a variety of participants. Many other states are determining the value of system services provided by emerging technologies such as rooftop solar; implementing reward mechanisms for utilities that meet peak reduction goals, energy efficiency, or affordability standards; and investigating the ideal grid structure that would ensure innovation, efficiency, and resilience.

Harmonizing Policy and Planning

Collaborative efforts between the United States, Canada, and Mexico happen with cross-border transmission projects and climate change (Krupnick et al., 2016). In 2014, the three countries signed a memorandum of understanding that allows the sharing of energy data. Cap-and-trade programs to reduce greenhouse gas emissions in Quebec and California, furthermore, demonstrate policy integration. Fuel economy policies in Canada and the United States share the requirement of increased stringency over time. Benefits of such collaboration include emission reduction, lower transaction costs, and coordinated decision making that facilitates additional projects. In addition, harmonization expands the size of energy markets, reduces energy costs to consumers, and creates economies of scale. While several efforts are underway to increase the scope of harmonization—including additional research on new transmission and pipeline links, the expansion of participants, greater climate policy integration, and closer coordination of electricity system planning—collaboration in North America offers a model to move forward in a more interconnected world.

Evolution of the Electricity Grid

Five trends are motivating a transformation of the electricity grid (U.S. DOE, 2015b):

- The incorporation of variable generators
- The changing of consumer preferences

- Growing expectations for a resilient electricity sector
- Upgrading an aging electricity infrastructure
- The integration of smart grid technologies

Incorporating Variable Generators

The United States' mix of electricity generation changed from the year 2000 to the present. In 2000, coal's share of the power generation mix exceeded 50 percent. Now it less than 40 percent. During the same time period, the share of natural gas grew from 16 percent to almost 30 percent. The share of renewables increased from below 10 to over 10 percent. The U.S. Department of Energy expects these trends to continue (U.S. DOE, 2015b). These trends demonstrate that variable generation, such as solar and wind, requires non-dispatchable technology. Because electricity is not easily stored, power generation managers must continuously match electricity supply with demand. With increasing variable generation, more resources and tools are necessary to maintain a reliable flow of electricity, while addressing the short-term need (during heat waves) for steep ramps in electricity demand.

Changing Consumer Preferences

Changing consumer preferences alter the delivery of electricity. The addition of renewable energy sources means greater generation from small-scale distributed sources, such as solar panels on rooftops or wind turbines on school properties. In addition, the demand for more energy-efficient appliances, buildings, and industrial equipment reduces the amount of electricity flowing from power stations. Moreover, changes in the marketplace from electromechanical to power-electronic-based components impact electricity consumption. This latter technology improves the controllability of the energy sector by enhancing power load regulation and performance of the power system. Variable speed drive systems, for example, in many consumer and industrial applications, have replaced induction motor loads. Many pumps, fans, and motors in processes, such as air conditioning, now use electronic drive systems that improve efficiency, enhance control, and regulate the flow of electricity. Finally, the demand for plug-in vehicles continues to rise. This trend could increase the demand for electricity but decrease the demand for petroleum. If sales continue to increase, electric vehicle charging will constitute an important new source of electricity demand. The implementation of smart meters, time-based electricity rates, and electric grid management encourage off-peak charging for electric vehicles and discourage the need for expensive additions to capacity.

Growing Expectations for a Resilient Electricity Sector

The billions of dollars of annual electricity disruptions endanger both safety and public health. During downtime, companies may stop production, slow distribution, and reduce communication. Households may experience accidents that require immediate attention. The downtime loss in labor productivity leads to higher costs for firms. The growing interconnectedness of the electricity grid with other infrastructures, including energy resources, transportation, information technology, and communications, increases the costs of electricity disruptions. Natural disasters often lead to costly power outages. But natural disasters are not the only threat: terrorism and cyberattack may also compromise the electricity sector, serving as high-risk sources of harm.

These and many other concerns demonstrate the need for new technologies to boost the resilience of the electricity sector. On transmission substations, new *equipment health sensors* help to prevent power outages and reduce system failures. *Microgrids*, discrete energy systems with distributed energy sources, commonly used in hospitals, universities, and municipal areas, operate independently from or parallel to the electricity grid. A microgrid connects to the electricity grid and maintains the same voltage; however, during an outage, a switch separates the microgrid from the main grid. The microgrid then functions independently and provides backup power. When outages occur, additional technology for power stations helps increase management capabilities and decrease restoration times (U.S. DOE, 2015b).

Upgrading an Aging Electricity Infrastructure

The electric grid is accommodating greater capacity for renewable energy resources. To continue this trend and reduce the nation's carbon footprint, the electricity sector requires thousands of miles of new transmission lines. This requirement is necessary to connect more renewable resources to electricity demand centers. The power grid must also evolve in order to balance fluctuating power flows from solar and wind generation, plug-in electric vehicles, and small-scale distributed sources.

The entire electricity grid is engineered to balance supply with demand at all points in time. With this as a priority, the transition to accommodate renewable resources, decentralized power sources, and plug-in vehicles is underway. But the transition impacts power companies in different ways. Firms that operate long-distance transmission lines—such as the Independent Systems Operators in New England and the Midwest—implement sensors, phasors, and other forms of technology that provide more control. More advanced technology that provides up-to-date information on the flow of electricity in the grid provides the opportunity to accommodate more variability (Weeks, 2010).

Electricity suppliers such as utilities that deliver power to businesses and homes focus on a different element: meters. The traditional electricity grid transmits information from the utility to the customer. Most meters display power usage for the current billing period. Power companies charge the same rate per kilowatt hour of electricity. Throughout the day and night, however, the cost of generating electricity varies. Because consumers may not observe this cost differential, they may not have the incentive to reduce electricity consumption during periods of time when the cost is high. To address this problem, advanced metering systems display to customers how much power costs at different times of the day. Using wireless communications systems and smart meters, the technology uses time-based pricing, reflecting the actual cost of power. The program intends to shift consumption away from periods of peak demand. But it also reduces the utility's cost of providing power when demand is high and decreases carbon emissions from the electricity sector, as reliance on coal-fired power stations declines (Weeks, 2010).

Integrating Smart Grid Technologies

The aforementioned problems and challenges with energy systems, in particular the electric grid, have given rise to an innovative idea called the *smart grid*—a network of integrated microgrids that monitor and manage themselves. In a smart grid, two-way communication occurs, thus improving efficiency and communication. Smart grids apply innovations from the information technology and telecommunications sectors to the utility infrastructure. Sensing mechanisms accompany automatic control for electricity transmission and repairs. Active and organized distribution networks provide better options for the integration of renewables. Greater potential exists for the incorporation of electric vehicles into the network. Advanced digital systems, automation, and control technologies allow both the continuous flow of electricity and an immediate notification of problems. If disruption occurs with electricity supply, the smart grid first isolates the problem and then adjusts supply.

A number of technologies highlight the advances of smart grid capabilities. High-bandwidth communication systems reduce costs, enabling more timely information about power lines and buildings. New tools for data management, analytics, and visualization improve both the ability to monitor the system and the flow of power from station generators to end-use customers. A greater use of phasor measurement units enhances the detection of oscillations in power generation that may be missed by supervisory control systems.

However, according to Biello (2010), the most important aspect of smart grid innovation is likely end-users. In the United States, the 150 million electric meters in homes, industries, and businesses employ the same basic technology that Elihu Thomson invented in 1888: they passively record the electricity used in kilowatt-hours. If smart meters display electricity consumption, how consumption relates to the behavior of neighbors, and the best time of the day to operate appliances, lower utility bills, and higher customer satisfaction will result.

But many challenges exist. Smart meters are not always reliable. Rate increases to pay for technology upgrades frustrate customers. Balancing electricity supply and demand continues to challenge power operators. In order to meet spikes in demand, utility companies generate *spinning reserve*—some electricity generation kept in standby mode. But this practice leads to the unnecessary burning of fossil fuels. The installation of smart meters and sensors throughout the hundreds of thousands of miles of the entire energy system requires decades of work. In one example, the smart grid city initiative in Boulder, CO, initiated in 2008, cost $2,000 per customer and included few homes (Biello, 2010). These realities made it impossible to use the example as a model for other communities.

Perhaps the greatest challenge is cybersecurity (Swanson, 2010). In traditional electricity grids, cybersecurity addresses bulk transmission lines from utilities to transmission substations. This part of the network is where worst-case scenarios could happen, such as large regional blackouts. With smart grid technology, however, power companies must consider protecting connections with homes, building, and factories. Security efforts must prevent hackers from infiltrating the network. The reason cybersecurity is a concern is that the grid generates a large amount of data. One innovation developed to handle data flow, *synchrophasors*, are measurement devices. Operating at a speed over 100 times faster than conventional capabilities, this application allows different locations, end-users, and utilities to be time aligned. Supplying synchrophasors, however, requires capital investment and network learning.

Electrification for the Environment

Five dimensions of security exist for an energy system: energy availability, affordability, resilience, governance, and environmental quality. But if the energy system satisfies the demand for electricity, pumps large quantities of carbon emissions into the air, exacerbates the climate crisis, and creates deleterious environmental outcomes, the system will not satisfy the environmental dimension. In addition, thermodynamic limits to the process of turning power sources such as natural gas, coal, or nuclear into electricity means only two-thirds of the energy from the sources makes it to the electric grid. Furthermore, once electricity is generated, electricity losses are equal to about 2 percent in transmission from power plants to substations and about 4 percent in distribution from substations to customers. Finally, efficiency losses occur for customers. Homes, factories, and buildings may experience losses, depending on the age of the infrastructure and connections to the energy system.

To address these challenges, a number of articles argue for specific programs and policies. Dennis (2015) argues that the energy system needs increased efficiency of end-use appliances, a long-term reduction in greenhouse gas intensity of the electric grid, and better management of end-use electric load to integrate more variable generation of renewables. Sternberg and Bardow (2015) make the case for distribution of surplus electricity into storage systems instead of producing in conventional ways. Dennis et al. (2016) conclude that a number of trends for environmentally beneficial electrification are already underway, including the implementation of public policies to achieve greenhouse gas emission reduction, lower emission rates, and higher efficiency of end-use devices, including space heating, water heating, and transportation.

If the country is to achieve ambitious levels of emission reduction, modernization of all aspects of the energy system must occur. Appropriate policies enhance the supply and demand for renewables; energy storage; cost-effective methods to capture, store, and re-use carbon dioxide; the efficiency of electricity transmission and distribution; incentive for greater use of variable generation; and the efficiency of end-use products and devices. The public policy and private sector framework necessary to make these changes will require an emphasis on long-term processes, integrated solutions, and enhanced communication networks.

Model of the Future Energy System

The model of the future energy system, adapted from U.S. DOE (2015b), includes all sources of power, a smart grid, variable generators, an advanced energy infrastructure, two-way communications between producers and consumers, and carbon capture and storage technology (figure 3.4). The model moves from a traditional, centralized framework to a hybrid system with greater computing and communication capabilities. Smart meters, storage capacity, and automated feeder switches facilitate system transition. New technologies for the delivery of electricity, including infrastructure improvements, fiber optics, and wireless networks enable a two-way flow of both information and electricity. In this framework, residential, industrial, and commercial customers will both consume electricity and serve as energy suppliers. But a modern grid incorporates protections against technical, human, and natural risk. As a result, this future system is characterized by flexibility, the ability to satisfy demand, technological advance, a method of fighting cyberattacks, and sustainable components.

Transmission and Distribution Centers

Transmission and distribution centers establish a network between energy suppliers and customers, coordinate communication, oversee electricity distribution, and provide base power, intermediate power, and peak load power. As resource capacity increases, these centers integrate renewable power sources.

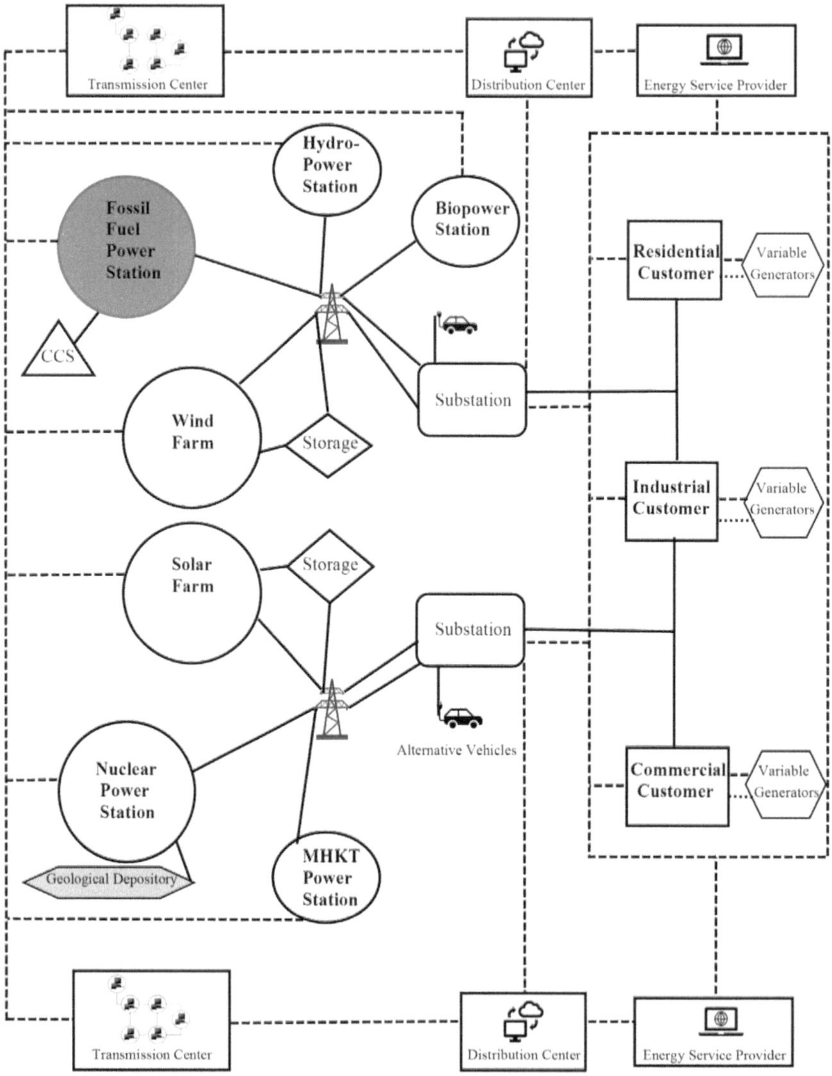

Figure 3.4 Model of the Future Energy System. *Source*: Author using information from U.S. DOE (2015b).

They also make sure the process of energy-efficient implementation of modern technologies, particularly with respect to the electric grid at all scales, integrates smoothly into the system. By providing real-time information, they ensure that the grid is resilient and secure in the presence of technical, human, and natural risks. Over time, grid modernization will continue. Smart grid technology will use communication and information technology to manage the flow of electricity more efficiently. Due to the size of the system, the number of participants on the supply and demand sides, and the evolving devices in the smart grid model, interoperability between the transmission and the distribution centers, power providers, and customers is the key to success.

Energy Service Providers

The model of the future demonstrates a more integrated energy system. The model does not displace the central grid, but new technologies are integrated in such a way to make electricity transmission more efficient on the supply side, responsive to the demand side, and resilient in the presence of risks. Currently, many private energy companies offer energy-efficient products and services to residential and business customers. However, in the model of the future, energy service providers have opportunities to provide more options: sources of energy, renewables, customer services, smart home technology, home security, and variable generators, including solar, wind, and geothermal. They could leverage data in smart meters to both understand customer preferences and provide new services. They could even offer multiple ways to retrofit, conserve energy, and manage market risk. If energy service providers offer these new technologies to customers, facilitate the integration of technological options on the supply side with changing customer preferences on the demand side, and maintain system goals, they could help create a more efficient and productive system.

Energy Storage

Electricity generated from renewable resources is growing worldwide. But it can rarely contribute to immediate changes in demand. It does not provide a constant supply. However, extensive research is addressing ways to store power, especially when it is generated by solar and wind. In the model of the future energy system, energy storage serves as a crucial element in the management of energy resources. For renewable energy sources to serve as stable contributors to the system, strengthen electricity networks, and maintain load levels, technology must overcome the inconveniences of variability and intermittency. Ibrahim et al. (2008) discuss a number of energy storage technologies. The reader is encouraged to read this article, as it provides a comprehensive discussion of many storage options. One example, *thermal energy storage*, first stocks thermal energy by heating or cooling a storage medium. Then, at a later time, the system may use the stored energy for power generation, heating, or cooling. Industrial processes and buildings primarily use this technology. Another example, *chemical energy storage*, achieved by using accumulators, provides a double function of storage and release of electricity. By alternating charge-discharge phases, this technology transforms chemical energy generated by electrochemical reactions into electricity, and vice versa. Portable, emergency backup and renewable energy storage systems often use this technology.

Alternative Vehicles

Market options for alternative vehicles are growing. New types of hybrid cars (diesel/electric; gas/electric; biofuel/electric) are available. Flexible fuel cars and trucks use more than one fuel (such as biofuels and gasoline). Hydrogen fuel cell vehicles use hydrogen as its onboard fuel for motive power. Electric vehicles allow drivers to plug them in to charge in off-board electric power sources. Natural gas vehicles are cost-effective for high-mileage and centrally fueled fleets. Neighborhood electric vehicles, first found in California, are one-to-four passenger, three- or four-wheeled vehicles that are designed for use in urban areas for commuting, errands, or local deliveries. The benefits of alternative vehicles include the reduction in oil consumption and combustion, contributions to environmental quality, and decreasing prices. Costs include ongoing maintenance, mileage that is only marginally better per gallon than high-efficiency cars, and a limited charging infrastructure for plug-ins.

Residential, Industrial, and Commercial Customers

Residential, industrial, and commercial customers demand stable and affordable electricity. In the presence of power outages, supply disruptions, and other problems, customers bear the burden. However, in the United States, the power sector and electricity grid are generally cost-effective and reliable. The challenge is that the share of electricity flowing to buildings (residential and commercial) has grown over time as a percentage of all electricity consumed in the economy. As a result, for the purpose of environmentally beneficial electrification, not only must we examine the sources of energy and their polluting implications, but we must consider the primary uses for electricity in buildings, including heating, cooling, ventilation, lighting, refrigeration, computers, and electronics. These processes must become more efficient.

Carbon Capture and Storage

The first step toward the reduction of carbon emissions from electricity generation is capturing the emissions in power stations or industrial factories such as cement manufacturing, refineries, steel making, and ethanol fermentation. The next step is storing it away from the atmosphere, thus completing the process of carbon capture and storage (CCS). The process works as follows: CCS technology secures, purifies, and concentrates carbon emissions at source. The captured carbon is then pressurized, forming a liquid that can be transported to a storage site. But the process requires large volumes of geological storage. Options include gas fields, oil fields, or aquifers. Deep below the surface, the fluid could be injected into porous rocks. The choice of stable storage sites without seepage would secure the carbon for thousands of years. But a number of challenges exist with CCS technology, including a lack of financial commitment, an increase in the monthly utility bills of households, and future monitoring.

Nevertheless, many benefits exist. One, CCS serves as an option for mitigation. Two, the process could reduce global emissions from energy by 20 percent (Haszeldine, 2009). Three, CCS technology makes fossil fuel combustion more sustainable. In terms of addressing the criteria for the evaluation of power technology, CCS increases the cost of electricity generation, but, by reducing carbon emissions, decreases the greenhouse gas footprint of the electric power grid.

SUMMARY

Through an interrelated network of power sources, power stations, transmission, and distribution connections, energy systems attempt to maintain an available, affordable, and resilient supply of electricity. Energy sectors, which include power sources and the electric grid, serve specific purposes within the energy system. In the United States, coal, natural gas, and nuclear power provide the majority of the generation capacity and power production. Although hydropower and other renewables are growing in importance, they remain small percentages of the total. With the traditional electric grid, maintenance and operating costs demonstrate the need for upgrades. Technological advances in clean power technology represent a way forward. In particular, renewables, fuel cells, and CCS offer methods of improving the environmental outcomes of the electric grid. Over time, public and private partnerships, financial incentives, emission reduction, clean energy, grid integration, and harmonizing policy and planning will help to usher in evolutionary changes to the electricity grid. Smart grid technologies, two-way communication between producers and consumers, and variable generation will advance the energy system. The future energy system will include these innovations, but will also maintain the fundamental priority of providing electricity to residential, industrial, and commercial customers in a reliable and affordable manner.

TERMS

Base load
Binary cycle plant
Carbon capture and storage
Chemical energy storage
Concentrating solar thermal power stations
Distributed energy resources
Dry steam plant
Energy resource capacity
Energy sector
Energy system
Equipment health sensors
Flash steam plant
Grid interconnection
Intermediate load
National standard
Microgrids
Peak load
Renewable energy standards
Re-sequester
Rotating devices
Smart grid
Soft costs of solar energy
Spinning reserve
Synchrophasors
Thermal energy storage
Transmission network
Wave energy converters

QUESTIONS

1. Describe the model of power sources and electricity generation. For individual countries, which sources of power generate the highest percentage of electricity? Why does this pattern exist? For Japan, graph the contribution of nuclear power for the supply of electricity from the year 2000 to the present. During this period of time, what happened? Explain the role of the Fukushima Power Plant disaster of 2011.
2. Conduct research on changes in electricity consumption in the United States. On its website, the U.S. Energy Information Administration has

helpful data: www.eia.gov. Over the last decade, what is the trend? Over the last five decades, what is the trend? Why are these trends occurring?

3. Look up U.S. State Renewable Energy (Portfolio) Standards and Goals at the National Conference of State Legislatures' website: http://www.ncsl.org/research/energy/renewable-portfolio-standards.aspx. Which states have standards? Which states have voluntary standards or targets? Which states have no standards or targets? Of the states that have standards, which are the most ambitious in terms of requiring the use of renewable energy?
4. Study the criteria for the evaluation of power technology. Explain each component. In terms of the three categories of electric requirements, siting characteristics, and environmental outcomes, what are the potential tradeoffs of each? Pick an individual form of technology, such as nuclear power, solar power, or hydropower. What are the specific tradeoffs? Given your discussion of the tradeoffs, do you believe net benefits exist when choosing this form of technology? Explain.
5. Unlike solar or wind technology, geothermal power provides a stable flow of electricity into the grid, day or night. The heat that flows to power stations contributes to an electricity sector's baseload power. However, geothermal is locationally specific. Globally, what countries incorporate the largest percentage of geothermal power in their energy systems? Pick one country. Research its geothermal power sector. In the United States, what states use the largest percentage of geothermal energy? Pick a state. Research its geothermal power sector. At the country or state level, do policies exist that encourage a greater use of geothermal energy?
6. Stationary fuel cells offer a number of benefits, including on-site power generation, resilience, reliability, and a small greenhouse gas footprint. What are the costs of stationary fuel cells? What are the technical challenges? Why are they not more widespread? Conduct research on an individual fuel cell plant. Is the plant cost-effective? Explain.
7. Research the process of CCS. Start with the article cited in the Bibliography section by Haszeldine (2009). Find related articles. Address the following questions: What are the technological requirements for the implementation of CCS technology? What are appropriate geological destinations? What examples of CCS technology are currently being used? Do the benefits of large-scale implementation of CCS technology outweigh the costs?

Chapter 4

Energy Sectors, Part II

Fuels, Buildings, Industry, and Transportation

AQUA TOWER

In 2009, when the Aqua Tower, an eighty-two-story skyscraper, was built in Chicago, it became the tallest residential building designed by an American firm headed by woman, Jeanne Gang of Studio Gang Architects. The building—with nonlinear balconies representative of waves—contains condos, apartments, a restaurant, and hotel. One reviewer wrote "the building seems to flutter with the winds that gust off nearby Lake Michigan" (Lasky, 2011).

In addition to adding a unique presence to the Chicago skyline, Gang identified environmental sustainability as an important factor in the design of the building. Examples include energy-efficient lighting, rainwater collection systems, and terrace extensions that maximize solar shading. The green roof helps to cool part of the building in the summer. The terrace provides a comfortable environment for both residents and tourists to recreate with a running path and an outdoor Jacuzzi. These and other aspects of efficient building design help to decrease energy requirements. The convenient location of the building near the bike path on Lake Michigan, the Magnificent Mile, and the city's downtown means building residents may ride their bikes to work.

The *Quadrennial Technology Review* of the U.S. Department of Energy (2015a) identifies four themes, convergence, diversification, confluence, and efficiency, which explain how energy sectors are intertwined. The themes also provide context and organization for the material in this chapter on the following energy sectors: fuels, buildings, industry, and transportation.

With *convergence*, energy sectors become more interconnected with each other and the economy. The buildings, industrial, and transportation sectors overlap in their demand for fuel. But all energy sectors are associated with energy markets, waste flows, and water systems. Properly integrated energy sectors may improve their operations but lessen environmental impacts.

Diversification means how the sectors are adapting and adjusting to changing market conditions. As one example, the power sector is adopting a greater use of renewables. Another example concerns demand for natural gas, electricity, and biofuels in the transportation sector.

The *confluence* of technical capabilities with software, computing power, modeling, and synthesis is creating a new era of analytics. Advances in computational modeling, big data management, and sensors are applicable across complex systems and therefore all energy sectors.

The achievement of *efficiency* gains in each energy sector, with greater output using the same energy resources, or the same level of output with fewer resources, may advance economic, environmental, and security goals. Efficiency gains in the value chain will help to reduce costs, improve the quality of the product or service, and reduce emissions.

THE FUEL SECTOR

Fuels are compounds with stored energy. Chemical bonds capture the stored energy through respiration and photosynthesis. A fuel, then, is a carrier of chemical energy that is released by a reaction to produce energy services, heat, or work. Coal, oil, wood, and natural gas have energy-rich chemical bonds that were created by energy from the Sun. They originated from the fossilized and decayed remains of plants and animals that lived millions of years ago. These fossil fuels are hydrocarbons with minor impurities. When the substances are burned, energy is released. The fossil fuels of oil, coal, and natural gas account for more than 80 percent of total U.S. primary energy use: they have high energy density, low costs of production, and are abundant. Oil is a mixture of carbon, hydrogen, nitrogen, oxygen, sulfur, and a few trace metals, consumed in vehicles, home heating, and industrial processes. Oil is also used to create thousands of petrochemicals, which are inputs in carpets, curtains, candles, milk cartons, detergents, food additives, and many other products. Coal is more of a polymeric substance than oil (the structure is composed of multiple repeating units), existing as a solid rather than a liquid. Natural gas is a light hydrocarbon fraction found in most oil deposits. Mostly made of methane and ethane, natural gas burns with high heat output, but produces fewer carbon emissions than oil or coal. *Biomass*, not categorized as a fossil fuel, refers to renewable organic materials burned directly or processed into biofuels, such as agricultural crops, municipal waste, or wood chips.

Fuel for Buildings

Building types include mercantile and service (malls, stores, car dealerships, dry cleaners, gas stations), office (professional, government, and banks), education (elementary, middle, high school, and college), health care (hospitals and medical offices), and lodging (hotels, dormitories, and nursing homes). By major end uses, buildings need energy for space heating, lighting, refrigeration, ventilation, cooling, computers, cooking, and water heating. Natural gas and electricity are the most common energy sources for heating and cooling systems in buildings. Many buildings possess individual units for these services, but when they cluster together, such as on college campuses, central power plants distribute steam, hot water, or cold water in the form of *district energy systems*. These systems often consume fossil fuels, but some use renewables such as solar, wind, and geothermal.

Fuel for Industry

In the United States, industry accounts for one-third of all energy consumption. Fuels are necessary to generate hot water or steam, process heating to raise the temperature of products in manufacturing, create feedstocks to make products, and many other applications. Natural gas, electricity, liquefied petroleum gas (propane), coal, and other sources such as wood, agricultural waste, and paper-related refuse serve as important fuel sources in manufacturing. Every industry uses energy, but, in the United States, a few energy-intensive industries use most of the energy, including petroleum refining, chemicals, paper manufacturing, and metals.

Fuel for Transportation

In the United States, fuels supply 99 percent of the energy in the transportation sector. Electricity contributes a small amount. An analysis of the transportation sector reveals the extent to which individual fuels are linked to specific forms of transportation. Petroleum refining, which creates gasoline, diesel, jet fuel, residual fuel oil, and liquefied petroleum gas, supplies these fuels for every form of transportation from automobiles to recreational boating. Diesel powers everything from automobiles to commercial shipping. Jet fuel is for general aviation and commercial aircraft. Ethanol is used in automobiles, light trucks, and medium and heavy trucks. Compressed natural gas is used in automobiles, trucks, and transit buses. A number of other fuels satisfy final energy needs in the transportation sector.

THE BUILDING SECTOR

In the future, an increase in economic activity will spur growth in the building sector. But technological advance may reduce energy consumption. Water heating, lighting, and space conditioning represent half of the energy consumption in the U.S. building sector. Advances in efficiency in these areas represent important recent breakthroughs. At the same time, the building sector's share of electricity consumption has increased from less than 50 percent in the 1970s to more than 75 percent today. This increase demonstrates why the building sector is important for energy efficiency, but also why future building design must consider technological advances that reduce energy demand. A number of forces are currently reshaping the industry, causing all phases of construction, operation, financing, policy, and insurance to adapt to changing conditions. These forces include a desire for green certification and a preference for sustainable construction.

Green Certification

Green certification adds integrity and accountability to the building process. In 1993, the establishment of the U.S. Green Building Council signaled a commitment of industry and government to high-performance building practices. To improve energy efficiency and environmental outcomes, the council transformed the way builders design, construct, and operate new buildings. To put these new values in place, between 1993 and 1998, a task force of the Council developed a rating system to evaluate the environmental impacts and level of resource efficiency of buildings. The system, Leadership in Energy and Environmental Design (LEED), serves as a certification program for communities and builders.

With sustainable development as a goal, LEED applies credits that must be met to achieve a specific level of certification, including Certified, Silver, Gold, or Platinum. It covers five categories: sustainable sites, energy and atmosphere, water efficiency, materials and resources, and indoor environmental quality. Additional credits are possible through innovation and regional priorities. Credits toward certification include locational characteristics, educational initiatives, the environmental footprint of construction, and building performance. Around the world, many communities adopt LEED for their verification process with almost 2 million square feet certified daily. Because LEED works for all building types—including office towers and homes—and all phases of development, the system provides a systematic method of evaluating environmental and energy performance.

Over the life of a building, higher levels of resource and energy efficiency lead to lower costs for operation and maintenance. But LEED certification creates other benefits. In a study of LEED certification, Matisoff et al. (2014) find that green building adoption is driven by two motivations: performance and marketing benefits. Better performance lowers operating costs. Marketing benefits result from consumer responses to green certification. Builders improve their reputation through perceived environmental performance. This activity enhances their economic standing in the marketplace. While all participants in LEED certification seek marketing benefits, the interest in this particular type of "green signaling" is significant, according to Matisoff (2014).

Sustainable Construction

Sustainable construction—using processes that are both resource efficient and environmentally responsible—is important for reasons of economy and functionality. Because more than half the world's population now lives in urban areas, the building sector could contribute to a sustainable future. But to achieve this goal when urban populations are swelling by more than 1 million people per week, architects and urban planners must optimize the design and performance of new structures. Incorporating elements of social responsibility, environmental performance, and economic efficiency, sustainable construction occurs when urban planning, architectural design, and capital financing share sustainability as a goal. The framework for sustainable construction, adapted from Kibert (2013)—an important text on the topic—provides a model to address energy and the building sector and includes principles, phases, and resources.

Principles of Sustainable Construction

The principles of sustainable construction provide guidelines. The principles (reduce, reuse, and recycle) guide builders when adopting resource inputs. These principles also complement the idea of protecting nature. For new buildings to rise, builders may target empty plots or old structures. An important principle concerns the elimination of toxics. Because good buildings last several generations, builders must choose resource inputs that do not poison the soil. An economic consideration, *life-cycle costing*, refers to the identification of all costs involved over the life of the building. Initial capital outlays; resource requirements for design, building, and maintenance; operational support; and many other costs are a part of process. These cost considerations help to determine potential profitability. They also determine the degree of sustainability. Building design, for example, may emphasize rainwater capture or passive cooling systems. The final principle, quality, emphasizes building contributions to neighborhoods. Buildings that contribute to the vitality of a city, a reduction in environmental impact, and efficient energy use, such as the Bank of America Building in New York City or the PricewaterhouseCoopers Building in London, contribute to a world that will experience a doubling of the urban population by 2050.

Phases of Sustainable Construction

The phases of sustainable construction address the entire construction life cycle from planning to deconstruction. When builders first begin the planning process, they have to work with a zoning committee to secure a specific site. Buildings may offer residential, commercial, office, manufacturing, or warehouse facilities. Cities zone specific plots to satisfy different needs, usually clustering plots together with the same zoning requirements. Cities then designate manufacturing districts, residential areas, commercial centers, etc. The choice of the specific site and building purpose guides the process. An important recent trend combines some of these elements, such as residential and commercial. This combination helps neighborhoods achieve higher urban density, especially when a residential building is close to public transportation and bike paths, such as the Aqua Building in Chicago.

After builders decide to offer office, residential, or another type of space, they must find investors and architects. While investors evaluate the potential for a new building to achieve a rate of return, architects consider space, materials, context, neighborhood, the environment, and other factors when establishing an appropriate design. The construction process employs the principles by securing the resources necessary to build a strong and appropriate structure. Market trends, the business cycle, and evolving macro conditions require building modifications. The iconic Willis Tower in Chicago, for example, once the tallest building in the United States, a 108-story, 1450-foot skyscraper, is known to many by its previous name: Sears Tower. In this building, renovations and updates have occurred with the name change, providing modern office space, technological capabilities, and reputational impacts that maintain both high occupancy rates and reasons for tourists to visit the Skydeck, with an enclosed and see-through ledge on the 103rd floor. With any structure, resource allocation for maintenance provides necessary funding for use and operation, a requirement that engineers deem appropriate for the life cycle of the building. The last phase, deconstruction, acknowledges that buildings do not last forever. Although buildings are present during most human life spans, even iconic buildings such as Penn Station in New York City (1910–1963) eventually meet their end.

Resources for Sustainable Construction

Sustainable construction requires resource-conscious design, according to Kibert (2013). Resource-conscious design aims to minimize both the consumption of natural resources and the impact on ecological systems. In terms of material selection, two goals exist: closing material loops and eliminating solid and liquid waste and gaseous emissions. A *closed-loop process* describes the ability to maintain resources in productive use. In this scenario, builders do not dispose of resources at the end of the building life cycle. Instead, resources in closed loops are disassembled and recycled. But not all resources recycle. As a result, to achieve the goal of sustainable construction, recycled materials must not be toxic in the natural environment. After deconstruction, many materials are appropriate for lower-value use, such as road or playground sub-base. But in most developed countries, construction and demolition waste constitutes an important part of overall waste flowing into landfills, increasing construction costs or threatening water supplies.

To estimate the potential for sustainable construction, designers and builders evaluate the composition of final structures in terms of life-cycle effects, considering the specific resource inputs used in the process. Two types of land resources exist: developed and undeveloped land. In urban areas, developed land may be reconstituted, rezoned, or altered in a way that satisfies planners' conceptions of economic development. A small building satisfying the commercial market may give way to a large building satisfying both the commercial and office markets. Alternatively, we may think of undeveloped land as a precious finite resource. Its development should be minimized. Some cities, such as Boulder, Colorado, address this issue by discouraging sprawl. Boulder establishes strict city boundaries that prohibit development beyond its borders.

Building material is used in the construction process, natural or synthetic. Natural materials, such as lumber, are unprocessed or minimally processed. Synthetic materials are manufactured and include substances such as petroleum-based paints or plastics. While natural materials are easier to recycle after deconstruction, synthetic materials, especially plastics made from oil, do not biodegrade.

In the building process, the supply of potable water may limit growth opportunities. The urbanization of sun-belt cities, for example, drains local water supplies. Over time, long-term planning for stable water sources, water conservation, low-flow plumbing, water recycling, and rainwater harvesting must accompany new construction. Taken as a whole, resource-conscious design, which includes land, materials, and water, must integrate with ecosystems. The reason is that sustainably integrated systems monitor building loads, design requirements, and waste so as not to disrupt the natural environment.

Finally, the resource process acknowledges that energy conservation must occur through effective building design. Many buildings employ renewable resources, heat transfer, and passive design. The latter includes assimilating a building into local elements of topography, climatological factors, wind, solar effects, and landscaping. Higher energy performance leads to more *energy-neutral buildings*. In these buildings, the amount of energy consumed equals the amount of energy generated on-site. These buildings may even become net exporters of energy, generating more energy than they consume.

Energy and the Building Sector

The building sector constitutes a major part of our economy's infrastructure. An improvement in energy performance serves as a goal for building design and operation. In the United States, more than 10 percent of primary energy sources, including fossil fuels and renewables, flow to the building sector. If we include the energy that first flows into the electricity grid and then to buildings, the building sector consumes 40 percent of the nation's energy. As a result, energy consumption serves as the most important challenge for sustainable buildings.

High-Performance Energy Design

High-performance energy design includes two fundamental goals: the consumption of fewer fossil fuels and the use of more renewables for heating, cooling, and ventilation. According to Kibert (2013), a number of innovations exist:

- Simulation tools to minimize energy consumption
- Passive solar design
- Thermal performance of the building envelope, which is the physical separator between the building's interior and exterior, including walls, floors, roofs, and doors
- Minimization of internal loads: equipment, appliances, processes, and lighting
- Heating, venting, and cooling (HVAC) systems that minimize energy consumption
- Maximization of the consumption of renewables
- The capture of waste energy through heat and power systems, cogeneration, ventilation/exhaust air energy recovery, and other processes

These innovations are part of an iterative process. But when optimizing innovations, tradeoffs occur. The developer's budget, priorities, and requirements evolve. A city's zoning board may vote to restrict the height of a residential tower. An architect may decrease operation costs with a phase change in materials. When implementing high-performance energy design, planners use energy targets, performance, and modeling practices.

Passive Design Strategy

A confluence of factors influences building design: place, function, goals, materials, and budget. Many designers advocate a *passive design strategy*—which incorporates a building's site, materials, and climate—to minimize energy consumption with respect to ventilation, lighting, heating, and cooling. It incorporates naturally occurring resources, including trees, plants, wind, and sunlight. It also evaluates the potential of developing these resources. Kibert (2013) explains that passive design "includes the use of all possible measures to reduce energy consumption prior to the consideration of any external energy source other than the sun and wind" such as:

- Local climate and site conditions
- Building aspect ratio (the ratio of the building's length to its width)
- Building orientation
- Building massing (the energy storage potential of materials)
- Building use and occupancy schedule
- Day-lighting strategy
- Building envelope (including shading, air leakage, and ventilation)
- Internal loads (including people, appliances, equipment, and lighting)
- Ventilation

While climate factors and passive design are applied, ideal energy performance requires factor integration. Computer modeling includes the evaluation of equipment, location, engineering details, orientation, shape, and building type. Collaboration between architectures and engineers promotes the optimal choice of building specifics. Finally, the application of passive design strategy differs with respect to geography. The dry climate of Phoenix, Arizona, for example, differs greatly from the rain-soaked climate of Seattle, Washington, and the elevated conditions of Denver, Colorado. Natural light for illumination, storing solar energy, and introducing landscaping (including green rooftops) to promote natural heating and cooling serve as cornerstones for this strategy.

THE INDUSTRIAL SECTOR

Energy is consumed by a diverse group of industrial divisions, including agriculture, forestry, and fishing; mining; construction; manufacturing; transportation; communications; wholesale trade; retail trade; finance, insurance, and real estate; services; and public administration. Because each industrial division varies with respect to output, pricing, and regulation, energy consumption and environmental impacts differ. The following discussion focuses on two divisions: agriculture and manufacturing. For the others, the reader is encouraged to investigate both the energy profile and environmental consequences.

Energy and Agriculture

During the last fifty years, the agricultural sector has created two impressive outcomes in the United States: less than 2 percent of the population is directly employed in food production, and this industrial division produces more than the domestic average caloric intake per person per day—about 2,500 calories—for all people in the country. What happens with the excess calories? Some calories are exported as processed or fresh food and others are wasted.

A food chain involves production, processing, distribution, consumption, and waste. It connects to every sector of the economy and requires fossil fuels for agricultural inputs, fertilizers, and irrigation in food production; processing practices such as packaging; distribution services such as cold storage and shipping; the use of refrigeration, preparation, and disposal in food service establishments, food retailing, and home kitchens; and the processes involved with waste. Dr. Michael Webber (2012), Department of Mechanical Engineering at the University of Texas at Austin, writing in *Scientific American*, explains that "the energy used to make food is vastly greater than the amount of energy we get out of it. The U.S. expends roughly 10 units of fossil energy to produce one unit of food energy." To decrease the energy requirements in the agricultural sector, Webber argues, we need to reduce the 10:1 ratio of energy inputs to food output (i.e., energy eaten). This reduction in the ratio would require a number of steps, including the conversion of agricultural waste products into power, drip irrigation, no-till agriculture, more precision farming with GPS-enabled technology, and more regional production systems.

Consider historical perspective. According to Tomczak (2006), three periods created the food system's modern reliance on fossil fuels. First, between 1900 and 1920, an increase in agricultural output was a function of more cultivated land with little technological advance. In the second period, the so-called Green Revolution, between 1920 and 1970, evolving technology took advantage of cheap and abundant fossil fuels and led to productivity growth. Examples included the synthetic fertilizers, hybrid crops, irrigation, herbicides, pesticides, and machinery that require fossil fuels. The third period, from 1970 to the present, is characterized by decreasing returns to scale. According to Tomczak (2006), larger amounts of fossil fuels are necessary to increase output and offset the negative environmental effects of pesticides and soil erosion.

In the United States, the food system accounts for an important share of fossil fuel consumption. During food production, petroleum is necessary for farm machinery, pesticides, transportation, and irrigation. In terms of processing, petroleum is required for packaging, plastics, food additives, and waste. With distribution, petroleum powers the vehicles that transport food items across hundreds or thousands of miles. With food consumption, the processes of driving to stores, storing perishable items in refrigerators, cooking, and running appliances require either petroleum or other fossil fuels. The stage of waste involves trash removal and recycling, both petroleum-intensive activities.

Food Production

The objectives of industrial food production include the minimization of consumer prices and the maximization of crop yields. The principles of standardization and specialization—predicated on the availability of inexpensive fossil fuels—have existed since the 1960s. Today, crop and livestock production differs with respect to the use of soil and water, resource inputs, farming practices, technology, and policy implications. Large land tracts planted in monocultures rely on capital-intensive equipment and manufactured inputs. Worldwide, thousands of large-scale concentrated animal feeding operations (CAFOs) rely on formulated feeds made from grains.

Fossil fuels are used to expand crop production in the form of synthetic fertilizer and agricultural pesticides. Pesticides are made from oil. Fertilizers are made from ammonia, which is created from natural gas. In the production process, farming equipment such as tractors and trailers require fossil fuels to prepare the soil, irrigate fields, sow seeds, and harvest crops. These technologies, bolstered by government subsidies, make the process of monoculture, especially corn, soybeans, and wheat, common practices in the industry.

On the industrial farm, energy-intensive inputs include fuel, electricity, fertilizer, machinery, and irrigation. Energy related to food production remains an important share of the total national energy budget. It increased during the first decade of this century, according to the United States Department of Agriculture (Canning et al., 2010). At the same time, the process of industrial livestock grew. Because of the prevalence of grain that is fed to livestock, feedlots continue to provide the majority of meat in the United States. Most dairy products, eggs, and meat are now produced on factory farms. These huge industrial operations raise thousands of animals in confined conditions. Because the animals cannot graze, factory farms require large quantities of feed from industrial crops, using energy-intensive farming techniques. But factory farms may pollute ground and surface water sources. These realities require municipalities to expend energy resources for water treatment.

An example demonstrates the energy requirements of large-scale food production: nonorganic salad mix. Grown in the agricultural valley of California, planters first drop seeds on the fields with precision seed planters attached to gasoline-powered tractors. When the salad crop is growing, diesel-powered spreaders apply herbicides, pesticides, and nitrogen-based fertilizers. These inputs are manufactured with electricity and natural gas, shipped in diesel trucks to local wholesalers. Local growers purchase the inputs from wholesalers. Also, during the growing period, farms employ electric-powered irrigation equipment. At harvest time, field workers pick the salad greens, pack them in boxes from a paper mill, load them in gasoline-powered vehicles, and ship them to regional processing plants. Each step with industrial food production requires extensive energy resources (Canning et al., 2010).

Food Processing

After food production, processed foods are created from the substances that are refined or extracted from whole foods. The processed substances include remnants of animal foods, variants of sugar, hydrogenated oils and fats, starches, and flours. Processing first involves breaking down commodity crops such as corn or animals like cows into their component parts. The parts are then reassembled into value-added food. In this stage, the array of processed food items brought to the market is a function of supply-driven processes, such as the ways to package and market the commodity crops and animals produced by industrial farms.

Modern food processing may be dated from the 1950s, when scientific advance enabled a wide range of food substances made from additives and inexpensive ingredients. Food processing has allowed the evolution, adaption, and urbanization of humankind, but it has also increased fossil fuel requirements. The important market trend for both food and energy consumption is that, per capita in the developed world, the consumption of processed calories is increasing as a percentage of total calories. One group of authors concludes that "ultra-processed products dominate the food supplies of high-income countries, and that consumption of these products is now rapidly increasing in middle-income countries. The general effect is displacement of dietary patterns based on regular freshly prepared meals, by constant snacking on relatively energy-dense . . . products" (Monteiro et al., 2013).

Consider the commodity crop of corn. This crop dominates the agricultural landscape of the Midwestern United States. The crop is not the sweet or white corn variety that people eat directly, about a bushel per person per year in the United States. This crop is what is turned into resource inputs such as corn sweetener, corn starch, and corn meal, pervasive in food processing. The industrial food chain that brings corn to the marketplace in the context of value-added products is rooted in the farms that grow the corn and the consumers that buy it. But very little money flows to the farmer for value-added products such as soda, often less than 5 cents per dollar spent by the consumer. At the other end, there is a natural limit to the amount of food that a person should consume, although an increase in population leads to greater sales of processed food.

Much of the industrial corn that is grown does not enter our bodies directly, but is heavily processed, broken down into simple compounds, consumed by animals such as steer (which we then eat), or sent to a processing plant. Processing plants reassemble the corn components and add other ingredients to produce pork, chicken, beef, soda, snacks, breakfast cereals, and many other products. Processing plants require fossil fuels. Moreover, more than one-fifth of the industrial corn produced in the United States flows to one of twenty-five wet mills, where a bushel of corn is turned into the building blocks from which companies like Pepsi, McDonald's, and General Mills create processed food. Wet milling, however, is energy-intensive: for every calorie of processed food, wet milling burns 10 calories of fossil fuels. Food processing, which has liberated food from the forces of nature through scientific manipulation, requires abundant energy resources.

Food Distribution

Over the past several decades, the world has experienced a growth in the trade of food products. In the United States, food imports account for almost 20 percent of total food consumed. More than 20 percent of fresh vegetables and 50 percent of fresh fruit is imported into the country. These examples of globalization result from the expansion of global trade and cheaper transportation. With global food distribution, produce often travels thousands of miles, requiring a large amount of petroleum. In the United States, food travels 1,500 miles on average to reach a household's dining table. In Canada, the average exceeds 5,000 miles. An emphasis on just-in-time delivery for perishable items means more trips are made.

Many examples demonstrate this point. Much of the world's garlic comes from China. The United States imports more than 100 million pounds of garlic from China annually. China also produces industrialized jumbo shrimp from its aquatic factory farms for export. Bananas are grown in warm climates. The world's top exported fruit, the global banana trade exceeds 4 billion dollars annually. Ecuador, Brazil, China, and India produce more than half of the world's bananas. In the case of corn, after harvest, it travels to grain elevators. It is then loaded onto trains or trucks, which transport the corn to processing plants or feedlots. Processed food, such as potato chips, crackers, or meat items, which often contain corn syrup, are brought to the marketplace via trucks, distribution centers, and local workers for shelving. Every year, the United States also exports some of its corn harvest. For perishable items, food distribution requires refrigeration. But refrigerators are manufactured in fossil-fuel-intensive processes, distributed across oil-intensive transportation systems, and powered by electricity.

From the perspective of food companies, tactical planning of multimodal distribution networks includes goals for efficient delivery time and cost minimization, but lead to significant energy impacts. When the price of a barrel of oil is low by historical standards, the food system produces a relatively inexpensive supply of industrial food.

Over time, the effects of globalization on both the world agricultural trade and the consumption of fossil fuels for distribution will depend on demand side factors such as population growth, food consumption patterns, income distribution, and urbanization; supply-side factors such as the cost of resource inputs, technology, and livestock, crops, fisheries, and aquaculture; and exogenous factors such as climate change and water scarcity.

In an article on the distribution of fresh food, however, Bortolini et al. (2016) argue for a multiobjective optimizer with respect to distribution: while cost minimization should remain a fundamental goal, food companies should also minimize their carbon emissions during transportation. Despite this environmental goal, many forecasts argue that global trade in agriculture will expand, not contract, over time. The consumption of fossil fuels for food distribution will most likely increase.

Food Consumption

Humans derive energy from food. Until the early twentieth century, food energy was derived from the sun through the process of photosynthesis. Food in the industrial system is now derived from fossil fuels. Because of energy requirements, the consumption of fossil fuels is reflected in our diets. The typical person in the United States consumes around 2,000 pounds of food per year, according to the U.S. Department of Agriculture. But we may break down this total by food category: more than 600 pounds of dairy; almost 200 pounds of meat and poultry; 415 pounds of vegetables; and around 275 pounds of fruit. But it's not all healthy: on average, we consume 140 pounds of sweeteners. Converting pounds into calories, the average person in the United States consumes 3,600 calories per day, exceeding both the 2,000 calories recommended and the world average of 2,700.

This intersection between the food system and fossil fuels suggests that market and policy decisions that affect one sector will have spillover effects on others. Currently to feed each person in the United States, it takes on average the energy of a gallon of oil per day. For perspective, fossil fuel consumption connected to the food chain accounts for more than 13 percent of carbon emissions in the United States (Canning, 2017). As a result, federal dietary guidelines with high fossil fuel inputs increase the interconnection between food consumption and fossil fuels. Changes in food consumption patterns such as switching to more local or regional food items or implementing a tax on carbon or sugary drinks would decrease energy consumption in the industrial food chain. As Anna Lappé (2010) argues in her book, *Diet for a Hot Planet*, the reliance on an industrial and global model for the food chain increases both the consumption of fossil fuels and emissions of greenhouse gases. A climate-friendly model of consumption, in contrast, involves fewer fossil fuel inputs, the choice of more locally sourced food options, diverse farming techniques that mimic the natural environment, a diverse array of local and regional food options, and policy incentives that encourage the consumption of less energy-intensive food items.

Food Waste

Getting food through the food chain requires 10 percent of the nation's energy budget and 80 percent of all the freshwater consumed annually (Gunders, 2012). A major problem, however, is that 25 percent of the food goes uneaten. This is a lot of waste! This waste is valued at more than $165 billion annually. Wasted food rots in landfills, serves as the largest component of municipal waste, and leads to methane emissions, an important greenhouse gas. Not only is waste a problem for food security, in which one in six Americans lack a secure supply of food, but it also represents wasted energy. Food waste entails 2.5 percent of annual energy consumption in the United States. Reducing the amount of food we throw away would decrease the consumption of fossil fuels. But this would require new attitudes, policies, and behaviors (Webber, 2012).

Gunders (2012) provides a fascinating account of food waste in the United States. To provide context for Gunders' analysis, the average American wastes 50 percent more food than in the 1970s and ten times more than someone in Southeast Asia. According to Gunders (2012), the inefficiencies that exist at every stage of the food chain lead to wasted energy. Waste occurs with a number of food items, including grain products, seafood, fruits and vegetables, meat, and milk. During the production stage, 20 percent of fruits and vegetables are wasted. During processing and packaging, 10 percent of grain products are wasted. Distribution leads to a 9.5 percent loss for seafood. At the level of the household, 33 percent of seafood goes to waste, followed by 28 percent of fruits and vegetables, 27 percent of grain products, 17 percent of milk, and 12 percent of meat (Gunders, 2012). Matching food production/processing/distribution with actual consumption for households would lead to a number of impacts: a reduction of food waste, less fossil fuels in the food chain, and lower levels of energy for trash removal and recycling.

Energy and Manufacturing

Manufacturing accounts for almost 80 percent of industrial energy consumption. As a result, principles of clean energy manufacturing—which involve new energy opportunities in manufacturing, production systems, and supply chains—are important for the reduction of future energy consumption, the utilization of material inputs, and the reduction in greenhouse gases that contribute to climate change.

Manufacturing

In manufacturing systems, facilities integrate machinery, equipment, and processes into workflows that transform resource inputs into finished products. Manufacturing processes require fuel and electricity for heating, cooling, electro-chemical practices, and other processes. Technologies for real-time energy adjustments, materials handling, waste heat recovery, energy conversion, and onsite energy generation enhance energy efficiency. The process of 3D printing or rapid prototyping, for example, now satisfies orders for same-day production and shipping. In the case of automobile manufacturing, companies with 3D printing capabilities design multiple prototypes for engines and test them simultaneously. Engineers then choose the optimal design based on model characteristics and performance standards and produce them to specification. A number of opportunities may reduce energy demand: the reduction of wasted energy, advanced equipment that enhances throughput (the amount of resources passing through a process or system), integration strategies, and equipment co-location (U.S. DOE, 2015b).

Production Systems

Production integrates equipment and practices in factories. Energy performance depends on organizational characteristics, institutional pressures, and environmental management systems (EMS). Adopted by thousands of companies worldwide, an EMS includes internal policies and assessments that determine the relationship between the factory and the environment. A reduction in the consumption of energy as part of a firm's EMS is a function of market forces, nonmarket forces, and regulatory demands. Market forces—such as competitors, consumers, employees, industries, shareholders, and suppliers—impact supply and demand. Nonmarket forces—such as communities, activists, and the media—pressure firms to enhance efficiency and increase resource management. Regulatory demands include environmental legislation and the monitoring of energy consumption and pollution. When these forces pressure plant managers to reduce the consumption of energy, a firm puts in place a focused energy strategy, which aligns with a company's mission. Goals that achieve the strategy of energy reduction are then established. At the level of the production facility, an action plan is operationalized into daily activities that achieve the goal of energy reduction.

Supply Chains

Manufactured products reach consumers on a global scale, making it imperative to consider the energy implications of global supply chains. Supply chain management (SCM) systems organize the information, finances, and materials that move in the production process from supplier to consumer. These SCM systems coordinate business functions and tactics for the purpose of improving the production, distribution, and consumption of final-end products. The goal of SCM systems is to produce value in the form of services and products in the hands of consumers. The phases of global supply chains have energy requirements, including suppliers, manufacturing, distribution, and customers.

Consider cell phones. Many suppliers in the cell phone market provide components such as batteries, audio chips, screens, flash memory, and touchscreen controllers. These suppliers are located in many countries, including Germany, South Korea, Japan, Taiwan, England, the United States, France, Malaysia, Mexico, Denmark, and others. Manufacturing of the iPhone occurs in the city of Zhengzhou in China. Distribution and consumption of the iPhone occur globally. Since the beginning of this century, technological advance has turbocharged the expansion of global networks of trade, particularly in the form of digital communication and software design. Therefore, while supply chains have become more sophisticated, they expand in the presence of inexpensive fossil fuels.

Worldwide transport of output accounts for 20 percent of global primary energy use. Energy costs impact not only the distribution of goods and services but also manufacturing operations, warehousing, storage at the retail level, packaging at distribution centers, and consumption patterns. Because the global forces of supply and demand may increase the price of fossil fuels and thus the cost of global supply chains, energy efficiency constitutes an important long-term incentive. Options include a reduction in the number of components, locating suppliers close to manufacturers, and implementing energy-efficient manufacturing procedures such as combined heat and power systems. A number of methods may reduce the amount of oil used in distribution: increasing value density (a product's economic value relative to its weight), decreasing average transportation distance, changing the mix of transportation modes (such as shipping instead of air freight or rail instead of trucking), adjusting the utilization of transportation systems to reduce congestion and increase speed and route planning, and increasing the scale of distribution by enhancing the cargo-carrying capacity of a transportation system relative to energy consumed.

THE TRANSPORTATION SECTOR

An efficient transportation sector is essential for a robust economy. While a range of technological advances, including vehicle efficiency, electric vehicles, hydrogen fuel cells, and light rail systems reduce energy consumption, problems remain. Examples include a dependence on oil, lower air quality, problematic health effects, and greenhouse gas emissions. As they relate to energy, this section evaluates the challenges, opportunities, technological advances, and energy patterns in transportation.

But, first, consider historical context. In the United States, President Dwight D. Eisenhower signed the Federal-Aid Highway Act in 1956, which created the Interstate System, a monumentally important public works project. Eisenhower considered it to be the most important achievement of his two terms in office. Many historians agree. For our purposes, what is essential about the Interstate System is that every person in the country has been affected by it. We either use it directly as motorists or benefit indirectly when we consume products that are transported on it. The country's reliance on the Interstate System and national modes of transportation lead to the need for stable, reliable, and affordable sources of fuel. Recognizing oil dependence, many cities have implemented policies and programs that decrease this fuel requirement and the resulting environmental impacts. Examples include congestion pricing on highways, carpooling incentives, charges for driving in the commercial center of cities, and the expansion of train, bus, and subway systems. But collectively, the country still relies on highways, driving, and oil.

Challenges in Transportation

The transportation sector is a complex network of roads, bridges, highways, train tracks, rivers, airports, and airplane routes. The sector includes the vehicles presented earlier in the section for fuels and transportation, including light-duty vehicles, trucks, aircraft, ships, and trains. The sector entails the infrastructure and vehicles for ground support, material handling, personal transport, and the movement of goods, agriculture, construction, mining, and all resource inputs and output in other industrial divisions. Transportation accounts for 10 percent of gross domestic product in the United States and considerable public sector investment for maintenance, development, traffic management, and expansion. The transportation sector consumes 25 quadrillion British thermal units of oil annually, 70 percent of all oil consumed in the United States (U.S. DOE, 2015b). The challenges of the transportation sector include the management of a vast, evolving, and critical part of the economy; a reduction in the reliance on oil; and policies that reduce environmental impacts. Any strategy to increase the country's energy security by decreasing our dependence on oil must address the transportation sector.

Opportunities in Transportation

The transportation sector needs improvements that create greater flexibility, fuel efficiency, and safety. Higher levels of flexibility give travelers more options. In urban areas, efficient trains, buses, and planes are crucial for strong local and regional economies. Many cities, including Denver, Colorado and Portland, Oregon are expanding light rails systems. In rural areas, trains provide both access to urban centers and links between farms and distribution networks for commodity crops. Fuel efficiency reduces the cost of driving, air pollution, oil dependence, and greenhouse gas emissions. Future transportation markets—with greater levels of technology and efficiency—will transform according to economic, social, and demographic trends. Economic advances will lead to greater use of information technology, which will reduce cost and energy intensity for vehicular transportation. Social changes will make plug-in vehicles a more appealing option. Demographic trends, which include a higher rate of urbanization, will provide incentive for cities to improve public transportation, biking, and walking options. Ultimately, technological advances in the transportation sector will offer opportunities across many dimensions, from information and services to energy reduction.

Technological advances in transportation are intended to increase vehicle efficiency, reduce cost, and decrease environmental impacts. These goals will exist as fundamental challenges over time due to market competition, complex consumer needs, the entrenched nature of the global oil market, and the long life of automobiles. Higher emission standards, for example, may take a decade to show improvements in energy consumption and environmental quality. Advanced technologies in light-duty vehicles may take longer. Other programs intended to reduce vehicle weight or increase combustion technology may possess multiple benefits, but require patience in terms of design, supply-side effects, and overall market impact.

Vehicle Efficiency

An improvement in vehicle efficiency entails greater fuel economy, the ability of a vehicle to achieve more miles per gallon. Rolling resistance, aerodynamics, and vehicle mass determine a vehicle's energy requirements.

Most of a vehicle's energy is translated into motion, but vehicle accessories such as controllers, fans, and pumps also absorb energy. To increase vehicle efficiency, mechanical engineers design more advanced combustion engines and more energy-efficient vehicle systems. In terms of increasing the efficiency of internal combustion engines, advances in drivability, reliability, and the capacity to use alternative fuels are required. Improvements in engine efficiency may increase fuel economy and decrease carbon emissions. These improvements decrease fuel costs.

Advances in onboard computing, sensors, and engine technologies enable improvements in clean combustion strategies and high-speed engine controls. Challenges to further advances in combustion technologies include accurate simulations of combustion processes, catalyst materials, and emission controls. In terms of efficient vehicle systems, advances focus on conventional powertrains, the portion of the vehicle system that changes—minus the engine and transmission—when the vehicle is front-wheel, rear-wheel, or four-wheel drive. Engineers address system design attributes, optimization, and load management. But driving style also influences a vehicle's consumption of energy. Methods that encourage more defensive driving techniques decrease the consumption of gasoline. Over time, improvements in these areas increase performance, reduce energy consumption, and enhance vehicle efficiency.

Zero Tailpipe Emissions

Zero emission vehicles (ZEV) emit no tailpipe pollutants. Polluting emissions from combustion technologies include carbon dioxide, carbon monoxide, particulates, hydrocarbons, lead, and different nitrogen oxides. The avoidance of these pollutants by ZEV represents an important environmental benefit. But the results are mixed. Even though the consumption of gasoline decreases with more ZEV, emissions are transferred to power plants that may burn coal, a fossil fuel with higher carbon content than oil. The damage effects of overall emissions into the environment, therefore, depend on the extent to which lower damage effects from the drivers of battery electric vehicles offset the higher damage effects from power plants. This overall impact is a function of the substitution of battery electric vehicles for fossil fuel combustion vehicles, the change in miles driven, and the extent to which power plants adopt cleaner fuel alternatives such as natural gas, wind, and solar. It may be the case that, as consumers switch to more battery electric vehicles while power plants simultaneously adopt cleaner energy sources, the environmental effect will be positive and increase over time.

Interestingly, in the early twentieth century, the most frequent propulsion system was an electric drivetrain with battery power. Beginning in the

1920s, however, battery electric vehicles became less desirable, due to longer recharging times relative to filling tanks with gasoline. Eight decades passed before concerns about greenhouse gas emissions encouraged many car manufacturers to design, produce, and market electric vehicles. Today, ZEV are gaining greater market share, although they still capture a small percentage of the market. As the transportation infrastructure evolves, charging stations become more ubiquitous, the demand for battery electric vehicles increases, and the benefits of zero tailpipe emission technology increase, the market will become more balanced between electric and fossil fuel combustion vehicles.

The Reduction of Energy Requirements in Transportation

The goal of a reduction in energy consumption may be achieved if the transportation sector is viewed as a network linked to the other energy sectors, including power, electricity, fuels, buildings, and industry. With this framework, improvements in one technology, such as battery storage or renewables, translate into a web of interdependencies and interactions that magnify the impacts. When a reduction in energy consumption occurs from technological advance, the results must be measured across the entire energy landscape. This system approach not only addresses interdependencies and interactions between and among sectors such as transportation and industry, it also describes important internal characteristics, external influences, and network boundaries (U.S. DOE, 2015b).

With the processes of urbanization, globalization, and industrialization gaining momentum, the future transportation sector will continue to evolve. In the second decade of this century in the United States, the production and delivery of electric cars increased from less than 0.06 percent of total car sales to more than 2 percent. While still a small percentage, this increase translates into tens of thousands of vehicles. It also has important energy system effects. An increase in the consumption of electric vehicles signifies changing consumer tastes and preferences. Many consumers demand greater fuel efficiency. In terms of external influences, global energy prices and climate change make consumers more cognizant of their decisions. With network boundaries between the transportation sector and the other energy sectors, a preference for greater energy efficiency translates into system-wide spillover effects. As the consumption of electric vehicles increases, more charging stations emerge. As more charging stations emerge, communities rethink how they want to organize the relationship between residential, commercial, and building divisions. This creates momentum for greater consumption of natural gas, renewables, and public transportation. Because the transportation system is within the mission of local, state, and federal jurisdictions, public policies may improve future outcomes. Examples include highway congestion pricing, city center pricing, and the expansion of public transit.

Highway Congestion Pricing

Commuters often suffer from highway congestion. Congestion carries a cost in terms of time lost. Commuters in the United States spend an average of more than 40 hours a year in traffic jams. This translates into $1,200 a year in wasted time and fuel. In Los Angeles and Atlanta, cities with higher-than-average congestion rates, the loss is greater. But most economists agree that cities cannot build their way out of the problem. More highways lead to greater traffic problems, as road capacity attracts motorists who previously took public transit, traveled at off-peak times, or used other routes. One policy to address the problem is *highway congestion pricing*, currently in place in San Diego, California, and many other cities. To increase efficiency, each motorist is charged a price that equals the cost of their contribution to the congestion problem.

In this context, congestion may be thought of as the mispricing of a public good: highway capacity at a specific place and time. Charging a price during high periods of congestion allocates a scarce resource to its most valuable use, that is, those people most willing to pay for the resource. The most practical method of establishing a highway congestion price is charging tolls that are higher during peak times, lower during off-peak times, and equal to zero at quiet times. As traffic patterns evolve and motorists avoid driving during peak periods, the tolls are adjusted. The evidence with existing programs suggests that drivers modify their schedules to avoid high tolls, choose alternative routes, or switch to public transit.

City Center Pricing

Similar to highway congestion pricing, city center pricing levies a charge on driving. The economic rationale is that motorists should pay for the external cost of greater congestion they impose on cities. The policy addresses the problem of unpriced traffic volume, which leads to economic losses. But in addition to alleviating congestion, the policy raises revenue for municipalities, provides funds for transportation infrastructure, reduces pollution, and encourages public transportation.

The city center driving fee, established in London in 2003, is the world's most famous. Central London, the commercial and financial hub, has limited road capacity. In the core area, the network of streets has not expanded much since the medieval ages. An increase in the volume of motorists during business hours results in severe congestion. But many travel alternatives exist, including subways, buses, and walking. Because 10 percent of peak-period trips are made by private vehicles, city center pricing in London impacts a small percentage of people traveling in the core. Motorists driving on weekdays between 7:00 a.m. and 6:00 p.m. in central London must pay £10. Exceptions are made for licensed taxis, motorcycles, vehicles used by disabled people, emergency vehicles, buses, and vehicles that use alternative fuels. London deploys closed-circuit cameras at numerous sites within the charging zone to record license plates. Spot payments are made via internet or kiosk arrangements. Since the establishment of the program, trips on the London Underground, buses, and bicycles have increased, while driving has decreased. Ongoing challenges include bicycle accidents and resources for public transportation. Other cities, including Milan, Singapore, Stockholm, and Gothenburg, implement similar pricing mechanisms.

Expansion of Public Transit

The expansion of public transit improves traffic flow, reduces energy consumption, and enhances the quality of urban life. Buses, trains, and subways contribute to a city's transportation network and reduce the consumption of fossil fuels. But many urban areas are turning to an old form of transportation to achieve these benefits: the light rail. The first streetcar lines in the United States opened in the 1830s and 1840s in New York City and New Orleans. With few exceptions, most of the original streetcar systems were dismantled by the middle of the twentieth century. (San Francisco is an exception.) In the 1980s, five metropolitan areas opened light rail systems: Buffalo, Portland, Sacramento, San Diego, and San Jose. For a much lower cost than subways, these systems provided much needed access between neighborhoods and downtowns. In 2016, Denver established light rail service from the airport to its central business district.

In these examples, billions of dollars have been spent by local, state, and federal governments. But they have not always resulted in higher transit use or the revival of downtown business districts. A number of reasons exist. The share of regional workers who ride transit has declined in some cities. The transportation system may encourage movement further away from city centers. Ultimately, the implementation or expansion of light rail networks enhances public transportation options, all of which become more appealing to motorists when cities implement complementary charges on driving and parking.

SUMMARY

The energy system contains six sectors: electricity generation, power sources, fuels, buildings, industry, and transportation. Energy efficiency gains in the fuels, buildings, industrial, and transportation sectors require technological advance and changes in consumer behavior. The fossil fuels that power buildings, industry, and transportation are compounds with stored energy. The building sector demonstrates important advances in green certification, sustainable construction, and energy efficiency. The industrial sector is comprised of many divisions, which possess different characteristics with respect to energy consumption. The transportation sector is crucial for well-functioning economies. While the challenges in the buildings, industrial, and transportation sectors reveal a dependence on fossil fuels, income, industrialization, and urbanization impact energy intensity, the level of energy consumption per unit of output.

TERMS

Convergence
Diversification
Confluence
Efficiency
Energy conversion devices
Fuels
District energy systems
Sustainable construction
Life-cycle costing
Closed-loop process
Energy-neutral buildings
Passive design strategy
Highway congestion pricing

QUESTIONS

1. In the context of fuels, discuss how the concepts of convergence, diversification, confluence, and efficiency apply. In addition to re-reading the section in this chapter on fuels, find relevant articles in journals such as *Fuel* and *Oil & Gas Journal* to help with your answer.
2. In the context of buildings, discuss how the concepts of convergence, diversification, confluence, and efficiency apply. In addition to re-reading the section in this chapter on buildings, find relevant articles in journals such as *The Electricity Journal*, *Energy and Buildings,* and *Building and Environment* to help with your answer.
3. In the context of industry, discuss how the concepts of convergence, diversification, confluence, and efficiency apply. In addition to re-reading

the section in this chapter on industry, find relevant articles in journals such as *The Electricity Journal* and *Journal of Manufacturing Systems* to help with your answer.

4. In the context of transportation, discuss how the concepts of convergence, diversification, confluence, and efficiency apply. In addition to re-reading the section in this chapter on transportation, find relevant articles in journals such as *Transportation*, *Transportation Journal*, and *International Journal of Sustainable Transportation* to help with your answer.
5. For buildings, study the components of high-performance energy design. Identify an example of a building process that exemplifies these components. Did the building designers minimize energy consumption? Why or why not?
6. With respect to industrial, organic, and local forms of agriculture, explain how demand side (population growth, changes in food consumption patterns, income distribution, and urbanization), supply side (changes in the cost of resource inputs, technology, and livestock, crops, fisheries, and aquaculture), and exogenous (energy prices, climate change, water scarcity, the availability of ecosystem services) factors impact food distribution and the consumption of fossil fuels. How does a focus on perishable or nonperishable food items impact the analysis?
7. Suppose a municipality suffers from traffic congestion. Governing authority proposes two solutions to the problem. The first entails expansion of highways to include more lanes. The other includes highway congestion pricing. Would these solutions have the same impact? Which do you think would work better?

Chapter 5

Energy Policy

Theory and Applications

CAP-AND-TRADE IN THE UNITED STATES

For many years, energy economists have argued for the merits of cap-and-trade policy, a market-based method of establishing a maximum allowable level of greenhouse gas emissions, which stem from the burning of fossil fuels. Regulators establish the emission cap, while polluters trade emission allowances in order to meet the cap. The problem is the policy has not always been politically feasible. To put the story in perspective, consider the brief history of cap-and-trade in the United States. With the 1990 Amendments to the Clean Air Act, the U.S. Environmental Protection Agency established a cap-and-trade system to regulate the emission of sulfur dioxide (a greenhouse gas) from coal-burning power plants. This policy has been a big success: since 1990, sulfur dioxide emissions have decreased dramatically, and the cost of the program is much lower than the original estimate. In his first budget, President Barack Obama spoke of the merits of cap-and-trade. In 2009, the House of Representatives passed a climate energy bill largely built around the policy. As a result, many experts believed it was only a matter of time until the United States formalized a national cap-and-trade system to regulate other greenhouse gases, most notably carbon dioxide; however, cap-and-trade was not implemented on a national scale for CO_2. What happened?

In 2009, cap-and-trade fell victim to a weak economy. The economy was in the midst of the Great Recession. Like all energy policies, cap-and-trade requires polluters to allocate scarce resources to reduce their environmental impact. Company lobbyists, who fought to keep cap-and-trade from becoming law, argued the policy would be too expensive for target industries, who could not afford to pay a price for pollution in a sluggish economy. Despite ample economic research that points to the benefits of cap-and-trade to regulate CO_2 emissions, many politicians sided with the lobbyists. After the lost opportunity to pass cap-and-trade legislation in 2009, Congress dropped it (Broder, 2010). Since then, politicians have debated other energy policies, including gasoline taxes, renewable energy standards, and carbon taxation.

The political death of cap-and-trade in 2009 is a fable about the conflict between economic reasoning and the process of political decision making. While economists may point to the efficiency gains from cap-and-trade policy, the moral of the story lies in a consideration of the political climate. As will become clear in this chapter, when implementing energy policy, various competing objectives exist. In the literature, economists have addressed these objectives, including an improvement in environmental quality, the ease of administration and compliance, and distributional consequences. As the cap-and-trade story makes clear, however, when advocating a particular energy policy, economists must also consider political feasibility.

To establish a rationale for policy intervention, this chapter first discusses externalities. The chapter then addresses the following questions: How much pollution abatement should occur? How much technological innovation should occur? Addressing these questions in an economics perspective, the answers may surprise some readers. This chapter then explores examples of federal, state, and local energy policies. The final section discusses the regulatory process and why political feasibility may serve as a roadblock to policy implementation.

EXTERNALITIES AND ECONOMIC EFFICIENCY

The combustion of fossil fuels creates polluting emissions. Pollution is one example of an *externality*, a cost or benefit that accrues to someone not involved in the production or consumption of a good or service. With pollution, a *negative externality* exists: humans are harmed when coming in contact to pollution in the air or water. Consider the case of smog in Los Angeles. The heavy use of automobiles is a well-known part of the culture of the City of Angels. On days with poor air quality, residents of the sprawling city and its suburbs inhale particulates and other pollutants that may compromise their health. As this chapter demonstrates, the presence of an externality creates *market failure*: when the private interests of individuals diverge from social interests of society. In this situation, the market does not establish the efficient level of output.

For a market system to function efficiently, governments must guarantee *property rights*. Property rights refer to the guarantee to individuals and businesses that they may use their property in an exclusive manner. The exclusive use of property such as land and original ideas is guaranteed by government;

however, in situations such as air quality, property rights do not exist or are difficult to guarantee. In the absence of property rights, a negative externality of air pollution may persist. Businesses and utilities may pollute and reduce air quality, but may not be held accountable for their actions.

How do governments regulate the environmental problems that stem from energy production? For the certainty of outcome, government may implement a *command-and-control approach*. Just as it sounds, this approach requires polluters to undertake specific actions—often mandated technology or standards—to comply with regulation. Because the command-and-control approach is often considered costly, economists advocate a second category, *cost-effective policy*. By establishing an emission price, this type of policy provides an economic incentive for polluters to adjust their behavior.

With electricity consumption, for example, consumers make decisions based on private cost, but the process of bringing electricity to the marketplace leads to an *external cost*. An external cost exists when others outside a market transaction are impacted in a negative way. In the case of electricity generation, power stations burn coal. Because of the resulting pollution, a negative externality is present. The problem is that, in the absence of government intervention, the market over-allocates resources in industries in which a negative externality is present.

NEGATIVE EXTERNALITY

In the marketplace, a negative externality reduces *economic efficiency*. A market achieves an efficient outcome when quantity demanded equals quantity supplied and all externalities are internalized. But in the case of electricity production, power plants assume private costs of production, but the external cost of pollution damage is borne by the public.

We learn in a principles of economics class that, in the presence of a negative externality, individuals make decisions on the basis of *marginal private cost* (MPC), but may not consider the *marginal external cost* (MEC) of their actions. MPC is the additional cost to the firm when producing one more unit of output. MEC is the additional cost of pollution damage to society, for example, when one more unit of electricity is produced.

Economic efficiency dictates that decisions should be made on the basis of *marginal social cost*: MSC = MPC + MEC. Without considering external cost, the supply curve equals MPC and represents the private cost that firms face when making production decisions. However, in the presence of MEC, market equilibrium is not efficient. But if firms assume all costs of production, including external costs, the supply curve equals MSC. When compared to the market outcome, the efficient equilibrium at the point where demand equals MSC leads to both a lower level of output and a higher price that internalizes the negative externality.

Energy Policy: Addressing the Negative Externality

The discussion of negative externalities leads to a specific argument: an increase in efficiency occurs with less output. A policy such as a gasoline tax both increases the price at the pump and discourages consumption of complementary products such as cars with low vehicle emission standards. If the cost-effective position is a reduction in activities that lead to negative externalities, what policies may achieve this result?

Thomas Covert, an economist at the University of Chicago, and his co-authors address this problem (Covert et al., 2016). They argue that, even though fossil fuels provide benefits for the economy, they create environmental costs. The first option in reducing polluting emissions is to capture carbon dioxide and store it. Possibilities include planting more trees and/or expanding capture and storage technology. The second option is to reduce both the production of fossil fuels and the polluting emissions with market forces and public policies.

The first of the market forces is a supply side effect. The production of fossil fuels could increase the marginal cost (MC) of extraction to the point that alternative and clean energy technologies become relatively less expensive. In this example, the MC of extracting a barrel of oil or a ton of coal would exceed the MC of providing wind or solar power.

The second of the market forces is a demand side effect. Research and science could advance to the point that newer and less expensive carbon-free technologies provide increasing returns to energy efficiency. The demand for fossil fuels would decrease as clean alternatives become more cost-effective. We would continue on our same energy consumption path, drive the same amount, consume energy at the same levels, but gradually adopt cleaner technology.

This analysis demonstrates that, to achieve a reduction in polluting emissions, public policy is necessary: "Our conclusion is that in the absence of substantial greenhouse gas policies, the United States and the global economy are unlikely to stop relying on fossil fuels as the primary source of energy" (Covert et al., 2016).

Framework for Emission Abatement: The Policy Option

Policy decisions require full information. But policy makers also require clearly defined objectives and resources for policy implementation, monitoring, and enforcement. The decision-making framework includes both the *marginal damage* (MD) *function* and the *marginal abatement cost* (MAC) *function* for an individual form of pollution. The MD function demonstrates the causal relationship between polluting emissions and damage to a target population. The MAC function demonstrates the additional cost to the firm from emission abatement.

Marginal Damage Function

Damages from polluting emissions may take the form of more frequent replacement and maintenance of equipment, diminished enjoyment of the outdoors, an increase in the prevalence of mortality and disease, and many other less-identified losses. MD increases with the amount of pollution. Two types of pollutants exist. The environment has little or no ability to absorb *stock pollutants.* They accumulate over time and include synthetic chemicals, heavy metals, and non-biodegradable plastics. However, the environment has some capacity to absorb *fund pollutants*, such as carbon dioxide, as long as the rate of emissions does not exceed the environment's absorptive capacity.

Research on the MD function reveals different shapes. With a toxic pollutant such as lead, the MD function may increase at a decreasing rate. When released into a contained body of water, lead may initially kill off most living organisms. Additional units of pollution do not provide much impact. In addition, a gradual increase in the ambient concentration of carbon dioxide in the air could lead to a MD function that increases at an increasing rate. Finally, the MD function may display a threshold effect, where the emissions of a certain pollutant such as particulates dramatically increases the potential for marginal damage. In this latter case, a certain quantity of emissions may cause the MD function to jump to a higher level of marginal damage.

Marginal Abatement Cost Function

MAC increases with the amount of polluting emissions that is abated or controlled. Abatement cost, associated with reducing pollution to lower levels in order to reduce damage, includes capital, labor, the opportunity cost from any reduction in production, and the energy needed to decrease emissions. To reduce emissions, polluters have to alter production decisions, install new technology, or adopt a different mix of resource inputs. MAC increases as cheaper options for pollution reduction are chosen first, followed by more expensive options.

The Optimal Level of Pollution Abatement

What is the optimal level of pollution abatement? The optimal level is a function of the social costs associated with pollution (figure 5.1). The first is

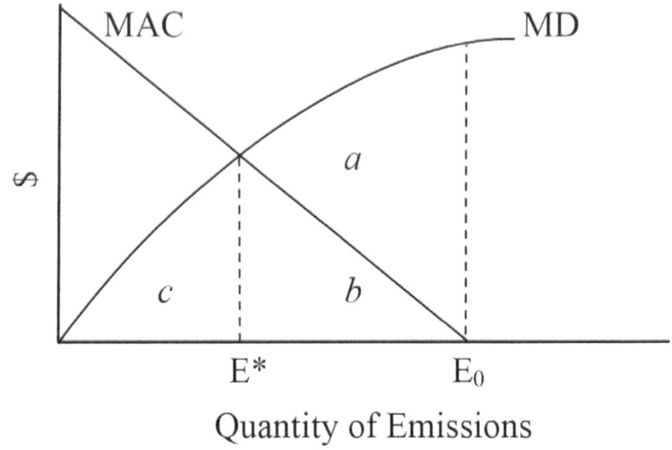

Figure 5.1 Optimal Level of Pollution Abatement. *Source*: Author.

represented by MD. The second is represented by MAC. In this framework, zero pollution is not desirable. A complete reduction in polluting emissions would have high opportunity costs in terms of lost production and output.

To find the optimal level of pollution abatement, first recognize that, in the absence of government intervention, the polluter operates at E_0, because MAC equals zero. But at E_0, the marginal benefit of pollution abatement (as measured along the MD curve) exceeds MAC, so society would benefit from emission reduction. Moving from E_0 to E^*, the total benefit of the reduction in damages from fewer emissions (area $a + b$) is greater than the total abatement cost (area b). Emission abatement should occur until MD = MAC. Why is this optimal? At E^*, the marginal benefit of reducing damage from polluting emissions equals MAC.

By demonstrating that E^* serves as the optimal level of pollution abatement, economists argue that society should not reduce polluting emissions to zero! Why? Emission reduction below E^* is cost-prohibitive, because MAC > MD. But a more comprehensive analysis of the problem reveals that individual pollutants differ with respect to their impact on humans and the environment. For example, highly toxic pollutants that pose a serious threat to human health and environmental quality possess MD functions with higher levels of damage per unit of emissions. Therefore, with highly toxic forms of pollution, E^* would exist closer to the origin. There are even cases when the MD of the first unit of emissions is greater than MAC. In this case, E^* would equal zero. Later in the chapter, we discuss specific policies that reduce pollution to E^*, including standards, technology mandates, energy charges, and cap-and-trade systems.

The concept of *net benefit* is important in this discussion. Net benefit represents the value to society of taking action when the benefits of the action exceed the costs. It is calculated by taking the difference between the total benefit of pollution reduction and the total abatement cost. The optimal level (E^*) leads to the maximization of net benefit from emission reduction (area *a*). What is important about net benefit? At any level of polluting emissions not equal to E^*, further gains to society are possible. When emissions exceed E^*, society would benefit from emission abatement: MD > MAC. When emissions are less than E*, further emission abatement is cost-prohibitive: MD < MAC.

Cost Minimization Means Equal Marginal Abatement Cost for Polluters

With respect to emission reduction, consider two important policy objectives. (A following section expands this list.) The objectives are interrelated, but we may analyze them in turn. First, policy should establish the optimal level of pollution abatement, where MD = MAC. Second, policy should achieve this objective with the lowest cost to society. But how does this occur? The least-cost policy outcome occurs when MAC is equalized across all polluters. The reason is the MAC functions of firms differ because of the technological potential of pollution abatement. For old plants with outdated technology, MAC is higher per unit of emission reduction than for new plants. But firms with lower MAC functions should reduce more emissions. Firms with higher MAC functions should reduce fewer emissions. This proposition provides a method to evaluate policy. The policies that equate MAC across polluters represent least-cost options. We will find that only one category of energy policy achieves this objective: cost-effective policy. But before we learn about this category, we must consider when policy implementation is appropriate.

Pigou, Coase, and Transaction Costs

Arthur C. Pigou, the British economist and acclaimed academic at Cambridge University, published *The Economics of Welfare* in 1920, explaining that the self-adjusting mechanism of the market sometimes fails to maximize economic welfare. Pigou believed that, because the size of national income influences economic welfare, unregulated firms decrease welfare through unintended actions: "It might happen . . . that costs are thrown upon people not directly concerned, through, say, uncompensated damage done to surrounding woods by sparks from railway engines" (Pigou, 1920). However, with this external cost, government may "put matters right." This theory, which argues for government intervention in the presence of an externality, holds true with either incomplete property rights or an inability to enforce property rights that already exist.

In 1960, however, Ronald Coase of the University of Chicago published a seminal article, "The Problem of Social Cost," in which he addressed Pigou. Coase argued that, in the absence of clearly defined property rights, victims should pay polluters to reduce pollution. In the presence of legal liability, in which firms are responsible for pollution damage, the firms should pay the victims for the right to pollute. In these cases, government intervention is unnecessary.

However, with pollution problems, many polluters and victims may exist. Because of high *transaction costs*—time and money necessary to exchange information—negotiation is not feasible. The *Coase Theorem* states that, if transaction costs are low, private bargaining between polluters and victims will lead to a suitable solution. In practice, however, transaction costs are normally high and a lack of full information exists. As a result, in these large numbers of cases, economic theory argues for policy intervention in the presence of negative externalities.

Government Intervention in the Presence of Negative Externalities

Five categories of government intervention represent different governing philosophies:

- *Moral suasion*: government influences behavior through argument
- *Direct production of environmental quality*: specific actions ameliorate environmental problems, including the cleanup of toxic waste and treatment of sewage
- *Pollution prevention*: programs address the market failure of imperfect information
- Command-and-control (CAC) regulation: constraints specify technology or limit resource inputs or output in the production process
- Cost-effective policy: actions align private interest with social interest by providing the incentive for polluters to reduce pollution with least-cost techniques

Only CAC regulation and cost-effective policy achieve the optimal level of emission abatement. But cost-effective policy also minimizes MAC.

Command-and-Control Regulation

The most straightforward way to achieve the optimal level of emission abatement for polluters is to mandate specific actions with CAC regulation. The idea is that regulators collect the information necessary to make decisions with respect to energy supply, demand, and pollution. The regulator then commands the firm to take specific steps. This form of regulation achieves a target level of emission reduction; however, it generates more abatement costs than necessary. The reason is that it does not equate MAC across polluters.

Technology Mandates

Technology mandates prescribe methods of pollution control. To reduce the release of greenhouse gases, the mandates require power plants to install specific scrubbing equipment on the end of smokestacks. In areas that do not meet air quality standards, the Clean Air Act requires polluters to use the best available control technology, as prescribed by the Environmental Protection Agency. From an economics perspective, the problem with technology mandates concerns the heterogeneity of firms. Because firms have different production methods, it is unlikely that a regulator would have enough information to establish a technology mandate that minimizes costs. In addition, technology mandates do not take advantage of the ability of firms to pursue all methods of pollution abatement, including the reduction of output or a cleaner mix of resource inputs.

Performance Standards

Performance standards restrict emissions either per unit of time (the maximum allowable level of airborne particulates every twenty-four hours) or per unit of output (tons of CO_2 per kilowatt-hour of electricity). With the former, output will be greater than optimal: The standard does not include the cost of environmental damage. With the latter, the resulting output will be greater than, equal to, or less than the optimal level: Consumers do not pay the full social cost of their purchases. Standards have another disadvantage. They force polluters to take the same action over time. But once the standard is reached, incentive does not exist for additional pollution control.

CAC Regulation and Efficient Outcomes

Even though CAC regulation does not equate MAC across polluters, it may lead to efficient outcomes in the presence of four conditions:

- When the optimal level of emissions is at or near zero
- When monitoring costs are extremely high
- When emergencies or random events establish a new relationship between emissions and MD such that low emission levels lead to high MD
- When abatement technologies have technical limits, but MAC < MD up to these limits

Cost-Effective Policies

One insight from the literature on energy economics is that CAC regulation does not protect scarce resources. The problem is associated with policy cost: with CAC regulation, government must use scarce resources to obtain information that polluters already possess. Cost-effective policies, in contrast, lead to least-cost resource allocation. They equalize MAC for all polluters.

Energy Charges

In response to climate change, many countries implement energy charges. For example, Denmark, Finland, and Sweden use carbon charges to discourage carbon emissions. From an economics standpoint, an energy charge serves as an appropriate policy when the charge links directly to the pollution source and the benefits of the improvement in environmental quality outweigh the costs.

An energy charge establishes an emissions price. Suppose the goal is to reduce emissions to the optimal level. How may the regulator achieve this result? As a profit-maximizer, the polluter will reduce polluting emissions when MAC is less than the per-unit charge. In figure 5.2, t is the energy charge levied per-unit of polluting emissions. Polluters must decide whether to pay the charge or reduce emissions and not pay the charge. Suppose an oil refinery is emitting at E_0. At E_0, $t >$ MAC, so it would be cheaper for the oil refinery to reduce emissions and not pay the charge. This process continues until the polluter reduces emissions to E^*, where $t =$ MAC.

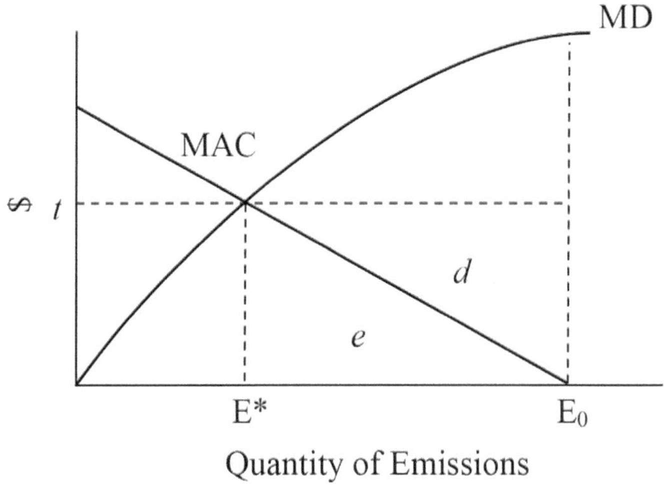

Figure 5.2 Energy Charge. *Source*: Author.

To emit pollution from E^* to E_0, the refinery's payment for the energy charge would equal area ($d + e$); however, to reduce emissions from E_0 to E^*, the firm's total abatement cost would equal area (e). When MAC < t, the refinery chooses abatement. At E^*, total payment for the energy charge = tE^*. At emission levels less than E^*, the oil refinery would choose to pay the charge on each unit of emissions rather than the MAC of reducing emissions below E*.

The strength of this energy policy concerns the flexibility of response. Polluters must react, but they decide *how* to react. A charge will promote technological innovation, cheaper methods of emission abatement—because the charge applies to all emissions—and a cost-effective allocation of resources. Firms will reduce emissions to the point where t = MAC. Because t is constant, MAC is equalized across polluters. Energy charges therefore lead to the optimal level of pollution abatement in a least-cost manner.

As an example, *carbon taxation* refers to a charge on the carbon content of fuel. It is the world's most important energy charge. To implement a carbon tax, the policy maker must determine the relative carbon content of fossil fuel. Per unit of energy (British thermal unit), coal has the highest carbon content, with oil second, and natural gas third. As a result, a carbon tax would levy the highest rate on coal and the lowest rate on natural gas.

By establishing a per-unit price on pollution and internalizing MEC, carbon taxation improves resource allocation. But as recent research makes clear, this process is not as straightforward as economists once thought. The idea proceeds as follows: after it is implemented, any new energy charge interacts with preexisting policies. Polluters pay the charge while they comply with other regulations. To serve as politically feasible policy, the charge may have to achieve *revenue neutrality* and not increase the overall tax burden of households (Goulder and Parry, 2008).

In this context, policy makers would use the revenue generated by the energy charge to finance lower rates on preexisting taxes on labor or capital. This way, the policy would both discourage an economic "bad" (pollution) and encourage economic goods (work and saving). Many economists conclude that energy charges could therefore create a double dividend: a cleaner environment and a less-distorting tax system.

To make a long discussion short (although the progression of ideas on the double dividend in the literature has been fascinating), the introduction of a charge on polluting emissions leads to three impacts: a positive environmental effect (EE) and two efficiency consequences related to the tax system. The first efficiency consequence is a tax interaction (TI) cost, as revenue from a charge on pollution cannot fully finance a lower rate on preexisting charges, because the tax base (pollution) decreases. The second efficiency consequence, a revenue-recycling (RR) benefit, means a lower tax rate on labor or capital encourages economic activity.

The potential for the double dividend depends on these impacts. When EE + RR > TI, the double dividend holds: a charge on polluting emission increases efficiency. The greater the value of EE, the more appealing are energy charges. In general, energy charges that raise revenue (such as carbon taxes) are more appealing than policies that do not. To this effect, many countries have implemented *ecological tax reform*, where energy charges finance lower tax rates on preexisting levies that distort economic decision making.

From society's perspective, an advantage exists with energy charges when compared to performance standards and technology mandates. Governing authorities implement CAC regulation on the basis of existing technology. But when firms develop more efficient production techniques, governing authority tightens the standards and mandates, increasing the cost of policy compliance. In this context, polluters have the incentive to hide new technology. But energy charges apply to all polluting emissions. Faced with an energy charge, polluters reduce tax payment by developing more advanced abatement techniques.

Suppose a firm's technology is characterized by MAC_1 in figure 5.3. The presence of an energy charge (t) provides incentive for the abatement of polluting emissions (E_0 to E_1*). By moving to E_1*, the firm's initial cost is the sum of tax payment and abatement cost:

$$\text{Firm s initial cost} = \text{tax payment}\left(l+m+n\right)+\text{abatement cost}\left(p+q\right).$$

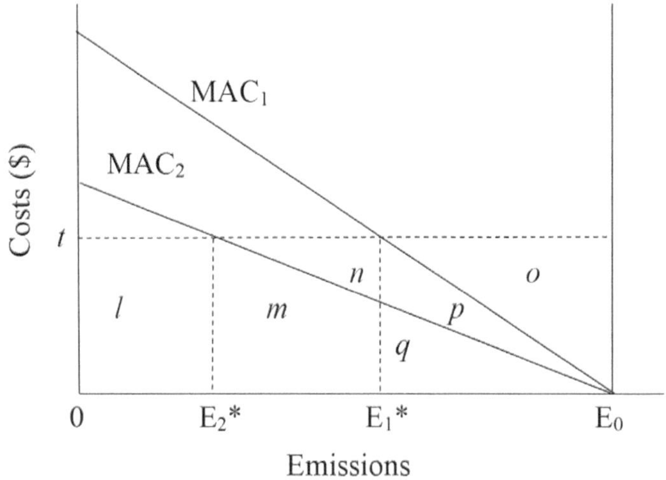

Figure 5.3 The Incentive for Research and Development. *Source*: Author.

However, an allocation of resources for research and development lowers MAC_1 to MAC_2. With constant t, the optimal level of emission abatement decreases to E_2^*. Moving from E_0 to E_2^*, the firm's new cost is less than the initial cost:

$$\text{Firm s new cost} = \text{tax payment}\left(l\right) + \text{abatement cost}\left(m+q\right).$$

The incentive to continually reduce emissions by updating abatement technology serves as an important advantage of energy charges over CAC regulation.

Cap-and-Trade

While the benefit of CAC regulation is the achievement of the optimal level of emission abatement, the benefit of energy charges is the equalization of MAC across all polluters. Another policy achieves both of these benefits: cap-and-trade. Because cap-and-trade achieves both benefits, many economists advocate this approach (such as Tietenberg, 2006). By limiting a target pollutant, a cap-and-trade system establishes a cap on emissions. Because cap-and-trade establishes both a pollution price and an incentive for pollution abatement, the regulator does not mandate polluter response.

In terms of policy specifics, cap-and-trade establishes a limit on a greenhouse gas pollutant, decreases that limit over time, and uses the power of the market to achieve low-cost emission reduction. In a cap-and-trade system, facilities such as oil refineries or power plants purchase *marketable permits* in order to pollute. Normally, the ownership of one permit allows the discharge of one ton of a specific pollutant such as carbon dioxide or sulfur dioxide. If a plant can reduce polluting emissions at a lower cost than another plant, it may sell the permit. The emissions cap and option for trading encourages both pollution abatement and clean technologies.

Effective policy requires two conditions. First, an individual form of pollution must be identifiable at source. This condition allows monitoring and enforcement. Second, total emissions must be less than the free market level. This condition creates a permit market. Polluters with high MACs may purchase permits and avoid the investment necessary to reduce emissions. Polluters with low MACs may avoid purchasing permits by reducing emissions. The total number of permits available in the market creates an upper limit for emissions. Polluters are free to buy and sell these rights to pollute. The exchange of permits re-allocates pollution rights. Over time, governing authority may reduce the number of permits in the marketplace, improving environmental quality.

Two options exist for the allocation of marketable permits. Permits may be auctioned to the highest bidders. Upon initial offering, this option generates revenue for government. In contrast, permits may be granted directly to polluters free of charge. This option establishes a market for permits, but it does not generate revenue. With both options, permits are tradable. The specific allocation of permits may be based on historic pollution levels, estimates of E^*, or some other allocation scheme.

For a successful cap-and-trade system, individual sources of pollution—such as power plants, oil refineries, and factories—must be clearly identifiable. While the regulatory authority has the responsibility to establish an acceptable level of environmental quality, polluters must alter their behavior. As Tietenberg (2006) explains, "The key to successful regulation is to design programs that harmonize the efforts of these two groups."

The world's largest emission trading system, the European Union Emission Trading System, was initiated in 2005. It puts a cap on CO_2 emissions of the power sector, aviation, and heavy industry (e.g., cement, aluminum, pulp and paper, and steel). In the system, the power sector generates half of the CO_2 emissions, while the other sectors are responsible for half. Overall, the system regulates 45 percent of total greenhouse gas emission in the EU. For each ton of CO_2 released into the atmosphere, the polluter must first obtain and then surrender a permit. Polluters trade the permits in the open market. With an incentive to reduce emissions, when MAC < permit price, cost-effective abatement occurs. Carbon dioxide emissions are transferred from sectors with inexpensive abatement possibilities to those with higher expenses. The sectors face a cap that declines each year. After implementing a trial period from 2005 to 2007, the second trading period lasted from 2008 to 2012. The third period, from 2013 to 2020, will be evaluated to determine whether a 21 percent reduction by 2020 occurs relative to 2005.

POSITIVE EXTERNALITY

To create new production methods or technology, firms may undertake a process of *innovation*. This refers to the process of translating an invention or idea into a good or service that is offered in the marketplace. But innovation generates a *positive externality*, a benefit to others not involved directly in economic activity. In this situation, firms make decisions on the basis of *marginal private benefit* (MPB), the benefit received from producing an additional unit of output. However, with innovation, firms may not consider marginal external benefit (MEB), the additional benefit that flows to society. For an efficient outcome, firms should make decisions on the basis of *marginal social benefit*: MSB = MPB + MEB.

In the presence of a positive externality, the demand curve represents MPB. The intersection of demand and supply leads to market equilibrium, which is a level of innovation that is too low from the perspective of society as a whole. But if firms internalize MEB in production, the demand curve equals MEB. When compared to the market outcome, the efficient equilibrium at the point where MSB equals supply leads to a higher level of innovation.

Energy Policy: Addressing the Positive Externality

With a positive externality such as innovation, the economy does not produce enough. Firms that innovate also allocate resources for research, design, development, and deployment. By creating more advanced technology, they benefit other firms. But in the absence of government intervention, too little innovation occurs.

Framework for Technological Innovation

From the perspective of society, how much innovation is efficient? Figure 5.4, which shows both the MC of innovation and the marginal benefit (MB), reveals the answer.

In figure 5.4, initially assume a position of no innovation, at I_0, where the MC of innovation equals zero. If firms are confident, innovation will generate an economic benefit; they will innovate and assume a short-term cost. At I_0, society would benefit from new innovation: MB > MC. From an economics perspective, additional innovation should occur to I^*, where MB = MC. Further innovation would not be cost-effective, because MB < MC.

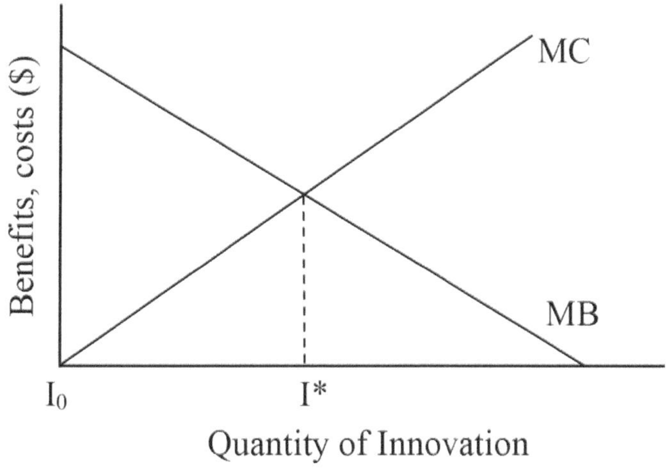

Figure 5.4 Optimal Level of Innovation. *Source*: Author.

Many governments at different levels of jurisdiction mandate a certain percentage of energy from renewable sources. Many U.S. states, for example, have proposed an 80 percent reduction of greenhouse gas emissions below 1990 levels by 2050 (Goulder and Parry, 2008). The EU has stated a goal of reducing greenhouse gas emissions by 20 percent by 2020, compared to 1990 levels (Delbeke et al., 2010). In order to meet these targets, renewable energy companies must bring cost-effective technology and equipment to the marketplace. Figure 5.4 reveals, however, a limit to the extent that new innovation creates efficiency gains. The efficient level of innovation at I^* means the MC of additional innovation beyond this point becomes cost-prohibitive. To further increase innovation, government intervention is necessary.

Government Intervention in the Presence of Positive Externalities

Advances in renewable energy technology reduce production costs, increase the demand for clean innovations, and improve the market penetration of emission reducing practices. Market forces motivate companies to implement these changes. But when firms focus their decisions on private benefits, the external benefits allocated to society remain unrealized, and innovation is too low.

A number of reasons exist. First, low potential returns (relative to social benefits) from the adoption of new technology may not justify the process of innovation. If innovators are unsure that uncertain long-run benefits justify upfront costs, they may hesitate in bringing new technology to the market. Second, firms may lack the incentive to create technological benefits. Even in the presence of a patent, innovators understand that legal methods of copying new technology exist. Third, the marginalization of new technologies may occur for smaller companies, due to the market power exerted by conventional energy firms. While higher energy prices trigger the adoption of energy-saving technology—such as fuel-efficient vehicles—stable prices may not provide ongoing incentive for invention, innovation, and diffusion. Finally, market barriers such as uncertainty over future energy prices, high discount rates, and capital-intensive investments exist.

Each of these barriers provides a rationale for government intervention. When market forces do not lead to the optimal level of innovation, energy policy must determine the path of technological change. This policy is a function of the target sector—such as manufacturing, power generation, and transportation—objectives, and the resources available for policy governance. If energy policy targets innovation in the transportation sector, for example, policy may focus on fuel efficiency. The objective may increase miles per gallon.

Policies that Decrease Marginal Cost of Innovation

Policies that decrease MC increase the optimal level of innovation. One such policy, a *subsidy for renewable energy production*, provides a per-unit payment to renewable energy providers (such as for solar and wind) for additional production. By reducing production cost, this policy encourages the production of electricity from clean sources.

Another policy that reduces the MC of innovation, a *subsidy for research, design, development, and deployment*, provides further incentive. If uncertainty exists as to the eventual realization of long-term benefits from innovation, firms need reasonable reassurance they will capture these benefits.

Policies that Increase Marginal Benefit of Innovation

Technology-specific policies increase the MB (demand) for clean energy technologies and spur innovation. One policy, *renewable portfolio standards*, serves as a regulatory mandate. Often implemented at the state level, the policy promotes renewable energy sources by mandating a certain percentage of electricity generation from renewable technology. Successful renewable portfolio standards create outcomes that increase innovation:

- Well-defined renewable energy generators and technologies
- Programs with long-term contracting
- Mandates that cover all load-serving entities
- Standards that increase over time
- Non-compliance penalties that apply to entities that do not meet increasing standards

Many states provide options for regulated entities. They may generate their own renewable supply of electricity or purchase credits from other suppliers. This latter option, participating in the *renewable energy credit system*, provides a market-focused incentive for innovation. The system also complements portfolio standards. The renewable energy credit system creates tradable energy certificates that provide proof of the generation of megawatt-hours of electricity from renewable sources. An agency certifies a certificate for every clean megawatt of electricity. But the certificate may be bought, sold, or traded. When the certificate is used by an energy provider, the certificate is retired. As a result, the system provides a mechanism in which clean energy contributes to the electric grid.

Increase in the Optimal Level of Innovation

With innovation: the first step involves research, design, and development of new technology. In this step, the MC per unit of innovation decreases. Early on, incentives for basic and applied research and demonstration initiate the creative process. The second step—the deployment of new technology, when equipment such as solar panels becomes more widespread—results in an increase in the MB per unit of innovation. Policies that increase the demand for clean technologies move the market toward full commercialization. Taken together, this double shift results in an increase in the optimal level of innovation. As a result, complementary policies that target all stages of innovation may increase the production of clean energy technologies.

Policy Objectives and Jurisdiction

In implementing policy to achieve a target level of emission abatement, governing authority considers different objectives:

- Efficiency—low-cost method to achieve the optimal level of emission abatement
- Equity—fairness across different socioeconomic groups
- Administration and compliance—minimization of administrative cost while ensuring compliance
- Policy Interaction—minimization of efficiency loss with broader interaction with preexisting policy
- Political feasibility—given a political climate, the likelihood of policy implementation

These objectives may compete with each other. Economists have advocated carbon taxation because it reduces greenhouse gas emissions in a cost-effective way; however, it may not be politically feasible. As the narrative at the beginning of this chapter explains, the failure to establish a cap-and-trade system in the United States to regulate carbon dioxide emissions serves as another example. An efficient policy is one that achieves a target level of change in a cost-effective manner. But fairness in energy policy means balancing costs and benefits across all affected parties. When energy policy distributes benefits fairly and allows those who benefit to pay an appropriate percentage of the cost, undue burden does not occur. However, energy policies that overwhelmingly impact a particular income group or geographical region limit policy effectiveness. In addition, energy policy should minimize the cost of administration while achieving a target level of compliance. But as the discussion on the double dividend debate makes clear, we must consider energy policy in the context of preexisting regulation. Because energy policy is written in the form of legislation and is subject to the political system, political feasibility represents the potential of energy policy to become law, given a country's political climate.

Satisfaction of Policy Objectives

How well do the energy policies addressed in this chapter achieve the policy objectives? Table 5.1 presents the results.

A number of policy realities exist. First, no energy policy is clearly superior to the others, given the competing policy objectives. Second, the choice of a given energy policy depends on the political climate. Third, given the reality of climate change, the most important objective of many policy makers will be the reduction of greenhouse gases. Fourth, given public budgetary constraints, cost-effective methods of pollution abatement are appealing. Fifth, energy policies that significantly reduce economic activity have little appeal. Sixth, significant tradeoffs occur with respect to policy instruments. In particular, the assurance of political feasibility may not lead to a choice of cost-effective policy. Finally, given the objectives and instruments of energy policy, the regulator faces a *portfolio choice*. A portfolio choice exists when the regulator faces both competing objectives and a number of policy options. A specific policy decision therefore depends on circumstance. While the efficiency objective is important, policy makers may not be able to implement a particular form of regulation without considering the entire policy landscape.

ENERGY POLICY AND THE POLITICAL PROCESS

The narratives in the chapter's introduction and in the previous section make clear that, when implementing energy policy, the policy maker must consider the political climate. A cap-and-trade system to regulate sulfur dioxide has been in effect in the United States since 1990; however, the political climate during the Obama Administration (2009–2017) was not conducive for a national cap-and-trade system for carbon dioxide. The executive branch favored cap-and-trade policy. But the legislative branch did not.

For perspective, Simon (2007) emphasizes five policy steps: (1) agenda setting, (2) policy formation, (3) policy implementation, (4) policy evaluation, and (5) policy termination or change. The first step involves prioritizing a specific issue and emphasizing its importance. To reduce oil consumption, policy makers may emphasize conservation. But industry executives may think additional oil drilling is the proper course of action. In the 2000 U.S. presidential election between Governor George W. Bush of Texas and Vice President Albert Gore Jr., for example, the governor argued for the opening of the Arctic National Wildlife Refuge for oil exploration and additional drilling in the Gulf of Mexico. The vice president argued for an acceleration of the supply of clean energy. Once in office, President Bush's identification with oil helped establish a policy agenda.

Table 5.1 Satisfaction of Policy Objectives

Policy Objective	*Mandated Technology*	*Performance Standards*	*Carbon Taxation (revenue-neutral)*	*Cap-and-trade (auction)*	*Cap-and-trade (freely allocated)*	*Subsidy for Renewable Energy*	*Subsidy for R&D*
Efficiency			√	√	√		
Equity	√	√				√	√
Administration/ Compliance			√	√	√	√	√
Cost Minimization: Policy Interaction			√	√			
Political Feasibility	√	√			√	√	√

Source: Author.

The second step of policy formation entails the choice of specific regulation. Given the portfolio of policy choices (performance standards, technology mandates, energy charges, cap-and-trade, subsidies for renewable energy, subsidies for R&D, and others), the policy maker must choose a policy that satisfies the most important objectives.

The third step of implementation exists in a specific policy environment, such as rising energy prices, the desire for energy security, or climate change. On June 22, 2011, when Steven Chu, the secretary of Energy of the United States, announced the release of 30 million barrels of oil from the U.S. Strategic Petroleum Reserve, the intent was to decrease price. Turmoil in the Middle East was impacting the global market. While this policy was short-term, policy implementation followed specific regulatory guidelines.

The fourth step entails evaluation of intended and unintended outcomes. Of particular importance are policy costs and benefits. The policy maker must weigh the costs of administration, compliance, and interactions with preexisting policy against the benefits of cleaner energy, greater fuel standards, job creation, and others.

The final step, terminating, altering, or renewing policy, entails a specific timeframe after which the policy must be reauthorized or ceases to serve as law. Energy policy depends on an annual allocation from government, which may change over time.

State and Local Energy Policies

Many energy policies exist at the national level. State and local policies also exist. In 2009, for example, California began regulating greenhouse gas emissions from vehicles within the state by requiring higher vehicle emission standards. The extent to which a state or local policy is successful depends on how well it achieves specific energy, environmental, and fiscal goals, which may differ from the objectives of national energy policies.

At state and local levels, the outcomes of new energy policies are often effective. The reason is that state and local policy makers have a high degree of familiarity with economic conditions. Policy makers take advantage of their knowledge of potential outcomes. State and local policies may build momentum for a shift toward a particular form of regulation. In this regard, the California vehicle emission requirement motivated many other states to adopt the same standard.

Energy policies at the state and local levels play a significant role in the dispersion of renewable energy systems. Households, businesses, and school districts often need financial incentive to adopt specific systems such as solar panels or wind power. Citizens may be unaware of the energy-producing potential of backyards or rooftops. Individuals or local groups may not allocate time and resources to determine the benefits and costs of renewable energy. But state governments may address these concerns by offering renewable energy subsidies, lowering private energy costs, and saving government money by reducing the electricity bills of public schools.

A movement exists in many regions to create more sustainable cities. Reforms in the use of land and zoning, public transportation, energy consumption, and conservation have been part of local regulatory efforts to promote more sustainable communities. Portland, Oregon, encourages cycling with the development of bike paths. Curitiba, Brazil, uses a rapid transit bus system, increasing the number of commuters using public transportation. In recognition of land constraints, Singapore uses congestion pricing. These and many other examples demonstrate that, at the local level, a movement toward more sustainable outcomes requires collaboration between citizens and government.

SUMMARY

To internalize externalities, national, state, and local governments may implement CAC or cost-effective policies. At the national level, examples include performance standards, technology mandates, energy charges, cap-and-trade, subsidies for renewable energy, and subsidies for research and development. States and municipalities may implement vehicle emission standards, improvements in public transportation, or changes in zoning requirements. Governments at all levels may design energy policy in an attempt to improve environmental quality, reduce the use of fossil fuels, or encourage technological innovation. Energy policies may also minimize the costs of administration and compliance, minimize interaction effects with existing regulation, and serve as politically feasible options. In the context of a portfolio problem of policy choice, policy makers must choose the energy policy that satisfies the most important objectives.

CONCEPTS

Cap-and-trade
Carbon tax
Coase Theorem
Command-and-control regulation
Cost-effective policy
Direct production of environmental quality
Ecological tax reform
Economic efficiency

Energy charges
External cost
Externality
Innovation
Marginal abatement cost function
Marginal damage function
Marginal external benefit
Marginal external cost
Marginal private benefit
Marginal private cost
Marginal social benefit
Marginal social cost
Marketable permits
Market failure
Moral suasion
Negative externality
Net benefit
Performance standards
Portfolio choice
Positive externality
Property rights
Pollution prevention
Renewable energy credit system
Renewable portfolio standards
Revenue neutrality
Subsidy for renewable energy
Subsidy for research, design, development, and deployment
Technology mandate
Transaction costs

QUESTIONS

1. The optimal level of emission abatement depends on the shape of both the MD function and the MAC function. In particular, the MD function may increase at increasing or decreasing rates or exhibit threshold effects. On separate graphs, show the shapes of these MD functions, keeping the MAC curve constant. What circumstances lead to a particular shape for the MD function?
2. Explain the Coase Theorem. When does it hold? Read Coase's famous article listed in the Bibliography. When choosing policy, why is it necessary to consider the Coase Theorem?

3. Contrast energy charges to cap-and-trade policy. How are they similar? How are they different? Identify countries or regions with energy charges or cap-and-trade systems. Which policies have reduced greenhouse gases?
4. Anyone may purchase sulfur dioxide allowances on the Chicago Mercantile Exchange. Many environmental groups have raised money to buy allowances. What is the impact on the overall level of sulfur dioxide emissions from these actions? What is the impact on price?
5. Study the objectives of energy policy. Why is it important to consider more than efficiency? With respect to equity, why do policy makers consider the distributional consequences on households with different income levels?
6. In the energy economics literature, identify examples of state and local energy policies. Do state and local energy policies ever create momentum for policy implementation at the national level? What are some examples?
7. Study the five-step policy process listed in the "Energy Policy and the Political Process" section. Consider a specific energy policy such as carbon taxation. Which steps might be vulnerable to an inhospitable political climate? Why?

Chapter 6

Energy Supply, Demand, and Markets

THE WORLD OF ENERGY

Global concerns about the environmental impacts of fossil fuel consumption, the development of renewable energy, and energy security have advanced energy economics to the forefront of policy discussions. But the world is not experiencing an "energy crisis." At current rates of consumption, fossil fuels will last for decades. It's more accurate to describe the world as relying on a variety of energy resources. Some countries such as China are building power plants—running on renewable and nonrenewable resources—at a rapid pace. Other countries consume high levels of nuclear power (France), solar power (Germany), and wind power (Spain). But the world is addicted to fossil fuels. Forecasts by the International Energy Agency demonstrate that over the course of the next few decades, the world will likely consume *more* fossil fuels, not less. This chapter argues that more solar, wind, and geothermal will also be incorporated into the global energy supply, but the production of fossil fuels will continue to grow. To demonstrate this point, the chapter discusses energy supply, demand, and markets. Because depletable resources are so prominent in the world, the chapter also establishes a model framework to analyze the economics of depletable resources. This framework is applicable for the depletable resources discussed in parts two and three of this book.

ENERGY SUPPLY

Many industries such as transportation and manufacturing use different energy resources. When the price of oil increases, trucking companies experience a higher cost of distribution. All else equal, this economic impact reduces profitability. In addition, even though companies in manufacturing consider monthly utility payments as variable costs, the price of electricity depends on the cost of bringing energy resources to the marketplace. When the supply of coal increases, for example, the price of electricity generated from coal-powered plants decreases. Stable energy prices help firms to forecast future levels of production.

The energy derived from renewable and nonrenewable resources provides power for our buildings and automobiles, warms and cools our homes, and helps to cook our food. Consider the supply of natural gas. Widely seen as a resource for heating and cooking, natural gas also flows to the power sector for the generation of electricity. But recent exploration of this fossil fuel has created a rift between the need for a stable flow of energy and the environmental quality. In order to drill for natural gas under land that is populated with housing developments, many drilling companies are offering home owners fixed monthly payments for the right to drill under their land. This practice is occurring in gas-rich states such as Pennsylvania, New York, West Virginia, and Texas. The problem is that many homeowners believe the drilling companies will not leave their property unharmed. But waste ponds from the practice of natural gas extraction—which hold toxic drilling sludge—may leak into the water table, potentially seeping hazardous waste. This example, while important to both drilling companies and homeowners, is typical of the potential friction between the extraction of energy in a cost-effective manner and the desire to preserve environmental quality.

The economic problem of allocating scarce resources for competing wants applies to energy investments. The energy system attracts investment funds. Those making investment choices evaluate competing uses for their funds. The decisions to invest in nonrenewables, renewables, or nuclear power entail the state of energy technology, price forecasts, and the policy environment. Cost/benefit analysis aids the choice, because energy investments possess important features:

- Capital intensive: Energy projects such as power plants are capital intensive. Initial investments are high. Energy economists use the concept of *overnight construction cost* to estimate the cost of building a power plant. Overnight cost is measured in dollars per kilowatt hour of energy production, $/kW, a common unit of measurement. According to the U.S. Energy Information Administration, overnight costs vary according to the type of technology. A coal-fired power plant might cost $5,000/kW, so a 1000-megawatt plant would have an overnight cost of $5 billion. A solar thermal plant might cost $4,000/kW with an overnight cost of $4 billion.
- Long building period: Energy projects often take several years to build. For example, a hydroelectric power station takes four to seven years.

- Long lifespan: Energy projects are intended to have long lifespans. In the case of coal-fired power plants, the average lifespan is forty years. Nuclear plants usually receive forty-year licenses to operate, but the majority of the reactors in the United States have received twenty-year extensions beyond their original forty-year operating licenses.
- Asset specificity: Energy projects have few alternative uses. A power plant generates electricity, but does not have other applications. Asset specificity means the extent to which an investment has higher value than if it's deployed for other purposes. Investment in a power plant may fund technology that incorporates both coal and natural gas, but renewable and nuclear plants possess high degrees of asset specificity.

ENERGY SUPPLY IN THE UNITED STATES

Primary energy production in the United States demonstrates the preeminence of fossil fuels. According to the U.S. EIA (2017), the following are the most prominent energy sources, including percentages of the country's total energy supply:

- Dry natural gas (32%)
- Oil (22%)
- Coal (18%)
- Nuclear/uranium (9%)
- Liquid natural gas (6%)
- Biomass (5%)
- Other renewables (4%)
- Hydro (3%)
- Other (1%)

For perspective, the United States is the world's third largest crude oil producer, second largest coal producer, and largest natural gas producer. Between 2001 and 2017, U.S. oil production increased by 69 percent, coal production decreased by 31 percent, and natural gas production increased by 40 percent. In percentage terms, uranium production has remained relatively constant during this century. With renewables, biomass is the largest, followed by hydro. But over time, growth in solar and wind will increase the percentage of renewables.

A forecast by the U.S. EIA (2017) shows healthy growth prospects for both natural gas and renewables. If this forecast is accurate, the next generation of electricity will be "cleaner," because the carbon content of natural gas is less than the carbon content of coal. In addition, expanding renewable energy capacity, especially solar, wind, biomass, and geothermal, will create industry opportunities. But the contributions from oil, coal, and nuclear power are forecasted to decline, which will alter the domestic energy landscape. Over time, fossil fuels will remain the most prominent portion of energy supply in the near term, but renewables will experience a growing share of total primary energy. The *Annual Energy Outlook* (U.S. EIA, 2017) projects the United States will become an overall net energy exporter in the 2020s. During the next two decades, the United States will continue to import oil but export natural gas and coal.

In the United States, renewables constitute a growing percentage of the total energy supply. More than half of this supply is for the production of electricity. Other uses include heating, steam for industry, and transportation. Two reasons exist as to why the supply of renewables is small relative to fossil fuels. First, historically renewables have been more expensive to produce than fossil fuels. Large-scale renewable energy sources, such wind or solar farms, are often located in remote, rural areas. This distance increases the cost of building power lines to power plants in urban areas. Second, renewable sources are intermittent. Drought reduces the amount of water available for hydropower; cloudy days limit the production of solar power; and periods of time without wind reduce the output of wind farms. Because of technological advance, battery storage, and the declining cost of distribution, however, renewables are becoming more competitive. Although renewables have played an important role in the economy for two centuries (wood supplied 90% of the nation's energy needs in 1850), only recently has the supply of renewables increased annually from multiple sources.

Four supply-side trends are important in the United States. First, total renewable energy production rose 105 percent during the ten-year period from 2006 to 2016. Second, during the same period, the production of wind increased 3,400 percent. Third, the production of solar grew 1,143 percent. Fourth, growth in energy production—led by natural gas and renewables—and modest growth in energy demand has reduced the reliance of the United States on energy imports.

GLOBAL ENERGY SUPPLY

Fossil fuels dominate global energy supply, according to the International Energy Agency (2015):

- Oil (32%)
- Coal (28%)
- Natural gas (22%)
- Biofuels and waste (10%)

- Nuclear (5%)
- Hydro (2%)
- Other (1%)

Over the past decade, these percentages have remained relatively constant. For years to come, we should expect fossil fuels to continue to fuel the global economy.

ENERGY DEMAND

Energy demand refers to the energy necessary to satisfy needs for heating, cooling, traveling, manufacturing, and power generation. The demand for energy is a function of the price of energy and other important variables, including income, prices of substitutes, and preferences. Substitute processes to produce the same end result may lead to the consumption of less energy or the use of alternative energy resources. The insulation of a home, for example, creates the same or a greater level of warmth. But more capital and labor to install the insulation is required to reduce energy consumption. Energy demand is derived from the consumption of products and services: heating, cooling, transportation, and lighting. During warmer months, higher energy prices that increase the cost of electricity encourage both the installation of more efficient cooling systems and less consumption of electricity.

Energy demand differs with respect to the short and long runs. In the short run with both fixed and variable resources, energy choices impact energy intensity, the energy efficiency of a nation's economy. Depending on market prices and personal circumstances, people drive the vehicles they own. In the long run, when all resources are variable, energy intensity may change, but consumers may also substitute newer, more fuel-efficient vehicles and appliances for their older counterparts.

The demand for energy also exists at specific locations. When the price of energy rises in one location relative to others, or industries migrate to other regions, the demand for energy declines in the initial location. But at the new location, energy consumption may increase, decrease, or remain unchanged.

In market economies, tradable energy commodities such as crude oil, natural gas, or gasoline are the most important parts of total energy flows. Energy demand consists of the aggregate purchases of these commodities in different markets. Energy demand is correlated with wealth and population growth. But variation exists between countries. On one hand, energy consumption increases as wealthier populations demand more energy resources. On the other hand, an increase in the demand for energy helps to increase wealth. In practice, these mechanisms are interdependent. Changes in technology, income, globalization, and the development of energy markets impact energy demand. Energy demand reacts to changes in energy prices, although price elasticities, regions under consideration, availability of substitutes, and energy eras (1970s vs. today, for example) influence the relationship.

Today, a reduction in the demand for energy—especially the demand for fossil fuels—is often couched as a means of promoting energy efficiency or mitigating climate change. Fundamentally, higher energy prices tend to reduce the quantity demand for energy, just as economic theory would predict. Therefore, the policies such as carbon taxation that raise fossil fuel prices have the greatest potential of reducing the quantity demanded of fossil fuels.

However, for three reasons, reducing the quantity demanded for energy is difficult. First, economic systems require large flows of energy. Second, the correlation between economic growth and energy consumption is strong. Third, increases in energy efficiency may not lead to corresponding reductions in energy demand. As a result, markets react to price changes, but policies that encourage energy efficiency may be as important (Sorrell, 2015).

Energy Demand in the United States

Fossil fuels account for the largest share of energy demand, followed by renewables and nuclear electric power (U.S. EIA, 2017):

- Natural gas (36%)
- Oil (32%)
- Coal (14%)
- Renewables (10%)
- Nuclear electric power (8%)

During this century, U.S. natural gas consumption has increased by 23 percent, while coal consumption has decreased by 36 percent. The total consumption of renewables shows a 113 percent increase during this century. The trend demonstrates growing demand for biomass, hydro, wind, and solar.

Global Energy Demand

As the global economy grows, global energy demand increases. Data gathered by the BP Statistical Review of World Energy from 2018 demonstrate that oil has the greatest share of global energy demand, followed by coal and natural gas:

- Oil (34%)
- Coal (27%)
- Natural gas (23%)

- Hydro (7%)
- Nuclear (5%)
- Other renewables (4%)

ENERGY MARKETS

In the most basic form, economists represent suppliers with an equation that demonstrates the quantity supplied of a specific form of energy (Q_s) as a function of its price (*P*):

$$Q_s = f(P).$$

Because of the Law of Supply, when the change in (Δ) *P* is positive, we expect the change in Q_s to be positive:

$$\frac{\Delta Q_s}{\Delta P} > 0.$$

The general equation for the supply curve includes the parameters a_1 (intercept) and b_1 (slope), where $b_1 > 0$:

$$Q_s = a_1 + b_1 P_c.$$

But in extended form, we may write Q_s as a function of price and other variables:

$$Q_s = f\left(P, P_r, P_{sg}, T, P_e, S, P_b\right), \text{ where}$$

- P_r : price of resource inputs, such as land, labor, and capital
- P_{sg} : price of similar goods, such as natural gas or coal
- T : production technology
- P_e : energy policy
- S : number of sellers in the market
- P_b : price of byproducts of the energy resource

In the most basic form, economists represent consumers with an equation that demonstrates the quantity demanded of a specific form of energy (Q_d) as a function of its price (*P*):

$$Q_d = f(P).$$

Because of the Law of Demand, a positive change in P leads to a negative change in Q_d:

$$\frac{\Delta Q_d}{\Delta P} < 0.$$

The general equation for the demand curve includes the parameters c_1 (intercept) and d_1 (slope):

$$Q_d = c_1 - d_1 P.$$

But in extended form, we may write Q_d as a function of price and other variables:

$$Q_d = f(P, P_s, P_c, P_o, T, P_e)$$

- P_s : price of substitutes for the energy resource
- P_c : price of complements to coal, such as coal turbines, generators, or cooling towers
- P_o : price of output
- T : technology for the consumption
- P_e : energy policy

At equilibrium, $Q_s = Q_d$. Price and the quantity of output are established. The market clears. But a number of factors may cause equilibrium to change. Supply and demand may shift. Government may implement a tax, subsidy, price ceiling, or price floor. Therefore, in the applications of energy markets in this book, we must acknowledge these possibilities. An important topic to address, however, is the economics of depletable resources. The following model provides a framework for depletable resources in parts two and three of this book.

ECONOMICS OF DEPLETABLE RESOURCES

Static Efficiency

Static efficiency assumes that the decisions we make today are independent of future decisions. In the absence of the consideration of time, total net benefit (discussed below) is an appropriate measure of static efficiency. In the absence of market outcomes or policy interventions that reduce efficiency, the total net benefit at equilibrium represents the greatest value to society from energy choices. This value leads to the largest efficiency gains for energy choices.

Social welfare includes both efficiency and *equity* (fairness). Up to this point, the assumption has been that equity is implicit. A dollar is the same, no matter who receives it. However, one could make the argument that the next dollar received is more valuable to a poorer person than a richer person. With this reasoning, the marginal dollar flowing to the poorer person adds more to social welfare than the same dollar flowing to the richer person.

In energy economics, this is a common perspective. For example, electric utilities may add a surcharge on electric bills to assist lower income customers. But weighing dollars unequally is difficult to quantify. Therefore, this model framework continues for now with the assumption that each dollar is weighed the same. At the end of the chapter, we will return to the idea of social welfare. We will evaluate whether an optimal path of resource extraction is fair to both present and future generations.

In an energy market without scarcity, market outcomes reflect the interaction between supply and demand. To demonstrate this concept, suppose a market for coal. We may characterize demand as downward-sloping, where *P* is the price per ton and *q* is the quantity of tons. Demand is the same as marginal benefit (*MB*). To simplify, the marginal cost of extraction is assumed constant (figure 6.1). In this example, if supply is 380 tons or greater and two periods are the relevant time frame, an efficient allocation would entail 190 in each period, regardless of the discount rate. Consumption in period one would not reduce consumption in period two. The static efficiency condition suffices. Resource allocation in period two is not temporally interdependent with resource allocation in period one.

At the point where *MB* = *MC*, what is net benefit (*NB*)? NB equals total benefit minus total cost. Total benefit (*TB*) equals the area under *MB* from the

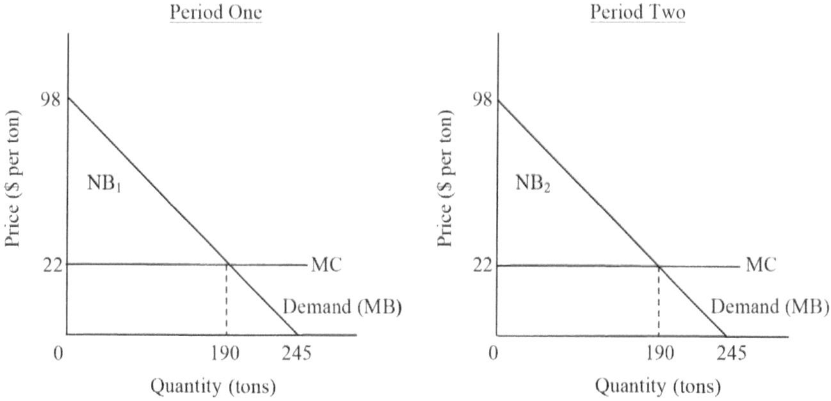

Figure 6.1 The Absence of Scarcity in a Two-Period Model. *Source*: Author.

origin to the quantity of 190. Total cost (*TC*) equals the area under *MC* from the origin to the quantity of 190. For both periods, total net benefit equals net benefit in period one (NB_1) plus net benefit in period two (NB_2).

Dynamic Efficiency

But if scarcity exists, the dynamic efficiency criterion applies. Dynamic efficiency refers to the productive use of depletable resources. The efficient allocation is the one that maximizes the present value of NBs from each period. Dynamic efficiency balances the present and future uses of depletable resources by maximizing the present value of total NBs over time.

Two resource categories are relevant for dynamic efficiency. The first is depletable and nonrenewable resources such as oil, coal, and natural gas. The second is depletable but potentially renewable resources such as wood, a source of bioenergy. With these categories, producers must balance the choice of extracting today versus extracting in the future. If producers maximize value over the life of the resource, they select an optimal path of resource extraction. But with renewable resources such as solar or wind, a dynamic framework is not necessary. These energy resources are renewable and nondepletable. The decision to produce more solar or wind power today does not preclude future production.

For depletable resources, two reasons exist for the application of a dynamic framework. First, the choice of resource extraction today entails foregone future opportunities. Second, a dynamic framework creates incentives for energy transition. For example, with a particular depletable resource, the producer must consider the level of proven reserves, the number of periods of extraction, and consumption patterns. This requires forecasts that incorporate advanced imaging techniques for underground reserves, current rates of production, and future levels of expected consumption.

With dynamic efficiency, we must compare dollar values over time. The method to convert a future value (*FV*) into a present value (*PV*) uses a discount rate:

$$PV = FV / (1+r)^n$$

where r = discount rate, n = number of periods for discounting, and $1/(1 + r)^n$ = discount factor.

Options for Resource Extraction

In a two-period model with scarcity, one option for resource extraction is to extract the market quantity in period one and the remaining reserves in period two. Another option is to extract an equal amount in both periods. A third option is to calculate the optimal level of resource extraction for both periods. Of course, other options exist, but we are going to compare these choices.

Continuing with the numerical example, suppose the introduction of a scarcity condition: total reserves equal 245 tons of coal, less than the market clearing level of 380 tons for two periods. We may characterize this constraint by showing the quantity extracted in period one (q_1) plus the quantity extracted in period two (q_2) must equal 245:

$$q_1 + q_2 = 245$$

The key to our problem is that suppliers may choose different quantities for q_1 and q_2. We will show, however, that the dynamic efficiency criterion leads to the optimal choice.

The First Option

The first option is to extract the market quantity in period one and the remainder in period two. With production of 190 in period one, production equals 55 in period two. In the presence of scarcity, we must calculate NB in each period, discounting the value in period two. (The recommendation here is to draw a new graph for period two with production equal to 55. This graph for period two differs from the period two graph in figure 6.1. At a quantity of 55, first calculate price by plugging $q = 55$ into the demand equation relevant for this problem: $P = 98-0.4(q) = 98-0.4(55) = 76$. Then for period two identify NB.) With a discount rate equal to 3 percent, total NB for both periods is $10,690.87 (example 6.1).

Calculation of net benefit in period one (NB_1) with production = 190 (Figure 6.1)
$NB_1 = (TB_1 - TC_1) = [(1/2)(190)(76) + (190)(22)] - [(190)(22)] = \$7{,}220$

Calculation of net benefit in period two (NB_2) with production = 55: Draw a new graph.
$NB_2 = (TB_2 - TC_2) = [(1/2)(55)(22) + (55)(76)] - [(55)(22)] = \$3{,}575$

Discounting NB_2 with a 3% discount rate by one period (from period two to period one)
$PV = FV/(1 + r)^n = \$3{,}575/(1 + 0.03)^1 = \$3{,}575/1.03 = \$3{,}470.87$

Calculation of Total Net Benefit
$TNB = NB_1 + NB_2 = \$7{,}220 + \$3{,}470.87 = \$10{,}690.87$

Example 6.1 The First Option: Calculating Net Benefit in the Presence of Scarcity.
Source: Author.

Calculation of net benefit in period one (NB_1) with production = 122.5. Draw a new graph.
$NB_1 = (TB_1 - TC_1) = [(1/2)(122.5)(49) + (122.5)(49)] - [(122.5)(22)] = \$6,308.75$

Calculation of net benefit in period two (NB_2) with production = 122.5. Draw a new graph.
$NB_2 = (TB_2 - TC_2) = [(1/2)(122.5)(49) + (122.5)(49)] - [(122.5)(22)] = \$6,308.75$

Discounting NB_2 with a 3% discount rate by one period (from period two to period one)
$PV = FV/(1 + r)^n = \$6,308.75/(1 + 0.03)^1 = \$6,308.75/1.03 = \$6,125$

Calculation of Total Net Benefit
$TNB = NB_1 + NB_2 = \$6,308.75 + \$6,125 = \$12,433.75$

Example 6.2 The Second Option: Calculating Net Benefit with an Equal Allocation.
Source: Author.

The Second Option

The second option is to extract an equal amount (122.5 tons) in each period. NBs equal the area under the demand (*MB*) curve and above the *MC* curve from zero to 122.5 units of output. (Draw new graphs with an output level equal to 122.5 tons in each period. At $q = 122.5$, price = \$49.) With a discount rate equal to 3 percent, total NB for both periods equals \$12,433.75 (example 6.2). Compared to the first option, the second option of extracting an equal amount in each period leads to a higher level of total NB. From society's perspective, extracting an equal amount is closer to the optimal path of extraction and the maximum of total NB.

The Third Option

With the third option, the dynamically efficient allocation must satisfy the following condition: the PV of the marginal net benefit (*MNB*) from the last unit in each period must be equal:

$$MNB_1 = PV\ MNB_2.$$

To calculate *MNB*, first identify MB, which is the same as demand. Then subtract *MC* at each quantity of output. Using this information, write the equation for *MNB*.

At a quantity of zero in figure 6.1, MB = 98 and MC = 22, so NB = 76. But at a quantity of 190, *MB* = *MC*: at this point, NB is zero and the willingness to pay for the unit of output equals its cost. Because the slope of *MNB* is the same as the slope of *MB*, we write the equation for *MNB* in the following manner: $MNB = 76 - 0.4q$.

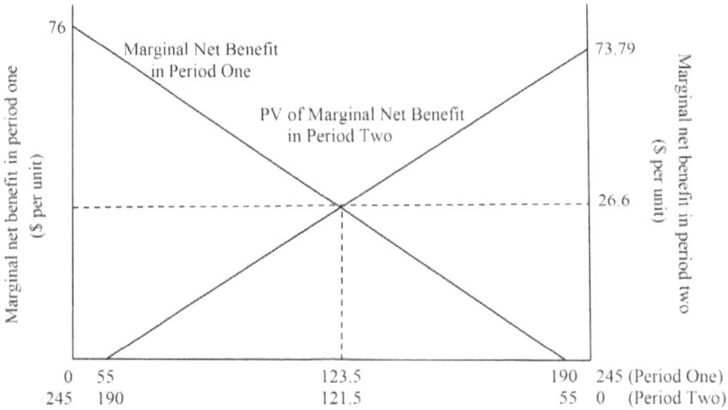

Figure 6.2 Dynamically Efficient Allocation of Resources. *Source*: Author.

Graphing *MNB* follows this procedure (figure 6.2). For period one, read the graph from left to right. For period two, read the graph from right to left. To graph *MNB* for period two, apply the discount factor to NB at each quantity. For example, at zero quantity, multiply NB of 76 by the discount factor $1/(1 + 0.03)^1$ to get 73.79, the vertical axis intercept.

The dynamically efficient allocation, the intersection, is where $MNB_1 = PV\ MNB_2$: $q_1 = 123.5$ and $q_2 = 121.5$. For the calculation of these quantities, see example 6.3. For the PV of total net benefits, calculate net benefits from period one (NB_1)—the area under MNB_1 from zero to the efficient allocation going left to right—and the PV of net benefits from period two (NB_2)—the area under PV MNB_2 from zero to the efficient allocation going right to left. With a 3 percent discount rate, total NB for both periods equals $12,434.24 (example 6.3). To summarize, the third option creates the most value:

- First option: $q_1 = 190$, $q_2 = 55$, total NB = $10,690.87
- Second option: $q_1 = 122.5$, $q_2 = 122.5$, total NB = $12,433.75
- Third option: $q_1 = 123.5$, $q_2 = 121.5$, total NB = $12,434.24

Marginal User Cost

In their discussion about dynamic efficiency, Tietenberg and Lewis (2018) note the importance of the concept of *marginal user cost*. This concept is the PV of foregone future production opportunities when depletable and scarce resources are extracted in the first period. The reason this concept is important is that, in the presence of scarcity, greater current extraction may not be appropriate. When resources are not subject to the scarcity condition, production always satisfies market conditions. But failure to consider higher levels of scarcity over time leads to greater inefficiency in future periods. According

Find the efficient allocation of the resource. That is, find the dynamically efficient quantities (q_1 and q_2) for each period. To begin, apply the following set of equations:

a. MNB = MB – MC (Marginal net benefit = marginal benefit – marginal cost)
b. MB = 98 – 0.4q (same as demand)
c. MB – MC = (98 – 0.4q) – 22 = 76 – 0.4q
d. MNB = 76 – 0.4q

To maximize the PV of total net benefits and achieve dynamic efficiency, marginal net benefits in period one (MNB_1) must equal the PV of marginal net benefits in period two (MNB_2). Total supply equals 245:

e. $MNB_1 = PV\ MNB_2$
f. $q_1 + q_2 = 245$

To solve the problem, plug in for MNB (line g) and then plug in for q_2 (line h):

g. $76 - 0.4q_1 = [1/(1 + 0.03)^1][76 - 0.4q_2]$
h. $76 - 0.4q_1 = [1/1.03][(76 - (0.4)(245 - q_1)]$
i. $(1.03)(76 - 0.4q_1) = (76 - 98 + 0.4q_1)$
j. $78.28 - 0.412\, q_1 = -22 + 0.4q_1$
k. $100.28 = 0.812q_1$
l. $q_1 = 123.5$
m. $q_2 = 121.5$

At the efficient allocation, calculate marginal net benefit:

n. $MNB_1 = (76 - 0.4q_1) = 76 - (0.4)(123.5) = 76 - 49.4 = 26.6$
o. $MNB_2 = (76 - 0.4q_2)/1.03 = [(76 - (0.4)(121.5)]/1.03 = 26.6$

To calculate total net benefits, sum the present value of net benefits from period one and the present value of net benefits from period two. This is the maximum level of value possible, given the optimal allocation of resources:

p. $TNB = NB_1 + NB_2$
q. $TNB = [(1/2)(123.5)(49.4) + (123.5)(26.6)] + [(1/2)(121.5)(47.19) + (121.5)(26.6)]$
$= [3{,}050.45 + 3{,}285.1] + [2{,}866.7925 + 3{,}231.9]$
$= [6{,}335.55] + [6{,}098.6925]$
$= 12{,}434.2425$

Example 6.3 The Third Option: Dynamically Efficient Allocation. *Source*: Author.

to Tietenberg and Lewis (2018), "This additional marginal value created by scarcity is the marginal user cost."

In our example, different assumptions concerning the scarcity condition illustrate marginal user cost. If scarcity does not exist and supply ≥ 380,

Calculate price by plugging the optimal quantities for each period (123.5 and 121.5) into the demand equations:

Period one: $P_1 = 98 - 0.4q_1 = 98 - 0.4(123.5) = 48.6$

Period two: $P_2 = 98 - 0.4q_2 = 98 - 0.4(121.5) = 49.4$

Then calculate marginal user cost by subtracting marginal cost from price:

$$MUC_1 = P_1 - MC = 48.6 - 22 = 26.6$$

$$MUC_2 = P_2 - MC = 49.4 - 22 = 27.4$$

Example 6.4 Marginal User Cost. *Source*: Author.

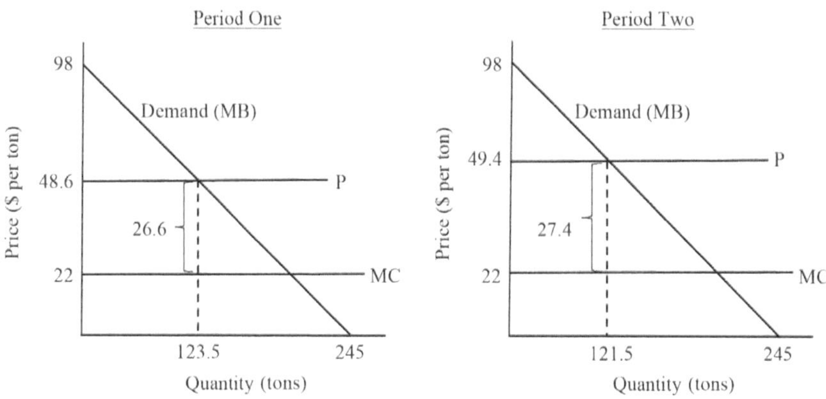

Figure 6.3 Marginal User Cost. *Source*: Author.

marginal user cost is zero. But if scarcity exists, supply < 380, and resource allocation in each period is less than the level that would occur in the absence of scarcity, marginal user cost is positive. Marginal user cost, revealed in example 6.4 and figure 6.3, is the same as MNB at the efficient allocation (26.6).

The analysis of an efficient market helps to illustrate the concept of marginal user cost. In an efficient market without scarcity, price equals the marginal cost of extraction. But in an efficient market with scarcity, price equals the sum of the marginal cost of extraction and marginal user cost (MUC):

$$P = MC + MUC.$$

The corresponding graphs are in figure 6.3. If we take the PV of the marginal user cost in period two $(27.4)(1/(1 + 0.03)^1 = 26.6$, we see the PV of marginal user cost is constant between periods, but the actual marginal user cost rises over time. In this context, the discount rate affects both the resource allocation between the two periods and the size of marginal user cost. The larger the discount rate, the more resources are consumed in the present period, because the future is given less weight.

Multiple Periods

A realistic framework involves multiple future periods. For oil, coal, and natural gas, the world has decades of proven reserves, given current rates of production. A number of points are important. First, continuous production with a depletable resource creates a condition of increasing scarcity. Second, with more future periods, the opportunity cost of current production increases, reflecting foregone future opportunities. Third, increasing scarcity and opportunity cost lead to rising marginal user cost. In response, the quantity of extraction decreases during future periods until it reaches zero. But this movement does not occur abruptly. In the presence of a positive marginal costs of extraction, an optimal path of resource allocation leads to a "smooth" transition to the depletion of the resource.

Transition to Renewable Substitutes

So far this discussion has not considered the availability of substitutes. The U.S. EIA (2018b) forecasts that renewables will increase as a percentage of total energy supply in the United States between today and 2040. Over time, power plants may produce output with less coal and more natural gas. In our model, with a readily available substitute, the exhaustion of a depletable resource would be less of a problem. The market would switch from one resource to another. The key is the marginal cost of extraction of the renewable substitute. As the marginal cost of the renewable substitute declines, the transition to the substitute accelerates.

The Consideration of Social Welfare

Do dynamic efficiency and the optimal path of resource extraction maximize social welfare? Recall from earlier in the chapter that social welfare includes both efficiency and equity. On one hand, the optimal path of resource extraction is the efficient outcome. But, on the other hand, it is not clear a priori whether the efficient outcome is an equitable outcome. We have assumed to this point that each dollar value of total NB is weighed the same, no matter where the dollar flows. The concept of equity, however, reveals that this assumption may not hold true.

A dynamically efficient outcome brings an optimal flow of energy to the marketplace. But coal combustion leads to higher levels of both carbon dioxide and air pollution. Lower income households are most vulnerable to these negative outcomes. As a result, we must acknowledge that an efficient allocation of resources is not necessarily equitable.

Many methods exist to address this problem. Throughout the book, we will use the sustainability criteria, established in chapter one, to consider equity, especially with respect to environmental impacts, atmospheric consequences, and health outcomes. When the consumption of fossil fuels compromises the ability of energy systems to establish positive environmental and health outcomes, fossil fuels will not be judged favorably with respect to equity.

We must acknowledge, however, that a method exists to address the problem, according to Tietenberg and Lewis (2018). One option in this chapter is the choice to extract an equal amount of coal in each of the two model periods. With this option, the NB in the first period is \$6,308.72 and the NB in the second period is \$6,125 (example 6.2). Another option is the optimal path of resource extraction. With this latter option, the NB in the first period is \$6,335.55 and the NB in the second period is \$6,098.69 (example 6.3). In the absence of sharing between periods, the optimal path of extraction makes people in the second period worse off compared to the equal extraction case.

But if sharing occurs, the outcome is different. Suppose society chooses the optimal path of extraction. To demonstrate the possibility of sharing to a future period, take the difference between the first period NBs: \$6,335.55−\$6,308.72 = \$26.83. If \$26.83 is invested at the market rate of 3 percent interest, society may save \$27.63 in period one for future use. Society in the future may then decide to use the money to reduce the negative environmental and health consequences of fossil fuel production and a more equitable outcome will emerge:

- Equal extraction in each period: Period two NB = \$6,125
- Optimal path of extraction: Period two NB + savings from period one = \$6,098.69 + \$27.63 = \$6,126.32

Allocating the savings makes society better off. But the key is whether society allocates the savings in future periods to the achievement of equitable outcomes. In this example, the amount of savings is low. However, with billions of dollars of value created in energy markets, society could address the inequalities that emerge from contemporary energy choices.

SUMMARY

Both renewable and nonrenewable resources are important in energy markets. The supply of and demand for energy are dominated by the fossil fuels oil, coal, and natural gas; however, the production of renewables, especially biomass, solar, and wind, is increasing. Of all forms of energy, the United States consumes the highest percentage of oil, followed by natural gas and coal. The country also consumes nuclear power and renewables, the latter growing as a percentage of the total. The world's consumption and production patterns further demonstrate a reliance on fossil fuels. With respect to the choice of the extraction of energy resources, the dynamically efficient outcome equates the PV of MNBs over time. Choosing this path of extraction maximizes total NB to society.

TERMS

Dynamic efficiency
Equity
Marginal user cost
Overnight cost
Social welfare
Static efficiency

QUESTIONS

1. How has the U.S. supply of energy changed over time? Why does the U.S. rely so heavily on fossil fuels? How important is nuclear power? What do forecasts for supply reveal? Using data from the U.S. Energy Information Administration, graph the supply of fossil fuels, nuclear, and renewables.
2. How has the U.S. demand for energy changed over time? What do forecasts for demand reveal? Using data from the U.S. Energy Information Administration, graph the demand for fossil fuels, nuclear, and renewables.
3. Suppose a FV of $10,000. Given $n = 1$ and the following discount rates, calculate PV: $r = 1$ percent, 3 percent, 5 percent, 7 percent, 9 percent. How does a change in r affect PV?
4. Characterize the global supply of energy. Which forms of energy are most prevalent? As a result of the nuclear disaster in 2011 in Japan, do you think the world will decrease its production of nuclear power? Why or why not?

5. What is the difference between efficiency and equity? In what circumstances are efficient outcomes equitable?
6. Suppose the demand for a depletable and nonrenewable resource is given by $P = 80 - 0.5q$ and marginal cost is constant at \$10. The scarcity level of the resource is 260 units. Assume a two-period model and $r = 2$ percent. For each of the three extraction options in this chapter, draw graphs and calculate total NB. Which option leads to the highest total NB? For the optimal path of extraction, calculate marginal user costs.

Part 2

TRADITIONAL ENERGY RESOURCES

Chapter 7

Oil

Fuel for the Global Economy

DEPLETION OR ABUNDANCE?

At least since the time of Malthus (1798), many academics have expressed concern about the adequacy of resources to support a growing human population. In recent years, some forecasters have predicted the inevitable exhaustion of one of our most important global resources: oil. If oil is consumed at the current rate, the thinking goes, it will be depleted. Richard A. Kerr (2011), for example, in *Science*, explained that a number of oil experts expressed concern around the year 2005 that high-technology exploration and drilling would not continue to increase oil production for OPEC (Organization for Petroleum Exporting Countries), the oil cartel. Then OPEC production would decline. Kerr (2011) also explained that, even though OPEC production accounts for less than 50 percent of the world's supply, non-OPEC production had not significantly increased between the years 2004 and 2011. An oil analyst was quoted as saying, "We believe—and pretty much everybody else believes—that non-OPEC [conventional] production has plateaued" (Kerr, 2011).

But what happened after 2011? Global oil production surged. In 2011, the world produced 84 million barrels per day. By 2019, world production exceeded 100 million barrels per day. Between 2011 and 2014, the price of a barrel of oil hovered around $100. This relatively high price encouraged exploration. In addition, political turmoil in the Middle East associated with the "Arab Spring" uprisings in 2011 shifted demand to markets outside the region.

There was another reason: new technology unlocking both Canadian oil sands and ultra-deepwater oil. These powerful forces, according to an IEA (2013) report, redefined the way oil is "produced, processed, traded and consumed around the world . . . with significant consequences for the global economy and oil security."

To explore the relationship between oil and the economy, this chapter first discusses oil in a historical context. The chapter then considers oil reserves and production. Next comes an analysis of the demand and supply factors that influence price. Following is a discussion of the mechanisms through which the price of oil affects the economy, the major players in the oil market, the type of market that exists, and relevant policies. The final sections consider sustainability and future prospects. As you read this chapter, keep in mind that the global oil market is dynamic. The price of a barrel of oil fluctuates daily. Considering this reality, the reader is encouraged to study historical price trends, current prices, and future forecasts.

OIL: HISTORICAL CONTEXT

For context, the energy expert Daniel Yergin (2012) explains that, in the last 150 years, there have been many periods in which people worried about the world running out of oil. The most recent was the beginning of this century. At the time, oil prices rose and the scale of global demand reinforced concerns about the adequacy of future supplies. However, as this chapter explains, the global supply of oil continues to rise, because of technological change, economic factors, and the availability of new resources. Recoverable resources in areas such as the Ghawar Field in Saudi Arabia, the Burgan Field in Kuwait, and the Bolivar Coastal Field in Venezuela are constantly moving targets. These and other fields have billions of barrels of recoverable oil.

The point is that, even with a growing global population and economy and the expansion of global networks of exchange, the world is not going to run out of oil over the course of the next few decades.

But even if the global supply of oil begins to slow, disaster will not immediately follow. It's true that the global economy now relies on oil; however, a decline in production provides incentive for the substitution of other forms of fuel. In the long run, this will gradually reduce the demand for oil. Production will be brought in line with the availability of the resource, even as short-term supply disruptions or imbalances continue.

Since the nineteenth century, oil has been important for the global economy. When we think of oil, we usually think of the refined products that are derived from oil, such as gasoline and diesel fuel. But we may trace the beginning of the oil revolution to kerosene, used for illumination. In 1846, geologist and medical doctor Abraham Gesner distilled coal and produced a clear fluid. When the fluid was placed in a lamp with a wick, it burned. Later made from oil, a more convenient resource, kerosene served as the impetus for the Rockefeller fortune in the late nineteenth century and marked the birth of Big Oil. In the twentieth century, the transition of oil from a fuel for illumination to a resource vital to the global economy started with Henry Ford putting the United States on wheels in the early 1900s. By World War I, when the country relied on tanks, vehicles, and fighter aircraft fueled by oil, the transition was complete.

Oil Reserves, Production, Price, and the Economy

Oil is derived from the process in which ocean plankton, algae, and other forms of marine life die and sink into oxygen-starved waters. Sediments from rivers mix with the partially decayed matter. The result is an organically rich concentration. Continued burying occurs with additional layers of sediment. When a mile or more of new sediment is buried over millions of years, the original sediment transforms into sedimentary rock. If the organic matter is buried deep enough to generate the necessary pressure and temperature, it transforms into oil.

The oil "window" is 7,000–18,000 feet below the Earth's surface. With 7,000 feet of overburden, pressure in the Earth is sufficient to increase the sediment's temperature to 150°F. This yields a heavy and generally undesirable grade of crude oil. As the depth approaches 18,000 feet and 300°F, preferred light crudes are produced. This depth requires one of three things. Sediments must be buried between 1.5 and 3.5 miles of debris to produce oil by (a) the ocean bottom sinking, (b) the surrounding land mass rising, or (c) a combination of both. Once formed, oil and natural gas, which are lighter than water, migrate vertically and laterally through migratory rock, extending as far as 200 miles from the source.

The rate of oil migration in rock depends on the permeability and porosity of migratory rock. *Permeability* is a measure of the extent to which fluids may pass from one pore (space) to another. *Porosity* is a measure of pores within the rock that may be filled with fluids. Both are important for determining the flow of hydrocarbons into a well. The reason is that the migration of oil and natural gas continues until it is interrupted by a solid rock formation or fault.

Once oil and natural gas are trapped in reservoirs within rock formations, the lightest, natural gas rises to the top and forms a gas cap. Saltwater, the heaviest, sinks to the bottom. Oil stays in the middle. However, a reservoir does not consist of a large, void space filled with oil. The space is migratory rock turned reservoir rock. The latter is saturated with oil and natural gas.

In the early exploration days, in the nineteenth century, oil drillers turned to geologists to help identify suitable fields. The land was examined for three necessary conditions: source rock that generates petroleum, migratory rock through which oil moves toward the surface, and reservoir rock which serves as an impediment to further migration. By the 1980s, computing capabilities had advanced sufficiently to analyze the seismic data necessary to generate a three-dimensional view of subsurface structures. It was possible to assess length, width, and depth. These cost-effective methods increased the probability of drilling successful wells.

Oil wells assume four forms. Wildcat wells are drilled at a distance from known oil fields. Exploratory wells are drilled near existing oil fields in search of extensions. If oil is discovered, an appraisal well is drilled to determine the extent of the oil field. Production wells are used to bring oil to the surface. In terms of economics, completing a production well, offshore or onshore, is more expensive than drilling an exploratory well.

Finally, the *recovery factor*—the amount of oil removed from a reservoir—depends on driving force. Driving forces include water (highest driving force), natural gas (next highest), or gravity (lowest). For oil fields, the average recovery factor is one-third. When a well is no longer economically viable, two-thirds of the oil is often left in the ground.

Oil Reserves

Before a drop of oil is extracted, exploration increases the reliability of future drilling. Though geophysical techniques are sophisticated, the data exist as scientific inference. In advancing their estimates of the size of an oil field, engineers and geologists project into the future. Inevitably, their estimates are updated over time.

Three concepts help define quantitative limits: *ultimately recoverable resources*, *proven reserves*, and *production capacity*.

Ultimately recoverable resources are the stock of oil that may be extracted over time. The estimates are derived from drilling activities, speculation, and deductions from previous findings. This is the quantitatively wider limit, but it is subjective and uncertain. The reason is that oil prospecting now extends to almost the entire Earth's crust, mapping all the potential areas, including ocean bottoms. According to the classification of oil, the ultimately recoverable resource includes all reservoirs that have been investigated and discovered, and others—undiscovered—which may be found.

The resources investigated and discovered are those that have already been identified with a high degree of certainty in location and quality and for which extraction is economically feasible. These proven reserves are a subset of the ultimately recoverable resource. Resources may be converted to reserves in the presence of different economic or technological factors. This conversion may take place, for example, in the presence of rising oil prices or new extraction technology. New sources of oil are counted as proven reserves if engineers are certain the oil may be recovered under current economic and technological conditions. When the price of a barrel of oil increases, marginal resources are transformed into reserves.

Resources and reserves are part of a dynamic system. In this system, the variables change. This is because of the uncertainty involved with geological conjectures concerning potential oil fields, political realities, and changes in the economic and technological conditions that continuously influence the results. The trend for both resources and reserves has been upward. But the upward trend will not continue indefinitely. That would nullify the finite nature of oil. The depletion of oilfields is real. It would be shortsighted to believe that depletion will never occur.

While the concepts of resources and reserves identify production limits and are expressed in terms of stocks—measured at one specific time—a third, more restricting concept exists: production capacity. This capacity is available at all times without compromising the potential for extraction. It is expressed as a flow variable over time and measured in terms of barrels per day. It is function of both the volume of investment made in exploration and development and the dimensions of the discovered oil fields.

Oil Production

In his book, *Crude Reality: Petroleum in World History*, Brian C. Black (2014), professor of history and environmental studies, argues that a pattern of dependence, closely tied to the supply side of the market, characterizes the world's relationship with oil. In the early twentieth century, oil flowed so freely that the marginal cost of extraction of a barrel was less than one dollar. Over the next several decades, a low output price encouraged the use of oil for fuel and everyday products, including toothpaste, trash bags, and house paint. Even though these and many other products were originally manufactured with resources other than oil, cheap crude made the products less expensive. A widespread use of petroleum integrated oil into our daily lives. By the end of the twentieth century, the oil market made many activities impossible without the resource. Examples include transportation, consumption, and entertainment. This dependence propelled the status of crude oil "beyond that of a mere resource to one of a critical actor, capable of shaping an entire way of life—a culture" (Black, 2014).

After crude oil is extracted, it is sent to a refinery. At the refinery, the crude oil is processed into different petroleum products. The resulting products include gasoline, diesel fuel, heating oil, jet fuel, petrochemical feedstocks, asphalt, waxes, and lubricating oils. A 42-gallon barrel of crude oil yields 45 gallons of petroleum products. The reason is that, in refineries, processing gains occur, similar to what happens with a bag of popcorn. The consumption of crude oil, therefore, is a derived demand. We demand gasoline for driving, diesel for trucking, jet fuel for flying, heating oil for cooking, and other forms of refined oil for additional activities.

U.S. Oil Production

Given current market conditions and technological capabilities, how long will oil last? The answer to this question has been debated for decades, at least since the geophysicist M. King Hubbert, an authority on energy, began discussing the concept of *peak oil* in the 1940s. Hubbert was interested in the physical limitations on extraction that exist for energy resources. The concept of peak oil is based on the idea that oil production follows a bell-shaped curve of a normal distribution. Peak oil refers to the maximum rate of production (extraction) of oil, after which it starts to decline. The implication of peak oil theory is that if the process of oil discovery follows a normal curve, the rate of production follows the same pattern.

Hubbert argued that, while aggregate production for an oil field usually increases at an increasing rate, peak oil refers to the moment in time associated with the maximum rate of petroleum production. After peak oil, the rate of production begins to decline, often rapidly, according to Hubbert, as the resource is depleted. In his 1949 article in *Science,* "Energy from Fossil Fuels," he wrote that fossil fuels develop over the course of hundreds of millions of years, but humans extract and consume fossil fuels in decades. As a result, we have "an essentially fixed storehouse of energy which we are drawing upon at a phenomenal rate" (Hubbert, 1949). In his 1956 presentation to the American Petroleum Institute, "Nuclear Energy and the Fossil Fuels," Hubbert charted the rise in world oil production from the late 1800s to the 1950s:

> The only a priori information concerning the magnitude of the ultimate cumulative production of which we may be certain is that it will be less than, or at most equal to, the quantity of the resource initially present. Consequently, if we knew the quantity initially present, we could draw a family of possible production curves, all of which would exhibit the common property of beginning and ending at zero, and encompassing an area equal to or less than the initial quantity (Hubbert, 1956).

The resulting "curve" that he drew was a symmetric logistic distribution curve, later known as "Hubbert's Curve" (figure 7.1). The curve approximates the production rate of oil over time, with three phases: build-up, peak oil, and decreasing production. Figure 7.1 includes a dotted line that intersects the curve. To the left of the dotted line, in the build-up phase, oil production is increasing. To the right is the declining production phase. An analysis of Hubbert's peak requires the consideration of time, but assumes that prices and technology are relatively stable. At any moment, the amount of a fossil

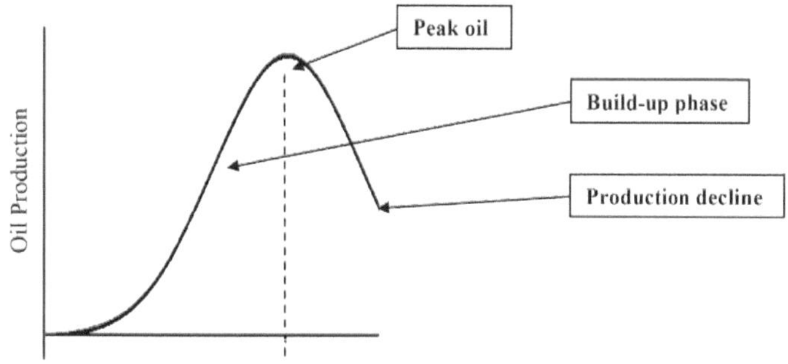

Figure 7.1 Hubbert's Curve: The Trend in Oil Production over Time. *Source*: Author.

fuel that remains in the ground equals the original level minus that which has been extracted. For a specific source of energy, future availability depends on current rates of extraction, the success of exploration, and the ability to develop cost-effective substitutes. As more oil discoveries supply the market with potential reserves, actual production occurs a number of years in the future. Therefore, a time lag exists between the pattern of discoveries and the pattern of production. Eventually, production must decline.

However, Yergin (2012) argues that a "plateau," not a peak, is a useful way to envision the trend of the future supply of oil. The world has decades of production growth in the oil market before it reaches a plateau, according to Yergin, perhaps around the middle of this century. When the market reaches the plateau, global output will remain relatively stable. After that, a gradual decline will occur.

Hubbert applied his theory to crude oil production in the lower forty-eight U.S. states. In the 1950s, he predicted that between 1965 and 1970 U.S. oil production would peak. He was right. U.S. oil production rose to 9.6 million barrels per day in 1970, the highest level for four decades. This prediction has been cited by many as proof of the accuracy of the model.

How well does the pattern of U.S. oil production fit the idealized Hubbert's Curve? Between 1950 and 2009, the answer is "well." Production increased, reached a peak in 1970, and then declined. However, starting in 2010, oil production began to rise (figure 7.2). In 2010, the United States was producing on average 5.475 million barrels per day. But by August 2018, crude oil production reached 11.3 million barrels per day, the first time that monthly production surpassed the 11 million mark.

What's lacking in the Hubbert's Curve framework is technological advance. The recent application of new and improved drilling and fracking technology demonstrates that Hubbert's model better suits conventional (not unconventional) petroleum production. The reason is that technological advance in exploration, development, and drilling continues to bring

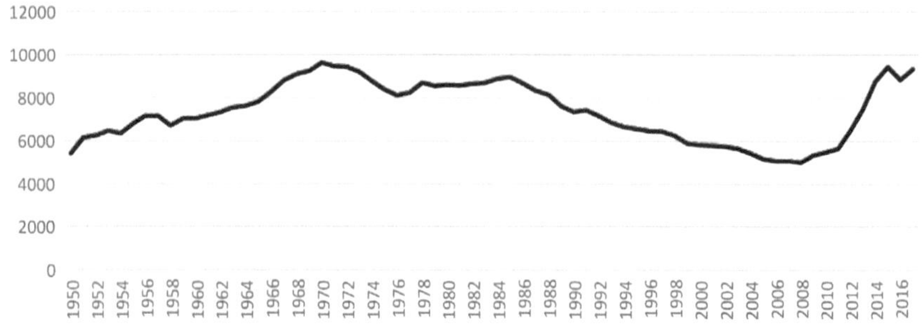

Figure 7.2 U.S. Oil Production: Barrels per Day—Thousands. *Source*: Author using data from the U.S. Energy Information Administration, https://www.eia.gov/dnav/pet/hist/LeafHandler.ashx?n=PET&s=MCRFPUS2&f=A.

unconventional sources to the market, such as tar sands from Canada and oil from ocean floors.

World Oil Production

One aspect consistent for several decades is the increase in global supply. In 1965, production equaled 31 million barrels per day. In 2015, world oil production reached almost 92 million barrels per day. The 196 percent increase in oil production from 1965 to 2015 reflects rising world demand, relatively higher prices during periods of expansion, technological advance, and the extraction of oil resources previously considered unconventional (figure 7.3).

Reserves-to-Production Ratio

The reserves-to-production ratio calculates the remaining amount of oil that exists in a specific area expressed in time: R/P, where R = proven reserves

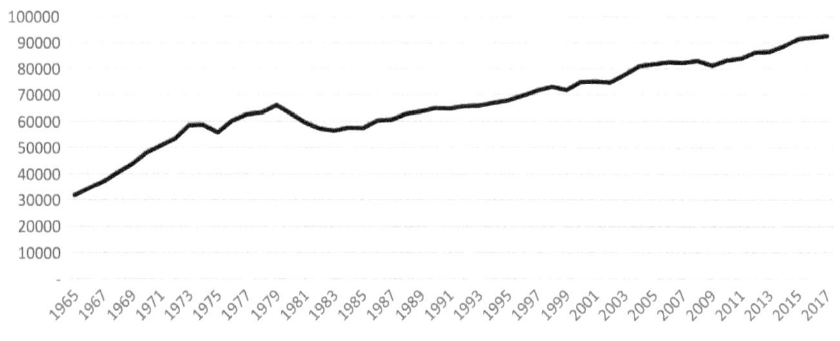

Figure 7.3 World Oil Production: Barrels per Day—Thousands. *Source*: Author using data from the BP Statistical Review of World Energy, https://www.bp.com/en/global/corporate/energy-economics/statistical-review-of-world-energy.html.

and P = the amount of oil produced, usually measured on a daily, monthly, or annual basis. At the global level, since the beginning of this century, the ratio of proven oil reserves to production has remained relatively stable at about fifty years. But we have to use caution when using this statistic as an indicator of the residual life of existing oil fields. We should think of it as a result of oil companies' policies of extraction and not as a concept beyond their control. The reason is that increasing costs of exploration have provided incentive for oil companies to invest in exploration technology as much as it is necessary to provide an adequate production horizon. Over time, because companies adjust their estimates for reserves, the ratio remains stable.

But for the R/P ratio to remain stable, proven reserves must increase when production goes up. Evidence exists for this trend. An increase in both world population and living standards leads to more production, which requires larger reserves to sustain the production. Reserves are larger now than they were decades ago. The reason is the time value of money. It is uneconomic to invest resources upfront to convert all identified or undiscovered resources into reserves. In practice, energy companies do not drill more than one or two decade's worth of reserves. Some areas have had about twenty years' worth of reserves for more than half a century as continuing exploration provides additional reserves.

Oil Price

With oil, two types of markets exist.

The *spot market* is where barrels of crude oil are bought and sold. In this market, the *spot price*, according to the U.S. Environmental Information Administration, is the "price for a one-time open market transaction for immediate delivery of (oil) at a specific location where the commodity is purchased 'on the spot' at current market prices." In the United States, the petroleum pipelines and refineries infrastructure are laid out in seven spot market regions. Though connected, the seven regions contain their own production, refinery, and distribution networks. Within each region, prices of refined products such as gasoline are influenced by local market and pricing conditions. A refinery problem in one region will impact price outcomes in that region. But regions may also influence each other's markets and pricing conditions. In the presence of natural disasters, the linking of regions is particularly acute. In the context of spot markets, a hurricane in the Gulf Coast may impact prices in the Pacific Northwest.

In *futures markets*, people buy and sell contracts that promise the future delivery of oil at set prices. But futures contracts normally do not impact the current price in the spot market. When we hear about a change in the price of oil in the news, it usually refers to the "front-month" oil futures contract trading on the New York Mercantile Exchange. In the United States, this is the de facto reference for oil prices and refers to contracts for the price of West Texas Intermediate-grade oil. The contract specifies a delivery date within the next month to a transfer hub in Cushing, Oklahoma. Interestingly, refiners normally purchase oil with futures contracts, either privately negotiated or from an exchange. Spot prices are not as important in global oil markets. But for either market, the price of a barrel of oil is determined by supply and demand conditions.

The futures market has grown to become the heart of the oil-pricing system. The futures market allows producers and refiners to hedge against their risks. Speculators use the futures market to define their positions. One reason is that the futures market is highly liquid. Compared to the spot market, it is less vulnerable to distortions. Another reason is that futures prices are determined by transactions in the futures exchange. Thus, the constant availability of futures prices, which are continuously updated, enhances price transparency.

Over the last fifty years, the oil market shifted first from governance by multinational oil companies to governance by OPEC. It then shifted from the spot market to the futures market. This transformation has had an enormous impact on the global marketplace.

Supply-Side Factors that Impact Price

The supply of oil is function of:

- Acute events and disruptions in production
- Geological factors and constraints
- Investments in new capacity or technologies

Acute events and disruptions in production include such unwelcome or intense events as war in the Middle East or other important oil-related areas of the world, changes in the supply of oil in the global marketplace by OPEC, or natural disasters such as hurricanes. Geological factors and constraints include the change in knowledge that alters the ultimately recoverable resource. The peak oil argument is relevant here. Conventional deposits peaked in the early 2000s, according to Kallis and Sager (2017), and extraction from operating conventional oil wells is decreasing. Moreover, production in eight of the top twenty producing nations has already peaked. Investments in new capacity or new technologies enhance the ability of oil companies to expand proven reserves from known reservoirs with engineering techniques.

Demand-Side Factors that Impact Price

The demand for oil is function of:

- Income
- Industrial activity
- Changing global demand for industrial commodities
- Future expectations

The energy economist, James Hamilton (2009), argues that "The single most important fact for understanding short-run changes in the price of oil is that income . . . is the key determinant." Petroleum consumption follows income growth. However, other factors provide a precautionary incentive to buy oil, especially forecasts of global growth, trends of rising demand for oil, and supply constraints. These factors put upward pressure on price.

U.S. Oil Consumption

U.S. oil consumption rose steadily from 12.1 million barrels per day on average in 1966 to 17.32 million per day in 1973. The first world oil crisis, in the years 1973–1974, saw the world price of a barrel of oil increase from 3 dollars per barrel to 12 dollars. This impacted consumption. In 1975, consumers demanded 16.33 million barrels per day, down by 5 percent in two years. In the latter half of the 1970s, consumption rose steadily, reaching 18.44 million barrels per day in 1979.

Then the second world oil crisis hit.

World oil production fell by over 4 percent during the period of 1979–1980, but prices rose by a greater percentage. United States oil consumption decreased from 17.06 million barrels per day in 1980 to 15.73 in 1985, a change of more than 8 percent. The remainder of the decade saw consumption rise again to 17.33 million barrels per day on average in 1989.

The 1990s and first decade of the new millennium saw a steady increase in consumption. Peak consumption occurred in 2007 with the country consuming 20.68 million barrels per day on average. Since 2007, however, an important trend has occurred: consumption has remained fairly steady between 18 and 20 million barrels per day. Interestingly, consumption in 2015 of 19.4 million barrels per day is lower than consumption in 2000 of 19.7 million, despite the fact that the economy grew almost 50 percent during this period.

In the early 2000s, the U.S. Energy Information Administration projected that oil consumption would grow steadily at almost a 2 percent annually rate for the next two decades. But the actual path diverges greatly from this forecast. The transportation sector accounts for most of the decline in the EIA's forecast, with the rest coming from the industrial, residential, and commercial sectors. In the transportation sector, declining vehicle miles travelled has had a greater effect on consumption than rising fuel economy.

World Oil Consumption

World oil consumption has been rising since the early 1980s, due to increases in both output per capita and population. World consumption increased from 62 million barrels per day in 1980 to over 95 million per day in 2015, a rise of more than 50 percent. During the same period, world GDP grew by more than 500 percent in current dollars. While developed countries were responsible for three-quarters of oil consumption in 1980, they will be responsible for less than half by 2030. Therefore, the focus of energy demand is shifting from developed countries (even though the United States is still the world's largest consumer) to emerging economies in India, China, and the Middle East. With this trend, an average person in developed countries consumes three tons of oil equivalent of energy per year. The value is below one in low-income countries in Africa, much of Asia, and Latin America.

Oil Price Expectations

Many of the oil price variations in the last forty years were unexpected. The rapid price decline at the end of 2014 and into 2015 is one example. The degree to which changes in oil prices are expected or unexpected depends on how we form expectations. Baumeister and Kilian (2016) describe four measures of oil price expectations, representative of economists, policymakers, financial market participants, and consumers:

- Economists' oil price expectations: future price expectations relate to past values and other determinants, including production, global GDP, and changes in oil stocks
- Policymakers' oil price expectations: future price expectations relate to the price of oil futures contracts
- Financial market oil price expectations: future price expectations relate to the value of the oil futures price minus the risk premium, which is the minimum amount of money the expected return on a risky assets must exceed the known return on a risk-free asset
- Consumers' Oil Price Expectations: future price expectations relate to household expectations, when future oil prices depend on changes in the nominal price of gasoline

How does the specific expectation influence the forecast? Consumers cannot expect to become experts in oil price forecasting. But the oil price expectations of households matter even if those expectations are not sophisticated. Alternatively, the expectations of policymakers and financial market analysts differ with respect to the importance of the risk premium. Finally, the forecasts of economists depend on the variables chosen for forecasts. A forecast may influence the price of oil, but may not exist as a generally accepted prediction.

What Is an Oil Price Shock?

An *oil price shock* is the unanticipated component of a change in the price of oil. Quantitatively, the magnitude of an oil price shock is calculated by comparing oil price expectations to subsequent outcomes. An oil price shock is normally caused by a decrease in supply.

The choice of measure of oil price expectations—economists', policymakers', financial market, or consumers'—determines the magnitude of the shock. That is, in analyzing historical data, a policymaker may conclude an oil price shock occurred of a certain magnitude, while an economist may conclude that a shock did not occur at all. Baumeister and Kilian (2016) argue this is common: "It can make a difference whether we take the consumer's perspective, the policymaker's perspective, the financial market perspective, or the economist's perspective in measuring oil price shocks."

Hamilton (2009) identifies five oil shocks from an economist's perspective since the early 1970s, the change in global supply (S), and the increase in price (p). This information provides a historical framework for the following discussion:

- October 1973–March 1974: 4 percent decrease in S, 41.3 percent increase in p;
- November 1978–July 1979: 1.3 percent decrease in S, 38.7 percent increase in p;
- October 1980–March 1981: 1.2 percent decrease in S, 25.8 percent increase in p;
- August 1990–October 1990: 2.9 percent decrease in S, 71.6 percent increase in p;
- December 2007–July 2008: 1.8 percent increase in S, 64.8 percent increase in p.

The 1973–1974 Oil Crisis

At first glance, the 1973–1974 oil price shock resulted from the war between Israel and a coalition of Arab countries, October 6 to 26, 1973. But the war occurred in Israel, Egypt, and Syria. None were major oil producers or members of OPEC. Thus, the disruption at the end of 1973 resulted from the Arab OPEC countries cutting production by 5 percent starting on October 16, 1973. This was ten days into the Israel/Arab War. The Arab OPEC countries then cut production by 25 percent on November 5, 1973, ten days after the war ended. This oil embargo targeted select Western countries and lasted until

March 1974. The oil embargo was an extension of the military conflict by other means, rather than an endogenous response in the region to economic conditions.

There was another reason for lower production and higher prices. In 1973, the price of crude oil received by Middle Eastern oil producers was fixed as a result of the Tehran/Tripoli agreement of 1971. Five-year agreements by OPEC fixed the price of oil received by host governments. In exchange, the governments granted foreign companies extraction rights. But when global demand increased in 1972–1973, many countries in the Middle East were operating at capacity. They could not increase production. Saudi Arabia and Kuwait, however, had spare capacity. They increased output, although reluctantly. The reluctance was attributed to the 1971 agreement, which was eroding, due to U.S. inflation and a depreciating dollar. This development led to Arab opposition to the Tehran/Tripoli agreement, leading to the repudiation of the agreement, on October 10, 1973. Middle Eastern oil producers cut production. This interpretation was motivated by the cumulative effects of a higher demand for oil, economic growth, dollar devaluation, U.S. inflation, and endogenous macroeconomic conditions. The $12 price of oil charged by Arab producers in early 1974, up from $3, was not an equilibrium. The price was set as a result of negotiation among OPEC and not by the market.

The 1978–1979 Oil Crisis

The second oil crisis occurred when the price of a barrel of oil rose from $15 in September, 1978 to almost $40 in April 1980. As in 1973–1974, governments responded to higher prices by rationing gasoline and enforcing price controls. This decision led to long lines at gas stations. The first reason for the second oil crisis was a change in oil price expectations. The Iranian Revolution started in late 1978, culminating in the departure of the shah in January 1979 and the arrival of Ayatollah Khomeini in February 1979. Iranian decreases in production occurred in January and February of 1979. Iranian oil production resumed in March, but at a lower rate. In response, Saudi Arabia increased production. In January 1979, the OPEC shortfall was 8 percent, relative to September 1978. By April 1978, the shortfall ceased. The price of oil did not increase until May 1979. But with the turmoil in the Middle East, consumers bid up the demand for oil in response to higher future price expectations. The Iranian disruption prompted a fear of further disruptions, spurring speculative hoarding. The second reason for the crisis was a strong global economy, which led to an overall increase in consumption. Therefore, much of the increase in the price of oil was due to a booming global economy and a sharp increase in precautionary demand.

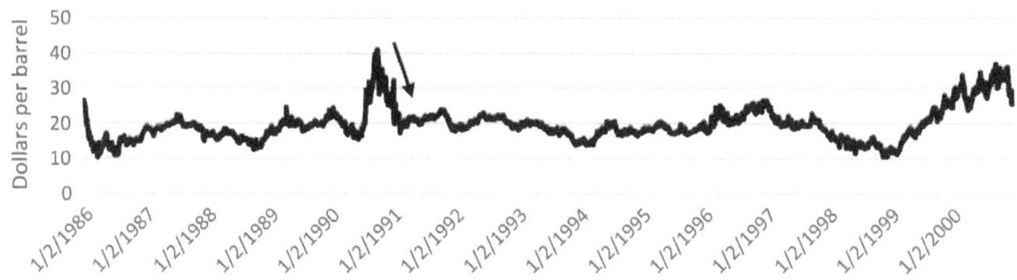

Figure 7.4 World Oil Prices, 1986–2000. *Source*: Author using data from the U.S. Energy Information Administration, Cushing, OK Spot Prices https://www.eia.gov/dnav/pet/hist/LeafHandler.ashx?n=PET&s=RWTC&f=D.

The 1980s and 1990s

The 1980s began with a brief upward movement in price during the 1980–1981 period and a decrease in output. However, the 1980s are characterized by a movement from over $35 per barrel in 1980 to below $10 in 1986.

The outbreak of the Iran/Iraq War, which lasted from 1980 until 1988, created an exogenous oil supply disruption. In late September 1980, Iraq invaded Iran. This caused the destruction of Iranian oil facilities. It also disrupted oil exports from both countries. The price of oil increased marginally as a result, rising from $36 per barrel in September of 1980 to $38 in January of 1981. After 1986 until the end of the decade, relative price-level stability existed (figure 7.4).

Then the First Gulf War began.

In August of 1990, Iraq invaded its small neighbor Kuwait, attempting to gain control over the latter's oil fields. The president of the United States, George H. W. Bush, immediately condemned the invasion, famously stating on August 5, 1990, that "This will not stand, this aggression against Kuwait." What followed was the first Gulf War, beginning on January 17, 1991. Coalition forces of thirty-five countries led by the United States pushed Iraqi forces out of Kuwait, liberating Kuwait and then advancing into Iraqi territory. On February 28, 1991, coalition forces stopped their advance and declared a ceasefire. The 1990 oil price shock, which occurred in response to the Iraqi invasion, lasted nine months. It was less extreme and of shorter duration than the two oil crises of the 1970s. The average monthly price of oil increased from $17 per barrel in July of 1990 to $41 per barrel in October.

Only in late 1990, after coalition forces moved enough troops to Saudi Arabia to forestall in invasion of Saudi Arabia, did the price of oil decrease. On December 31, 1990, the price of a barrel of oil stood at $28. But by the end of February 1991, the price fell to $17, demonstrated by the downward arrow in figure 7.4.

The Great Surge of the 2000s to the Oil Shock of 2007–2008

The beginning of this century saw a steady increase in price, but a rapid change started on November 17, 2005, when the price of a barrel of oil was $56, and ended on July 3, 2008, when the price peaked at $145. The price peak occurred at the beginning of the Great Recession, the largest economic downturn in the U.S. economy since the Great Depression. In this case, the negative effects of rising oil prices took time to appear. This explanation offers an answer to the question of why higher oil prices in the 2000s did not impact the economy before the end of 2007. It was because global growth and higher industrial demand eventually caused oil prices to rise. In contrast, shifting price expectations caused an immediate and large change in the real price of oil that reached a maximum after about three years (Kallis and Sager, 2017).

The End of the Oil Shock of 2007–2008 to the Present

After July of 2008, the price of oil decreased dramatically. After peaking at $145 per barrel at the beginning of July 2008, the price fell to $30 in December 2008. This is a rapid decline in a short period of time! By the middle of 2008, the global economy slowed, the demand for energy declined, and price adjusted. During the period between 2009 and 2014, the global economy recovered from the Great Recession, industrial and commercial demand rose, and oil prices increased.

Oil Price and the Economy

Oil prices affect the economy through the supply and demand sides of the market. This process works via production, consumption, and interest rates (figure 7.5). Changing oil prices may alter the cost of production, especially energy-intensive firms (*a*, figure 7.5). Higher oil prices, for example, increase the cost of production, reducing economic activity. Changes in oil prices may also alter labor productivity, which in turn impacts the cost of production (*b*, figure 7.5). Higher oil prices reduce labor productivity, increase the cost of production, and reduce economic activity. Changing oil prices impact the economy through consumption—that is, through firm and household expenditure (*c*, figure 7.5).

Kilian (2008) has a useful method of explaining complementary paths between oil prices and expenditure, which are relevant here: an income effect, when households adjust spending in other areas to account for a different share of energy in their budgets; an uncertainty effect, when consumers alter the purchase of durables until energy prices settle; a precautionary effect, when households alter their spending patterns when faced with changing oil prices; a durables effect, when households alter their consumption of

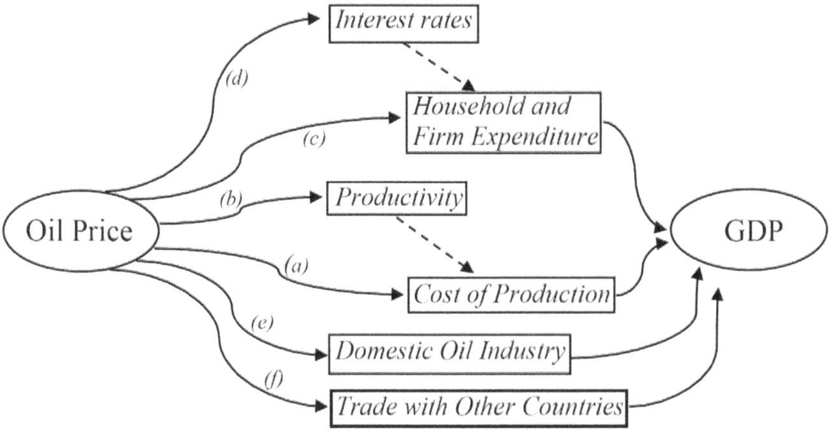

Figure 7.5 Oil Prices and the Economy. *Source*: Author using information from Kallis and Sager (2017).

energy-intensive durable goods, such as vehicles; an energy-intensity effect, when firms alter their expenditures in response to changes in oil prices; and a reallocation effect, when sectoral changes in related industries impact employment and consumption as a result of changes in oil prices.

Many macroeconomists have identified another reason that oil prices impact economic activity: bad policy choices. One popular argument for the recession in the late 1970s and early 1980s was not the increase in the price of oil per se, but from the decision of the Federal Reserve Bank to implement contractionary monetary policy to fight oil-induced inflation. The increase in interest rates reduced household and firm expenditure, resulting in a lower level of economic activity (*d*, figure 7.5). In the early 2000s, this argument was mobilized in an attempt to minimize the relationship between oil prices and the economy. The reason was that inflation policy changed: Monetary authorities would not make the same mistakes of the 1970s. However, the escalation of oil prices in 2008 and the subsequent recession undermined the assertion that oil prices no longer affect the economy. By 2010, it was clear that higher oil prices contributed to the Great Recession of 2008–2009.

Changing oil prices impact countries differently, depending on whether they are net-exporters or net-importers of oil (*e*, figure 7.5). For countries that do not produce oil, low prices increase economic activity. Higher prices increase economic activity for oil-producing countries.

Finally, oil price changes impact trade with other countries (*f*, figure 7.5). When the price of oil increases, economic growth in oil-producing countries increases the demand for oil domestically and from the rest of the world (ROW). This impact may offset recessionary effects in the ROW. As Kallis and Sager (2017) explain, with the exception of the United States and Japan, in 90 percent of the world's countries, oil prices and exports move in the same direction. This reality renders the adverse effects of high oil prices lagged and mild. Moreover, the expansionary effects of low oil prices may be tempered by decreasing exports to oil-producing countries.

In sum, it is not easy to predict how changes in oil prices will impact economic activity. The results depend on whether a particular country has a sizable oil industry compared to the overall economy and whether it exports to oil-producing countries. In addition, we must question the causality posited by figure 7.5. Do lower oil prices spur economic activity by decreasing production costs, increasing consumption, or both? Or is it the case that an increase in economic activity raises the demand for oil, thus increasing consumption? In the 1970s, an economic contraction followed the steep rise in oil prices. But in the second half of the 1980s, falling oil prices were not accompanied by strong economic growth. It may be the case that the impact of changing oil prices on the economy is "asymmetric." That is, higher oil prices may reduce economic activity while lower prices on a similar scale do not increase economic activity to the same extent.

THEORY OF OLIGOPOLY

The market for oil is characterized as an *oligopoly* market, in which a large market share is controlled by a few firms. The firms sell a homogeneous product (oil). Each firm recognizes that it must consider the actions of its rivals in a process of mutual interdependence. Significant barriers to entry in the market exist. Because a few major firms supply most of the output, each possesses substantial market power. However, because the product is homogeneous, the actions of one firm affect the ability of others to successfully price their output.

The Cartel

The *cartel* is a special case of oligopoly. A cartel is a group of producers that attempt to increase their collective profits by means of restrictive practices such as limiting supply or fixing price. In theory, a cartel could be established in any industry, but it is only practical in oligopoly markets when a small number of large firms exists.

With a cartel, a few firms (or countries) collude to operate like a monopoly. They attempt to maximize market power, set a monopoly price and level of output, and share in monopoly profits. There may or may not be a price leader; that is, a firm or country that possesses the most market power and influence in the group. In the United States and the European Union, cartels are illegal. However, the world's most famous oil cartel—OPEC—is a group of countries mostly from the Middle East, including Iran, Iraq, Kuwait, Libya, Saudi Arabia, and others.

For over half a century, from the end of World War I until the oil crisis of 1973, the world's seven major oil companies controlled the industry: British Petroleum (BP), Chevron, Exxon, Gulf, Mobil, Shell, and Texaco. These were fully integrated multinational companies, controlling every facet of the business. Upstream activities included exploration and the development of oil fields. Downstream activities included refining crude oil and distributing the refined products by trucks, tankers, and pipelines to gas stations and residential, commercial, and industrial end users. These companies both competed with each other over market share and cooperated in exploration and development. Even if an oil field was located in a foreign country under a concession agreement, the business assumed ownership of the field. Production volumes and prices were set, but this framework collapsed in 1973, a pivotal year in the oil industry.

In the meantime, countries in the Middle East, led by Saudi Arabia, were developing their oil fields. So was the Soviet Union. In fact, by the late 1950s, cheap Soviet crude was cutting into the profits of the Big-Seven oil companies. The companies began to lower their prices to maintain market share, which decreased profits. In 1959, in order to preserve its profit margin, Exxon cut prices to oil producers. Other oil companies followed. At the same time, the Arab oil producers organized the first meeting of the Arab Petroleum Congress, the result of discussions between the oil ministers of Saudi Arabia and Venezuela. A second round of cuts by Exxon provided impetus for stronger unity among oil producers.

OPEC was formed on September 14, 1960, at a meeting in Baghdad, the Iraqi capital. The meeting of the oil ministers of Saudi Arabia, Iraq, Iran, Kuwait, and Venezuela provided the foundational structure for OPEC. The original purpose of OPEC was not to increase prices but to prevent prices from going down. But by the second OPEC meeting, in 1962, each OPEC country sought to garner a larger export share. The incentive to cheat on the cartel had begun. Today, the organization has fourteen members. The group became influential on a global scale during the 1973/–1974 oil crisis, but competition today from non-OPEC countries in North America, Africa, and Asia is reducing the power of OPEC.

OIL POLICY

In the United States, public policy with respect to the oil market exists in four categories, although some contemporary policies do not resemble their historical antecedents: the regulation of production, import quota restrictions, fiscal policy, and price controls.

The Regulation of Production

In the twentieth century, quota restrictions were implemented. In Texas, for example, production was allowed for 261 days in 1952, 194 days in 1954, and 122 days in 1958, leading to higher costs. Costs rose because the restrictions hit cheaper production, increasing average total cost. Oil companies then turned their attention abroad, in an attempt to increase profit. Today, these oil restrictions do not exist. Oil companies make production decisions based on market conditions.

Import Quotas

The Mandatory Oil Import Quota Program, established by Presidential Proclamation in 1959, set a maximum level of imports as a percentage of domestic production. The idea was to minimize U.S. dependence on imported oil. The results of the program, however, were higher energy prices for U.S. consumers, greater exploitation of oil reserves, and the flow of cheap Middle Eastern oil into Europe and Asia. While the quota program ended in 1973, some American oil producers in 2016 argued for a return to the president Eisenhower-era import quotas, for two reasons. Saudi Arabia and other countries in OPEC were flooding the market with cheap oil, thus handicapping U.S. oil producers. Foreign producers were also crippling the ability of the United States to produce and consume our own natural resource.

Fiscal Policy

Fiscal policy as it relates to oil takes three forms: *depletion allowances*, *deduction of intangible costs*, and *foreign tax credit*. These policies reduce the effective federal income tax rate for U.S. companies.

The depletion allowance, introduced in 1926, focuses the tax code on the depletion of oil reserves. Since 1975, only small companies may claim it. The idea is that annual depreciation may be offset (as a capital loss) against income. Under the law, an oil producer may deduct 15 percent (originally 27.5 percent) of any gross income from an oil well. Companies are therefore encouraged to produce more than they would otherwise.

The deduction of intangible costs refers to a 1916 Congressional rule in which companies may expense "intangible drilling costs" in the first year of a well's life. This includes equipment used or work done. Today, oil prospectors almost always find wet wells, but the tax break remains. Oil companies may expense 70 percent of their drilling costs and depreciate the rest.

In terms of foreign tax credit, the United States taxes corporations according to global income, regardless of the source. Because U.S. companies are taxed by other countries on foreign income, income from foreign sources is subject to double taxation. As a result, since 1918, the United States has allowed a credit against U.S. taxation of foreign taxes paid. Alternatively, companies may deduct foreign tax payments from their foreign income.

Overall, these polices provide investment incentives and make the oil industry highly profitable when measured by return on investment.

Price Controls

Not until the early 1970s did a shift occur in the price setting power from multinational oil companies to OPEC. A number of factors were responsible. The most important was the tight demand and supply conditions that emerged in the early 1970s. Between 1970 and 1973, global demand for oil increased, but was met by OPEC countries. This market response enhanced the power of OPEC at the expense of multinational companies. As a result, the governments of OPEC began seeking higher stakes in their oil sales.

At the center of the new system was the reference price, the price of Arab light crude. Member countries would set their prices in relation to this marker.

In the early 1980s, in response to higher prices, new oil discoveries in non-OPEC countries increased global supply. Between 1975 and 1985, non-OPEC countries increased their share of global oil production from 48 percent to 70 percent. Most of the increase came from the Soviet Union, the North Sea, and Mexico. This increase in non-OPEC supply led to non-OPEC countries setting prices more responsive to market conditions.

OIL AND SUSTAINABILITY

We may evaluate oil with respect to the sustainability criteria established in chapter 1. With the six sustainability criteria, coal satisfies one: contribution to economic performance. Because it is a nonrenewable resource, oil will not last indefinitely. It does not provide baseload power for electricity sectors. Because of the pollution and atmospheric modification caused by the combustion of oil, it does not lead to limited environmental or atmospheric consequences. These effects also impact human health. For decades, however, the contribution of oil to economic performance has been steady, especially with transportation and manufacturing.

Future Prospects

For cartels such as OPEC to maintain power, they must limit membership, develop a similar cost structure for members, and exhibit significant barriers to entry into the marketplace. With OPEC, each of the provisions is satisfied except the last. Hamilton (2009) identifies the period between 1973 and 1996 as the "age of OPEC." But with the growth in oil production since the beginning of this century in the United States, Russia, China, Canada, Brazil, and Mexico—six of the world's twelve top producers and all non-OPEC members—the power and influence of OPEC has declined.

SUMMARY

The levels of oil resources, reserves, and production capacity help to establish the supply of oil. Whether the market will experience peak production in the upcoming decades will help determine future prices. Most estimates demonstrate a world oil reserve to production ratio of around fifty years. Shifts in demand and supply have altered the price of a barrel of oil, creating periods of volatility. Oil prices affect the economy through a number of mechanisms, including the cost of production, productivity, expenditure, interest rates, the domestic oil industry, and international trade. While the oil market exists as an oligopoly, the OPEC cartel is not as influential today as it was in the 1970s. Oil policies such as the regulation of production, import quotas, fiscal policy, and price setting have all played a role in the development of the oil industry.

CONCEPTS

Cartel
Depletion allowance
Deduction of intangible costs
Foreign tax credit
Futures markets
Hubbert's peak
Oil price shock
Oligopoly
Peak oil
Permeability
Porosity
Production capacity
Proven oil reserves
Recovery factor
Spot markets
Spot price
Ultimately recoverable resources

QUESTIONS

1. Plot oil production data for a number of countries and regions. For each country and region, does production pattern the shape of Hubbert's Curve? Why or why not?
2. For a particular country or region, estimate the oil reserves-to-production ratio. One particularly useful source of data is the BP Energy Charting Tool, available online. For your country or region, answer the following questions: is the ratio increasing, decreasing, or remaining relatively constant? Why?
3. For a particular country or region, plot oil production and GDP. It is helpful to index each at the same starting point for a given year. Over time, is the change in production or GDP higher?
4. Go to the U.S. Energy Information Administration's website at https://www.eia.gov. Look up the data on Oil Spot Prices in the section on Petroleum and Other Liquids. Download the data. Graph the data for the last two decades. Answer the following questions: during what periods of time did price increase? During what periods of time did price decrease? Using a supply and demand framework, graph the price-level changes. For your graphs, pay attention to the specific time frame under consideration.
5. Calculate the annual production of oil of OPEC countries. Compare the OPEC total to the global production of oil. How has the percentage of OPEC production to global production changed? Based on this percentage, do you believe the market influence of OPEC is rising or falling? Why?
6. Given the different theories of oil price expectations, how may an economist's expectations differ from the expectations of a policymaker?
7. How worried should OPEC be about the growth of renewable energy?

Chapter 8

Coal

Fuel for the Power Industry

MOUNTAINTOP REMOVAL

In 2008, a battle over the future of Coal River Mountain in West Virginia surged. On one side of the debate, the coal industry was planning to use a process known as *mountaintop removal mining*, an economically efficient procedure that blasts large portions of mountains away to reveal coal seams inside. Bulldozers first clear trees from the site. The detonation of thousands of tons of explosives then topples the mountain top into valleys below. Coal seams are exposed. Extraction begins.

On the other side of the debate, a local group of coal-mining families and environmentalists joined forces to form the Coal River Mountain Watch, a group that attempted to safeguard both the mountain and the local community of Rock Creek. They launched the Coal River Wind Project, a breakthrough initiative designed to transcend the perceived stranglehold on local jobs of the coal industry. The idea was to build a wind farm on Coal River Mountain. According to its proponents, the local wind potential blew away the short-lived economic benefit of coal mining. The wind farm would create hundreds of local jobs during construction and dozens of permanents jobs during the life of the wind farm. One study demonstrated that, in terms of jobs, the wind farm would serve as a feasible alternative to coal mining. In the process, it would consist of over 100 wind turbines and provide 440 megawatts of electricity, enough energy for 150,000 homes. It would provide property taxes to the local county, far in excess of the amount provided by coal mining. As reported by Tom Zeller, Jr. (2010), writing in the *New York Times*, a local resident concluded, "If we don't stop this (mountaintop removal), one day we'll be standing on a big pile of rock and debris, and we'll be asking, 'What do we do now?'"

Mountaintop removal mining is conducted in the Appalachian Mountains in the eastern United States. It is a form of surface mining at the summit of a mountain. Mountaintop removal mining is controversial because it destroys the local environment. Explosives remove hundreds of feet of mountain in order to reveal coal seams. The debris resulting from the process—a mixture of dirt, rock, and other "leftovers"—is dumped into streams and valleys. When hundreds of feet of elevation are removed from the mountaintops, equal amounts are filled in valleys below. The result, a peculiar landscape in various stages of development, includes partially forested "peaks" and wide plateaus in various stages of redevelopment.

What happened at Coal River Mountain? Massey Energy, then the fourth largest producer of coal in the United States by revenue and the largest coal producer in Central Appalachia (bought in 2011 by competitor Alpha Natural Resources for $7.1 billion), soon began blasting away at the mountaintop, despite the threat to the health and welfare of area residents. Over time, active surface mining occurred in parts of the contiguous Workman's Creek, Collins Fork, and Middle Ridge areas. Despite the bankruptcy of Alpha Natural Resources in 2015 and the declining demand for coal, the subsidiary of Alpha, Republic Energy, continued to actively mine several areas of the mountain. Meanwhile, the Coal River Mountain Watch group continued to work to protect the mountain, local communities, and the watershed from mountaintop removal. But the plan to replace coal mining with a wind farm never materialized.

The reason that mountaintop removal mining in Appalachia continues, despite competition from natural gas and the health impacts resulting from millions of pounds of strip-mining explosives, is our appetite for electricity. Coal, a biomass fuel from ages past, is currently irreplaceable. It is essential when we flick on light switches and charge our devices. According to the U.S. Energy Information Administration, in 2017, of the 4.01 trillion kilowatt hours (kWh) of electricity that were generated at utility-scale facilities in the United States, 63 percent came from fossil fuels (oil, coal, and natural gas). Natural gas generated 32 percent of the total, while coal was a close second, generating 30 percent. Nuclear provided 20 percent, with renewables at 17 percent and oil at 1 percent. This country relies on a steady flow of coal.

This chapter addresses the importance of coal for the power industry. The chapter's thesis is that, while the benefits of using coal are steadiness, reliability, and cost-effectiveness, the costs entail environmental and health impacts. In a world in which substitutes for coal are growing—especially natural gas, wind, and solar—we must evaluate coal in a comprehensive manner. On one hand, the level of coal consumption is substantial. On the other hand, coal production in the United States decreased throughout the second decade of this century. Coal production in 2018 was the lowest level since 1978. The share of coal in the generation of electricity is also decreasing: in 2010, coal contributed 44.8 percent of the total share of electricity in the United States, but in 2018 that percentage was 27.4.

To address these trends, this chapter considers the history of coal and the industry, coal reserves, production, price, and the economy. A discussion of contemporary challenges is followed by an analysis of coal from the perspectives of climate change and sustainability. The final section considers the future prospects of coal.

HISTORY OF COAL AND THE INDUSTRY

About 400 million years ago, the first primitive life forms, multicell algae, appeared in oceans. Fifty million years or so later these algae moved onto land. They evolved into mosses, plants, and trees. It is the remains of this period, which geologists call the Carboniferous Period, which gave rise to fossil fuels, including the giant coal seam that runs from Alabama to Pennsylvania.

The evolution of coal is a function of heat, pressure, and time. The organic matter from the plants and trees created vast piles of trunks, branches, leaves, and stems that were periodically covered with seawater. The seas rose and fell in glacial cycles. Over very long periods of time, the weight of the organic matter compressed into peat, a mixture that resembles chewing tobacco. When the peat was covered by seawater, it was cut off from the supply of oxygen. This prevented decay. The evolution of these swamps was aided by the fact that, 350 million years ago, the microbes, fungi, and bacteria that today chew dead organic matter into smaller bits did not yet exist. When the peat was buried under the water's surface and squeezed, heat was created. This process forced off the hydrogen, oxygen, and nitrogen. Continued burying by rising oceans added weight to transform the peat into coal.

Top-grade coal requires a long gestation period. For perspective, the formation of a one foot coal seam requires a three to seven feet layer of compacted plant material. The average time required to accumulate this compacted plant material to eventually form coal is more than 1.5 million years. But some coal veins are 100 feet thick. This size demonstrates both the amount of plant life and time necessary to create this fossil fuel.

Had the bacteria that currently devours wood been around 350 million years ago, it would have broken the carbon bonds. Carbon would have released into the air. Instead, carbon stayed in the wood. This was an extremely large amount of carbon! In fact, the rate of coal formation back then was several hundred times the average rate. As a result, around 90 percent of the coal we burn today comes from the Carboniferous period. That's why the period is called "carboniferous," because so much carbon was produced. Therefore, by not being there 350 million years ago and not arriving for 50 million more years, the absence of wood-eating bacteria contributed to the evolution of coal seams around the world that now provide energy for light and heat.

But the production of coal has an important environmental consequence. Living plants and trees absorb carbon dioxide from the air. The CO_2 is released when the plants and trees decay. For a sustainable system, CO_2 is recycled between living biomass and dead matter. In this system, the overall CO_2 content in the atmosphere stays relatively constant. But over time, atmospheric concentration of CO_2 changes. When trees grow, atmospheric concentration of CO_2 decreases. With deforestation or coal combustion, CO_2 increases. Around 350 million years ago, the interruption of plant decay by the formation of peat blogs removed huge amounts of CO_2 from the air. This cleared the way for a more hospitable atmosphere for living organisms.

Today, coal is classified into four main categories, lignite, subbituminous, bituminous, and anthracite, depending on the carbon it contains and the heat energy it produces (considered later in the chapter). Each category has different characteristics. Lignite, the closest to peat, 25–35 percent carbon, resembles black dirt with its soft and flaky texture, generates power, is largely produced in Texas and North Dakota, serves as 17 percent of world coal reserves, and exists as 10 percent of total U.S. coal production. Subbituminous, also soft with a brownish-black appearance, contains 35–45 percent carbon, generates power, cement, and industrial application, is largely produced in the Powder River Basin in Wyoming, serves as 30 percent of world coal reserves, and exists as 45 percent of total U.S. coal production. Bituminous coal—45–86 percent carbon, with a black and hard appearance, generates power, cement, and industrial application—is largely produced in West Virginia, Kentucky, and Pennsylvania, serves as 52 percent of world coal reserves, and exists as 44 percent of total U.S. coal production. Very rare in the United States, anthracite contains 86–97 percent carbon, is black, hard, and glossy, used for domestic and industrial purposes, is largely produced in Pennsylvania, serves as 1 percent of total world reserves, and exists as 1 percent of total U.S. coal production

In the United States, most of the coal in the West, such as Wyoming, is subbituminous. In the East, the most common is bituminous, found especially in West Virginia, Kentucky, and Pennsylvania. Subbituminous and bituminous are also the leading forms of coal produced in the United States, constituting almost 90 percent of the market.

Coal found in the western part of the country has a lower heating value than the coal in the East. This is the resource's stored energy potential. Because most of the coal in the West was created in freshwater swamps, it is also generally lower in sulfur content. This gives western coal a market advantage. While the best seams in the East are eight to 10 feet thick, some seams in the West, including those in the vast Power River Basin in southeast Montana and northeast Wyoming, are ten times thicker. In the middle of the basin lurking thousands of feet below the surface is the "Big George" seam, over 200 feet thick in places. When it is fully mined, it will be one of the richest coal seams in the world.

Coal creates an external cost: air pollution. In 1882, when Thomas Edison fired up the first coal plant on Pearl Street in Manhattan, residents complained about pollution and soot. Edison figured out how to generate electric light using coal. Edison's power plant or "dynamo," as it was called at the time, lit up several blocks of Manhattan, including the offices of the *New York Times* and the financier J.P. Morgan, an early backer of Edison. After three years, Edison had also designed the first incandescent light bulb and electric power system. These innovations influenced the trajectory of the global economy during the next 100 years.

Just as Edison was putting the finishing touches on his power plant, Samuel Insull arrived in the United States from Great Britain and worked in all areas of Edison's business, including securing a steady supply of coal from Pennsylvania and overseeing Edison's electric operations. In 1892, when Edison Electric was purchased and merged with a rival company, Thomas-Houston, it became General Electric. Insull ran Chicago Edison, one of the fastest-growing power companies, arguing against competition among power companies. He proposed that they were natural monopolies, subject to regulation by the state. A radical idea at the time, the idea persisted.

Over time, coal-fired power plants moved to the outskirts of cities. The reason is that the pollution from coal contributes to foul air and adverse human health effects such as asthma. But in the early twentieth century, coal mining progressed when machinery replaced miners. Pollution was not at the forefront of industry policy or regulation. Mining machines banished many picks and shovels, doing the same work in one-third the time. In the last few decades, productivity has increased along with the size of the machinery: earthmovers, haul trucks, conveyor belts, and coal trains extract and transport millions of tons of coal around the world. Some coal mines now sprawl over thousands of acres. The difference between today and 100 years ago is how we regulate pollution from the coal industry with both command-and-control and cost-effective policies. But we still live in Samuel Insull's world. Our electricity flows from large, centralized power plants. We pay a flat rate for inexpensive power. We plug in electronic devices, but we don't pay attention to the amount of power they use.

Deposits of coal are now excavated on six continents. This geographic balance enhances the level of energy security. From 2001 to 2016, global coal consumption increased by 54 percent. But the low cost per kilowatt-hour of energy that flows from coal-fired plants largely ignores hidden environmental and capital costs. Therefore, to this day, coal is aligned with the paradigm of large and centralized power plants. Part of this reality is necessity. The movement of huge quantities of coal from mines to power plants is difficult and expensive. In addition, coal-fired power plants burn massive amounts of coal. The largest coal-fired power plant in the Western hemisphere—the Scherer Power Plant in Georgia—burns more than 1,200 tons of coal every hour and receives the resource in 124-car-long trains. Similar to a nuclear plant, a coal plant is still expensive to build but relatively inexpensive to operate. Considering these market characteristics, advocates of coal argue the merits of industry characteristics:

- Abundance—coal reserves will last for decades, given the current rate of consumption
- Cost-effectiveness—historically, coal has been the least expensive source of energy
- Safety—unlike natural gas, coal will not explode during combustion
- Security—for many countries, coal supplies minimize imports

COAL LIFECYCLE

The first four steps of the coal lifecycle demonstrate why advocates argue for the merits of coal. But the last step is a problem from an environmental perspective:

- Mining
- Transportation
- Pulverizing and drying
- Electricity generation
- Carbon dioxide emissions

Mining

In the 1200s, the English discovered coal in their land. During an early period of deforestation around London, people gathered coal lying on the ground on the banks of the River Tyne near Newcastle. They then began digging in the hillsides for exposed seams. The process of coal mining started when the exposed seams created holes which eventually led to tunnels. A new profession then emerged: coal mining. The miners extracted coal and sent it down the River Tyne on water vessels to London. During the nineteenth century, this led to a transportation system with steam engines. Coal also fueled the steam shovel and became the fuel for its own excavation. By the end of the nineteenth century, coal replaced charcoal in the production of steel and iron and became a source of energy for the generation of electricity.

Miners extract coal from the surface and underground. But coal miners are at the mercy of mine owners, safety provisions, the dangerous nature of the work, and the global economy. Mine owners may not implement sufficient safety provisions. A decrease in the demand for coal may throw miners out of work. The contribution of these workers, however, helped save many forests from devastation, by giving urban areas a fuel they could consume besides wood.

Oil eventually replaced coal as the fuel for transportation, but coal is still important for electricity generation. Only until recently in certain parts of the world, including the United States, has employment in coal mining decreased. One reason is mining has become more capital-intensive. Another reason is power plants consume more natural gas. Employment in the coal mining industry in the United States decreased from 89,600 workers in 2011 to 51,800 in 2017 (figure 8.1). An article in the *Washington Post* by Christopher Ingraham (2017) noted that the U.S. coal industry employs fewer people than both the company Arby's and the used car industry.

Breaking down employment by the type of mine demonstrates the trend of declining employment. Underground mining entails two methods: *longwall mining* and *room-and-pillar mining*. The first involves a large machine with a rotating drum that moves back and forth and excavates coal. The second involves digging "rooms" into the coal seam and establishing "pillars" of coal that support the roof of the mine. Surface mining includes mountaintop removal mining, *open-pit mining* (extracting coal from an open pit), and *strip mining* (the practice of mining a seam). In general, with surface mining, workers remove the rock and soil overlying the mineral deposit with heavy equipment such as earthmovers. They then use dragline excavators or Bucket

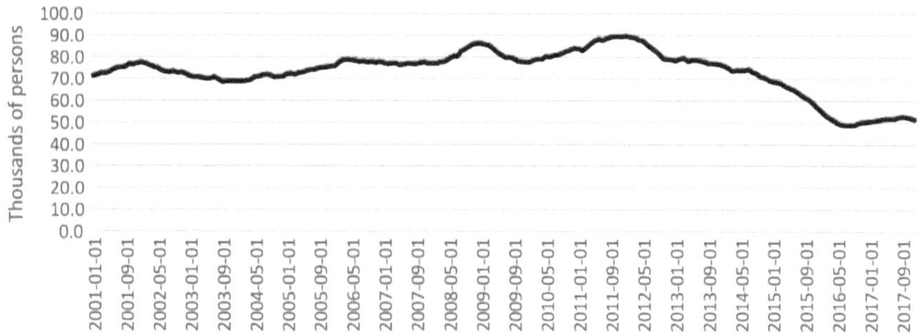

Figure 8.1 United States Employment in Coal Mining. *Source*: Author using data from the Federal Reserve Bank of St. Louis, https://fred.stlouisfed.org/series/CES1021210001.

wheel excavators to extract the coal. In the United States, underground mines employ more workers than surface mines, but employment in both has been decreasing.

From the miner's perspective, a problem is potential injury. Cave-ins may trap miners. Rescue efforts may fail. Suffocation, gas poisoning, and explosions may occur. Ever-present health dangers include dust, radon, welding fumes, mercury, noise, and heavy loads. During the twentieth century, more than 100,000 coal miners were killed in the United States. But over 90 percent of the fatalities occurred in the first half of the century. Over time, the industry became safer. Improvements in mining methods, hazardous gas monitoring, ventilation, and electrical equipment reduced the risks of poor air quality, explosions, and rock falls. Black lung disease, which may be fatal, has almost been eliminated with improvements in ventilation. Another safety innovation is the use of closed-circuit escape respirators. This is the equipment in which the miner breaths after the carbon dioxide is removed, restoring a suitable supply of oxygen. In the United States, 1,489 mining fatalities occurred in 1900. In 2000, the number decreased to thirty-eight. For perspective, coal mining is a much more dangerous industry than nuclear energy, which has a safer historical record.

Transportation

After mining, most coal is transported to electricity-generating plants, but some is sent to coke producers, commercial or institutional producers, other industrial activities, or export ports. In strip or surface mining, coal is loaded onto huge trucks by large mechanical shovels. The trucks transport the coal directly to power plants, railroad cars, or barges. In the past, not only did early railroads transport coal, but steam locomotives that were fueled by wood soon switched to coal. One reason was deforestation. The other reason was the availability of coal as a common commodity. Diesel engines eventually replaced coal; however, the transportation of coal on trains remains a common sight today. In the United States, more than half the coal supply is transported by railroad, often by trains with 100 cars, each holding 100 tons of coal. At the end of the trip, hoppers unload coal onto conveyor belts or giant rotary dumpers empty 100 tons of coal at a time by turning the coal cars upside down, like toys. The coal that is not moved on trains is transported by barge. In the United States, over 25,000 miles of inland waterways serve as routes.

Transportation costs contribute to the delivered price of coal. For long-distance shipments such as from mines in Wyoming to power plants on the east coast, transportation costs may exceed the price of coal at the mine. Transporting coal by truck, barge, or train uses diesel fuel. Changes in the price of diesel fuel therefore affect the final delivered price of coal. For example, the average sales price of coal in 2016 at the mine was $31.83 per ton. During the same year, the average delivered price of coal to electric power plants was $42.58 per ton. The resulting average transportation cost, $10.75 per ton, was about 25 percent of the total delivered price.

Pulverizing and Drying

After coal arrives at a power plant, it is piled until needed. When it is needed, a conveyor belt transports the coal into the plant, where it is crushed and pulverized into fine powder, drying it completely. In this process, coal is ground to the size of fine grain. It is then mixed with hot air, blown by large fans into the combustion chamber of a boiler, and burned at 1300°C–1400°C. The idea with pulverized coal is to use the entire furnace for fuel combustion. Burning in suspension, the mixture of air and coal creates both the maximum heat possible and most complete combustion. During the process, the mineral matter contained in coal is converted to ash. Bottom ash is removed at the bottom of the furnace. Fly ash, a fine and powdery substance, is made up of non-combustible inorganic material, but also contains some carbon. Because fly ash is so fine, the removal and collection from combustion gases (flue gases) requires special equipment. An example is a baghouse, an air pollution control device that removes particulates out of flue gas.

Electricity Generation

Primary energy is obtained from the burning of coal, oil, or natural gas, and electricity with a nuclear or hydro origin. The generation of electricity in coal-fired power plants, however, is a secondary energy source. The energy content of coal used to generate electricity is greater than the energy content of electricity: the boiler that burns coal has an efficiency rate less than 100 percent. In the process, heat energy from coal becomes a form of energy transfer from one location to another. The heat energy dissipates when the coal is burned, increasing the temperature of water and creating steam. The steam from the boiler turns a turbine, transforming heat energy from coal into the mechanical energy that spins the turbine. The spinning turbine powers a generator, transforming mechanical energy into electrical energy.

Here it is important to again distinguish between power and energy. Energy is the capacity to do work, measured in kilowatt-hours or megawatt-hours. For example, the energy unit for electricity in utility bills is the kilowatt-hour. Power is the *rate* of doing work: the amount of energy transferred per unit of time. Power is measured in kilowatts or megawatts. Energy production is a function of the amount of power a plant generates multiplied by the time it operates. The letter *j* signifies the basic energy unit joule. It may be converted into any other unit of energy. For example, 1 *j* = 0.0009478 British thermal units (Btu). A watt is the *flow* of one *j* per second. A kilowatt is 1,000 joules per second. Moving from seconds to hours, 1 watt hour (Wh) = 3600 *j* = 3.412 Btu. In terms of kilowatt hours, 1 kWh = 3,412 Btu.

We may calculate the number of light-bulb hours generated from coal. Suppose a ton of coal contains 27,790,000 Btu of heat energy. (The actual number of Btu may differ. Different grades of coal have different heat contents.) Suppose a light bulb is 1,000 watts or 1 kW. If all of the energy in the coal is converted into electricity with no efficiency losses, the coal would power the light bulb for 8,145 hours. A two-ton pile of coal would generate 16,290 hours (example 8.1). If efficiency losses occur, the number of hours would decrease.

With electricity generation, the *capacity factor* of a power plant is the ratio of actual electrical energy output over time to the maximum level. In the United States, nuclear plant capacity is normally highest, followed by geothermal, natural gas, and coal. In addition, when coal is burned, it releases thermal energy. The stored energy potential of coal—*heating value*—is the amount of potential energy that a power plant may convert into actual heating ability, expressed in Btu per pound. The heating values for specific grades of coal vary with respect to carbon content: bituminous (13,840 Btu/pound), anthracite (12,910 Btu/pound), subbituminous (9,150 Btu/pound), and lignite (6,900 Btu/pound). Finally, the *heat rate*—expressed in Btu/kWh—is a measure of energy conversion efficiency of a power plant or generator. According to the U.S. Energy Information Administration, the heat rate is "the amount of energy used by an electrical generator or power plant to generate one kilowatt hour (kWh) of electricity." It is how much energy a power plant must expend in order to generate a unit of output.

In a perfect system, 1 kWh = 3,412 Btu. But a power plant's heat rate may be more. In 2017, for example, the average operating heat rates for coal (10,464 Btu/kWh), petroleum (10,834 Btu/kWh), natural gas (7,812 Btu/kWh), and nuclear (10,459 Btu/kWh) differed. What determines the heat rate? It is a function of the plant's technical capabilities:

- The boiler: fuel is converted into steam heat
- The turbine: steam heat is converted into mechanical rotational energy
- The generator: rotational energy is converted into electric power

The heat/loss method then determines the efficiency of each conversion process. The product of these three conversion values results in the overall power plant heat rate. Because the mathematics is beyond the scope of this chapter,

Basic conversions between units demonstrate how much heat energy in coal may power a light bulb. Suppose a light bulb is 1,000 watts or one kW. In step one, identify the equivalency between one watt hour—the measure of electrical energy equivalent to power consumption of one watt for one hour—and Btu. The Btu is a traditional unit of heat: the amount of heat required to raise the temperature of one pound of water by one degree Fahrenheit. In step two, calculate the Btu equivalent of one kWh: 1 kWh = 3,412 Btu. In step three, calculate the Btu equivalent of coal, if one ton of coal = 27,790,000 Btu. Multiply this number by the tons of coal. In step four, calculate the number of hours of operation of the light bulb, assuming no efficiency losses between the burning of coal, the generation of electricity, and the transmission of electricity. In step five, with efficiency, calculate the number of light-bulb hours.

Step one: Identify the equivalency between one watt hour and Btu.

One Wh = 3.412 Btu

Step two: Identify the equivalency between one kilowatt hour and Btu.

One kWh = 3,412 Btu

Step three: Calculate the Btu equivalent of coal. Suppose two tons are available. One ton equals 27,790,000 Btu.

(2)(27,790,000) =
55,580,000 Btu

Step four: Calculate the number of hours of operation of the light bulb, which is 1000 watts or one kW.

55,580,000 Btu/3,412 Btu =
16,290 hours of operation

Step five: Assuming different levels of efficiency loss, calculate the number of hours of light-bulb operation.

Case 1—If 100% of the heat energy in the coal is converted into electricity and transmitted to the light bulb, 16,290 hours of operation occur.

Case 2—If 50% of the heat energy in the coal is converted into electricity and transmitted to the light bulb, the light bulb will operate for (16,290)(0.50) = 8,145 hours.

Case 3—If 25% of the heat energy in the coal is converted into electricity and transmitted to the light bulb, the light bulb will operate for (16,290)(0.25) = 4,072.5 hours.

Example 8.1 The Conversion of Heat Energy to Power. *Source*: Author.

the following describes each part of the calculation. First, boiler efficiency focuses on the process of burning fuel such as coal to create steam energy. A plant may reduce losses by installing combustion controls to adjust the air level in the furnace or reduce the excess oxygen in the furnace. Second, the turbine converts steam into rotational energy at around 50 percent or higher efficiency. Improvements include better blades, condensers, cooling towers, pumps, and piping. Third, generator efficiency is normally close to 100 percent. The little inefficiency that may exist is due to equipment systems. Overall, engineers focus on these parts of the generation process, trying to reduce inefficiencies.

To calculate the thermodynamic efficiency of a power plant as a percentage, divide the Btu content of a kWh of electricity in a perfect system by the heat rate. Assume a power plant requires triple the rate of a perfect system. This would correspond to 33 percent efficiency:

$$\textit{Power plant efficiency} = \frac{\textit{Maximum Btu content of a kWh of electricity}}{\textit{Heat rate}}$$

$$= \frac{3{,}412 \text{ Btu}}{10{,}236 \text{ Btu}} = 0.33.$$

Given heating values, heat rates, and power plant efficiency, we may calculate the fuel requirements for coal-fired power plants (example 8.2). Suppose a plant operating at 100 percent capacity generates 1,000 megawatts (MW) of electricity per hour. If 1 MW = 1,000,000 watts = 10^3 kilowatts, the power rating of the plant equals 1,000 MW or 10^6 kilowatts. The expected energy for 1 hour equals 10^6 kWh. In a perfect system, it takes 3,412 Btu to generate 1 kWh of electricity. But because of heat loss and other thermodynamic realities, it may require 10,236 Btu (the "heat rate") to obtain 1 kWh. As a result, 10^6 kWh = $(10^6)(10{,}236)$ = 10,236,000,000 Btu. If bituminous coal has a heating value of 13,840 Btu per pound, a ton (2,000 pounds) has a heating value of 27,680,000 Btu. If 10,236,000,000 Btu is required per hour, the amount of coal needed equals 10,236,000,000 Btu / 27,680,000 Btu = 369.79 tons per hour. This calculation provides perspective for coal extraction and transportation. In the United States, about 555 coal-fired power plants exist, requiring a large amount of coal extraction and transportation per hour.

Caron Dioxide Emissions

Carbon dioxide emissions result from a chemical reaction during the burning of fossil fuels. Carbon dioxide emissions contribute to global warming. But

By identifying the generating capacity of a power plant, we may calculate the coal requirement. Operating at capacity, suppose a coal-fired power plant generates 1,000 megawatts of electricity per hour. In step one, given the MW, calculate the number of kilowatts. In step two, identify the amount of energy expected in one hour. In step three, provide the heat rate, the amount of Btu necessary to generate one kWh of electricity. In step four, calculate the number of Btu necessary to generate the energy in one hour. In step five, calculate the heating value of coal. In step six, calculate the amount of coal the power plant needs per hour.

Step one: Given the number of MW, calculate kilowatts (kW).

1,000 MW = 1,000,000 kW = 10^6 kW

Step two: Identify the amount of energy expected in one hour.

10^6 kWh

Step three: Provide the given heat rate, or number of Btu necessary to generate one kWh of electricity.

Suppose 10,236 Btu = one kWh (This number differs with respect to the technological capabilities of the power plant.)

Step four: Calculate the number of Btu necessary to generate the energy in one hour.

(10^6 kWh) (10,236 Btu) = 10,236,000,000 Btu

Step five: Calculate the heating value of coal.

If bituminous coal has a heating value of 13,840 Btu per pound, a ton has heating value of (2,000) (13,840) = 27,680,000 Btu

Step six: Calculate the amount of coal needed per hour to generate electricity.

If 10,236,000,000 Btu is required per hour, the amount of coal needed = 10,236,000,000 Btu / 27,680,000 Btu = 369.79 tons per hour

Step seven: As an extension, calculate the tons of coal needed per day or per year for the power plant or the amount needed for the industry as a whole given a specific unit of time.

Example 8.2 Fuel Requirements for Coal-Fired Plants. *Source*: Author.

stationary coal-fired plants may capture and store CO_2. A typical 1,000-megawatt plant generates about 6 million tons of CO_2. This is equivalent to 2 million automobiles. (In the United States, there are more than 260 million vehicles.) Flue gas, a byproduct of combustion, is roughly 15 percent CO_2. Rather than discharging flue gas into the atmosphere, it is passed through a baghouse, an air pollution control device that removes particulates released from fuel combustion. The question then becomes: what should the plant do with the rest of the CO_2? One option is to discharge it into the atmosphere. This is the most common choice.

Another option is to capture it at source. If the power plant sits atop impermeable rock, the CO_2 may be injected into a porous sand formation filled with brine. A vertical pipeline reaches the formation. A horizontal extension then disperses the CO_2. If the brine is of sufficient depth, usually 800–1,000 meters, the pressure on the CO_2 will push it to a place where its density is similar to the brine it displaces. The brine absorbs some of the CO_2. After CO_2 saturates the formation, horizontal pipelines then establish new depositories.

A third option, the avoidance of CO_2 emissions, involves switching from coal to another source of energy. Switching to natural gas is cost-effective. Switching to oil is not as efficient. Switching to nuclear, hydropower, or other renewable sources would eliminate CO_2 altogether.

To forecast how CO_2 emissions from coal-fired power plants may change, a number of industry characteristics are important. Examples include the average age of power plants, the rate at which new plants are built, average efficiency ratings, the types of coal burned during combustion, and how the consumption of coal is correlated with both GDP and population growth. The forecasting of CO_2 emissions over the course of the next decade and beyond is an uncertain exercise. Any specific forecast will certainly be incorrect. But analyzing how these variables may change over time will help establish a framework for addressing the problem. It may be the case that, if the consumption of coal continues to decline over time as both GDP and population rise, CO_2 emissions from coal-fired power plants may also decline.

COAL RESERVES, PRODUCTION, PRICE, AND THE ECONOMY

Coal Reserves

Because the supply of coal in the United States is so vast, the first attempt to quantify recoverable reserves didn't occur until 1909. At the time, the coal industry possessed a growing level of influence, which corresponded to higher levels of coal consumption. A question naturally arose about the number of years of existing supply. After extensive evaluation, the U.S. Geological Survey (USGS) determined the country had over 3 trillion tons of coal, but at least 2 trillion were thought minable. This estimate was way too high. But the study wasn't superseded until 1974 with the publication of a revised report. The new report included updated information, such as the quality of the coal, thickness of coal seams, and amount of earth to extract in order to access the coal. What was the report's conclusion? The United States had less than 500 billion tons. Less than 50 percent of that was recoverable. But this was still enough for 400 years.

Today, estimates of recoverable reserves consider more sophisticated information, most importantly how much coal may be extracted given existing economic and technological conditions. The important question with all fossil fuels is not how much may be extracted, but how much may be extracted at a profit given current prices.

Unlike oil or natural gas, which gathers in reservoirs deep underground, coal rises and falls in the earth's folds. It often exists at or close to the surface, where it may catch fire and burn for dozens or hundreds of years. This geology differentiates coal from oil and natural gas. It also affects the estimates of proven reserves, which are recoverable under existing conditions.

Over time, the estimate of proven reserves changes. For oil, the discovery of offshore fields impacts estimates. For natural gas, advanced fracking technology and horizontal drilling make previously unobtainable reserves attainable. With coal, U.S. total reserves were estimated to equal 476 billion short tons in 2017, according to the U.S. Energy Information Administration. But recovery rates vary between surface and underground mining. The actual amount of coal that may be recovered from undisturbed deposits varies from 90 percent at some surface mines to less than 40 percent in some underground mines. The reason is that some underground mines are difficult to access for geological reasons such as narrow coal seams or rock intrusions. They may also be under state and national parks, towns, roads, or other barriers. As a result, according to the U.S. Energy Information Administration, the United States had recoverable coal reserves of 254 billion short tons in 2017, slightly higher than the two previous years.

In order of proven reserves, more than 80 percent of the world's coal exists in ten countries: United States, Russia, China, Australia, India, Germany, Ukraine, Kazakhstan, Colombia, and Canada. The United States holds the world's biggest reserves, more than 25 percent of the world's total. The United States is also the second largest consumer and producer of coal. In terms of reserves, the world's largest mine is the Peabody Energy-operated North Antelope Rochelle mine in the Powder River Basin of Wyoming and Montana, employing more than 1,000 people. Since its inception in 1984, it has produced more than 1.8 billion tons of coal. Coal from the mine is delivered to more than eighty power plants across the country.

Coal Production

In the United States, the production of coal declined after 2008 (figure 8.2), due to the reduced share of coal in the mix of power generation and lower global demand for coal exports.

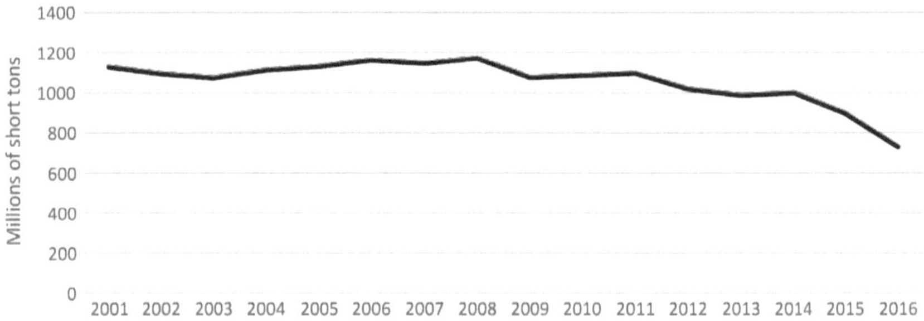

Figure 8.2 U.S. Coal Production. *Source*: Author using data from the U.S. Energy Information Administration, https://www.eia.gov/coal/data/browser/.

In terms of the share of total electricity generation from individual power sources, the percentage for coal in the United States is decreasing. At the same time, the percentage of natural gas and non-hydro renewables is increasing. These trends demonstrate an increasing contribution to electricity generation from non-coal sources. When compared to coal, natural gas, solar, and wind have become more cost-effective. But President Donald J. Trump campaigned in 2016 on a revival of the coal industry. Time will reveal which influence is greater.

Globally, coal production increased during the first decade of this century, plateaued, and then decreased. China, the world's biggest producer and consumer, is burning less coal. The demand for coal is declining in the United States. Because many countries and companies are working toward the goal of the Paris climate agreement of 2016, which seeks to reduce greenhouse gas emissions, coal production is falling and the production of cleaner-burning natural gas is rising.

An important concept is the number of years the world may continue to provide coal at levels similar to today. The ratio of proven coal reserves to production provides this information: Coal Reserves to Production Ratio = R/P, where R = proven reserves and P = the amount of coal produced, usually measured on a daily, monthly, or annual basis. The data show that world proven coal reserves are currently sufficient to meet more than 150 years of global production. This is about three times more than natural gas and oil. Therefore, in upcoming decades, the world will not face scarcity problems with coal. For global electricity generation, the incentive to switch from coal to renewables or even natural gas will occur for reasons of environmental quality and/or cost-effectiveness, not scarcity.

Coal Price

Most coal sold for the generation of electricity is through long-term contracts. Coal futures are a method for coal producers and utility companies (coal consumers) to limit their exposure to the risk of price fluctuations. As per the contract, buyers agree to purchase a standard quantity of coal using a (pre-specified) *futures price* on a specific date. Sellers agree to deliver the coal at the price on the future date. These coal contracts specify quantity, grade, and date of delivery so they may be traded on organized markets. A standardized contract, a coal future is traded on several global exchanges. But the supply of coal is supplemented with spot purchases, shipments of fuel purchased for delivery within one year using *spot prices*. While changes in spot prices are a function of short-term market conditions, futures prices are more stable. The average price of coal delivered to different end-use sectors declined in the second decade of this century.

As this chapter explains, coal is primarily consumed for electricity generation. In developed nations, electricity from coal, heating oil, and natural gas cooks food and heats homes. But in many developing countries such as China and India, coal is still burned for cooking food and heating homes. World coal consumption, essentially stagnant in the 1990s, surged at the beginning of this century. But that trend did not continue. By 2011, the consumption of coal started to plateau. In 2015 and 2016, it declined. The reasons are twofold. In electricity generation, many countries are substituting natural gas for coal. Global consumption of natural gas for electricity generation increased during the same period of time. In addition, many countries are trying to reduce air pollution from coal-fired power plants by closing them or implementing carbon capture and storage technology.

In the United States, after the turn of the century, the consumption of coal remained steady. But soon after coal consumption began to decline. Between 2008 and 2016, U.S. coal consumption declined by more than 50 percent. In the first decade of this century, productivity gains with natural gas technology decreased the price of electricity fueled by natural gas and generated a fundamental shift away from coal. Productivity gains in solar and wind, while smaller than natural gas, have made important inroads into electricity generation. Therefore, productivity gains in natural gas and certain renewables have been the primary forces of change. But another force exists. The buildup of alternative technologies for electricity generation resulted in the retirement of old coal-fired generating units. In 2017, in the United States, twenty-seven coal-fired plants totaling 22 gigawatts of capacity were closed or converted. Given market trends, this pattern will most likely continue.

From this demand-side perspective, we may calculate the price of coal per kilowatt hour (example 8.3). If we identify the heating value of the coal burned in the power plant (let's say bituminous) to equal 13,840 Btu/pound, we may calculate the heating value for 1 ton. Identifying the efficiency value of the power plant (suppose 33%), we may then calculate the heat rate at 10,340 Btu/kWh. The number of kWh in a ton of coal is therefore equal to the heating value of a ton of coal divided by the heat rate: 27,680,000/10,340

We may calculate the price of coal per kilowatt hour (kWh). In step one of the problem, identify the type of coal used in the power plant and find the corresponding heating value of per ton. In step two, identify the average efficiency value of power plants. In step three, calculate the heat rate, given the maximum Btu per kWh of electricity and the average efficiency value. In step four, calculate the number of kWh in a ton of coal. In step five, identify the average cost per ton of coal. In step six, calculate the number of kWh per dollar and the price of one kWh from power plants.

Step one: Identify the type of coal used in the power plant and find the heating value per ton. Suppose a medium-volatile bituminous grade.

Heating value per pound = 13,840 Btu/pound
Heating value per ton = (13,840) (2,000) = 27,680,000 (Btu/ton)

Step two: Identify the average efficiency value of power plants.

Suppose the efficiency value = 33 percent.

Step three: Calculate the heat rate

$$\text{Heat rate} = \frac{\text{Maximum Btu content of a kWh of electricity}}{\text{Power plant efficiency}}$$

= 3,412/0.33 = 10,339 Btu/kWh

Step four: Calculate the number of kWh in a ton of coal.

Number of kWh in a ton = 27,680,000 Btu/ton / 10,339 Btu/kWh
= 2,677 kWh

Step five: Identify the average cost per ton.

The average cost of coal delivered to power plants in the U.S. from 2008 – 2016 was $43.77 per short ton. (For this information, visit the U.S. Energy Information Administration website: https://www.eia.gov/coal/annual/).

Step six: Calculate the number of kWh per dollar and the price of one kWh.

One dollar will buy 2,677 kWh / $43.77 = 61 kWh.

Price per kWh = 100 cents / 61 kWh = 1.64 cents from power plants

Example 8.3 The Price of Coal. *Source*: Author.

= 2,677 per kWh. According to the U.S. Energy Information Administration, the average cost per short ton of coal delivered to power plants in the country from 2008 to 2016 was $43.77. Therefore, 1 dollar will buy 2,677/$43.77 = 61 kWh of electricity. We may then calculate the price per kWh for electric power generation. An extension of the problem is to calculate the cost per kWh for other uses of coal, including industrial, coke producers, and commercial/institutional applications.

Coal and the Economy

A decrease in both the U.S. production and consumption of coal impacts coal-extracting regions. Lower employment in coal mines, less labor force participation, lower average income levels, and higher rates of poverty are all apparent in areas such as eastern Kentucky, West Virginia, and parts of Pennsylvania. The economic effects include fewer jobs in the railroad industry transporting coal and declining resources for education in areas impacted by the coal industry.

In a general framework, however, we must consider that overall U.S. electricity production increases over time. Therefore, economic losses in the coal industry correspond to gains in other industries, especially natural gas and renewables. As a result, from the perspective of the economy as a whole, economic growth in competing industries may offset losses in coal. One area that has remained strong, however, is the coal export market. The United States has been an exporter of coal to countries such as India, the Netherlands, South Korea, and many others.

Contemporary Challenges

As an important source of energy, coal elicits polarized attitudes. On one hand, proponents of the fossil fuel argue that coal will continue to be the world's most important fuel for electricity generation. In the second decade of this century, global demand for coal grew about 2 percent annually. Even in the United States, where low-priced natural gas provides competition, coal is projected to continue to be an important component of the country's energy mix. For example, even though little new coal capacity is projected, the 2017 U.S. EIA Annual Energy Outlook still forecasts coal generating 1 trillion kWh of electricity in 2040 in the country, down from 1.5 trillion kWh in 2017. On the other hand, the consumption of coal is at odds with efforts to address the climate crisis. The question is not about discontinuing the consumption of coal, at least not yet, but how to make it compatible with climate change goals. Before addressing the issue of coal and climate change, however, consider two other contemporary challenges: mountaintop removal and air pollution.

Mountaintop Removal

The story of mountaintop removal at the beginning of the chapter brings to light the inherent problems with mining. In the story, the idea was that the introduction of a wind farm would replace coal-mining jobs. But what sparked the debate over coal and wind, at least in part, was the devastating effects of mountaintop removal. The reality is that mountaintop removal is regional, occurring in Appalachia in the United States. It takes place in Tennessee, Virginia, Kentucky, and West Virginia. It began as an extension of conventional mining techniques. From an economic perspective, the method is used because it leads to a complete recovery of coal seams. It also reduces the number of workers necessary for extraction. The process occurs when coal companies first remove vegetation and topsoil. They then blast away hundreds of feet of the mountaintop, often using thousands of pounds of explosives. Massive earth-moving machines (draglines that stand twenty-two stories tall) remove Earth and coal, displacing miners. The dirt and excess biomass is dumped into nearby valleys, burying streams, polluting land, and creating "sludge dams" that create leaky impediments to newly created lakes. These effects lead to the contamination of drinking water. The technique costs a fraction of conventional extraction.

Given its environmental effects, why does mountaintop removal persist? The answer is the insatiable market for electricity. Mountaintop removal companies attempt to minimize cost. Cost minimization entails any production process that reduces resource inputs, including labor. As long as consumers demand inexpensive electricity, the market will incentivize inexpensive coal. Mountaintop removal persists for another reason: participants in energy markets are willing to sacrifice small areas in certain parts of the country—in this case parts of Appalachia—to ensure a stable electricity marketplace. Even though it leads to local environmental degradation and global climate change, regulation has not eliminated mountaintop removal.

Air Pollution

By the early 1600s, the adoption of chimneys in London homes encouraged a transition from wood to coal for heating. The chimneys kept heat inside. They funneled smoke outside. When indoors, this was beneficial. When outdoors, this was costly. The smoke and resulting air pollution eroded and blackened stone in buildings, impacted human health, and stunted plant life.

Later during the Industrial Revolution and beyond, in the 1800s and 1900s, Manchester in England became the center of British textile manufacturing. Pittsburgh in the United States became the center of American steelmaking. These cities suffered from air pollution. But the impacts in other cities were not equally felt. Philadelphia and New York City, both industrial powerhouses during the twentieth century, were originally spared from foul air. Nearby anthracite coalfields in eastern Pennsylvania provided a source of coal of almost pure carbon that burned little smoke. However, by the middle of the twentieth century, the demand for coal was so high that anthracite reserves were not sufficient. Power plants turned to bituminous coal, which fouled the air. Early utility managers, when possible, burned anthracite coal during the day and bituminous coal at night.

Coal combustion releases more than seventy harmful chemicals. When coal burns, the chemical bonding that holds carbon atoms in place is broken. Energy is released. Other chemical reactions occur that release toxic airborne pollutants. Some solids go into the atmosphere but others are left at the plant as coal ash. The modern argument against the combustion of additional coal reserves is couched in terms of these polluting effects. Every year, thousands of people in the United States die from air pollution generated by coal-fired power plants.

Despite the remaining problems of air pollution and human health, U.S. air quality has been improving for decades. An unequivocal success story involves sulfur dioxide (SO_2). The U.S. Environmental Protection Agency (EPA) has developed national ambient air quality standards for SO_2. The 1990 amendments to the Clean Air Act created a permanent cap on the total amount of SO_2 emissions from electric power plants. Using state and local agencies, the EPA monitors the concentration of SO_2 in parts per billion (ppb), which determines the number of units of mass of SO_2 that exist in the air per 1 billion units of total mass. For SO_2, the ambient standard is 75 ppb, so the United States became compliant with the Clean Air Act in 2006. Since 2006, the concentration of SO_2 in the United States has declined, reaching 20 ppb in 2016. The reasons for the decline include changes in the electricity generation mix (electricity generation from coal decreased), the installation of environmental equipment such as scrubbers, and a lower utilization of the highest polluting power plants.

Coal and Climate Change

The most important long-term impact of coal is on climate change. Human-induced global warming stems from the emissions of heat-trapping gases that are absorbed in the atmosphere and warm the earth's surface. The most important greenhouse gas results from the combustion of coal: carbon dioxide. When fuel is burned, the amount of CO_2 produced is a function of its carbon content. Interestingly, CO_2 emissions have a higher atomic weight than the original fuel. The reason is that, during combustion, carbon dioxide forms when one carbon atom (C) unites with two oxygen atoms (O). The atomic weight of CO_2 is 44, or 3.667 times the atomic weight of carbon, which is 12. As an example, the carbon content of bituminous coal is 65.5 percent on average. The carbon of a short ton (2,000 pounds) is therefore 1,310 pounds. The CO_2 emissions from the combustion of a short ton of bituminous coal is 4,804 pounds, 3.667 times the weight of carbon in the short ton. But the world consumes billions of short tons of coal annually. This leads to a lot of CO_2 emissions.

In the United States, the percentage of electricity production from coal continues to decline. But in an article published in the journal *Environmental Research Letters*, Edenhofer et al. (2018) find that "Reports of coal's terminal decline may be exaggerated." In the article, the authors estimate the cumulative future emissions expected to be released by coal power plants that are planned, announced, or under construction. They conclude that, even in the presence of declining coal consumption and a lack of increasing capacity in coal-fired power plants, the construction of the plants that are planned, announced, or under construction could endanger international climate targets. (The international target cited is the Paris Agreement, the 2016 voluntary accord among 196 nations that intends to stabilize global mean temperature increases at 2° C from preindustrial levels and provide a framework for more ambitious climate policies.) The reason is the continued reliance on coal-fired plants in the world's emerging economies could prove to be a major impediment for climate change mitigation. Moreover, all new plants will generate a substantial amount of CO_2 emissions in addition to those already locked in by existing infrastructure. As a result, the article argues that "dedicated policies to phase out coal are needed to . . . allow for credible commitment to ambitious long-term mitigation targets" (Edenhofer et al., 2018).

For climate reasons, how likely is the world to "phase out" coal? Not likely, in the mind of this author, at least any time soon. On one hand, in the second decade of this century, the amount of coal power capacity under development worldwide declined. But, on the other hand, more coal plants are under development in Japan, Indonesia, Turkey, and other countries. For the production of electricity, the world continues to rely on coal.

Coal and Sustainability

We may evaluate coal with respect to the sustainability criteria established in chapter 1. Does the market for coal contribute to our current needs without compromising the ability of future generations to meet their needs? With the six sustainability criteria, coal satisfies one: the provision of baseload power. This chapter argues that there is over a century's worth of coal left in the ground on a global scale. But as a non-renewable resource, the world will eventually deplete it at the current rate of consumption. The provision of baseload power for the generation of electricity is why coal remains an important energy resource. The largest objection to coal is related to environmental and health effects. Coal-fired power plants make the largest contribution to CO_2 emissions. They are the largest contributor to global warming. In the United States, employment in the coal industry is declining. The overall assessment for sustainability, therefore, ranks coal at the bottom of the list of energy resources.

Future Prospects

Taking these points into account, the future prospects of the coal industry are uncertain. On one hand, coal has been the fuel of choice for the power industry since the beginning of the twentieth century. On the other hand, coal is the fossil fuel that generates the largest level of CO_2 emissions. In addition, the global energy system is on a transition pathway with the emergence of renewable technologies. Some countries are actively reducing the share of coal in electricity production. The U.K. plans to close all unabated coal power stations. The Australian government plans an energy transition with the eventual retirement of coal-fired plants. Even the Chinese are planning to reduce the consumption of coal and implement a cleaner energy system. Because of energy transition, the negative environmental impacts of coal, and moral reasoning, some academics such as Paul Collier and Anthony Venables (2014) are advocating an extreme position, the end of the coal industry: "Closing down the global coal industry meets the key features that give an action moral force. It is a concrete event, readily observable, and directly under the control of identifiable actors. It is also manifestly material to the global problem of carbon emissions."

Which future prospect is more likely? Global trends favor the industry-on-the-decline viewpoint. Employment in coal mining is decreasing. Natural gas and renewables are producing a greater share of electricity. Coal lobbies and industry groups do not have the same financial strength and political muscle of old. Natural gas and alternative fuels are more competitive. However, even though coal's market share is declining, coal is part of the world's energy and economic foundation. Transitioning away from that reality will require technological advance, new energy policies, and a lot of time.

SUMMARY

This chapter reveals that the global production and consumption of coal have stopped increasing. But given that coal is an inexpensive fossil fuel, it is important for present and future energy scenarios. In most coal-producing countries, coal is not being phased out, but it is on the decline. In the United States, many old and inefficient coal-fired power plants are closing. No new coal-fired plants are being built. This trend is influencing an important transformation in the electricity sector: a movement to natural gas and renewables.

Air quality would improve if the world used less coal, but the electricity sector may be able to mitigate the harmful emissions more than other sectors with necessary investments in carbon capture and other technologies. The problem is that power generation is a leading cause of air pollution and the single largest source of greenhouse gas emissions contributing to global warming. The chapter's conclusion is that coal has a declining share for electricity generation in the United States, but remains relatively stable worldwide.

CONCEPTS

Anthracite
Bituminous
Capacity factor
Forward prices
Heat rate
Heating value
Lignite
Longwall mining
Mountaintop removal mining
Open-pit mining
Room-and-pillar mining
Spot prices
Strip mining
Subbituminous

QUESTIONS

1. Graph the level of employment in coal mining in the United States over time. Is there a difference between underground and surface mining? Discuss the trends for each. What are reasons for the trends? Explain.
2. How has the share of coal in electricity production changed over time? Use data to support your answer. What are the reasons for the trend?
3. For individual countries and regions of the world, review the data on reserves to production ratio (R/P). A good source of data is the BP Global Statistical Review, available online. The R/P ratio gives the remaining amount of a resource that exists in a specific area expressed in time. For the individual countries are regions, how would you characterize the R/P ratio? What is the implication for energy transition from coal to other sources such as natural gas and renewables? Explain.

4. Using data from the U.S. Energy Information Administration, how has the average price of coal delivered to end-use sectors changed in recent years? What are the reasons for this trend?
5. Given the environmental costs of coal, why does the resource continue to serve as a major source of energy?
6. What are the future prospects of coal? Will coal serve as an important source of electricity production over time? Why or why not? Before answering these questions, read the articles by Dai and Finkelman (2018) and Leipprand and Flachsland (2018) listed in the Bibliography.

Chapter 9

Natural Gas

A New Horizon in Energy

MARKET SURGE

In the United States in 2006, natural gas production entered its fifth year of decline. The *natural depletion rate*—the decrease in production capacity of a gas deposit that is caused by past and present production—was forecasted to rise. Energy economists thought the United States would increase its level of natural gas imports. But the market changed. For the next decade, the production of natural gas soared, transforming the country's energy future.

The impetus was unanticipated growth in the production of shale gas. According to the economist Paul Joskow (2013), this growth resulted from market development, deregulation, and industry reform. This platform supported pipeline expansion and technological advance. A surge in innovation encouraged the extraction of natural gas from previously unattainable shale deposits. Engineering ingenuity unlocked a large storehouse of natural gas buried beneath the ground from New York to Texas. Producers capitalized on two newly viable technologies: hydraulic fracturing (*fracking*) and *horizontal drilling*. Fracking injects high-pressure fluid to release gas from shale rock formations. Horizontal drilling allows operators to turn their drilling instruments from vertical to horizontal.

These changes drove up natural gas production, promising larger homegrown supplies of energy. Environmentalists envisioned a replacement for coal. Security analysts favored fewer imports. Economists supported lower consumer prices. Climate change activists argued that natural gas yields 45 percent of the carbon dioxide emissions of coal.

The increase in production was dramatic. Between January 2007 and January 2016, United States shale gas production rose by almost 50 percent. Natural gas terminals in the Gulf and the northeast designed to import *liquefied natural gas* (LNG)—which has been converted from gas to liquid for ease and safety of transport and storage—were reconfigured for exports. The resulting abundance reduced the U.S. price to one-third of the global average. According to Robert A. Hefner (2014) of the Harvard University Kennedy School:

> Natural gas has been a godsend for the United States. Already, gas has spurred a manufacturing renaissance, with investors spending and planning hundreds of billions of dollars on new facilities such as chemical, steel, and aluminum plants. . . . Moreover, because natural gas supplies about 25 percent of the total energy consumed in the United State (a figure that is rapidly growing), the boom is saving U.S. consumers hundreds of billions of dollars a year. Combined with other benefits, those savings have given the United States a long-term economic advantage over its competitors and helped the country recover from the Great Recession.

Furthermore, Robert D. Blackwill and Meghan L. O'Sullivan (2014) of the council on Foreign Relations and Harvard University, respectively, in *Foreign Affairs*, argued that, thanks to higher natural gas production, in 2013 the United States surpassed Russia as the world's leading energy producer. But other countries will struggle with replication: U.S. investors display a patience for risk. According to Hefner (2014), "In the United States, any company can strike a deal with a willing landowner to lease the rights to . . . gas beneath his land and start drilling, a setup that has spawned Darwinian competition among entrepreneurs in order to survive and grow."

The United States boasts thousands of independent gas and service companies, compared with far fewer in other countries. At each well, 3D models of subsurface seismic activity monitor drilling technology in real time. They explore prolific areas of shale formation and optimize fracking. In Europe and China, large shale resources exist, but the lack of an entrepreneur-friendly environment discourages both exploration and production.

Natural gas may contribute to a country's strategic position. With the exception of Canada, no other country boasts an energy environment as favorable as the United States. In the United States, fewer imports and more exports improve the country's trade position. Because the U.S. price has been among the lowest in the world, domestic industries such as steel and petrochemicals that rely on the natural gas for *feedstock*—a substance that may be used directly as fuel—experience competitive advantage. Around the world, lower natural gas prices benefit China and India, among other developing countries. They are already major natural gas importers.

The increase in supply in the United States impacts global markets. In 2012, gas prices averaged $17 in Japan per million Btu, $11 in Germany, and

$3 in the United States. But as the United States exports greater quantities of LNG, "the integration of North American, European, and Asian gas markets will require years of infrastructure investment and the result, even then, will not be as unified as the global oil market, the increased liquidity should help put downward pressure on gas prices in Europe and Asia" (Blackwell and O'Sullivan, 2014).

By examining the costs and benefits of natural gas, this chapter addresses these issues. The chapter first considers the history of natural gas, reserves, production, price, and the economy. In both economic and environmental perspectives, the next section addresses the contemporary challenges of fracking and horizontal drilling. After the consideration of climate change and sustainability, the final section addresses future prospects. The chapter's thesis is that an increase in the supply of natural gas leads to lower energy prices and reductions in greenhouse gas emissions (when natural gas replaces coal). But the consumption of natural gas disrupts more far-reaching reforms. Shifting from coal to gas does not solve the climate change problem. But a relatively greater reliance on natural gas could provide time for the deployment of renewable technology, while reducing carbon dioxide emissions.

NATURAL GAS HISTORY

Natural gas—primarily made of methane, a carbon atom with four surrounding hydrogen atoms—is the cleanest burning fossil fuel. Electricity generation from natural gas has a higher level of thermal efficiency than oil or coal, decreasing carbon dioxide emissions per unit of electricity.

Historically, natural gas was extracted from shallow wells using the traditional technology of vertical drilling. But three periods characterize industry evolution (Wang et al., 2014). The "infant period," 1821–1970, began with the drilling of the Devonian Dunkirk Shale in Chautauqua County, New York. Production, transportation, and consumption occurred locally. During the 1800s, shallow wells were drilled along Lake Erie and southeast from the lake. In the 1900s, major wells were developed in western Kentucky, West Virginia, and Indiana. By the 1970s, production of onshore gas fields declined. The fields became "mature."

In the "large demonstration period," 1970–2000, oil shocks increased the price of oil, propelling the U.S. government to invest in alternative energy, including natural gas from shale formations. During the 1980s, research, development, and investment expanded supply, transmission, distribution, and consumption. In the 1990s, natural gas prices increased. Companies learned that underground deposits in the United States possessed large volumes of natural gas. They tried early fracking techniques, but were not profitable. Then a market-changing event occurred. George Mitchell, a Texas natural-gas baron, explored around Fort Worth in a thick layer of rock thousands of square miles called the Barnett Shale. Mitchell's innovation was to drill horizontally into the shale. This process exposed thousands of feet of gas-bearing rock, rather than the dozens of feet common in a vertical well. When gas prices were higher and horizontal drilling techniques improved, Mitchell's company profited. (In 2002, Devon Energy bought Mitchell's company, increased innovation, and developed the Barnett formation. Other independent companies, including Chesapeake Energy, joined the market, launching the shale revolution.)

In the "industrial-scale period," 2000–present, two factors contributed to an increase in producer confidence in natural gas in general and shale gas in particular: advanced drilling techniques and the rise in gas prices after 2003. By the beginning of this century, U.S. companies had drilled more than 150,000 horizontal wells, costing more than $1 trillion, and fracking drilled more than 150,000 miles of shale (Hefner, 2014). In addition, Chesapeake Energy passed ExxonMobil as the largest supplier of natural gas in the United States. Not long after, the United States became the world's largest producer of natural gas, surpassing Russia.

The extraction of natural gas from shale rock has served as a landmark energy event. *Shale gas* is in shale deposits, typically found in floodplains, river deltas, or lakes. Shale gas is one type of "unconventional" gas. (The others are coal-bed methane, tight gas, and gas hydrates.) Shale gas is classified as unconventional because it is situated in rock formations with low permeability that makes it difficult for gas to flow. Alternatively, natural gas deposits are conventional if they are in rocks with high permeability. With high permeability, gas flows freely into well boreholes.

In the first decade of this century, the United States went from being one of the world's largest gas importers to self-sufficiency. In 2000, shale gas was 1 percent of the United States natural gas supply. By 2010, it was 20 percent. At the same time, total unconventional gas—from coal beds, low-permeability sandstone, and shale—rose to 50 percent of the total supply.

In the second decade of this century, it became clear that natural gas would serve as a major energy source for heating, electricity generation, and cooking. In the process, the extraction of natural gas from shale formations offset the decrease in conventional gas output. Even more, partly due to some replacement of coal by natural gas in electricity generation, carbon dioxide from fossil fuel consumption was lower than what it would be otherwise.

In 2017, in the United States, production exceeded 90 billion cubic feet (bcf) per day, up from 58 bcf in 2008. According to the U.S. IEA (2015), this total is expected to both steadily increase in the next few decades and serve as a growing share of the world's total supply. Gas producing states such as Texas, West Virginia, and Pennsylvania are exporting natural gas. An important reason for the increase is that natural gas provides consumers with convenient access on the front end. By turning on the main valves that deliver gas from the pipeline system, end users enjoy a number of industrial, commercial, and residential applications.

NATURAL GAS LIFECYCLE

The natural gas life cycle includes:

- Exploration
- Extraction
- Production
- Processing
- Liquefaction
- Tanker transport
- Liquid natural gas gasification
- Transmission and storage
- Distribution
- Combustion in power plants or direct end uses

The lifecycle begins with the exploration of a gas reservoir. A promising discovery leads to investments in drilling and extraction. Pumping equipment (compressors) and pipelines are then installed for production. The gas flows from the well until reaching a "peak." During the period of production, costs include the maintenance of pipelines and compressors and the gas used as fuel to run the compressors. Adding compressors (a variable input) to the system increases output. But this procedure increases per unit cost. As a result, it is economical to increase pipeline capacity instead of continuing to add compressors.

After production, natural gas is sent to processing plants. Before dry natural gas is distributed to consumers, undesirable components are removed. By decreasing the share of heavier hydrocarbons, a suitable quality is attained. Liquefaction creates a form safe and efficient for transport. Gasification converts the substance back into dry form. It then enters the transmission and storage system. Storage opportunities include salt caverns, aquifers, or depleted gas reservoirs. This helps to meet seasonal and/or short-term demand. From the transmission and storage system, natural gas flows to large-scale consumers such as power plants and to local consumers via low-pressure, small-diameter pipelines.

There are four main components of a mature natural gas industry: production, transmission, storage, and distribution. Before programs of market deregulation in the 1980s and 1990s, the components were either independent or integrated. But in the current era of deregulation, production, transmission, storage, and distribution are independent. A mature industry develops distribution networks around transmission lines. For example, some natural gas collected in fields of Siberia is transported in a large transmission pipeline to a hub in Germany with storage capacity. There it is transferred to smaller pipelines. Finally, it is transported to power plants, businesses, and households. For these end users, natural gas generates electricity and heat and serves as fuel for cooking. In this supply chain, the producers in Russia act as wholesalers. The German distributors act as retailers.

The key is this relationship. A retailer may sign a contract with a wholesaler for a monthly shipment, equal to the retailer's estimate of demand by power plants, businesses, and households. Because the estimate is unlikely to equal actual demand, the two sides arrange for the delivery of additional *swing gas*. Swing gas is natural gas bought on short notice to meet unexpected changes in daily demand not covered by long-term contracts. Every morning, a short-term contract for the price and quantity of swing gas is set for delivery the next day. An even smaller component is *spot gas*, natural gas bought in the morning for delivery later that day. Full-scale deregulation, which does not exist, would do away with all long-term contracts: Transactions would be made on a daily basis. But retailers have found that long-term arrangements in conjunction with short-term contracts provide flexibility in meeting demand.

Natural Gas Pipelines

An important part of the life cycle is the movement of natural gas through pipelines. Unlike oil, natural gas requires little processing to become pipeline ready. Pipelines both onshore and offshore are an economical method of transportation, especially with the advent of metallurgical improvements, enhanced welding techniques, and an increase in global pipeline networks. Pipelines distribute natural gas with almost the same flexibility and efficiency as grids distribute electricity. As a result, in many countries, electricity and gas are considered substitutes.

In recent decades, a new method has emerged that involves the shipping of natural gas in a liquefied state. When gas is shipped by sea, it must be liquefied first. After reaching a terminal across an ocean, it must be de-liquefied. Liquefied natural gas export plants, import terminals, and LNG carriers monetize the industry and help provide output to consumers. LNG is transported in huge amounts between continents on tanker ships and flatboats.

But for short to medium distances, pipelines are more economical. Pipelines exist in regions such as North America, where more than 300,000 miles of transmission pipelines and more than one million miles each of distribution and gathering pipelines connect producers with consumers. The location, construction, and operation of natural gas pipeline systems are usually regulated. But in countries such as the United States, Brazil, and Canada, the network of natural gas pipelines is privately owned and independently operated.

Three types of pipelines range in size from four inches to four feet: gathering systems (from production wells), transmission systems (from preprocessing plants or storage facilities to distribution systems), and distribution systems (to businesses, buildings, and houses). The main differences are the specification of pressure and the physical properties.

To reiterate, the natural gas lifecycle begins with extraction. It proceeds to a pipeline with some gas removed for further processing, storage, or sale. More than 400 storage sites exist in the United States. In a deregulated market, natural gas is drawn from storage or obtained directly in supply hubs or interstate transmission companies. One reason is that storage is held when prices change. When price escalates, inventories are sold. This helps to moderate price increases. When output price declines, inventories are augmented. Taking output out of the market helps to moderate the decrease in price. Another reason is the market "watches" whether storage reaches levels of abundance or shortage. In the case of abundance, higher levels of gas that may appear in coming months put a downward pressure on gas prices. With shortages, the opposite occurs. Finally, storage increases flexibility for inventory owners. Output may increase with inventories but without incurring the expenses associated with production. Hence, the storage of gas functions as a hedge against uncertainty with both price and quantity.

Natural gas is stored during off-peak periods. If peak demand jeopardizes the ability of the market to satisfy consumption, gas is removed from storage. With long- and medium-term contracts, natural gas is delivered on specific dates. The market entities uncertain about pipeline quantities carefully consider the level in storage. Overall, storage increases the level of efficiency of the system because it optimizes off-peak capacity. Having storage available transfers parts of consumption from low-value periods to high-value periods (peak production). If a company stores gas and withdraws it at high value, then its economic position improves.

Natural Gas Hubs

Hubs are physical transfer points, sometimes called pipeline interchanges. Operating independently of production, transportation, and storage, they provide a locale where traders, shippers, and buyers may purchase and sell gas. They redirect gas from one pipeline to another. Hubs bring together interstate pipelines in a common network. Hubs are market centers, where brokering, insurance, and the provisions of transportation services occur. Consumers using one interstate pipeline may consume natural gas from suppliers hooked into other interstate pipelines.

In the United States, a dozen major hubs exist, the most important for pricing being the Henry Hub in Louisiana. There, pipelines establish one large common network. As a pricing hub, it establishes base price. Hubs in New York City and elsewhere then add transmission costs and local market variations. If a pricing gap appears among transmission hubs, consumers close the gap by bargaining with suppliers in different regions.

But consumers know that demand exists away from natural gas' point of origin. This reality provides different options. For example, it is economical for China and India to import LNG instead of building additional local pipelines. For distribution, natural gas is "frozen" in the country of origin, transported in LNG carriers, re-gassed, and ready for use.

National gas suppliers, on the other hand, who are no longer regulated to the degree to which they once were, try to sell at the highest price. Suppliers look at the market price at different destinations and subtract the cost of liquefaction, shipping, regasification, and pipeline transportation. The result gives the *netback price*. Suppliers sell to the pricing hub with the highest netback value. A vast number of daily transactions occurs between buyers seeking the lowest delivered cost and sellers seeking the highest netback price.

In a transparent market without a price leader, *commoditization* occurs. The natural gas is both extracted from different areas and distinguishable in terms of geological conditions. But for consumers, it is one commodity. With final transactions, natural gas prices are set by market conditions that reflect supply and demand, not cost-plus pricing, which is determined by regulators. The regulators' role is to increase the transparency of transactions, ensure no price manipulation occurs, and eliminate market controlling behavior.

In a commodity market, suppliers differentiate with respect to value-added services. A buyer will select a supplier based on dependability and reliability. The relationship may include maintenance and repair of equipment or advice with respect to the efficient use of natural gas. Over time, companies bundle natural gas with other energy resources, electricity, and even market information that differentiates the company from competitors.

Pipeline Model

In a simple pipeline model, natural gas moves from supply hubs (transfer points that initiate delivery) to transshipment nodes (junctions) and to compressor stations (operations that alter pressure). Pipeline arcs represent pressure changes for commercial, electric, industrial, residential, and transport end users (figure 9.1).

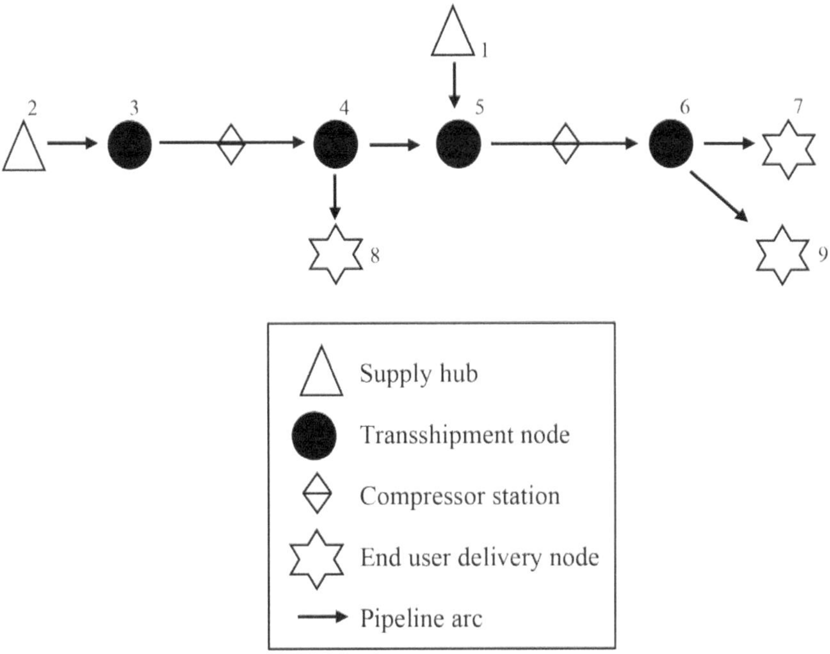

Figure 9.1 Model of a Natural Gas Pipeline System. *Source*: Author using information from Rios-Mercado and Borraz-Sanchez (2014).

For optimal flow, network reconfiguration removes compressor stations. System components merge into super nodes (S_1, S_2, S_3, S_4). Compressor stations are re-introduced into the network, completing the system. With optimal organization, three types of network topologies exist (figure 9.2): (a) linear—corresponding to a linear arrangement of compressor station arcs, when the reduced network exists as a single path; (b) branch—when the compressor station acres are arranged in branches; and (c) cyclic—when compressor station arcs form cycles with other compressor stations (Rios-Mercado and Borraz-Sanchez, 2014).

NATURAL GAS RESERVES, PRODUCTION, PRICE, AND THE ECONOMY

Ultimately, the question is whether the benefits of natural gas exceed the costs. The first benefit is that natural gas is an abundant source of energy for electricity generation, home heating and cooking, and production in many industries. Another benefit of natural gas is the positive spillover effects

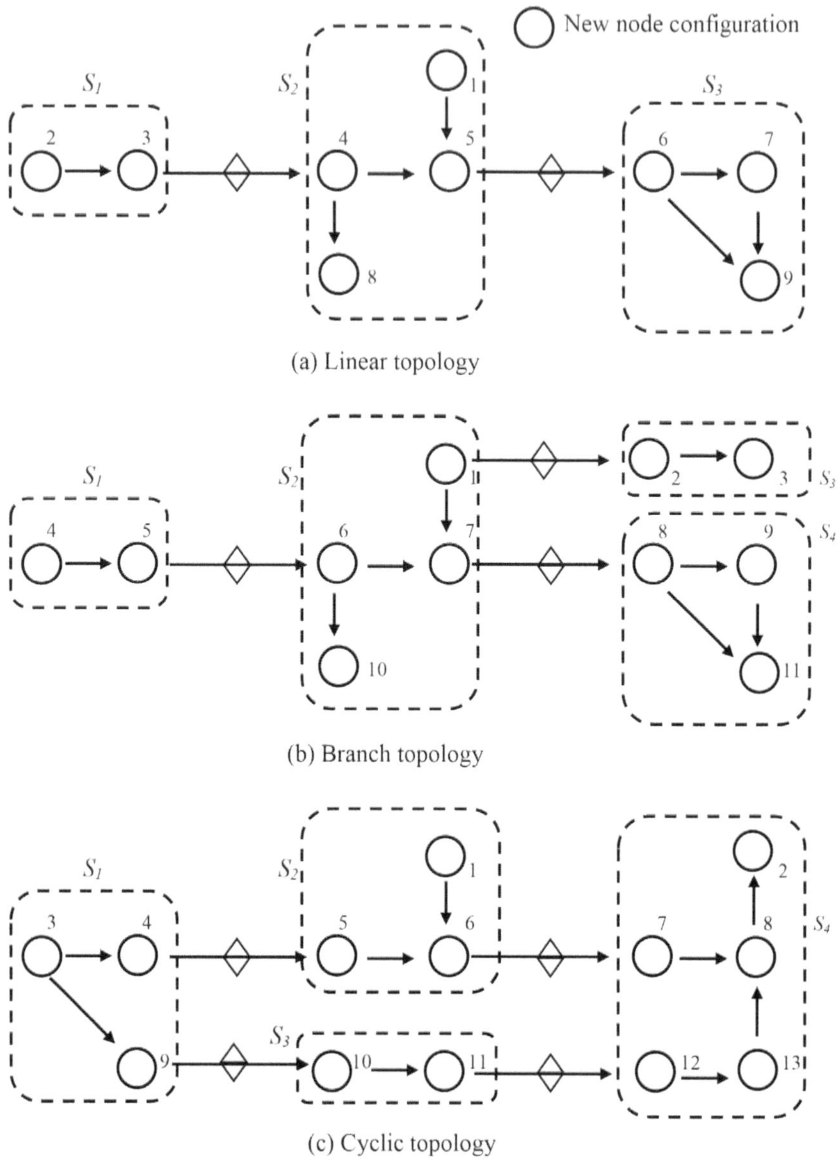

Figure 9.2 Pipeline Network Topologies. *Source*: Author using information from Rios-Mercado and Borraz-Sanchez (2014).

relative to coal. Measured according to its carbon content, natural gas is "cleaner."

Costs include spending on raw materials, pipelines, capital equipment, and labor. Another cost is the loss of privacy to the property owners hosting drill pads. The lease agreement establishes royalty payments that compensate land owners. A sufficient level of competition in the industry is required to ensure proper compensation. The industry generates a user cost. Extracting natural gas in the present reduces extraction for future generations. (This holds true for all nonrenewable resources.) If property rights are well defined, user costs are internalized in the natural gas industry. The industry will extract gas today if the current price exceeds the expected future price. But as a result of this decision, the extractor imposes a user cost on itself, reducing the future availability of the energy resource. The final cost is the value of economic damages imposed on humans and the environment. Fracking involves the use of local water sources. Water backflow contains high levels of elements such as sodium that are dangerous for the environment, especially aquifers. The natural habitat surrounding well pads is segmented with pipelines and service roads, which is dangerous for wildlife. With the general nuisance and vehicle traffic for neighbors not compensated by the industry, a negative externality persists.

To conclude, both economic benefits and costs exist. The value of each determines the extent to which the extraction of natural gas creates net benefits to the economy.

The consumption of natural gas is most important in three sectors: electricity generation, industry, and residential/commercial. Over the course of the next few decades, the demand for electricity will increase. In order to meet growing demand, the economy will need hundreds of new gigawatts of new electric generation capacity. Because of the relatively low capital requirements for the construction of natural gas power plants and the reduction in greenhouse gas emissions that occurs when natural gas replaces coal, a large percentage of new electric generation capacity will be natural gas combustion turbine generation. With industrial demand, the primary force that is shaping the consumption of natural gas is the movement away from energy-intensive manufacturing processes. In terms of residential/commercial demand, the consumption of natural gas is expected to increase, because of multifamily buildings being built with natural gas heating.

However, natural gas travels a long way before it arrives at its final destination. Even though dependable and economic pipeline systems preserve a continuous supply, a number of challenges exist. Mechanical malfunctions disrupt the flow of natural gas. Short-term demand is uncertain. Seasonal demand fluctuations occur: demand is higher in the winter than the summer.

A strategy to address these challenges is to recognize that pipelines serve as both transportation links and storage units. Due to the nature of dry gas, operators may store large reserves inside pipelines on a short-term basis. During off-peak times, they accomplish this by injecting more gas into the pipelines with higher pressure. Then during periods of high demand, they withdraw gas when flow elsewhere in the system is at capacity.

In this context, suppose the existence of two transmission lines between one producer and one community. Assume the amount of gas required by the community is satisfied with 80 percent of maximum capacity for several periods. The market solution is to meet the customer demand. However, suppose demand increases to 120 percent of maximum capacity for one period. In this case, the producer does not have the capacity to meet demand. But if the producer stores excess natural gas whenever it is not needed, satisfying demand beyond system capacity is possible.

Natural Gas Reserves

Natural gas fields have double the reservoir recovery (up to 80%) of oil fields (up to 40%). Proven reserves are recoverable under existing conditions. (Ultimate reserves, which are much larger, equal cumulative production + proven reserves + undiscovered reserves.) The estimates of proven reserves change. One reason is the reserves of some deposits are difficult to estimate, especially offshore. For example, in the Barents Sea, north of Norway and Russia, the financial rewards from exploration are enormous, but the risks of exploring in such deep water are large. For investors, financing exploration in the presence of such uncertainty may not occur without price guarantees. As another example, shale gas is unconventional today, but as technology improves, it may become conventional. New discoveries lead to the appraisal of existing fields, new prices, the production of existing reserves, and new estimates.

Changes in supply impact prices and the incentive for further exploration. When the supply of natural gas increases, prices decline and the incentive for further exploration goes down. In this case, it is likely that the estimate for reserves will decline. Since 1965 in more than 400 storage sites in the United States, total proven natural gas reserves have fluctuated between 150 trillion cubic feet and 400 trillion cubic feet. In the second decade of this century, U.S. proven natural gas reserves soared to record highs.

Jude Clemente (2015), a contributor to *Forbes*, argues that the increase in reserves is a function of the gains from the Marcellus shale field in the Appalachian Basin, located in West Virginia and Pennsylvania. The proven reserves of these two states more than quadrupled between 2010 and 2015. In fact, the states accounted for 60 percent of new natural gas reserves. Texas

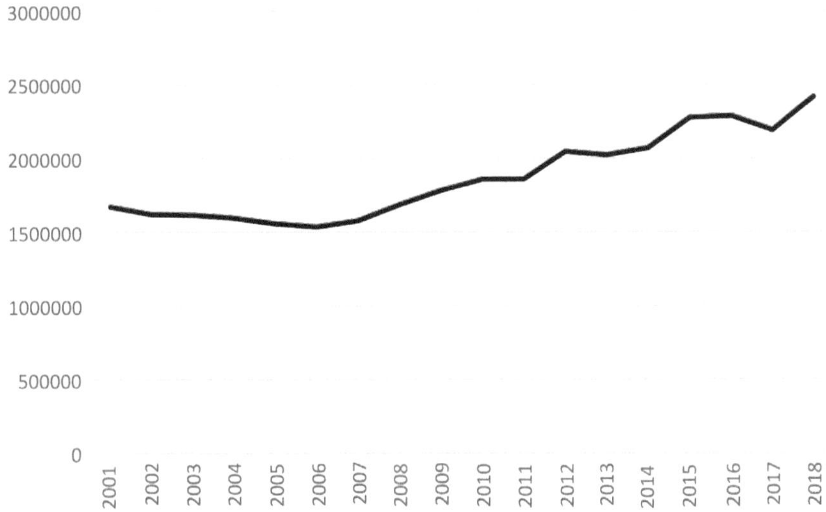

Figure 9.3 U.S. Dry Natural Gas Production (MMcf). *Source*: Author using data from the U.S. Energy Information Administration, https://www.eia.gov/dnav/ng/hist/n9070us2m.htm.

also contributed. The increase in proven reserves occurred with relatively low prices. In 1996, the BP Statistical Review estimated the world's proven shale gas reserves to be more than 120 trillion cubic meters, which increased to 160 trillion cubic meters in 2006 and over 180 trillion cubic meters in 2016.

Natural Gas Production

In the United States after 2006, natural gas production surged (figure 9.3). With unit conversions, 1 Cf (cubic foot) = 1,015 Btu (British thermal units) or 0.01015 therms (unit of heat equivalent to 100,000 Btu). The unit MMcf equals 1 million cubic feet:

$$\text{MMcf} = 1{,}000{,}000 \text{ Cf} = 1{,}015{,}000{,}000 \text{ Btu} = 10{,}150 \text{ therms}$$

In 2006, conventional wisdom was that U.S. production was in decline. But in the following decade, it increased by almost 50 percent. Pipelines able to carry significant amounts of natural gas—such as the 7 billion cubic feet a day from the prolific Appalachian region—grew the market. Rising oil production in the Permian shale basin in Texas also increased supply.

Over time, the cost of producing gas from shale and tight rock formations should continue to decrease, given the current pace of technical advance. Two reasons exist. Large efficiency gains signify that increases in capital expenditures will trigger even more growth in production. In addition, vast amounts of hydrocarbons have migrated from their original rock sources. They have become trapped in shale and tight rock formations on a scale that exceeds all of the world's proven oil reserves, about 1.5 trillion barrels. If the technology for shale extraction extends globally, there is reason to believe that decreasing cost and greater efficiency will serve as important factors in the global economy. Because of the increase in U.S. production after 2006, other countries who import natural gas, such as Turkey, China, and England, are now developing their domestic natural gas resources. Over time, this trend will spread to other countries: shale gas investments will increase on a global scale.

At the global level, natural gas production has steadily increased. This trend reflects a general increase in demand for energy resources but also an increasing preference for energy resources with a lower carbon content.

In 2018, the United States was the world's top producer of natural gas hydrocarbons for the seventh straight year. Forecasts, including the U.S. EIA (2017), show that, to meet rising demand, the world's producers will increase supply by more than 50 percent from 2015 to 2035, concentrated in Europe, Asia, and North America. The largest increases in production will most likely occur in the United States, China, and Russia.

Reserves to Production Ratio

An important concept is the number of years the world may continue to provide natural gas. The relevant figure is the ratio of proven natural gas reserves to production (*R/P*), which determines the remaining amount of natural gas expressed in time, where R = proven reserves and P = the amount of natural gas produced, measured on a daily, monthly, or annual basis. Calculations for the R/P ratio may occur at the global, regional, or country level. For the world, at the beginning of this century, the R/P ratio exceeded sixty years, but in two decades that figure declined to below fifty-four years. The reason is an increase in production.

Given current technological and economic conditions, the world is not going to run out of natural gas at any time soon. Natural gas, a cleaner energy source when compared to coal, is abundant. These realities support the argument that the transition to renewable energy may be slow. But a change in the price of natural gas could alter this forecast. A sustained decrease in price could both discourage exploration and decrease potential reserves. Given current production trends, this could lower the world R/P ratio over time. But while possible, this forecast is unlikely. Because the energy infrastructure uses natural gas as a major fuel source in the production of electricity, the world will continue to demand new sources of natural gas for the foreseeable future.

Natural Gas Price

At the time of the first oil shock in 1973–1974, the regulation of natural gas wellhead pricing had already been in place for twenty years. Introduced by the Federal Power Commission, the regulation was causing significant shortages by keeping prices below equilibrium. The initial response involved non-price rationing, which allocated scarce supplies among existing customers. New customers were turned away. During the 1970s, shortages continued as oil prices climbed. In 1978, Congress passed the Natural Gas Policy Act, intended to reduce shortages by gradually bringing wellhead prices to equilibrium levels. Wells with different cost characteristics were to charge different ceiling prices. Pipelines then averaged these multiple wellhead prices to determine the prices charged to service customers and local gas distributors.

During the time of the second oil shock, 1979–1980, when real crude oil prices doubled, shortages in natural gas initially increased. Pipeline companies responded by negotiating long-term contracts with gas producers at higher ceiling prices. As a result, pipelines expected to sell the gas to customers at the blended price of the average of the "old gas" and "new gas" contract prices.

By 1986, real crude prices fell by nearly two-thirds. Natural gas was less economical compared to oil at the higher regulated bundled price charged by pipelines. This led to the "take-or-pay contract bubble": the demand for natural gas by direct service customers and local gas distribution companies was greater than the obligations of the pipelines.

In response, new regulatory policies changed the structure of the industry. Pipeline companies created special marketing programs to retain customers. The programs allowed customers to purchase unbundled transportation services from pipeline companies. The customers bought gas directly at lower prices in producing areas. They paid the pipeline companies to transport the gas, bypassing higher regulated prices.

This process largely ended the traditional structure of the pipeline system. It was originally built around the bundled sale of natural gas and transportation services. But the 1989 passage of the Natural Gas Wellhead Decontrol Act accelerated the deregulation of wellhead prices. It integrated intrastate and interstate markets. The natural gas market evolved to its current state in the 1990s, developing spot and derivative markets, liquid gas trading hubs, and market integration that decreased geographic differences. The regulation of wellhead gas pricing ended in 1992, eliminating shortages and allowing natural gas prices to increase and then stabilize. Prices rose in the first decade of this century, but then stabilized.

Here we may put the price of natural gas in context. Recall that Btu means "British thermal unit," which is the energy content of fuel. Dimensionally, 1 million Btu (1 mBtu) ≈ 1,000 cubic feet of gas = 1,000ft^3 = 28 cubic meters. With this equivalence, we may translate a price in dollars per thousand cubic feet of natural gas into dollars per million Btu. Because the average barrel of oil contains 5,800,000 Btu in terms of heating value, the price of $9.00/mBtu for natural gas is the oil equivalent of (9.00)(5.8) ≈ $52.20/barrel.

Comparing prices of natural gas and oil provides context for energy markets. The comparison also provides perspective with respect to why investments in fuel-switching capacity have become attractive for producers in energy-intensive industries such as petrochemicals. This technology provides the physical capacity to permit the use of different energy inputs, such as gas, oil, and coal. When energy equivalents demonstrate similar prices with different fossil fuels, producers are indifferent to which energy input they use. But if the price of natural gas is below that of oil, producers will consume more natural gas in their production processes. Market prices will then adjust.

The new market structure removed barriers for the extraction of natural gas. By 2006, the new structure provided a platform that led to the shale gas revolution. But it also encouraged producers to evaluate market conditions. For example, as the price of natural gas fell between 2014 and 2016, the number of rigs focused on drilling for natural gas decreased.

After the new millennium in the United States, natural gas consumption was steady for six years and then increased for ten. The increase in consumption patterned general decreases in price, especially after the year 2005. Between 2005 and 2015, the price of natural gas declined, resulting from the expansion of shale gas flowing into the market. During this same period, consumption increased. In the year 2000, the United States consumed 23 trillion cubic feet (Tcf) of natural gas. In 2018, that figure increased to more than 27 Tcf, equivalent to more than 28 quadrillion Btu.

With respect to U.S. natural gas consumption by major end users, electric power generation consumes most, followed by industrial, residential, and commercial users. Over time, natural gas will continue to serve as an important source of energy for electricity generation. The consumption of natural gas may increase as a percentage of the total among residential users as new homes adopt natural gas heating systems.

In terms of global consumption, a steady increase occurred from 2004 to 2018, except for a decline during the Great Recession of 2008–2009. In upcoming decades, natural gas may account for the largest increase in world primary energy consumption. Robust production technology and abundant natural gas resources will contribute to a strong competitive position. Strong growth is projected in India and China, where expansion of the energy sector will fuel economic growth.

NATURAL GAS AND THE ECONOMY

The recent innovations in fracking and horizontal drilling have powered the shale revolution, but the narrative that natural gas is a transition fuel to a low-carbon economy is debatable. The reason is this narrative has not manifested itself on a global scale. To be sure, the growth in natural gas production has put downward pressure on price. But changing market conditions could reverse the trend. The competition between natural gas and other energy sources—especially coal, nuclear power, and renewables—benefits consumers. The competition also provides incentive for producers to become more efficient. In addition to the importance of shale gas, the growth in production has led to the coming of age of LNG. The expansion of natural gas markets globally includes growing LNG trade. The LNG from high production areas allows the energy sector to respond to growth in energy demand in other regions.

In the United States, industry growth has made a dramatic impact on exports. In the year 2000, the United States exported very little natural gas. But the United States is now the world's largest natural gas producer, having surpassed Russia in 2009. Since that year, exports have increased. In the first decade of this century, U.S. production was short about 9 billion cubic feet a day on average, relative to its level of consumption. The country made up the difference through imports. But in 2017, the United States became a net exporter of natural gas. This condition occurred because of increasing exports to Mexico in pipelines between the two countries and increasing exports of LNG to the rest of the world. The United States exports to Chile, China, Mexico, and fifteen other countries. The exports to Chile, China, and Mexico, however, account for 40 percent of the total U.S. LNG exports. Therefore, growing exports of natural gas in pipelines and tankers are a bright spot for the U.S. energy market. Moreover, new pipelines spreading out from the eastern United States will allow producers in West Virginia, Pennsylvania, and other states to tap into favorable market conditions. In terms of U.S. imports, more than 95 percent of the total comes by pipeline from Canada.

CONTEMPORARY CHALLENGES

Fracking

Fracking—the process of injecting water, chemicals, and sand into shale rock in order to crack and open the rock for the release hydrocarbons—is a method that increases the flow rate of gas wells. The first step in the process, building the site infrastructure, includes well construction. Production wells are drilled to a depth of around 10,000 feet. They may have horizontal sections. By pumping the fracturing fluid into the wellbore at a sufficient rate, a hydraulic fracture is created. The technology then pumps the fracturing fluids into a geological formation at high pressure. After the creation of fractures, fracture width is maintained by injecting a *proppant*—solid material such as sand that keeps the hydraulic fracture open—when the pressure of the fluid reduces. Natural gas is then extracted. After the completion of the process, internal pressure causes recovered fracturing fluids ("flowback") to rise to the surface, where it is stored in pits or tanks.

Fracking poses environmental risks. Examples include possible contamination of drinking water from leaky wells or spills, local air pollution from drilling sites called well pads, spilling waste products during aboveground transport, dust and noise from trucks serving drilling sites, and seismic activity. It is nearly impossible to decontaminate groundwater, for example, so continuous appraisal of the process must accompany extraction and production. The triggering of micro-seismic activity from fracking, moreover, has gained attention because of low-magnitude earthquakes near injection disposal wells that do not occur in the absence of fracking. These earthquakes occur because of faults and their reactivation.

In response to the risks of fracking, many groups have turned to the legal system. In 2013, citizens in Boulder, Colorado, voted for a five-year moratorium on new gas exploration. In 2014, New York State outlawed high-volume fracking. This result is interesting for one reason: New York States sits atop the Marcellus Shale, a rock formation that holds vast amounts of natural gas. Recent estimates show 140 trillion cubic feet of recoverable natural gas, enough to supply the entire country for decades. Also, in 2014, Colorado adopted the first rules in the United States that regulate methane emissions. In 2016, California implemented a moratorium on fracking on the coast, where high levels of biodiversity in the ecological world reign. However, federal agencies in the same year determined that fracking poses no significant impact, ending the moratorium. After years of hype in Europe over the economic benefits of shale gas, Scotland, Germany, and France banned fracking.

Until recently, many energy analysts predicted natural gas would create net benefits for the economy. Unlike coal-fired power plants, natural gas plants produce negligible amounts of sulfur dioxide (which causes acid rain), mercury, and other pollutants. When burned, natural gas produces less carbon emissions than coal. But the burning of natural gas creates methane emissions, which threaten to offset any benefits from lower emission levels of other pollutants. In the United States, about one-third of total methane emissions come from the gas and oil industries. But no one (not even the U.S. Environmental Protection Agency) knows with certainty how much methane leaks from natural gas facilities, pipelines, processing plants, and wellheads (Krupp, 2014). It may be that the environmental costs of fracking plus the potential of natural gas production crowding out investments in solar and wind lead to a negative overall assessment.

What is needed is better monitoring of the construction and maintenance of wells, mitigation of methane leaks, rules requiring companies to disclose which chemicals they use for fracking, and emission controls (Krupp, 2014). These improvements are important because other countries are likely to follow the U.S. lead in developing shale gas reserves. As a result, the regulations in Colorado and elsewhere may guide the industry beyond U.S. borders. China, for example, has the world's largest natural gas reserves, over 1,000 trillion cubic feet. This amount is larger than the reserves of Canada and the United States combined.

To be sure, shale gas will not solve the world's climate change problem. But if environmental costs are minimized, shale gas will help reduce the consumption of high-carbon coal in the United States, Europe, China, and around the world. Reforming the industry, however, must not overshadow the transition to a cleaner energy system.

Horizontal Drilling

From the offshore gas and oil industries, the onshore natural gas industry borrowed the technique of horizontal drilling. The purpose is to expose significantly more reservoir rock than would occur with vertical drilling. Horizontal drilling is a two-part process. It first entails drilling a well from the surface to a subsurface location above the target gas reservoir. It then entails deviating from the vertical plane around a curve to a near horizontal inclination in the reservoir. Instead of drilling into 100 vertical feet, the operator is now drilling into 5,200 or more horizontal feet. This multiplies the expected natural gas well recovery rate. Drillers also use sensory technology to detect gas reserves in promising rock intervals. They may drill up, down, left, or right as they continue horizontally through the rock formation. This technological achievement allows the maximization of returns from each well, higher royalty payments to mineral owners, and higher tax revenues for state and local governments. It may extract gas from a broad area with one drill pad, improve the productivity of a well, and broaden the underground zone of extraction. With this technology, a larger level of extraction is possible than an offshore drilling platform. According to Richard Kerr (2010), in *Science*, horizontal drilling out to 2.5 kilometers multiplies the length of a well by up to ten times.

The results of horizontal drilling are mixed. A single process of horizontal drilling may replace dozens of vertical wells. Larger wells use more sand, water, and other additives, but the technology leads to fewer wells being drilled overall. Compared to conventional drilling, this means fewer greenhouse gas emissions and less water usage. Less land is impacted. The benefits therefore include the avoidance of surface sites that are environmentally sensitive, targeting larger gas reserves with a single well, reducing the costs of surface impacts, and enhancing gas production by drilling in a way that exposes more of the reservoir. But a horizontal well may cost 100 percent more than vertical drilling. It may compromise underground aquifers. Whether or not net benefits exist depends on the size of these costs and benefits.

NATURAL GAS AND CLIMATE CHANGE

With electricity generation, natural gas emits about half as much carbon per unit as coal in efficient power plants. In a study that compares the lifecycle air emissions of coal, natural gas, LNG, and synthetic natural gas (SNG)—produced from coal that serves as a substitute for natural gas and is suitable for transmission in natural gas pipelines—researchers at Carnegie Mellon University (Jaramillo et al., 2007) argue that the demand for natural gas is projected to grow the fastest for electricity generation. When compared to coal, LNG, and SNG, they find that, for electricity generation, greenhouse gas emissions are the least with natural gas combustion.

However, the effects of shale gas on climate change are complex. The reason is uncertainty with respect to methane leaks. Methane is a more potent greenhouse gas than carbon dioxide, but methane stays in the atmosphere only one-tenth of the time. Viewed over a 100-year period, methane has a global warming potential that is thirty-three times greater than carbon dioxide, according to the analysis of Wang et al. (2014).

With the expansion of global trade, the natural gas supply chain is more prominent in a climate change perspective because of the role of methane emissions. In exporting countries, the production of natural gas and the natural gas infrastructure contribute to greenhouse gas emissions. In importing countries, emissions associated with the lifecycle of natural gas depend on how efficient the resource is used.

With this information, the magnitude of methane leaks from natural gas production provides reason to question the climate benefits of substituting natural gas for coal. On one hand, estimates of the lifecycle of greenhouse gas emissions of shale gas are generally lower than coal for the production of electricity. Although uncertainty exists with the emission estimates due to production volumes and transportation, the favorable estimates hold true in the absence of any effective carbon capture and storage technology. But for realistic estimates of leakage rates, shale gas has a smaller global warming impact than coal: "For leakage rates less than two percent, the impact of shale gas approaches one third that of coal" (Wang et al., 2014).

On the other hand, if the methodology includes slightly different assumptions, it may be that the greenhouse gas footprint of shale gas is larger than coal. In a study of natural gas obtained by high-volume fracking from shale formations, the scholars Robert Howarth, Renee Santoro, and Anthony Ingraffea (2011) found that 3.6 percent to 7.9 percent of the methane from shale-gas production escapes to the atmosphere in leaks and venting of the lifecycle of a well. These methane emissions may be 30 percent higher to 50 percent higher than emissions from conventional gas. The higher emissions result from the time shale gas wells are hydraulically fractured and during the drilling process following the fracturing. On a time scale of two decades, methane emissions from shale gas dominate the greenhouse gas footprint: "Compared to coal, the footprint of shale gas is at least 20 percent greater and perhaps more than twice as great on the 20-year horizon" (Howarth et al., 2011).

NATURAL GAS AND SUSTAINABILITY

We may evaluate natural gas with respect to the sustainability criteria of chapter 1. Does natural gas contribute to our current needs without compromising the ability of future generations to meet their needs? With the six sustainability criteria, natural gas satisfies two: the provision of baseload power and contribution to a country's economic performance. In 2016, 1,793 U.S. natural gas-powered electricity plants generated 34 percent of the nation's electricity, surpassing coal (30%), nuclear (20%), and renewables (15%). Overall, the satisfaction of two of the six sustainability criteria does not place natural gas highly in the sustainability rankings, especially compared to renewables.

Future Prospects

According to James Taylor (2017), in *Forbes*, "natural gas is the wave of the future." First, no other power source is even close to matching the potential of natural gas over the next few decades. Second, even though coal-fired power plants generate more electricity than natural gas on a global scale, the share of coal in global electricity production will likely fall from 40 percent (in the second decade of this century) to 30 percent in 2030. The reason is that many countries are trying to reduce the effects of debilitating air pollution, including China and the United States. Third, in the United States, natural gas is competitive with coal.

But Joel Stronberg (2016), in *Renewable Energy World*, argues that "Adopting natural gas as a go-to transitional energy source is fraught with danger." Natural gas is by no means a panacea for the environmental problems that result from our energy choices. To combat the worst possible effects of climate change, carbon reductions on a global scale of up to 80 percent by 2050 are necessary. Switching to natural gas from coal-fired power plants will not bring about this reduction. In addition, the continued production of new shale gas resources will exacerbate preexisting water management and methane emission problems.

The reality is that clean-energy alternatives to natural gas (and coal) such as wind, solar, and energy efficiency will slow the increase in carbon emissions from power plants even more. But Stronberg (2016) worries that today's "bridge technology" of natural gas to a cleaner future will become tomorrow's "barrier" to progress on the environmental front. As we invest in the natural gas industry, our future dependence on natural gas will rise. This will make it harder to switch to clean energy.

SUMMARY

Natural gas is an important component of the overall energy mix. The abundance of natural gas and its multiple applications means it will continue to contribute to global energy demand. The production of shale gas in the United States has reached a mature stage. But it will continue to grow globally. The future of shale gas is subject to environmental uncertainties, such as groundwater contamination, greenhouse gas emissions, and increased seismic activity. From a technical perspective, the shale gas experience in the United States does not guarantee the same success in other countries. But in upcoming years, natural gas production and consumption will most likely accelerate. A greater share of natural gas in the global energy mix will depend on how well the industry prevents the most important environmental impacts, especially with respect to fracking and horizontal drilling.

CONCEPTS

Commoditization
Exploration
Extraction
Feedstock
Fracking
Gasification

Horizontal drilling
Liquefaction
Liquefied natural gas
Natural depletion rate
Netback price
Shale gas
Spot gas
Swing gas

QUESTIONS

1. One argument states that more production of shale gas will improve climate change. Another states that more production will exacerbate climate change. Which argument do you think is correct?
2. On the internet, look up the BP Energy Charting Tool for natural gas and the *R/P* ratio. Using data from the website, graph the *R/P* ratio for the Middle East and other regions of the world. What do your data show?
3. How closely related is the price of natural gas to the "rig count"?
4. Discuss the economics of pipelines. For your answer, research compressor stations and transshipment nodes.
5. Over the next two decades, do you believe global natural gas production will increase, decrease, or remain relatively constant? Why? For your answer, develop a specific forecast, going five, ten, fifteen, and twenty years into the future.
6. Is natural gas an important part of our energy future? Why or why not? (In terms of the generation of electricity, contrast the prospects of natural gas with coal and renewables.) Read the articles by Taylor (2017) and Stronberg (2016) listed in the Bibliography.

Chapter 10

Nuclear Energy

The Controversy Continues

DECARBONIZATION

With the *Paris Agreement* of November 4, 2016, nations of the world came together to combat climate change. The central aim of the agreement is to limit the increase in global temperature during this century to 2°C above preindustrial levels. But if this does not occur, runaway feedback effects will generate billions of dollars of damage, including agricultural losses, water shortages, rising sea levels, and massive refugee relocation.

In order to achieve the goal of temperature stabilization, the world must establish a number of pathways to decarbonization of the global economy. In this context, a pathway is a way of achieving a specific result, or a course of action. In order to meet the goal, the world needs an increase in the supply of low-carbon electricity. The best way to achieve this is with a portfolio of advanced technologies, including renewables, carbon capture and sequestration, energy storage, and nuclear energy, which creates zero carbon emissions during the process of electricity generation (Ford et al., 2017; Lester, 2016; IPCC, 2014b; IEA, 2014b). But problems of cost, safety, proliferation, and radioactive waste hinder a global scale-up of the nuclear energy industry. In addition, a lack of public support for nuclear energy in the years after the Fukushima accident in 2011 has important nontechnical dimensions, including fear of expansion of the industry and philosophical opposition to this technology.

In the United States, the Department of Energy's Office of Nuclear Energy oversees the process of technical advance. But the office has lacked both the funding and the programmatic focus to carry out its plan to develop more nuclear reactors, according to Ford et al. (2017) in an article in the journal *Energy Policy*. Difficulties in fulfilling this goal highlight fundamental challenges with energy transformation: how can scarce public resources encourage energy transition in general? Specifically, what drives innovation in nuclear technology? The first question is an ongoing topic in this book. The second question is considered in this chapter.

The world is approaching the so-called fourth-generation of nuclear energy with advances in fission technology and fuel processing systems (Goldberg and Rosner, 2011):

- Generation One: mid-1950s–mid-1960s
- Generation Two: mid-1960s–mid-1990s
- Generation Three: mid-1990s–2030
- Generation Four: 2030–beyond

To consider how innovation in nuclear energy could contribute to global decarbonization, this chapter considers the fundamentals of nuclear energy, contemporary challenges, and other important topics, including climate change, sustainability, and future prospects. The chapter's thesis is that if the world wants both a strong global economy and pathways to decarbonization, it must consider an expanding role for nuclear technology.

FUNDAMENTALS OF NUCLEAR ENERGY

In the 1930s and 1940s, when scientists recognized the possibility of nuclear fission, they realized that nuclear technology could produce a large amount of energy from little material. The Manhattan Project, launched during World War II as one of the largest scientific projects of the twentieth century, propelled the United States forward with nuclear technology. The first experimental nuclear reactor was built in 1942 at the University of Chicago. With a small budget and an abandoned squash court, Enrico Fermi demonstrated the possibility of a self-sustaining nuclear reaction. A nuclear "pile" entailed the slotting of pellets of uranium into a pile of graphite bricks. In a carefully arranged geometry, embedded cadmium control rods absorbed neutrons. The pile grew to a sufficient size to create a nuclear reaction when the control rods were withdrawn from the pile. After the demonstration, the large nuclear reactors built in the United States, Great Britain, China, and the USSR were initially designed to make weapons grade plutonium for atomic bombs.

The progress of this technology, however, with its potential for energy gave rise to the commercial nuclear power industry. In 1946, the Atomic Energy Commission was created in the United States to oversee both civilian and military applications. Early forecasts of rising energy demand, the depletion of fossil fuels, and long-lasting uranium reserves served as arguments for nuclear power. But nuclear technology could make a decisive contribution to the power sector only with the construction of nuclear power plants.

As this process began in the 1950s, the argument for nuclear energy became stronger. Research addressed both submarine propulsion, a strategically important application, and electricity generation. The first electricity generated by nuclear power occurred in 1951 at a small reactor in Idaho. But in 1958, the world's first commercial nuclear reactor, the Shippingport Atomic Power Station in Pennsylvania, began operating during the administration of President Dwight D. Eisenhower, part of his Atoms for Peace program.

The Shippingport station, a 60-megawatt unit, was modified from a submarine design, which evolved into the most commonly used reactor types: the pressurized water reactor and the boiling water reactor. These are referred to as "light water reactors," as opposed to reactors that use heavy water moderators, mediums that reduce the speed of fast neutrons in generating chain reactions. But a major problem with the design of light water reactors is environmental risk. Any incident or accident that releases steam could potentially spread radioactive contamination.

As the industry grew in the 1960s, the Atomic Energy Commission anticipated the building of 1,000 reactors in the United States by the year 2000. That did not happen. But by 1974 the country had 54 operating reactors and another 197 on order. Enthusiasm for nuclear power existed during this period, with high prices for coal. The problem was that, after 1974, utilities suspended construction of many existing orders. Concerns about safety and the environment persisted.

In 1974, the Nuclear Regulatory Commission replaced the Atomic Energy Commission. It was charged with maintaining the safety and security of the industry, including licensing new reactors, handling radioactive waste, and disposing spent fuel. But when communities challenged nuclear energy for safety reasons, it became more difficult to construct new plants. Then, in 1979, the Three Mile Island incident, in which a nuclear plant suffered a partial core meltdown, further jeopardized the industry. By the middle of the 1980s, the nuclear industry came to a standstill. The United States never built 1,000 reactors; as of 2019, ninety-nine were operating. During this time, the nuclear industry has been characterized by four themes: nuclear hype, a rush of new technology to the market, the absence of learning effects, and higher reactor construction costs (Cooper, 2014).

On a global scale, nuclear energy generates more than 11 percent of the world's electricity. It produces almost 2,500 terawatt-hours annually. North America accounts for one-third of the total, with the European Union providing another one-third. Over the course of the last sixty years, global commercial plant operation has given rise to over 17,000 reactor years of operation in thirty-one countries.

Nuclear energy generates electricity without greenhouse gas emissions and air pollutants such as particulates, nitrous oxides, and carcinogenic hydrocarbons. Today, a pound of reactor-grade uranium oxide produces the same amount of electricity as 16,000 pounds of coal, enough to meet the needs of an average household in the United States for more than a year.

The problem is that the world will not forget the nuclear incidents and accidents at Three Mile Island (1979), Chernobyl (1986), and Fukushima (2011). But for expansion in the industry, the world must address this apprehension. In reality, in a given year, there is a low but positive risk of catastrophic damage from individual nuclear reactors.

NUCLEAR ORIGINS

While the pre-Socratic Greek philosopher Democritus conjectured that the world is made of invisible substances called "atoms," scientists now know atoms are divisible. They may be split into parts. The two main parts are the nucleus, the atom's core, and the "cloud" of electrons that surround the core. The nucleus contains both protons (positively charged particles that exert forces on other charged particles) and neutrons (elementary particles having no charge, but slightly greater mass than protons). Electrons, with a much smaller mass than protons, are the negatively charged particles that form the cloud (figure 10.1).

Sources of Nuclear Energy

The sources of nuclear energy are *fusion*, *fission*, and *radioactive decay*. They transform mass into energy. First, when light atoms are forced together to make heavier atoms, nuclear fusion occurs. In this process, electricity is

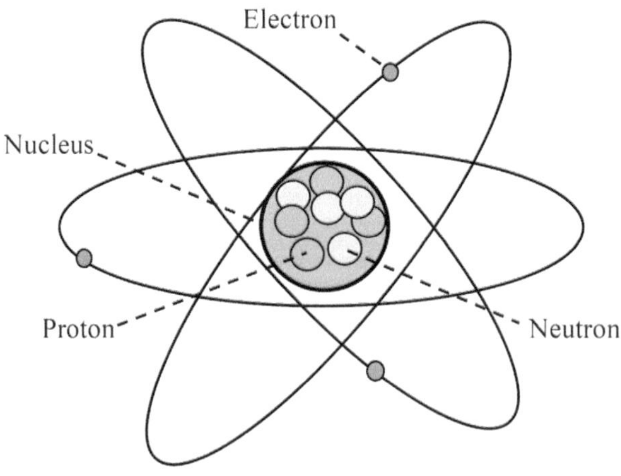

Figure 10.1 Composition of an Atom. *Source*: Author.

generated by using fusion reactions. Fusion reactions fuse two lighter atomic nuclei to create a heavier nucleus, thus releasing energy. Second, when heavy atoms become unstable and split, nuclear fission occurs. Nuclear power plants obtain the heat necessary to produce steam through this process, which entails the splitting of uranium atoms in a nuclear reactor. Bundles of uranium fuel, consisting of small, hard pellets, are packaged into long tubes and inserted into the reactor. Most uranium fuel, composed of protons and neutrons, is unstable. As the nuclei break apart, neutrons are released. When neutrons slam into other uranium atoms, those atoms split, releasing additional neutrons and heat. Ultimately, this process creates a chain reaction, and fission becomes self-sustaining. Third, when unstable atoms emit energy to become more stable, radioactive decay occurs. This process is governed by the weak nuclear force. The first two sources of nuclear energy are governed by the strong nuclear force. During radioactive decay, when unstable atomic nuclei lose energy by emitting ionizing particles and radiation, energy is released. The loss of energy, or decay, results when an atom of one type, the parent nuclide, transforms into an atom of a different type, the child nuclide.

Nuclear Fuel Cycle

The *nuclear fuel cycle*—the demonstration of how uranium ultimately powers nuclear plants—entails several stages:

- Mining
- Milling
- Conversion
- Enrichment
- Reactor fuel fabrication
- Reactor operation
- Removal of spent fuel
- Permanent storage

Uranium Mining

Uranium mining entails the extraction of uranium ore from open-pit or underground mines. According to the website of the U.S. Energy Information Administration, the three largest uranium mining countries, Kazakhstan, Canada, and Australia, account for more than 72 percent of global supply. The United States, the ninth highest producer, supplies the global marketplace with more than 1,000 tons of uranium, almost 2 percent of the world's total. The world's largest uranium mine, discovered in 1988, is McArthur River in Canada.

Uranium exists in rocks near the Earth's surface, including autunite, uranophane, and tobernite. Phosphate rock, monazite sands, and lignite also contain uranium. Uranium comes in several *isotopes*, forms of the element with different numbers of neutrons. Some isotopes are more radioactive and may give off energetic particles. Others may be more fissile, or likely to produce nuclear fission. The most abundant isotope is uranium-238, found in rocks and seawater. But the most radioactive, uranium-235, is best known for the creation of nuclear reactions. According to the World Nuclear Association, global uranium mining produced 59,462 tons in 2017, an increase of more than 26 percent since 2008.

Uranium reserves are recoverable deposits, regardless of isotope. The identification of uranium reserves initiates uranium mining. Most reserves are identified by the mineralization of uranium near the surface. Uranium production depends on these reserves. According to the Nuclear Energy Agency, uranium reserves total 7 million metric tons. The planet's economically accessible uranium reserves could power reactors for 200 years at current rates of consumption. In this century, exploration expenditure has risen. The recoverable reserves equal more than 5 million metric tons. But this estimate may eventually rise: the extraction of uranium from seawater could make available more than 4 billion metric tons.

Uranium Milling

After uranium is delivered to a mill, the process of milling separates uranium ore from rock. The rock is crushed and ground up. Water is added, resulting in a substance referred to as "slurry." Then, in a process known as "leaching," sulfuric acid or alkaline solutions are added to leach out the uranium from the ore. The substance is then recovered from the solution and dried. The outcome is uranium oxide, often called "yellowcake," because of its yellowish color. Radioactive waste left from the milling process is called "tailings," which contain lead, polonium, radon, radium, and arsenic. The waste is stored in special ponds called "impoundments."

Uranium Conversion

In reactors, the yellowcake is not usable by itself. It requires conversion to a chemical form suitable for the production of fuel or the provision of material for enrichment plants. As a result, after the mill produces uranium ore concentrate, the substance is packaged in 55-gallon drums. It is sent to the uranium conversion plant. The conversion plant processes the yellowcake by mixing it with fluorine. The result is uranium hexafluoride, which exists as a gas. It is then cooled to a liquid. It is drained into storage and transport cylinders and transitions into a solid. In a solid form, the substance is suitable for enrichment. The cylinders are shipped to enrichment plants. In this state, the risk of contamination is more chemical than radiological, involving chemical forms that contribute to potential problems of inhalation. Commercial conversion plants operate in Canada, China, France, Russia, and the United States. In the United States, the conversion plant is operated by Honeywell International, Inc., in Metropolis, Illinois. It began operating in 1958.

Uranium Enrichment

Most of the world's nuclear reactors require enriched uranium with a higher concentration of the U-235 isotope than in uranium hexafluoride. Light water reactors require a higher concentration in order to sustain a chain reaction. The result is low-enriched uranium fuel. Advances in enrichment technology could reduce the uranium needs of light water reactors as much as 30 percent. In the United States, the Urenco USA facility, operating outside of Eunice, New Mexico, enriches uranium. But the International Atomic Energy Agency, in conjunction with the United States, has proposed the creation of international uranium enrichment centers. Because uranium enrichment could lead to nuclear proliferation, the international centers would undertake enrichment activity under international oversight, encouraging global scrutiny of the process.

Reactor Fuel Fabrication

In the last stage of uranium transformation, fuel fabrication facilities convert enriched uranium into fuel for nuclear reactors. (A 1,000-megawatt nuclear reactor requires about 27 tons of fresh fuel. In contrast, a coal-fired power plant requires two-and-a-half million tons of coal to produce the same amount of electricity.) First, uranium hexafluoride is converted into uranium dioxide powder. Second, the powder is pressed into small fuel pellets, which are heated into a hard ceramic material. Finally, the pellets are inserted into fuel rods, which are grouped together and measure several meters in length. These fuel assemblies are loaded into the reactor core and used to generate nuclear power. In a typical reactor, the nuclear core contains 157 fuel assemblies, each possessing over 45,000 fuel rods and 15 million fuel pellets.

Reactor Operations

Of the thirty-one countries with nuclear power plants, five use nuclear for a majority of the domestic supply of electricity: Belgium, France, Hungary, Slovakia, and Ukraine. Spain, the United Kingdom, and the United States generate about 20 percent of their electricity using nuclear power. Globally, the 2.8 trillion kilowatt-hours of electricity generated from nuclear power in light water reactors use low-enriched uranium fuel (LEU). About 10 metric tons of uranium produce 1 metric ton of LEU. This fuel generates about 400 million kilowatt-hours of electricity. As a result, the nuclear reactors in the world today require about 70,000 metric tons of uranium annually.

The electricity from nuclear power is generated mostly in light water reactors: pressured water reactors (main design) and boiling water reactors. They both use enriched uranium oxide and water as coolant and moderator (medium that reduces the speed of neutrons in order to turn them into thermal neutrons for chain reactions). To enable high operating temperatures, they have steel pressure tubes. In pressured water reactors, water is heated to over 300°C in its primary circuit. In its secondary circuit, steam is generated. Boiling water reactors, in the primary circuit, create steam above the reactor core. Temperatures and pressures are similar with both designs.

Removal of Spent Fuel

Once the reactor core is loaded, fuel remains for up to four years, depending on the operating cycle. Refueling occurs at intervals of twelve, eighteen, or twenty-four months. During refueling, most reactors are shut down, so maintenance may open the reactor vessel. During this process, one-fourth to one-third of the core, about forty assemblies, is removed and placed in a water-filled spent fuel pool and replaced by fresh assemblies. The spent fuel is stored in 40-foot deep pools for a year or more. The pools possess concrete walls several feet thick with steel liners. The bottom holds storage racks with the fuel assemblies. The idea is to cool the spent fuel rods and provide shelter from radioactivity. As the pools reach capacity, utilities remove some of the older fuel assemblies into dry cask storage spaces, which are steel cylinders, bolted or welded closed, and surrounded by additional steel or concrete that shields plant workers from radiation.

Permanent Storage

Radioactive waste, a by-product from nuclear reactors, presents a unique long-term problem. This problem does not exist with fossil fuels or renewables. High-level radioactive waste, primarily uranium fuel, which has been used in the nuclear fuel cycle, is spent or no longer efficient in generating electricity. But spent fuel is thermally hot. It is highly radioactive. It requires remote handling and permanent separation from the human population.

During short periods of direct exposure, high-level wastes are hazardous: they create lethal doses of radiation. Although radioactive isotopes eventually decay, some have long half-lives: the amount of time in which half the radioactive material will decay. Plutonium-239, for example—which is discussed below—has a half-life of 24,000 years. Reprocessing separates residual plutonium and uranium from fission material. The plutonium and uranium may then be used again as fuel. Other than spent fuel, most high-level waste in the United States has come from reprocessing fuel from plutonium reactors.

In the United States, the Nuclear Regulatory Commission (NRC) regulates the storage and disposal of commercially generated radioactive waste. All nuclear power plants in the United States store their spent fuel in pools on-site. But the NRC believes the on-site pools are temporary. At some future date, spent fuel must be moved to a permanent storage location. None exist.

Planning for the disposal of nuclear waste has occurred for six decades. But trust in the federal government has not overcome local fears. In 1986, the Department of Energy recommended three sites for permanent waste disposal: a basalt site in the Hanford Reservation in the state of Washington, a bedded salt site in Texas, and Yucca Mountain in Nevada. In 1987, Congress seemingly resolved the issue with the Nuclear Waste Policy Amendments Act, designating Yucca Mountain for storage. The site is a desert area in southern Nevada, 100 miles northwest of Las Vegas, sitting on federal land. The site offers multiple natural barriers, an arid climate, and remoteness. The geologic setting could potentially isolate waste for tens of thousands of years. It was the only site studied in great detail and determined to be feasible.

In the spring of 2002, President George W. Bush endorsed the Yucca Mountain site, including a facility 100 stories below ground, stainless steel casks for uranium waste, and tunnels for the casks. But facing groundwater penetration, a vulnerability to earthquakes, and economic obstacles, an inadequate level of funding doomed the location. In 2010, Congress approved a budget proposal from the Obama administration that eliminated funding for the Yucca Mountain site. Because typical nuclear power plants generate 20 metric tons of waste annually; the nuclear industry generates more than 2,000 tons annually. As a result, the United States needs a new long-term solution for the 100,000 tons of spent nuclear waste.

Plutonium

Plutonium-239 (Pu-239), an isotope of the element plutonium, is the primary fissile isotope in nuclear weapons. It also may be recovered as a by-product of uranium fuel. Like all other heavy elements, plutonium has many isotopes. Each of the fifteen differs with respect to the number of neutrons in the nucleus. But they are unstable and therefore decay. When they decay, they emit radiation. Therefore, all are radioactive. When plutonium is integrated into the nuclear fuel cycle, it is an impressive energy source: the fission of one atom of Pu-239 creates 8 million kilowatt hours of electricity. It is also one of the three most common isotopes used as fuel in nuclear reactors, along with uranium-235 and uranium-233. More than one-third of the energy produced in conventional power plants comes from plutonium.

The fission of one atom of uranium-235 in power plant reactors produces two or three neutrons. The isotope uranium-238 absorbs these neutrons and produces Pu-239 and other isotopes. In a reactor, Pu-239 can also absorb neutrons. Within the uranium fuel load of a typical 1,000 MW power reactor, potential plutonium exists. If the typical reactor creates 25 tons of used fuel annually, almost 300 kilograms of plutonium may be manufactured. Interestingly, although it is not found in the Earth's crust, plutonium exists in the atmosphere, a legacy of nuclear weapons testing. According to the World Nuclear Association, four of the six Generation IV reactor designs are "fast neutron" reactors that will use plutonium. Therefore, while plutonium remains a concern for weapons proliferation, it has an important future with nuclear energy.

Electricity Generation

Nuclear power contributes to baseload electricity generation. In 2002, nuclear energy supplied 20 percent of the United States' and 17 percent of the world's electricity. Fifteen years later, in 2017, the percentages were 19 and 11, respectively. In the United States, the history of electricity generation from nuclear energy shows a growth trend, although production has stabilized in recent years (figure 10.2). In 1957, the one U.S. nuclear reactor produced 10 million kWh of electricity. In 2017, the ninety-nine U.S. reactors produced 804,950 million kWh of electricity.

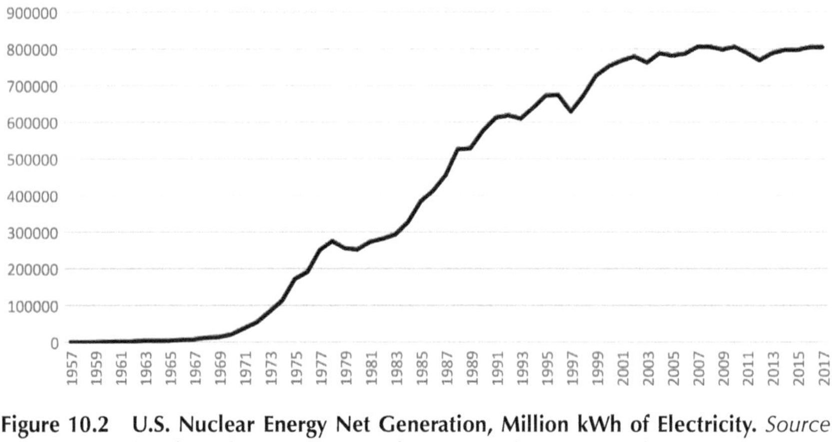

Figure 10.2 U.S. Nuclear Energy Net Generation, Million kWh of Electricity. *Source*: Author using data from the U.S. Energy Information Administration, https://www.eia.gov/totalenergy/data/monthly/.

Contemporary Challenges

The limited prospects for an expansion of nuclear power are a function of four unresolved problems, according to an MIT study by John Deutch and Ernest Moniz (2003):

- Proliferation
- Radioactive waste management
- Cost
- Safety

Proliferation

Strategies of nuclear *proliferation* affect both the likelihood of success and the global nuclear landscape. They also impact how we evaluate this unresolved problem. The objective is to minimize the risk of proliferation. According to the International Atomic Energy Agency (IAEA), thirty-one countries have nuclear energy, but nine countries have nuclear weapons (table 10.1). Seven have both. Israel and North Korea are the only countries with nuclear weapons but not nuclear energy programs. Several others, including Bangladesh, Vietnam, Turkey, and Abu Dhabi, are pursuing nuclear energy.

Table 10.1 Countries with Nuclear Capabilities

Country	*Nuclear Energy*	*Nuclear Weapons*	*Country*	*Nuclear Energy*	*Nuclear Weapons*
Argentina	√		Mexico	√	
Armenia	√		Netherlands	√	
Belgium	√		North Korea		√
Brazil	√		Pakistan	√	√
Bulgaria	√		Romania	√	
Canada	√		Russia	√	√
China	√	√	Slovakia	√	
Czech Republic	√		Slovenia	√	
Finland	√		South Africa	√	
France	√	√	Spain	√	
Germany	√		Sweden	√	
Hungary	√		Switzerland	√	
India	√	√	Taiwan	√	
Iran	√		Ukraine	√	
Israel		√	United Kingdom	√	√
Japan	√		United States	√	√
South Korea	√				

Source: Author using information from the International Atomic Energy Agency.

Other countries are backing away from existing programs, such as Sweden and Germany.

The problem is that, even though global concern has led to the creation of institutions that prevent proliferation, none have proved satisfactory. The IAEA verifies compliance with generally accepted principles concerning the nuclear fuel cycle, but it is constrained by both the scope of its authority and the growing divergence between funding and responsibilities. Different types of nuclear proliferators exist. The distinction helps determine which countries may obtain nuclear capabilities. It also elucidates methods of deterrence.

Vipin Narang (2017) of MIT argues that pursuit often occurs under duress. One reason is that, when a nuclear weapons program gets close to fruition, other countries might attempt to destroy it. In addition, the anticipation of nuclear weapons may embolden efforts to deter retaliation. Finally, proliferation may lead directly to duress, which encourages proliferation in a feedback loop. When pursuing nuclear weapons, a country or rogue group must therefore consider whether it wants to fully weaponize its capabilities. Reasons of security, prestige, domestic politics, terrorism, deterrence, or regional influence may drive the decision. In this context, Narang (2017) provides a useful framework, discussed in the following sections.

Hedging

Hedgers develop nuclear technologies that may be used for either energy programs or weapons. They establish the intent to develop a bomb, but defer the decision. If the desire to obtain nuclear weapons appears, then nuclear weapons may complement a program of nuclear power. Hedging countries, such as India, decide to pursue an active proliferation strategy, while others, like Sweden, do not. Varieties of hedging include technical hedging, when technological capabilities allow a future military option; insurance hedging, when further advances allow a reduction in time necessary to build a bomb; and hard hedging, when threshold capabilities make a functional weapons program looming (Narang, 2017).

Sprinting

Sprinters develop nuclear weapons quickly. They undertake a program of "tactical obfuscation," which protects the integrity of both research and production. They do not hide their intent. They create organizational structure for the management of nuclear weapons. If a country is in good global standing and immune from military or economic sanctions, it may develop nuclear weapons. But sprinting is a rare strategy. Few countries after the first generation of proliferators (the five permanent members of the UN Security Council—China, France, Russia, the United Kingdom, and the United States) start and finish as sprinters (Narang, 2017).

Hiding

Hiders choose a clandestine approach. They prioritize secrecy, shun speed, and fear actions that prevent progress. They sacrifice efficiency in order to maximize secrecy. They do not want the world to discover their program, because rivals could destroy it or economic sanctions could cripple the economy. The key is choosing a pathway that is easier to conceal, not an approach like plutonium reprocessing. The risk is that if caught, a hider could face military, economic, or diplomatic mobilization against it. The world would perceive the actions as illegitimate. In historical context, hiding has rarely been successful as a strategy: maintaining a secretive program is difficult in the presence of a global community trying to detect hidden weapons programs. However, both North Korea and South Africa used this strategy (Narang, 2017).

Sheltered Pursuit

Sheltered pursuers obtain nuclear weapons by cultivating the protection of a major power. Rather than a meeting of allies, the relationship takes a client-patron approach. The major power tolerates the development of nuclear weapons by the client and expects a transactional arrangement. The client offers geographical reasons to override nonproliferation. The pursuer develops nuclear weapons capability before the major power abandons the idea. Quintessential sheltered pursuers include Pakistan and Israel, under the protection of the United States. Israel seeks active protection from the United States, while offering a geographical connection to the Middle East. Pakistan, after the Soviet Union invaded Afghanistan in 1979, sought protection from the United States, which became an ally in the fight against communism. As long as support from the major power continues, sheltered pursuers experience a high degree of success (Narang, 2017).

Nuclear Acquisition

Which strategy will a country choose? To answer the question, Narang (2017) argues that a country must consider security, the domestic context, and international constraints (figure 10.3). With these options, nuclear simulation tools, and the ability to disguise proliferation activities, the potential for future nuclear proliferation—especially in the developing world—exists:

> The current nonproliferation regime must be strengthened by both technical and institutional measures with particular attention to the connection between fuel cycle technology and safeguardability. Indeed, if the nonproliferation regime is not strengthened, the option of significant global expansion of nuclear power may be impossible, as various governments react to the real or potential threat of nuclear weapons proliferation facilitated by fuel cycle development (Deutch and Moniz, 2003).

Nuclear Energy and Proliferation: Conventional Wisdom

Does a nuclear energy program provide the incentive for a country to develop a nuclear weapons program? According to Nicholas Miller (2017) of Dartmouth College, the answer is "yes." He argues that three pathways between nuclear energy and weapons exist: the means, motivation, and political cover.

First, a nuclear energy program requires the training of scientists in nuclear physics and engineering. This training involves the provision of technical

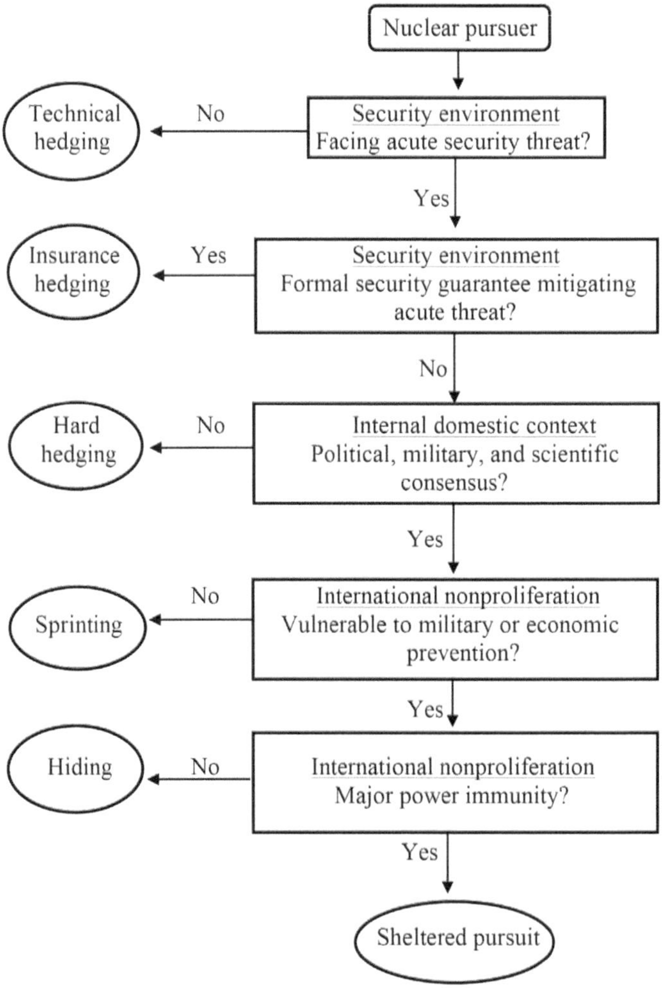

Figure 10.3 The Choice of Nuclear Weapons Acquisition Strategy. *Source*: Author using information from Narang (2017).

know-how and skills, which decreases the cost of developing nuclear energy programs (Miller, 2017).

Second, the development of a nuclear energy infrastructure increases the potential for nuclear weapons. For reasons of power, prestige, or the public budget, the existence of a nuclear energy program could empower a country to push for weapons (Miller, 2017).

Third, a nuclear energy program could provide cover for the acquisition of nuclear enrichment and reprocessing technology. Interestingly, Article 4 of the global Nonproliferation Treaty (NPT), which entered into force in 1970, may provide a framework for such action. The NPT's objective, to prevent the spread of both nuclear weapons and nuclear weapons technology, does not impact the right of countries to develop nuclear energy. In theory, proliferators could use the NPT as cover for the acquisition of fissile material, a step toward the development of nuclear weapons (Miller, 2017).

Nuclear Energy and Proliferation: The Reality of Restraint

But policymakers in countries that favor nonproliferation, notably the United States, understand the link between nuclear energy and weapons. As a result, they have weakened it. Two restraints counterbalance the potential to use nuclear energy technology for weapons proliferation: the likelihood of detection and costs from sanctions. With the first restraint, nuclear energy programs face global scrutiny. When a country without nuclear energy announces its intention to develop a program, the world takes notice. With the second restraint, nuclear energy programs increase the potential costs of nonproliferation sanctions, which are harmful to programs that rely on the light water reactor technology, which is globalized and dominated by a small number of large suppliers. In 2019, twelve countries produced fuel rods for light water reactors, but thirty-one countries had operational light water reactors. Countries with this technology may choose to import enriched uranium fuel and risk disruptions in global supply or develop enrichment technology and acquiesce to international scrutiny and pressure (Miller, 2017).

RADIOACTIVE WASTE MANAGEMENT

Many decades after the first nuclear power plant, countries grapple with the problem of permanent storage for radioactive waste. The preferred approach is the construction of repositories in rock formations hundreds of meters below ground. But Finland is the only country with this preferred approach. Located on a sparsely inhabited island off the west coast, the facility exists nearly 1,500 feet down into bedrock. According to Andrew Curry (2017), writing in *The Atlantic*, the facility will house spent fuel packed into 25-ton, cast iron canisters wrapped in pure copper. The canisters will keep the radioactive waste from leaking. Stored in specially carved chambers sealed with bentonite clay, which will absorb water that may seep in over the course of centuries, the radioactive isotopes will degrade to a form that does not pose an environmental threat. The only catch? The waste will remain radioactive for at least 100,000 years. As a result, planners must address the question of how to warn future generations about the underground site.

Future visitors to nuclear waste sites may not be able to read warnings, so signs must be creative. (What symbols should the signs include?) The Finns have chosen the opposite approach: no warning sign at all. They hope an inconspicuous spot will be sufficient to "hide" the waste. The site in bedrock should not interest future prospectors, because of a lack of oil, ore, or metal deposits. As radioactive waste fills the 137 tunnels, they will be backfilled with absorbent clay blocks. But in the early 2100s, the site will reach capacity. The idea is that it will not need oversight. Forest will cover the site. Future generations may forget about it.

Cost

An analysis of nuclear power plants by the U.S. EIA (2016) reveals three important issues. First, many nuclear plants around the world were originally (a) state-owned or (b) regulated, investor-owned, and vertically integrated utility monopolies. However, the industry today relies primarily on investors in a competitive market. In this market, risk associated with the future value of electricity is shifted to consumers in the form of utility prices. However, some market risk, all construction and operating costs, and performance risk is held by investors. As a result, nuclear technology competes with investments in fossil fuel and renewable technologies.

Second, construction costs are lower today than in previous decades. The article by Lovering et al. (2016) in the journal *Energy Policy* offers perspective. Early analyses of historical construction costs of nuclear power reactors focused on France and the United States in the 1970s and 1980s. However, these countries suffered from first-mover disadvantages with early technology. The countries built most of their reactors before 1985, so dozens of global reactors have subsequently come online. Therefore, cost trends vary (Lovering et al., 2016).

Third, even if investors value an expansion of nuclear generation capacity, they must address political, social, and regulatory challenges. They must obtain licenses to build on specific sites. They must address local opposition, water sources, and obtaining discharge requirements. Many plants incur large development costs only to be canceled.

To compare electricity-generating technologies, energy economists use the concept *overnight construction cost* (OCC). "Overnight" refers to costs if construction occurred instantaneously. This concept normalizes costs, in order to compare different forms of energy technology. With nuclear power, OCC represents the largest component of total levelized cost, accounting for more than 50 percent. For vendors and architect-engineer teams, OCC includes the costs of construction services, resource procurement, and direct engineering. Indirect owner's costs include commissioning, contingencies, project management, site preparation, and training.

The value of OCC, crucial in the decision to invest in nuclear versus other technologies, is not the only decision input. Intangible factors include the political and social environment, projected fuel costs, changes in energy policy, and forecasts for future energy demand. With nuclear power, political and social attitudes may ebb toward or flow away from this technology. Leaders may value decarbonization and advocate nuclear technology. In contrast, skepticism of the risks of proliferation or radioactive waste management may influence decision making as much as overnight costs.

Investment in nuclear generation therefore depends on two factors: OCC and intangible costs. Investment occurs when these costs are less than risk-adjusted costs of alternative technologies. To assess this choice, the U.S. EIA (2016) has compiled useful statistics concerning the relative nature of OCC for different technologies. (It is hard to quantify the intangible factors, especially the political and social environment and changes in energy policy. It may be that future energy policy such as production tax credits may favor the expansion of the renewables market.) The U.S. EIA (2016) study finds that OCC for nuclear power plants is relatively higher than OCC for most forms of coal, natural gas, biomass, wind, solar, and hydroelectric technologies. For practical purposes, OCC is a roadblock for the expansion of the nuclear industry.

Safety

Nuclear safety refers to the prevention of incidents and accidents. Nuclear plants vary with respect to their safety assessment, commitment to a safety culture, maintenance of equipment, and worker training. Today, the biggest safety risks exist with the eleven Chernobyl-style reactors that still operate in Russia. If harmful incidents occur, such as the release of radiation, the goal is to mitigate the impact on humans and the environment. Safety procedures to reduce this risk entail the retrofitting of reactors with quality safety systems, designing future reactors with high safety standards, training plant workers, and preventive maintenance. A particular challenge is that safe operations of the global fleet of nuclear facilities are paramount for success. The world learned with the Three Mile Island, Chernobyl, and Fukushima accidents that the industry could face public backlash. A worst-case scenario would entail public pressure to shut the entire industry down. Zero tolerance for accidents is not realistic, but an important goal is to minimize risk.

At nuclear facilities, a multilayered system provides several layers of protection. First, the fuel is designed to avoid rupture. Second, the covering or coating of material around the uranium or plutonium fuel is made with an alloy such as zirconium that helps prevent the release of fission products. Third, the reactor pressure vessel is typically made of steel, resistant to cracking. Fourth, the airtight containment structure, made of thick and reinforced concrete, is intended to prevent the release of radioactive gases. Finally, the emergency core-cooling system is intended to keep the reactor from melting down. To quantify the industry's safety record, we may compare the number of major accidents (three) to the amount of time all nuclear reactors have been in operation (17,000 reactor years).

In the United States, the Nuclear Regulatory Commission ensures that reactors establish a culture of safety. The Commission requires nuclear plants to have a probability of significant reactor damage to be less than one in 10,000 years. For perspective, in the presence of 10,000 reactors, one would have a major accident each year. With ninety-nine nuclear reactors in the United States and 450 in the world, this outcome is unlikely. The most efficient nuclear plants face a probability of core damage of about once every million years. This should be acceptable, especially compared to higher risks in the coal industry. But with nuclear power, all is not equal. Problems remain with the availability of trained personnel, fuel cycle safety, threat of terrorist attacks, and natural disasters. But before we address these risks, consider the details of the three most famous nuclear power accidents.

Three Mile Island (1979)

On the morning of March 29, 1979, in Reactor Unit 2 at the Three Mile Island Nuclear Power Plant, in Londonderry Township, Pennsylvania, the flow of feedwater to a steam generator was interrupted. (Condensed steam creates feedwater. Steam is used to turn the turbine that powers the electric generator. A continual flow of feedwater prevents the overheating of the reactor core. When the temperature is maintained, the core does not overheat.) On this morning, the flow stopped, because the condenser pump turned off. Within 2 minutes, the steam generator boiled dry. This resulted in the buildup of heat and pressure. To counter the problem, the pressure valve in that part of the plant opened. Once pressure decreased to an acceptable level, the valve should have closed; plant operators believed that it did, because an indicator light showed that it was closed. But the valve did not. The operators did not have correct information. More than 45 minutes after the start of the accident, supervisory personnel arrived, the pressure relief valve was closed, and a site emergency was announced. While the release of radiation was small, the impact was large. Substantial disposal costs of the partially melted reactor existed. Negative perceptions of the accident fueled resistance to new plant construction. The containment building around the plant prevented a greater release of radiation. No one was killed in the accident. But in terms of negative perception, the damage was done.

Chernobyl (1986)

In the early morning, April 26, 1986, the world's worst nuclear disaster began. At the Chernobyl Nuclear Power Plant, in the Ukraine, four reactors were operating. The previous night, the maintenance team was testing a safety feature of reactor four. They were trying to determine whether the electric generator could provide enough electricity to run the coolant pumps at lower power. In this situation, the reactor would normally have backup power from offsite supplies and diesel generators. The idea was not to rely on offsite power, but to factor in the slight time delay of the diesel generator. During the delay, the coasting down mode of the generator should have supplied enough power to maintain safety. But many hours elapsed before operators reduced the electric generator. Meanwhile, xenon, a product of fission that acts in a radioactive manner, built up in the reactor. Xenon absorbs neutrons and makes it more difficult to sustain a controlled chain reaction. To compensate for this problem, operators increased control rods in the reactor, violating an operations guideline. Because control rods absorb neutrons, more neutrons increased the propensity of reactivity in the nuclear reactor. The operators continued. At this point, a reduction in the flow of water put the plant at a high risk of an accident. That is exactly what occurred. The control rods were in a harmful position. Steam pressure decreased to the turbines. Water flow declined to the reactor core. Formation of additional steam in the core triggered reactivity. The reactor had more neutrons available for fission. But water was not available to capture them. Reactivity surged. To fight the surge, operators inserted additional control rods; however, flaws in the rods led to an additional surge in reactivity. Two large explosions occurred. The roof of the reactor building was blown off. Firefighters raced to the spot and put out the fire, preventing it from spreading to other reactors. But thirty-one firefighters and emergency responders died of radiation exposure. More than 100,000 people living within 30 kilometers of the reactors were evacuated. Massive levels of radioactive contamination covered the region. Many people suffered and died from cancers. The disaster contributed to the slowdown in the nuclear industry in the late 1980s, especially in Austria, Sweden, and Germany. Austria, in fact, banned nuclear energy.

Fukushima (2011)

On March 11, 2011, a massive earthquake measuring 9.0 on the Richter scale—the largest ever recorded in Japan's 140-year history of monitoring seismic activity—occurred in northeast Japan. A movement of the Pacific tectonic plate triggered a gigantic tsunami. The fast-moving wall of water—up to 128 feet high—slammed into the Fukushima Daiichi Nuclear Plant. Three of the plant's six reactors were operating when the earthquake struck. A shutdown procedure began. But flooding overwhelmed the emergency diesel generators. Offsite electrical power failed. After the shutdown, the reactor core still generated thermal power. Without electricity to operate the cooling pumps, the reactor core began to overheat. The water near the core turned to steam, and the steam reacted with coating material on the fission products to produce hydrogen gas, which was flammable. To reduce the pressure, plant operators vented steam and hydrogen gas, trying to prevent the primary containment structure from rupturing. But after a few days, the hydrogen gas in the secondary structure ignited. It blew holes in reactors one and three. The cores were not exposed, but the spent fuel pools were. Reactor two experienced a hydrogen explosion, and small amounts of radioactive material flowed out of the plant with every release of steam.

Although no one died of radiation, many disaster-related fatalities occurred, mostly elderly residents. Radioactive material was detected in the soil and food supply; in Tokyo, it was detected in the water supply. In April 2011, the federal government increased its assessment of the accident, putting it second to the 1986 Chernobyl explosion in terms of severity. By the end of 2011, however, an unanticipated result occurred: many countries acknowledged they must continue to rely on nuclear power. With the exception of Germany, few countries expressed a desire to shut down nuclear plants. This accident, more significant than Three Mile Island but not as impactful as Chernobyl, has led to greater awareness of the dangers of natural disasters.

Probabilistic Risk Assessment

A systematic evaluation of risk from nuclear reactors is important to ease public concern. One such method, *probabilistic risk assessment* (PRA), identifies the probability that operational failures may occur in a reactor, traces the events that follow, and establishes the likelihood of core damage. With nuclear oversight, PRA is considered helpful, but not without controversy. The reason is that the database on nuclear accidents is small. This is fortunate, but computer simulations—not real-world observations—are used to determine the probability of risk. The upside is that these simulations assign relative values of risk to possible nuclear accidents. Thus, nuclear facilities use this information to both identify the weakest aspects of plant operations and strengthen them.

In this framework, risk = (probability)(consequence), where probability is a function of initiators and system failures. Initiators include natural disasters, breaks in reactor pipes, losses of multiple power systems, problems with engineered safety features, and human failure. Consequences entail the physical responses of nuclear plants, offsite releases, and health and environmental effects. The equation determines the probability of some accident sequence. According to the U.S. Nuclear Regulatory Commission, three levels of risk exist:

- Level 1 PRA: estimates the probability of damage to the reactor core
- Level 2 PRA: starts with Level 1 core accidents and estimates the probability of the release of radioactivity
- Level 3 PRA: starts with Level 2 releases and estimates the probability of damage to the environment and human health

While no set of safety precautions may insulate facilities with 100 percent confidence, a number of preemptive measures may minimize the risk from tsunamis, hurricanes, earthquakes, flooding, and tornadoes. These include the geographic location of plants, suitable backup power systems (electrical power for reactor safety in the United States comes primarily from the offsite grid), continuous re-training of personnel, innovation in design, and containment of radioactive waste. But Spencer Wheatley, Benjamin K. Sovacool, and Didier Sornette (2016), writing in *Energy Research & Social Science*, argue that large disasters may continue. But they ask: how often and with what severity? They address these questions by quantifying four dimensions of risk:

- Historical frequency of accidents
- Historical costs
- Presence of extreme events
- Expected future costs

They find a "1% probability each year that an accident occurs that leads to a loss of at least $331.6 billion" (Wheatley et al., 2016). Therefore, the possibility of a Chernobyl- or Fukushima-sized accident remains.

NUCLEAR ENERGY AND CLIMATE CHANGE

To significantly reduce greenhouse gases, how could the nuclear industry contribute? To answer this question, we may turn to the Wedge Model, developed by Stephen Pacala and Robert Socolow (2004) of Princeton University. A "stabilization wedge" is a strategy or campaign that results in 4 billion tons of carbon dioxide not being emitted into the atmosphere by 2050. To serve as a wedge, nuclear power would have to generate 700 additional gigawatts of energy, double existing capacity, and expand by 700 new reactors with 1,000 megawatts each. In addition, by midcentury, the entire world's fleet of existing reactors would require upgrades.

To serve as a technological option to fight climate change, the world would need 1,000 new and upgraded reactors by 2050. If this occurred, one new plant would have to be connected to the electricity grid every two weeks. In the wedge framework, this would contribute one-seventh of the technological change necessary to stabilize CO_2 emissions. In the 1980s, nuclear power was added to the global grid on the equivalent of about one 1,000-megawatt reactor every two-and-a-half weeks. So this pace is possible. But how likely is it to happen? The author's answer? Not likely.

However, nuclear power is time-tested and concentrated: ten countries operate more than 80 percent of the world's nuclear reactors. Nuclear power could therefore be deployed as a climate mitigation strategy. But four challenges remain (Socolow and Glaser, 2009). First, the accumulation of plutonium stockpiles must cease. Second, cost reductions must increase the competitiveness of nuclear power. Third, the nuclear industry must manage nuclear waste. Fourth, research and development must support industry growth. Almost fifty countries without nuclear energy programs have approached the International Atomic Energy Agency for assistance. Many plan to build reactors, but lack technical expertise and face economic constraints.

NUCLEAR ENERGY AND SUSTAINABILITY

We may evaluate nuclear energy with respect to the sustainability criteria from chapter 1. With the six criteria, nuclear energy satisfies four: baseload power generation, limited atmospheric consequences, limited impact on human health, and contribution to economic performance. But nuclear energy does not satisfy long-term energy supply or limited environmental impacts. Is it possible for nuclear power to serve as an element in a more sustainable energy future? Because of the mixed result concerning the sustainability criteria, especially with respect to radioactive waste, the question is not settled.

Future Prospects

Moving forward, it may be that the necessity of reducing greenhouse gas emissions outweighs both the threat of nuclear proliferation and the problem of hazardous waste. But forecasts of radiation exposure, waste depositories, and accident probabilities serve as important variables in the evaluation of nuclear technology.

A ROADMAP FOR NUCLEAR ENERGY INNOVATION

In a compelling essay, Richard Lester (2016), the Japan Steel professor and associate provost at MIT, an expert in innovation strategy and management, argues that meeting the world's growing appetite for electricity while reducing greenhouse gas emissions "will be impossible without rapid nuclear energy growth." But he is concerned about the lack of innovation in the United States. As the fleet ages, new reactors coming online will be insufficient for growth in the industry. Lester's (2016) framework entails three waves of innovation. The first, from the present to 2030, focuses on innovations that reduce the cost of operating and maintaining existing reactors. The second, beginning in 2030 and lasting until the middle of the century, entails a rapid increase in scale, to achieve deep cuts in carbon dioxide emissions. The third wave, after 2050, advances nuclear technology to further reduce carbon dioxide emissions.

NUCLEAR ENERGY POLICY

To complement innovation, public policy must address externalities and waste management. Levelized cost estimates reflect private costs of investing in different forms of electricity generation. These estimates help determine which plants are built. But the estimates may not include external costs. Using a policy simulation, Davis (2012) demonstrates that the relatively high external cost of pollution from fossil fuel plants improves the prospects of nuclear energy. With coal-fired plants, the external cost from particulates, nitrogen oxides, and sulfur dioxide averages 3.5 cents per kilowatt hour. Nuclear energy does not entail this external cost. However, the incorporation of external cost in the policy framework does little to close the gap between nuclear technology and natural gas. The external cost from natural gas plants averages 0.1 cents per kilowatt hour of electricity (Davis, 2012).

In terms of waste management, policy must address a number of unresolved issues, especially the standards that limit the risk of cancer from radioactive exposure, the protection of future generations, and intergenerational and intragenerational equity. At the moment, these questions are unresolved.

For specific areas of energy policy, Lester (2016) recommends that, with his first era of nuclear innovation, from the present to 2030, "Nuclear 1.0," government should attach a value to nuclear power generation, compared to wind and solar, whose intermittency creates a cost in terms of reliability. In the second era, 2030–2050, "Nuclear 2.0," policy should promote advanced power systems and modular construction techniques. In the final era, beyond 2050, "Nuclear 3.0," nuclear policy should help to mitigate climate change. Advanced nuclear technology serves as insurance, in case other technologies either fail to materialize or lose their economic viability.

THE NUCLEAR DEBATE

On one hand, nuclear technology is established, contributes to the supply of electricity, does not generate greenhouse gas emissions during operation, and remains an important contributor to the world's energy supply. According to Lester (2016),

> A new generation of nuclear technologies holds promise. . . . The outcome is far from certain, but no worthwhile innovation initiative ever is. Moreover, the need for nuclear innovation is global, since the current generation of nuclear technologies is struggling to compete with fossil fuels in much of the rest of the world. . . . The innovation roadmap . . . has the potential to restore U.S. leadership in a field that, notwithstanding the hopes of many environmental activists and the gloomy prognostications of some pundits, is most likely still in the early stages of development.

On the other hand, opposition to industry expansion includes NIMBY, vested interests, intellectual opposition, and opportunistic opposition (Herring, 2010). The not-in-my-backyard argument entails local opposition. Vested interests include opposition by competing industries such as natural gas. Intellectual opposition provides explanations as to why nuclear technology should not expand. Opportunistic opposition by social groups attacks nuclear policies that encourage industry expansion. For this side of the debate, Cooper (2014) argues that

> the failure of nuclear economics is not just bad luck. Nuclear power is inherently uneconomic because it relies on a catastrophically dangerous resource that is vulnerable to human frailties and the vicissitudes of Mother Nature. The severe threats to public safety posed by nuclear power and the evolving demands of safety result in an extremely complex technology that requires long lead times and large sunk capital costs. The technology suffers constant cost escalation and does not exhibit cost reducing processes that are observed in other industries. Therefore, any nation that claims to have the wherewithal (technical expertise and economic resources) to build a "safe" nuclear reactor will have the wherewithal to meet its needs for electricity with alternatives that are less costly and less risky.

Over time, the winning argument will influence the trajectory of the industry. Whether one takes the pro- or anti-nuclear side depends on how one values the arguments. By the end of the second decade of this century, in the United States, five aging reactors retired early, two dozen more were at risk for early closure, and many major upgrades in the industry were canceled.

But China, India, and South Korea have ambitious plans for industry expansion. Many reactors are in the pipeline (more than twenty in China and sixty worldwide). But national plans for nuclear expansion do not match the expected retirement of the global fleet. As a result, the share of nuclear power in global energy is likely to decrease. We have to keep in mind, however, that the first demonstration of nuclear fission came sixteen years before the first photovoltaic cell. Solar cells are still considered new technology. Nuclear technology, therefore, will continue to develop for decades, especially with respect to a promising new reactor design for small modular reactors.

NEW REACTOR DESIGN: THE CASE OF SMALL MODULAR REACTORS

An evolving technology, the small modular reactor (SMR), has capacity below 300 megawatts electrical (MWe). The current generation of baseload nuclear plants has capacity of 1,000 MWe or higher. The SMR technology is intended to reduce capital costs, provide power away from electricity grids, and integrate advanced nuclear technologies with production capabilities. SMRs could replace decommissioned coal-fired power plants. SMRs have small size and modularity; standardized and fabricated components; simplified deployment; transportation capability by truck or rail to a nuclear power site; cost control for manufacturers; passive safety design; integration of major systems into a single unit; below ground deployment that eases safety concerns and costs; and the ability to meet small increases in demand in power generation.

Given their characteristics, SMRs are built in factories, transported, and installed on-site. Because of modular design, the possibility exists of linking multiple units together, which would lead to economies of scale. SMRs are in an advanced stage of development, closer to production than Generation IV large reactors. According to Vegel and Quinn (2017), potential demand in the United States could support the construction of a factory that would manufacture SMRs. But the viability of SMRs depends on cost, especially when compared to large reactors. In addition, safety concerns of SMRs persist, including close proximity to population centers, shrinking containment, staffing concerns, inspection, and flooding. Over time, SMRs may be economically competitive on a per-kilowatt hour basis, but regulatory fees from the NRC would have to be adjusted to reflect smaller output from SMRs.

SUMMARY

Nuclear power generates baseload electricity and contributes to a country's energy needs. But the problems of construction cost, safety, proliferation, and radioactive waste prevent global expansion. As a result, its relative share in global primary energy is declining, although nuclear electricity generation will continue to rise in absolute terms. With privatization and liberalization of the power sector, investors often do not invest in nuclear technology. Reasons include high financial risk, capital-intensive operations, an uncertain timeframe for construction and licensing, and safety liabilities. It is difficult to estimate construction cost before a plant becomes operational or exactly how long it will take to build. The nuclear industry has not achieved cost savings through commercialization that often occurs with innovation. More stringent regulations, a lack of standardization, and uncertain future environmental regulations contribute to the lack of cost savings. These factors are compounded by safety concerns that resulted from three major nuclear accidents: Three Mile Island, Chernobyl, and Fukushima.

CONCEPTS

Fission
Fusion
Isotopes
Light water reactors
Nuclear fuel cycle
Overnight construction costs
Paris Agreement
Probabilistic risk assessment
Proliferation
Radioactive decay
Uranium reserves

QUESTIONS

1. To help contain radioactive releases, should nuclear power plants be sited underground?

2. Why would a country pursue nuclear weapons but not a nuclear energy program?
3. In his article on nuclear proliferation, Narang (2017) argues that proliferation strategies are important. Why does he make this claim? Do you agree?
4. What countries have both nuclear power and nuclear weapons programs? Why do nuclear energy programs rarely lead to proliferation? Are there examples of countries with nuclear power that may develop nuclear weapons? What factors are important?
5. Study the process of PRA. What are the core features and levels of risk? For Three Mile Island, Chernobyl, or Fukushima, draw an "event tree" that maps the sequence of events from initiating problem to consequences. At each step, show the implication of system failure.
6. Of the four challenges of nuclear technology—proliferation, radioactive waste management, cost, and safety—which is the most important? Why?
7. What kinds of risks originate outside of nuclear power plants?
8. Over the next decade, do you think nuclear power will contribute more or less to electricity generation in the United States and the world? To aid your answer, construct a forecast.

Part 3

MOVING FORWARD

Chapter 11

The Rise of Renewable Energy

NEW ENERGY

Alternatives exist for the pollution-belching, environmental degrading, and climate abasement that results from the consumption of fossil fuels. Fossil fuel power creates hundreds of billions of annual dollars of negative externalities (Sovacool and Watts, 2009). Alternatively, Sovacool and Watts (2009) argue that two countries, the United States and New Zealand, are already equipped to produce 100 percent of their electricity using *renewable energy*, collected from renewable resources and replenished on a human time scale. Germany and Iceland are close. Finding ways to generate electricity with renewables would create economic, environmental, and social benefits.

Public policies and private sector initiatives contribute to the growth of renewable energy. For example, renewable portfolio standards, already in place in many states, specify the amount of electricity that must come from renewable sources. In addition, many tech companies use hydropower technology. Many retailers employ solar power.

Renewable resources may be exhaustible or inexhaustible. Renewable but *exhaustible energy resources,* such as bioenergy, geothermal, and hydropower, are vulnerable to depletion if the rate of extraction or usage exceeds the rate of replenishment. Renewable and *inexhaustible energy resources*, such as solar and wind, do not face the same constraint.

In 2017, fossil fuels accounted for the largest share of energy demand in the United States, according to U.S. EIA (2018a):

- Natural gas (36%)
- Oil (32%)
- Coal (14%)

- Renewables (10%)
- Nuclear electric power (8%)

In terms of renewables in the United States, in 2017, hydropower accounted for the largest share, according to U.S. EIA (2018a):

- Hydro (25%)
- Wind (21%)
- Biofuels (21%)
- Wood (21%)
- Solar (6%)
- Biomass waste (4%)
- Geothermal (2%)

Marginal cost provides additional context. The marginal cost of electricity is the additional cost of providing the next unit of output, measured in cents per kilowatt hour. Renewables such as wind and hydropower are more competitive than fossil fuels (Sovacool and Watts, 2009):

- Offshore wind (2.6 ¢/kWh)
- Hydroelectric (2.8 ¢/kWh)
- Onshore wind (5.6 ¢/kWh)
- Geothermal (6.4 ¢/kWh)
- Biomass combustion (6.9 ¢/kWh)
- Coal (7.2 ¢/kWh)
- Gas oil combined cycle (8.5 ¢/kWh)
- Solar thermal (18.8 ¢/kWh)
- Nuclear (24 ¢/kWh)

Generating electricity from renewables leads to three clear benefits. First, from an environmental perspective, renewables offer a method to reduce greenhouse gas emissions when they replace fossil fuels. Second, from an energy perspective, a greater production of renewables helps to diversity the country's energy supply. Third, from an economics perspective, less dependence on fossil fuel imports decreases the exposure of economies to international price and market fluctuations.

Given these benefits, this chapter argues that the way forward is to increase the supply of renewables. Currently, hydropower accounts for the greatest share of global and renewable electricity production (16%). Other renewable technologies, including bioenergy, geothermal, solar, tides, and wind, account for more than 6 percent (figure 11.1). To address these issues, the chapter first analyzes policies for renewable energy. It then considers

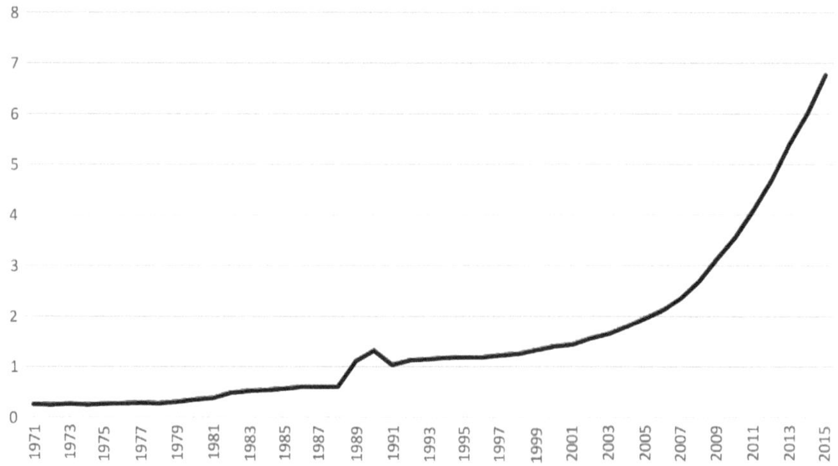

Figure 11.1 Percentage of Global Electricity from Renewable Sources, Excluding Hydroelectric. *Source*: Author using data from The World Bank, https://data.worldbank.org/indicator/EG.ELC.RNWX.ZS.

individual forms of renewable energy from technological, economic, and sustainability perspectives.

PUBLIC POLICIES FOR RENEWABLES

To establish a clean energy economy, large-scale investment must occur in renewable energy technologies. Public and private partnerships must serve as the main drivers for growth. The labeling of "clean" electricity and reliance on consumer choice must provide alternatives to obligatory processes. If consumers could choose between clean/renewable and dirty/nonrenewable, they would make informed decisions. To encourage this movement, policy must eliminate existing barriers and deliver financial support to renewable projects.

Feed-in-tariffs reduce cost, accelerate the diffusion of green technologies, foster learning, and attract investment. With feed-in-tariffs, the public sector purchases energy above market price. A long-term offer guarantees a purchase agreement for green energy producers. The tariff equals the difference between purchase and market price. The producers then sell electricity to the grid. Over time, the tariff is adjusted downward. The decrease in the tariff traces the reduction in cost of renewable technology. The policy maintains profitability for newly commissioned projects. But policy success depends on both the size of the tariff and how it adjusts over time. Among the global policy mechanisms for renewable energy, feed-in-tariffs are the most prevalent. They are responsible for encouraging more than half of global solar photovoltaic output and wind production (Alizamir et al., 2016). They are in place in almost 100 regions in the world.

Renewable portfolio standards, offered at the state level, mandate that utilities provide a percentage of electricity from renewable sources. The standards promote domestic energy production, diversify the supply of energy, reduce greenhouse gas emissions, and lead to economic development. The majority of U.S. states have either mandatory or voluntary renewable portfolio standards. The States of Hawaii and California have the most aggressive renewable portfolio standards, requiring 100 percent electricity production with renewables by 2045.

At the federal level, two tax credits encourage electricity production from renewables. The *Renewable Electricity Production Tax Credit*—implemented on a per-kilowatt-hour basis—applies for the first ten years of a facility's operation and encourages growth in the wind industry. The *Renewable Investment Tax Credit* applies to certain renewable energy investments, including solar and geothermal. The level of the credit is determined by the value and type of technology.

BIOENERGY

Humans have used *bioenergy*—energy from organic matter—throughout history. The process began with the burning of wood for heating and cooking. Today, wood still serves as the largest source of energy from biomass. But bioenergy power plants derive biofuels directly from energy crops or indirectly from industrial, commercial, domestic, or agricultural wastes. A variety of bioenergy resources are used to produce heat, transportation fuels, and electricity.

Bioenergy resources are agricultural, forest, and secondary. Agricultural resources include grains; oil crops; crop residues from small grains, wheat, and corn; perennially grown trees and grasses; annual crops; and woody crops grown on pasture and cropland. Forest resources include fuelwood; residues from the harvesting of commercial timber; thinnings; and forest residues from land conversion. Secondary resources include residues from wood processing mills; pulping liquors; unused mill residue; crop processing residue; waste greases and oil; urban wood waste, and animal manure. Collectively, these resources meet a growing demand for bioenergy. However, concerns about both the energy requirements necessary for production and the environmental implications of consumption require a careful consideration of costs and benefits.

Bioenergy Technology

Two types of bioenergy technology exist. Traditional technology entails the process of burning charcoal and wood. Charcoal and wood have been used for fires and cooking since the early days of human existence. In rural areas, they remain an important source of energy. Some of the health and environmental costs associated with this traditional technology include deforestation, pollution, and smoke inhalation. More advanced stoves that offer better ventilation and require less fuel both improve efficiency and reduce emissions.

Modern bioenergy technology includes resources for electricity generation, vehicles, and heating boilers. For example, power plants may generate electricity using solid, liquid, or gaseous biofuels, such as starches from corn, sugar cane, or wheat. Biomass conversion occurs with biochemical, chemical, or thermal processes. Biochemical conversion uses bacteria, enzymes, or other organisms to convert biomass into gas, solid, or liquid fuels. Chemical conversion uses chemical interactions to transform biomass into different forms of energy. Thermal processes use heat to convert biomass into energy. These applications create different biofuels.

The process of cogeneration creates both heat and electricity. In a power station or heat engine, this small-scale process uses *feedstock*—a raw material used as input for an industrial process—and attempts to minimize carbon emissions. Furthermore, *biodiesel*—fuel from crops such as soybeans, sunflowers, canola, and mustard—contains no petroleum, but may be blended with petroleum diesel to reduce the release of hydrocarbons, carbon monoxide, and particulates. Applications of biodiesel include vehicles, railways, aircrafts, heating oil, and generators.

Economics of Bioenergy

Currently, more than fifty countries have implemented mandates, blending targets, or biofuels quotas. In upcoming decades, global demand for biofuels is therefore expected to increase. Bioenergy production reflects the inclusion in energy systems of multiple bio-based forms of energy. Appropriate policies for land expansion must therefore balance the need for food production with bioenergy expansion. With direct land use changes, new cropland is developed for the production of biofuels feedstocks. With indirect land use changes, existing cropland is developed for the production of biofuels feedstocks, creating other uses for new cropland.

Global markets for biomass are volatile, diverse, and differ with respect to the technology involved. The power and industrial sectors consume more than half of the world's biomass supply. Biodiesel and ethanol from agricultural crops are the most commonly produced transportation biofuels, although ethanol production is higher. With respect to feedstocks, corn, sugarcane, and soybeans make sizable contributions to biofuels production.

Economic influences include new technologies, the renewable properties of bioenergy, and public policy. The competitiveness of bioenergy depends on conversion efficiencies, production costs, the price of fossil energy feedstocks, and the world price of oil. Considering these factors, few markets of bioenergy production are economically viable in the absence of government intervention. Economic viability requires blending mandates and tax credits. In the United States, corn-based ethanol is competing with gasoline, but blending with gasoline serves as the economic model. The United States exports corn-based ethanol. If residues or wastes are used, electricity generation is more competitive, especially with respect to combine heat and power technologies.

The economic consequences of increasing bioenergy capacity involve the relationship between bioenergy markets and conventional markets for agricultural commodities. Over time, biofuel production is forecasted to consume a growing share of the world's grains, vegetable oils, and sugarcane. Higher global demand for biofuels is driving conversion of native ecosystems and forests into crops for biofuels feedstocks. This trend could put upward pressure on the prices of industrial food varieties. In poorer regions, it could also increase food insecurity. The impacts on fresh water resources, biodiversity, economic growth, and employment will depend on the extent to which bioenergy is integrated into energy systems.

Bioenergy and Sustainability

As an energy resource, bioenergy satisfies one out of the six sustainability criteria from chapter 1: long-term energy supply. If the cultivated land for bioenergy is managed, bioenergy provides a renewable and long-term source of energy.

But bioenergy does not satisfy the other criteria. It does not contribute to baseload electricity generation. It does not satisfy the environmental impacts criterion. Commodity crops such as corn and soybeans require fields of monoculture, rather than crop variety. Monoculture deprives the soil of nutrients that occur through crop rotation, leads to chemical applications, and damages local water supplies. In addition, the expansion of land dedicated to bioenergy production, including palm oil in Southeast Asia, contributes to deforestation. Bioenergy does not satisfy the atmospheric impact criterion. When the land is cleared of carbon-holding vegetation to grow energy crops, carbon is released. Bioenergy satisfies neither the human health nor the economic performance criteria. Large-scale monoculture re-allocates land from food production to bioenergy production. This reallocation increases both food prices and insecurity.

Future Prospects of Bioenergy

Moving forward, a number of issues will influence the growth of bioenergy markets. First, current policies are driving the expansion of biofuels, including the U.S. Renewable Fuel Standard, the EU's Renewable Energy Directive, California's Low Carbon Fuel Standard, and both Indonesia's and Brazil's biofuels mandates. The extent to which these policies incentivize bioenergy production will determine market trends. Second, when compared to fossil fuels, the greenhouse gas emissions of biofuels are lower. An important issue here is whether biomass is used as a feedstock for transportation or as a biofuel in energy systems. Another important issue is whether biofuels in energy systems replace coal, natural gas, or nuclear power. Third, policies that encourage renewables will increasingly address the problem of climate change. Because of this factor, many energy analysts are opposed to growth in crop-based biofuels. Some even favor phase-outs or caps on biofuels. The reason is that bioenergy harms the environment more than other forms of renewable energy. Considering these factors, the future prospects of bioenergy depend on whether bioenergy feedstocks gravitate to the highest value markets; whether they compete with fossil fuels, nuclear power, solar, and wind for electricity generation; and whether they compete with wood products, food production, and wildlife for land.

GEOTHERMAL ENERGY

Geothermal energy is the use of heat or thermal activities from the Earth. Geothermal energy is renewable but exhaustible. The reason is that, for geothermal systems, it is possible for the rate of extraction to exceed the average rate of heat flow to the thermal reservoir rising from the Earth's magma. If the rate of extraction is less than or equal to the rate of replenishment, geothermal energy is stable over time. But this is often not the case. Extraction from both wells and downhole pumps may lead to continuous withdrawal, which creates conditions of both reduction and depletion. Typical geothermal reservoirs have a life span of thirty to fifty years, as the geothermal technology wears out or the heat supply is depleted. Even though reservoir modeling shows that the process for many geothermal systems will create a continuous flow of heat for decades, the assumption of exhaustibility highlights the potential of future scarcity conditions at specific sites.

Thermal activity from inside the planet is driven by the heating of the mantle and lower crust by the thermal decay of radioactive isotopes. The deeper into the Earth, the hotter is the temperature. But for many areas that are close to the surface, the temperature is too low for geothermal processes. Some parts of the upper crust, however, experience high flows of heat. They are accessible in standard economic processes. Modeling of geothermal activity demonstrates that the amount of heat energy available within 3 kilometers of the surface is greater than the installed generation capacity of the world's electricity networks. But geothermal processes contribute 1 percent of global energy supply. The challenge is to tap into the vast potential of geothermal reserves.

Geothermal Technology

Geothermal technology is ubiquitous but marginally developed throughout the world. It provides power for buildings, greenhouses, industry, farms, and many other processes. The best sites for expansion are high-temperature hydrothermal systems with recent volcanic activity. Other productive sites are near active plate tectonic boundaries, including convergence and subduction zones. But many geothermal sites currently in use include crustal and mantle hot spots.

The Earth's mantle is composed of a number of elements, including iron heated to high temperatures. In some places, this superheated material rises to the Earth's crust. Two forms of technology take advantage of this geological reality: *convective* and *conductive* technologies. Convective systems use heat from the mantle flowing through the crust or magma within the crust. Most of the world's geothermal systems are convective, such as the liquid reservoirs in Iceland and Japan. With some of these systems, wells are drilled in areas of geothermal activity. Hot water known as *brine* is extracted and its energy is used. When developed as a closed system, surface contaminants do not pollute the brine. After the brine is used, it is injected back into deep wells within the Earth.

Conductive systems, in contrast, exist when high levels of heat create extremely hot rocks. Radioactive decay and insulating sedimentary layers supplement this process. In other situations, conductive heat is transferred to groundwater, creating warm springs. Finally, thermal blankets may emerge from rapid sedimentation, trapping conductive heat in strata.

Geothermal technology is used for thermal purposes—including heat pumps and direct heat—and electricity generation, which is measured in kilowatts or megawatts. The technical feasibility for these applications depends on the quantity and quality of geothermal resources. In the United States, heat pumps are the most widely used geothermal technology, involving wells, piping, and circulatory pumps. To meet the geothermal requirements of a house or building, underground water must achieve a sufficiently high temperature. When the water pumps through pipes, optimal systems minimize efficiency losses. In cooler months, the geothermal system transfers heat into surrounding air in the home or building. In hotter months, warm air is transferred to antifreeze or other chemicals in the piping system, cooling down the structure. But the ability to install heat pumps in a cost-effective manner is a function of both geological conditions and policy incentives.

Around the world, the direct use of heat from geothermal sources continues to grow. This technology has the potential for reducing thermal heating costs, because it may be employed in a decentralized manner. Increasingly common applications include greenhouses—especially where conditions are not conducive for outdoor crop production—aquaculture fish farms, and resorts with spas and swimming pools.

For electricity generation, operators employ either steam directly from geothermal sources or a hot pressurized liquid to generate a boiling point fluid for turbines. Closed-system binary turbines, used in medium-temperature environments, do not expose geothermal water to the surface environment. Over the long term, this structure has a better record in maintaining the quality of the geothermal reservoir, when compared to steam turbines. The binary system draws water from a geothermal source and runs it through a heat exchanger on the surface. The system transfers the heat to organic substances such as butane or pentane with low boiling points. The superheated butane or pentane is then sent to a turbine, which spins a generator for electricity generation. After this process, the system sends the butane or pentane through a condenser, cools it to a liquid form, then sends it back through the heat exchange, where it is converted back into steam and used in the next round of electricity generation. The system injects the geothermal brine back into the reservoir, and the process repeats.

Steam turbines are used in high-temperature environments. In these situations, steam emerges directly from wellheads. The pressurized steam passes through a turbine and is then condensed and cooled into liquid form. The turbine spins, a generator turns, and electricity is produced. The liquid resource is then injected back into the geothermal reservoir, which alters its average temperature and impacts future productivity. In fact, this process, when applied at high application rates for long periods of time, has reduced the capacity of some geothermal reservoirs to produce steam for electricity generation.

Long-term energy system decentralization will influence geothermal technology. The traditional model of the electric utility as a centralized and unidirectional source of power is changing. New network platforms are growing in importance. They are supporting smaller-scale geothermal technologies such as ground-sourced heat pumps, district heating systems, and smart thermal grids. Often developed by private companies, these smaller-scale technologies employ deep thermal heat extraction, but incorporate growing storage capacities.

Economics of Geothermal Energy

The economics of geothermal energy reflect market conditions, investment realities, and declining costs. Since the 1990s, privatization in the electricity market has transferred much of the world's geothermal capacity to private companies. This has minimized the ownership split between the power company and the resource. Exceptions exist in developing countries that reduce risk.

Global investment opportunities exist. While annual investment in geothermal energy is less than solar, wind, and bioenergy, investment opportunities include electricity production, surface exploration, field development, production drilling, and the direct use of heat. Countries with the highest levels of investment include Australia, China, Indonesia, Italy, Kenya, New Zealand, Philippines, South Korea, and the United States. In fact, with its geological landscape, the United States has the world's largest geothermal potential, followed by the Philippines and Indonesia.

Along with growing capacity, an important aspect of geothermal energy is its declining cost. Geothermal is generally considered costlier than gas-fired or coal-fired plants, onshore wind, and solar photovoltaic utilities. It is less expensive than solar photovoltaic from rooftops. On a per-kilowatt-hour basis, the cost of providing electricity using geothermal technology varies by continent, due to generation capacity, energy infrastructure, geology, and other factors. But on an average kWh basis, the cost is becoming more competitive with fossil fuels, nuclear, and renewables, according to the World Energy Council (2016b): $0.08 per kWh in Africa, $0.07 per kWh in Asia, $0.12 per kWh in Europe, $0.08 per kWh in North America, and $0.08 per kWh in South America.

The economics of geothermal energy are also influenced by government incentives, land access and use, and shifts in market power. With respect to renewable technologies, geothermal does not receive the same policy focus as solar and wind. As a result, with the exception of renewable portfolio standards that encourage a greater production of renewables in general, geothermal technology is not on the forefront of energy policy. This is one reason geothermal technology is not increasing as a share of total renewables. Another reason is the provision of geothermal energy requires substantial areas of land. To formalize land rights and compensation, developers work within the legal environment. But the consideration of legal systems serves as an economic risk for countries attempting to attract independent power producers.

Geothermal Energy and Sustainability

Of the six sustainability criteria established in chapter 1, geothermal energy satisfies three: energy supply, human health, and economic performance. But numerous studies and meteorological records indicate two important realities: the warming of subsurface temperatures in urban areas and geothermal energy as an untapped resource. First, around the world, warming trends in urban areas result from climate change and the process of urbanization. In turn, this effect of warmer urban areas has influenced nearby underground temperatures. The extra heat stored in underground aquifers serves as a potential thermal reservoir for space cooling and heating. Second, the amount of untapped thermal energy stored underground is capable of fulfilling part of the rising global demand for heating and cooling. With respect to human health effects, geothermal fluids—after the removal of heat—are reinjected into geothermal reservoirs below the levels of potable water. To the extent to which the process is successful, it avoids the contamination of water supplies. With economic performance, pressure to improve production and safety incentivize innovations in exploration, process modeling, and larger thermal operations.

Geothermal technology does not satisfy three sustainability criteria: baseload power, environmental impacts, and atmospheric consequences. With environmental impacts, geothermal technology leads to a number of chemical discharges into water and land and gas discharges into the air. It may also induce seismic activity. With atmospheric consequences, power production from geothermal resources results in the emission of greenhouse gases. With baseload power, geothermal produces a small percentage of electricity output.

Future Prospects of Geothermal Energy

The benefits of geothermal energy include availability, distribution, and total potential. Worldwide electricity production from geothermal is expanding, but opportunities for greater regional distribution exist. The total potential of geothermal energy is vast, because the Earth supplies an enormous amount of heat. Geothermal energy could supply many times the amount of electricity currently generated by the technology. Even though individual geothermal sites face geological constraints, over the next half century growth in geothermal energy will not be constrained by the availability of the resource. Climate change is not expected to reduce the ability of energy systems to expand the scope of geothermal technology.

HYDROPOWER

Hydropower, the world's largest source of renewable electricity with respect to investment and installed capacity, is generated by dams that channel flowing water. For more than 5,000 years, humans have been building dams. More than 2,000 years ago, the Greeks used hydropower to spin wheels to grind grain. Today, hydropower is a cost-effective method to generate electricity. The marginal cost of providing electricity from hydropower is lower than all sources of energy except offshore wind. China has the world's largest hydropower capacity, followed by the United States, Brazil, Canada, India, and Russia.

The world's installed capacity continues to grow. With almost 1,000 hydropower stations, Norway generates more than 95 percent of its electricity from hydropower. The world's largest hydropower station is the Three Gorges Plant in China, which holds the capacity to generate 100 terawatt hours per year, enough to power 80 million homes. Sovacool and Walter (2018), in an informative article in the journal *Energy*, note that hydropower dams supply a greater source of commercial energy than all the nuclear power plants in the world. The percentage of global electricity production from hydropower exceeds 15 percent, making it the world's most important renewable source of electricity (figure 11.2).

In recent years, a resurgence of hydropower has occurred around the world. More than 150 countries generate some hydroelectricity. In developing countries, hydropower offers the possibility to supply electricity to underserved populations. According to The World Bank (2014), nine countries

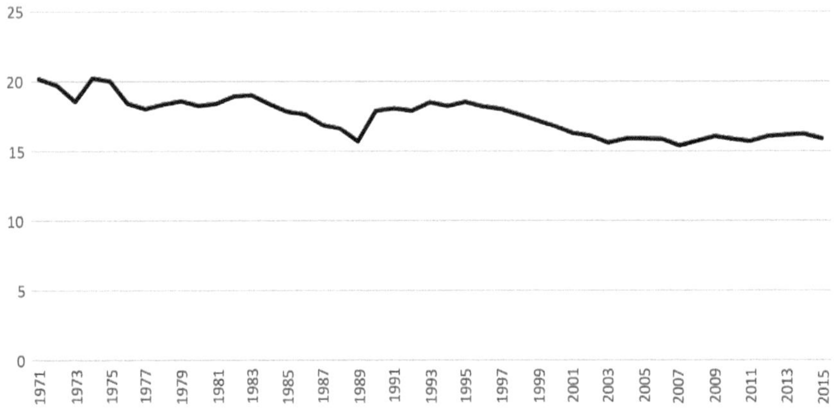

Figure 11.2 Percentage of Global Electricity Production from Hydroelectric Sources. *Source*: Author using data from The World Bank, https://data.worldbank.org/indicator/EG.ELC.HYRO.ZS.

generate more than 90 percent of their electricity from hydropower: Albania, Democratic Republic of Congo, Ethiopia, Kyrgyz Republic, Mozambique, Namibia, Nepal, Norway, and Paraguay. More than sixty countries generate at least 50 percent of their electricity from hydropower. The reality, however, is that the increase in hydropower capacity will partially but not fully close the global electricity gap, not substantially reduce carbon emissions, and continue to fragment many of the world's largest rivers. Dams fundamentally impact both human settlement patterns and the environment. As a result, we must evaluate the benefits of the expansion of hydropower capacity against the ecological, economic, and social costs.

Hydropower Technology

Hydropower technology consists of the generation of power by harnessing energy from flowing water. The technology generates electricity through the transformation of hydraulic energy into mechanical energy. The process activates a turbine, which powers a generator. According to the World Energy Council (2016c), hydropower plants are site-specific, but exist in four categories:

- Storage hydropower: when a dam impounds river water and then releases it to generate electricity. This technology may operate independently of hydrological flows for weeks or months. It is used to provide both baseload and peak load power to the electric grid.
- Run-of-river hydropower: when a facility channels flowing water through a floodgate or canal to generate electricity. This form of technology has short-term water storage and little land inundation. It is used to provide baseload power to the electric grid.
- Pumped-storage hydropower: when a facility cycles water between an upper and lower reservoir by pumps to generate electricity. When the demand for electricity is high, water released to the lower reservoir spins turbines. It is used to provide peak load power to the electric grid.
- Offshore marine hydropower: when a facility uses the power of currents or waves or the characteristics of large bodies of water to generate electricity. These newer technologies are emerging, but include rivers, oceans, tidal streams, and ocean thermal technologies.

Economics of Hydropower

An economic evaluation of hydropower includes the sources of investment, capital outlays, the cost of electricity, and risk. Investment in hydropower technology has normally been the responsibility of the public sector, because these projects require major capital outlays. But recently many private companies have entered the market, building hydropower capacity in order to power aspects of their production processes. Many technology companies serve as examples. In terms of capital outlays, hydropower plants sometimes come under criticism for cost overruns. But this is not unique to hydropower technology. In general, smaller hydropower systems are relatively more expensive. Construction costs include engineering, designs, materials, labor, grid connections, and access upgrades. The largest maintenance task is keeping the intake screen clear of objects floating in the river.

With respect to the cost of generating electricity, hydropower offers a large benefit. With hydropower technology, no expenditure is required for fuels. This contrasts with expenditures for uranium (with nuclear power) and natural gas or coal (with fossil steam). As a result, data from the U.S. Energy Information Administration on average power plant operating expenses demonstrate much lower operating costs for hydropower, when compared to nuclear and fossil steam (the data are easy to find with an internet search).

Risk results from the costs of unforeseen problems. During operation, low maintenance cost and zero fuel requirements mean revenues are stable. These factors make the life of typical hydropower plants long (50–100 years). But climate change and unpredictable patterns of rainfall and snowfall may alter the hydrological potential of many of the world's rivers. Therefore, once the plant is operational, short-term risks decline; however, long-term risk exists in the form of changes in both hydrological and environmental conditions.

Hydropower and Sustainability

In terms of the six sustainability criteria from chapter 1, hydropower satisfies three: energy supply, baseload power, and human health. Hydropower capacity will exist over the course of the long term. The technology contributes to baseload power, particularly in run-of-river hydropower plants. Hydropower is nonpolluting, so human health effects are minimal.

But hydropower does not satisfy three other criteria: environmental impacts, atmospheric consequences, and economic performance. With respect to environmental impacts, on one hand, hydropower may bring benefits with flood protection, drought management, and irrigation. On the other hand, hydropower dams lead to the fragmentation of large rivers systems, eliminating their classification as free-flowing. This water resource exploitation generates inexpensive electricity, but causes the loss of biodiversity, natural habitats, fish migrations, and ecosystems. In terms of the atmospheric criterion, hydropower leads to methane emissions, when the decay of vegetation left in reservoirs produces this greenhouse gas. Hydropower does not satisfy the economic performance criterion. According to Sovacool and

Walter (2018), countries that rely more heavily on hydropower have lower economic growth rates, higher rates of poverty, more internal conflicts, and higher rates of public debt.

The implication of these results is that we must carefully scrutinize all aspects of hydropower, including construction, production, and impacts. With respect to costs and benefits, hydropower projects are site-specific. Medium- and smaller-scale hydroelectricity projects may contribute more effectively to a country's mix of electricity-generating options. Dams that are built on reservoirs in mountain or remote areas with no local populations may generate electricity with minimal impacts. Others built in low-lying plains may increase food insecurity. These latter dams may minimize the cost of connecting the plant to the grid, but lead to human resettlement, as in the case of the Three Gorges Dam in China. The net benefit of hydropower, therefore, is not predetermined, but depends on context and its degree of equity.

Future Prospects of Hydropower

Global population growth, climate change, and the need to boost electricity production have increased the demand for renewable forms of energy. But an increase in hydropower capacity, fueled by dozens of new dam projects, is planned or underway. Many of these projects exist in countries with emerging economies. In particular, the development of future hydropower is concentrated in Africa, South America, and Southeast Asia. The Ganges-Brahmaputra basin (in Nepal and India) and the Yangtze basin (China) will experience most of the new dam construction in Southeast Asia, while the Amazon and La Plata basins (Brazil) will have most of the dam construction in South America (Zarfl, 2015). Over time, how much new hydropower capacity is developed will be a function of competing renewable options, government policy, and market conditions.

SOLAR

Solar energy is renewable and inexhaustible. Although two forms of technology, *photovoltaic* (PV) devices and *concentrated solar* plants, may harness the power of the sun, the technology that attracts the most research focus is PV devices. The reason is that solar cells exist as a pure form of renewable technology. Sunlight is abundant. The process entails the direct conversion of sunlight into electricity. After production, no complex industrial process is required. In a short period of time, solar panels may be installed on the roofs of houses or buildings. These connections do not require complicated transmission lines or grids. As a result of these benefits, no technology among the portfolio of renewables generates as high expectations as directly harnessing the power of the sun. Ultimately, it may be the case that solar energy will serve as the fundamental source of electricity. When the time comes, both PV and concentrated solar systems will transform the entire energy system.

Solar Technology

Solar technology provides two conceptual options: a decentralized network where buildings and houses are power generators with solar panels or a network of generating stations (concentrated solar), where the dispatched electricity stems from solar power. A probable option in moving forward is the expansion of both of these forms of technology. But any pathway requires an increase in scale. Greater scale, in turn, necessitates lower costs. Lower costs depend on continuous innovation.

Photovoltaic modules generate power directly from sunlight. They come in two types, thin film, which uses non-crystal, semiconducting materials coated on glass panels, and crystalline PV, which uses silicon as the main material. With each of these technologies, tradeoffs exist. Thin film technology is cheaper to make but less efficient in converting sunlight into energy. Scientists are even experimenting with nanotechnology to manufacture solar cells. Nanomaterials possess desirable characteristics such as stability, high catalytic activity, and easier preparation techniques. Over time, the introduction of solar cells manufactured from nanomaterials could revolutionize the solar marketplace.

The production cost of solar cells has decreased because of innovations with thin film technology. With this technology, sunlight descends on solar cells. In the process, photons—one form of energy—are absorbed. In a semiconductor, the photons first dislodge and then displace electrons—another form of energy. The loose electrons flow along miniature channels as electric current. Thin film solar panels, made with solar cells with extremely small absorbing layers for sunlight, provide light PV cells, high levels of durability, and low costs of installation.

Photovoltaics offer a promising growth market. But they are not the only pathway forward. Concentrated solar is similar to traditional electricity production. This process is like electricity generation from fossil fuel plants, but the input is sunlight and no carbon emissions exist. Once a concentrated beam of light is converted into heat, it generates electric power. It offers an environmentally friendly method of power generation without large operating costs.

Concentrated solar systems generate power using mirrors, which reflect sunlight onto receiver tubes. A heat transfer fluid such as synthetic oil absorbs the sun's energy. The fluid is heated to very high levels, often 750°F or more. The heated fluid passes through a heat exchanger, which heats water and produces steam. The steam powers a conventional steam turbine, generating electricity. A typical concentrated solar farm uses hundreds of parallel rows of mirrors, connected as a series, and placed on a north-south axis. The mirrors then track the sun from east to west. Concentrated solar power stations are in operation in the southwest of the United States, Spain, India, South Africa, Morocco, and China. Because the systems possess high capital costs, the technology is suited for large solar power stations.

Ultimately, the success of solar technology depends on the installation of utility- and commercial-scale installation and PV panels. The larger the solar system, the greater the reduction in both capital and installation costs. In terms of output, concentrated solar technology generates higher levels of electricity production than PV panels. But PV panels require smaller spaces.

Economics of Solar Power

The market for sunlight, while growing annually during this century, is smaller than the market for wind. When compared to other renewables, industry growth has been more volatile. The sentiment of investors and manufacturers has swung from positions of optimism to pessimism and back. The introduction of public incentives often propels these sentiments. But greater global capacity, lower production costs, and the persistence of government subsidies have contributed to a growing market. With global capacity exceeding 400 gigawatts and rising every year, China, the United States, India, and members of the European Union lead the world in additions to capacity. For perspective, the production of 1 terawatt (1,000 gigawatts) of solar power would equal the output of 3.125 billion PV panels.

The decrease in the cost of PV technology is a function of three factors. First, the increase in global manufacturing capacity for solar cells has outstripped demand. This has led to price competition on a global scale. China, for example, annually exports dozens of gigawatts of solar panels. Chinese manufacturing is set up as a growth industry, but is affected by global demand conditions and protectionist policies. Second, there has been a dramatic decrease in the price of silicon, the raw material used in solar panels. Because of this market reality, end-users have benefited from less expensive solar electricity. Third, as the solar industry grows, so does investment from venture capitalists. As the preference for clean power expands globally, competition from both established and venture capital funded start-ups propels efficiency gains.

Solar and Sustainability

Both PV and concentrated solar technologies use the sun's energy. These technologies satisfy five of the six sustainability criteria: long-term energy supply, limited environmental impacts, limited atmospheric consequences, positive health effects, and contributions to the economy as a growth market. Currently, solar technology does not have the capacity to provide baseload power. From a sustainability perspective, a major advantage of solar power is the satisfaction of both the environmental and the atmospheric criteria. Once solar panels and concentrated solar systems are operational, no harm to the environment or atmosphere occurs. Because of the high sustainability rating, solar power offers primary technology for the transition to a clean energy economy.

Future Prospects of Solar

Since the inception of both PV and concentrated solar technology, continuous growth in the marketplace has occurred. These technologies create highly sustainable forms of energy. But each technology possesses its own incentives, marketplace, and prospects. The economic returns of concentrated solar plants are higher; however, the capital costs for PV are lower. Moving forward, future growth in the market for each technology will depend on increasing capacity, decreasing costs, government support, and changing preferences for solar technology. Each technology is appropriate for different contexts: PV for decentralized markets such as homes and buildings and concentrated solar for centralized but clean forms of power generation.

WIND

Wind power is renewable and inexhaustible. While sunlight leads to life on Earth and is destined to become a major global source of renewable power, wind technology has already arrived. Buoyed by declining costs and climate principles, the global market for wind is characterized by increasing capacity. At the end of the second decade of this century, total installed global solar capacity grew to more than 400 gigawatts; however, total installed global wind capacity grew to more than 500 gigawatts, rising by more than 50 GW annually. This trend is expected to continue.

Wind Technology

The main reason for the growth in global wind capacity involves advances in mechanical engineering. The preeminent wind technology incorporates three rotors or blades shaped like propellers, elevated on a tower, and a drivetrain that includes a gearbox and generator, necessary components for electricity generation. With this technology, power is transmitted from the rotors to the generator through the main shaft and drivetrain. When wind is harvested by turbines, electricity flows into local grids.

The allocation of research, development, and deployment funds have improved the design of rotors, which were formally made of lightweight steel but are now made of fiberglass or composite materials such as carbon fibers with high levels of durability. The largest machines feature blades as long as football fields, standing twenty stories tall. They produce up to 750 kilowatts, enough electricity to power 1,400 homes. Smaller but common versions stand 30 feet, have rotors up to 25 feet in diameter, and produce 50 kilowatts. They supply the power needs of a business or home. The most efficient turbines today average 30 percent efficiency, a percentage that increases over time. The modular design of contemporary turbines means they may be installed in a few days. Technological challenges include operational limitations (because wind turbines generate power less than half the time) and the potential for storm damage.

Wind farms are built in a variety of locations, including shallow coastlines of oceans and lakes, rows of hills, open plains, deserts, mountain ridges, agricultural fields, and the rims of river gorges. To maximize the amount of harvested wind, hundreds of turbines are arranged in patterns. For the sake of example, 500 wind turbines, each producing 1 megawatt of power, could replace one typical coal plant, which is about 500 megawatts in size, providing power for 1,500 homes. One problem, however, is the amount of space necessary to build such a wind farm. It requires extensive use of territory. As a result, the offshore option is promising. Another problem is wind speed. Harvestable energy is proportional to the cube of wind speed. As a result, a small increase in speed creates a large increase in power. For this reason, mapping wind speeds by region provides guidance for the optimal location of wind farms.

Economics of Wind Power

With respect to economic considerations, wind power is stronger at night. But this trend corresponds to a period of lower demand. Some countries such as Germany, the United Kingdom, and France have addressed this issue by locating wind farms in many different areas. For the European Union as a whole, the development of a supergrid allows integration of renewable energy sources from both remote and common locations. From the Baltic Seas in the North, the coasts of Ireland in the west, and the Bay of Biscay in the south, the system would incorporate wind power from offshore and onshore locations to electricity load centers. The idea is to balance wind power from different parts of the system, solar energy from as far away as the Sahara desert, and hydro power from France, Italy, Norway, and Spain. When it is completed, the supergrid will have a capacity of hundreds of gigawatts. In this framework, wind power is viewed as one of many sources in a growing portfolio of renewable energy options.

In the global wind industry, capacity continues to rise with specific growth areas in China, India, Europe, and offshore. Wind technology is in a process of rapid transition to full commercialization, declining subsidies, and successful competition with fossil fuels and nuclear. Capital costs continue to decline, averaging about $1,000/kWh onshore and about $1,500/kWh offshore. Falling prices to as low as $0.03/kwh make wind competitive in most markets but reduce profits along the supply chain. In the United States, wind energy has provided around 6 percent of total electricity generation. For the world, the percentage is five. With low fossil fuel prices, wind energy has not been competitive in the marketplace. But that trend is changing. The wind industry has advanced to the point where new capacity is cheaper than incumbent generation. It provides carbon-free electricity with falling costs.

Wind and Sustainability

From a sustainability perspective, a number of characteristics make wind appealing. Industry growth, falling costs, and the spreading of wind technology to all continents have moved wind power beyond a niche industry. It is one of the most environmentally friendly technologies. When it is used to replace fossil fuels, wind energy reduces both air pollution and greenhouse gas emissions. It also preserves water resources by not consuming the millions of gallons of water used by the electric power sector. On a global scale, it continues to lead to job creation, supporting a strong supply chain. It also increases community revenues. Land lease agreements and property taxes lead to additional forms of revenue. But some challenges exist. Siting and land use concerns remain. Near urban area, resorts, and habitats for endangered species, objections to wind technology persist. It is possible that wind turbines remove land from alternative uses, but their height and design allow for grazing and farming to continue. In terms of the six sustainability criteria from chapter 1, wind power therefore satisfies five: energy supply, limited environmental impacts, no atmospheric consequences, human health, and economic performance. But it does not currently contribute to baseload power generation. Nevertheless, its overall sustainability ranking is high compared to other energy resources.

Future Prospects of Wind

Future prospects for wind are bright. Because of growing markets, development of offshore sites, and growing concern about climate change, global capacity is expected to rise. While wind power is becoming more reliable in Asia, North America, and Europe, developments in Latin America, the Middle East, and Africa are expected to expand global capacity. A large wind farm in Latin America, for example, the Reynosa Wind Farm, operates in the state of Tamaulipas in Mexico. Opened in 2018, possessing more than 100 turbines, it generates 400 megawatts of electricity. While the North American Development Bank finances wind projects, the private sector provided funds. In examples such as this, it is challenging to predict future wind patterns so investors may recoup their investments. Another challenge is the cost of transmission. Some of the best locations for wind are not close to important population and industrial centers. Therefore, for the foreseeable future, wind will serve as a vital supplement to but not a major source of global electricity.

SUMMARY

Renewable energy resources provide an alternative to the traditional forms of energy: fossil fuels and nuclear power. While the renewable market is growing, hydropower, wind power, and bioenergy currently account for the largest shares. Public policies for renewable energy—including feed-in-tariffs, renewable portfolio standards, and renewable tax credits—incentivize greater levels of production. Bioenergy resources are used for electricity, transportation fuels, and the production of heat. Geothermal energy provides power for farms, industry, homes, buildings, and greenhouses. For many places in the world, hydropower serves as an important source of electricity. Solar technology, although a small percentage of the market, is growing in terms of capacity. Wind power offers the potential for electricity generation with little environmental impact. Each form of renewable energy scores highly in terms of sustainability criteria with the exception of bioenergy.

CONCEPTS

Biodiesel
Bioenergy
Brine
Concentrated solar
Conductive geothermal systems
Convective geothermal systems
Exhaustible energy resources
Feed-in-tariffs
Feedstock
Geothermal energy
Hydropower
Offshore marine hydropower

Photovoltaic
Pumped-storage hydropower
Renewable Electricity Production Tax Credit
Renewable energy
Renewable Investment Tax Credit
Renewable portfolio standards
Run-of-river hydropower
Storage hydropower

QUESTIONS

1. With bioenergy conversion, what sustainability questions emerge, especially with respect to environmental and atmospheric consequences?
2. What are the different types of geothermal power plants? What are their costs and benefits? In particular, what sites are suitable for geothermal development?
3. With respect to hydropower technology, should cost-benefit analyses of new projects consider both ecological and social impacts? On a new hydro project, conduct a cost-benefit analysis. Do net benefits occur?
4. What technological differences exist between solar photovoltaics and solar thermal systems? How do these technological differences translate into economic assessments of the technologies?
5. What are the economic and environmental barriers to greater wind power capacity? What public policies may address the barriers?
6. In a global context, is it possible for renewable energy technology to replace the electricity generated from fossil fuels and nuclear power? Explain whether you think the world will ever experience this transition.

Chapter 12

Energy, Economics, and the Climate Crisis

A CLIMATE IN CRISIS

The planet is smoldering. Wildfires in the Amazon and California, heat waves in Texas and Japan, droughts in Germany and Ethiopia, once rare, are now commonplace. As an example, nine of the ten deadliest heat waves ever recorded have taken place since 2000. These impacts of climate change are becoming more pronounced. Climate change—a change in global or regional climate patterns attributed to a higher atmospheric concentration of greenhouse gases (GHG) from the burning of fossil fuels—constitutes the major global environmental challenge of this century. An increase in GHG—gases in the atmosphere that absorb radiation within the thermal infrared range—are linked to higher average global temperatures. "This period is now the warmest in the history of modern civilization" (U.S. Global Change Research Program, 2017a).

Climate scientists have warned that, as the Earth warms, weather patterns will deviate from existing norms. Today, it is roughly 1°C hotter than when the first Industrial Revolution furnaces were fired up. To keep the increase in temperature below a 2°C threshold, relative to preindustrial levels, as required by the Paris Agreement of 2016, GHG emissions will first have to stabilize and then decrease. In other words, a massive movement to global decarbonization must occur, a monumental challenge for the world.

An important impact of climate change, global warming—the long-term rise in the average temperature of the Earth's climate system—poses a unique threat: This century has given rise to many years of record heat. Global warming is costly, involves scientific uncertainties, and will impact human societies for decades to come. To take one example explored in this chapter, a higher average global temperature is increasing the rate of melting of major ice sheets, particularly in Greenland. Because Greenland has the largest ice sheets in the world, the freshwater runoff from ice melt leads to a rise in sea levels. But around the world hundreds of millions of people live along coastlines. Even more, many island countries, such as the Maldives in the Indian Ocean, may become completely submerged. Major metropolitan areas, including New York City, Miami, Shanghai, Mumbai, and Bangkok, face this long-term threat.

The debate over both the potential for decarbonization and mitigating the long-term effects of climate change has proponents. Optimists say the world has the technological means to decarbonize the global economy. But pessimists conclude that, even if the world agrees on and enforces global targets for GHG emission reduction, change is difficult. First, energy demand continues to rise, especially in developing countries in Asia. Second, economic and political inertia means that the more fossil fuels the world consumes, the harder it is to choose another path. Third, the technical challenge of decarbonizing specific sectors, such as electricity, buildings, industry, and transportation, is proving to be difficult: over half of global carbon emissions stem from transportation, farming, cement, and steel production, industries that are growing.

This chapter uses the tools of economics to analyze energy and the climate crisis. Of particular interest is the impact of our energy choices on the climate. As we will see, not only does the consumption of fossil fuels lead to a warmer planet, but higher atmospheric concentrations of GHG lead to climate volatility. When making future decisions concerning energy systems, we must consider this reality. As James Hansen et al. (2007)—one of the world's leading climatologists—and his co-authors explain:

> The Earth's climate is remarkably sensitive. . . . Positive feedbacks predominate. This allows the entire planet to be whipsawed between climate states. One feedback, the "albedo flip" property of ice/water, provides a powerful trigger mechanism. A climate forcing that "flips" the albedo of a sufficient portion of an ice sheet can spark a cataclysm. Inertia of ice sheet and ocean provides only moderate delay to ice sheet disintegration and a burst of added global warming. Recent greenhouse gas emissions place the Earth perilously close to dramatic climate change that could run out of our control, with great dangers for humans.

Every major professional scientific society and National Academy of Science and almost 100 percent of climate scientists argue that a higher atmospheric concentration of GHG poses long-term threats to humans and the environment. As Scott L. Montgomery (2010) explains in his important book, *The Powers that Be*, "Science . . . is the only domain where . . . consensus exists." Every day, humans pump more than 90 million tons of greenhouse gases—mainly carbon dioxide (CO_2), methane, and nitrous oxides—into the atmosphere. With the atmosphere's heat-absorbing capacity, this buildup of GHG has increased the surface temperature of the Earth.

To address the topic of energy and climate change, this chapter first puts the topic in context by addressing the theory of public goods, and then develops an integrated assessment model, which provides a framework for analysis. The chapter then considers each part of the model, including economic and energy activity, GHG emissions, change in atmospheric concentration, the rise in temperature, and damage effects. The last section discusses strategies in moving forward. For readers curious about the science of climate change beyond this chapter, IPCC (2014a, 2014b, 2013) are excellent places to start. In terms of energy, economics, and climate change, the articles by Nordhaus (2019) and Stern (2008) and the books by Nordhaus (2013) and Goodstein and Intriligator (2012) provide thorough discussions.

THE CLIMATE AS PUBLIC GOOD

In 2018, the economist William Nordhaus, of Yale University, shared the Nobel Prize in Economic Sciences, along with Paul Romer, of New York University. For Nordhaus, the prize was awarded for his pathbreaking work in integrating climate change into the field of economics. In his Nobel Prize speech, delivered in Stockholm, in December 2018, Nordhaus said that the climate is a "public good. . . . Such activities are ones whose . . . benefits spill outside the market and are not captured in market prices" (Nordhaus, 2019). The two key attributes of public goods are *non-rivalry*—when the costs of an additional person experiencing the good or service are zero—and *non-excludability*—when it is impossible to exclude people from the good or service. With climate change, we are considering a "public bad," in the form of GHG, a particularly difficult global problem. The reason is that, in this context, a global externality exists (global warming), but it differs from local or national externalities because it "resists the control of both markets and national governments" (Nordhaus, 2019).

In order to address the climate crisis, large up-front expenditures are required. Compounding the difficulty is uncertainty. While scientific understanding advances and economists implement sophisticated climate modeling techniques, a complex link exists among energy consumption, climate change, and economic outcomes. As part of the Fourth National Climate Assessment, the U.S. Global Change Research Program (2017a) reported on the state of science relating to climate change. This is a very important report. A number of conclusions are relevant to this chapter:

- For 200 years, human activity has been the most important cause of climate change.
- Global average temperature will likely increase more than 2°C during this century.
- The magnitude of temperature change will depend on atmospheric GHG concentration.
- The melting of ice sheets and glaciers will combine for a rise in sea levels.
- Coastal submersion, flooding, and scarcity could displace almost a billion and a half people, 20 percent of the world's population.

The challenge in moving forward is implementing the appropriate form of collective action. In an essay, Gernot Wagner (2011), an economist at the Environmental Defense Fund, argues that, to address climate change, "the changes necessary are so large and profound that they are beyond the reach of individual action." Wagner is not arguing that we should stop making choices that decrease our personal impact, such as choosing greater energy efficiency, conservation, and renewables. Wagner is saying that we are pumping so much CO_2 into the air—over $400 worth of damage annually per American—that we are paying for it on a global scale.

INTEGRATED ASSESSMENT MODEL OF CLIMATE CHANGE

Integrated assessment models (IAMs) combine economic and scientific aspects of the problem of climate change into a single framework. As Nordhaus (2019) explains, with climate change and the application of IAMs, "it is increasingly necessary to link disciplines together to develop effective understanding and efficient policies." The IAMs are based on solid economic and scientific theories, but in practice rely on numerical dynamic models of different levels of complexity. (For further discussion of the role of IAMs and climate change, see Nordhaus, 2019.)

The model (figure 12.1) in this chapter first demonstrates that GHG emissions flow from economic and energy activity. The GHG emissions increase atmospheric concentrations of these gases. Higher atmospheric concentrations of GHG emissions are, in turn, translated into global mean temperature changes. These changes then link to physical and biological impacts and economic damages. Damages are translated into economic values. In this framework, a policy that impacts one part of the model subsequently influences all other parts. The following sections discuss each component of the model, starting with economic and energy activity.

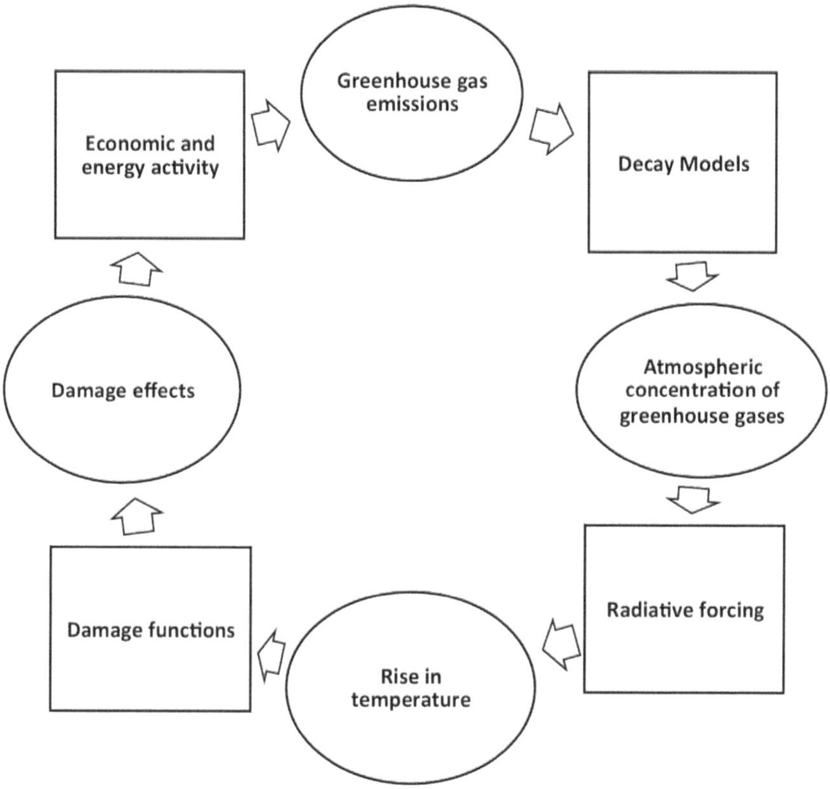

Figure 12.1 Integrated Assessment Model of Climate Change. *Source*: Author.

Economic and Energy Activity

Throughout history, changes in climate patterns have led to human development. Five million years ago, a major cooling period led to the appearance of the first hominids, who foraged in forests and walked on two legs. After four ice ages, Homo sapiens appeared 100,000 years ago. This period put a premium on larger brains, necessary to adapt to ecological changes. Around 20,000 years ago, a migration led to human settlement in North and South America. During the last Ice Age with large ice sheets, the ocean was 300 feet lower than it is today. The shallow Bering Strait—between what is now Russia and Alaska—served as a land bridge for migratory routes. Ten thousand years ago, as the temperature climbed and the ice melted, Native Americans had already populated the new continents. The point is that the climate may vary according to natural processes: cycles of warming and cooling that occur over time.

But in the last two centuries, industrialization, globalization, and modernization have altered the climate system. The reason is that the burning of carbon-based fuels such as oil, coal, and natural gas, so important for the expansion of the global economy, lead to GHG emissions. These gases accumulate in the atmosphere and remain for decades or centuries. Initially the increase in the atmospheric concentration of GHG above preindustrial levels was caused by deforestation and other land-use changes. But by the beginning of the twentieth century, "human activity, especially emissions of greenhouse gases, (were) the dominant cause of the observed warming" (U.S. Global Change Research Program, 2017a).

Anthropogenic emissions occur on top of the natural carbon cycle that circulates carbon between the terrestrial biosphere, ocean, and atmosphere. According to IPCC (2007), three forms of evidence exist. First, there are human "fingerprints" on the carbon content of the atmosphere. The burning of fossil fuels and the act of deforestation create carbon molecules that are lighter than the molecules from other sources. Scientists identify an increase in the lighter molecules, corresponding to the anthropogenic trend in emissions. Second, sophisticated computer models, such as in Nordhaus (2018) and Stern (2008), cannot accurately reproduce observed temperature changes with natural climate drivers such as volcanic eruptions and the intensity of the sun. But when human-induced climate drivers are included, such as the burning of fossil fuels and deforestation, the models accurately capture temperature changes since the beginning of industrialization. When natural climate drivers are compared to human-induced climate drivers, the accumulation of carbon from human sources serves as the most important factor. Third, the troposphere, the lower level of the atmosphere that contains carbon, is expanding. As heat-trapping gases accumulate and the troposphere warms, the atmospheric layer surrounding it expands. At the same time, less heat escapes into the stratosphere, the higher layer of atmosphere, and so the stratosphere cools. If the sun were the sole climate driver, both layers would warm.

Greenhouse Gas Emissions

Since the beginning of the Industrial Revolution, the world has burned large quantities of oil, coal, and natural gas in vehicles, power plants, furnaces, and steel mills, creating increasing levels of CO_2. On a global scale, CO_2 is generated from fossil fuel combustion, industrial processes, forestry, and other land uses. Global CO_2 emissions in 2018 were more than 37 billion tons, almost 3 percent more than the previous year (figure 12.2).

To put this trend in perspective, if you drive 10,000 miles and your vehicle gets 28 miles to the gallon, your vehicle will emit about one ton of carbon. Or consider that the typical U.S. household uses 10,000 kilowatt-hours of electricity annually. If generated from coal, these kWh release three tons of

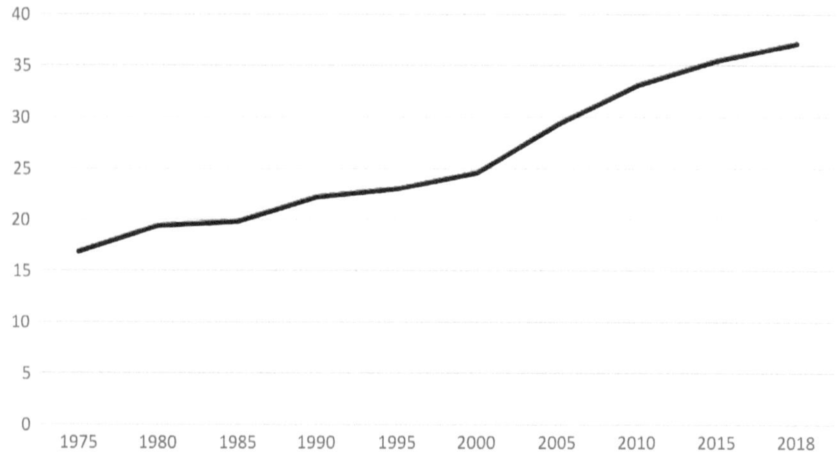

Figure 12.2 Global CO_2 Emissions (Gigatons), 1975–2018. *Source*: Author using data from the Global Carbon Project, http://folk.uio.no/roberan/GCB2018.shtml.

carbon. Carbon dioxide has a weight of 3.67 times the weight of carbon, so with driving and consuming electricity at home, you would release about 15 tons of CO_2 annually.

Before the industrial revolution, human activity led to negligible CO_2 emissions. In 1850, the United Kingdom was the world's top CO_2 emitter. Between 1850 and the beginning of this century, industrialized countries dominated the world's emissions. But in 2007, China became the world's largest emitter of CO_2, passing the United States. In the same year, CO_2 emissions from the developing world exceeded emissions from industrialized countries. Today the top 10 emitting countries make up 80 percent of the world's total. Global CO_2 emissions have reached record levels, leading the United Nations secretary general Antonio Guterres to conclude that "we are in deep trouble with climate change. It is hard to overstate the urgency of our situation" (Dennis and Mooney, 2018). In all, about 25 percent of global GHG emissions come from electricity and heat production, 24 percent from agriculture, forestry, and other land uses, 21 percent from industry, 14 percent from transportation, 10 percent from other energy categories, and 6 percent from buildings (IPCC, 2014b).

Electricity and Heat Production

Powering the economy means electricity generation. For fossil fuel power plants, the resulting CO_2 emissions depend on technology, the carbon content of fuel, and the rate of *fuel efficiency* (efficiency of turning fuel into energy). With constant technology and fuel efficiency, coal leads to a greater level of CO_2 emissions than oil or natural gas. The greater a country's reliance on fossil fuels for baseload power generation (as opposed to renewable energy sources or nuclear power), the greater is its CO_2 emissions.

Agriculture, Forestry, and Other Land Use

The writer and activist Anna Lappe (2010) in her book *Diet for a Hot Planet* summarizes the challenge of agriculture and climate change: "The dominant story line about climate change—the sectors most responsible for emissions and the key solutions to reducing those emissions—diverts us from understanding not only how the food sector is a critical part of the problem, but also, and even more important, how it can be a vital part of the much-needed solutions." Why does industrial agriculture play a significant role in heating the planet? Although industrial agriculture is not universally practiced, many farmers adopt the techniques of monoculture, pesticides, machinery, and equipment. With a commodity crop such as corn, the first stages in the production process—planting, growth, and harvesting—require fertilizers and pesticides. The next stages involve transferring the crop to a grain elevator and then to factory farm feedlots, wet mill processing plants, ethanol plants, or foreign countries. The next stage, processing, involves the use of corn as an input for bio-energy, food for animals, and processed food. The final stage, human consumption, involves demand for the value-added form of output, including meat, processed food, fast food, and ethanol. Each stage requires fossil fuels and leads to GHG emissions. How could adjustments take place? A focus on eating more regionally sourced food reduces the fuel requirements of commodity crops.

In terms of forestry, an important process is the *carbon cycle*: all carbon atoms in existence rotate through the atmosphere, inorganic matter, and living organisms. Carbon is stored in the atmosphere, ocean surface, and biota; in carbonate rocks; as deposits of oil, coal, and natural gas; and as dead organic matter. Carbon enters the biotic world when living organisms extract carbon from the nonliving environment. Plants and trees use CO_2 and sunlight for food and growth. By the processes of respiration, burning, and decay, carbon returns to the atmosphere and bodies of water in the form of CO_2. The global problem concerns large-scale deforestation. Land-use change such as this accounts for an increasing portion of CO_2 emissions. Deforestation sends more carbon into the atmosphere by felling trees; however, it also decreases the potential of the natural environment to absorb CO_2. Sustainable forestry management, natural forest plans, forestry standards, and certification systems are necessary to mitigate the problem.

Industry

Since the beginning of the Industrial Revolution, fossil fuels have powered manufacturing industries. Many factories were established along waterways to take advantage of hydropower, including flour mills on the Mississippi River and cement factories on the Ohio River. But the emergence of coal made railroads cost-effective. Manufacturers were free to build factories away from waterways. As long as trains provided service to manufacturing centers, factories took advantage of these markets.

Today, manufacturing requires the use of fossil fuels in a multiple of the weight of the final product. Fossil fuels provide heat to produce metals and related products. Coal serves as the largest source of energy for the generation of electricity. In the steel industry, GHG emissions result from the burning of fossil fuels during production. Even the production of ethanol requires a heavy use of petroleum.

Globalization—the widening and deepening interconnections of people worldwide—leads to GHG emissions. As an example, Dell manufacturing plants in Penang, Malaysia, Xiamen, China, Bracknell, the United Kingdom, Manila, Philippines, Bangalore, India, Hortolandia, Brazil, Limerick, Ireland, Austin, Texas, Nashville, Tennessee, Peoria, Illinoi, and other locations obtain resource inputs in surrounding regions to produce Dell's products. As consumers worldwide purchase the company's output, GHG emissions are part of the global supply chain.

Transportation

Technology allows people and goods to travel faster and farther, increasing GHG emissions. Railroads, commercial aircraft, trucks, and cars lead to end-use sector emissions. In the transportation sector, light-duty vehicles (including passenger cars and light-duty trucks) are the largest contributors to GHG emissions. In the United States, GHG emissions from transportation are increasing more in absolute terms than commercial, residential, agriculture, industry, and electricity sectors. The reduction of transport-related GHG emissions requires the reduction of transportation activity, higher levels of fuel efficiency, blending low-carbon fuels with gasoline, increasing vehicle occupancy rates, the expansion of public transportation, greater opportunities to walk and bike, changing land-use patterns through planning and design, and the implementation of carbon-pricing policies. Programs of smart growth in urban areas, where commercial and residential opportunities are linked to systems of public transportation, may achieve the goal of emission reduction. With existing technologies, the fuel economy of new passenger cars and light trucks could rise for years to come. The interconnections between transportation and economic activity and the external costs associated with energy use mean that all of these actions and policy applications will be necessary to reduce transportation-related GHG emissions.

Other Energy Categories

Greenhouse gas emissions come from areas of the energy sector that are not associated with electricity or heat production. Examples include fuel extraction, refining, processing, and pipeline transportation. In terms of fuel extraction, GHG emissions stem from the extraction of coal, oil shale, tar sands, natural gas, and crude oil. Methane emissions result from the drilling of oil wells. The process of refining means chemically or physically transforming materials from one state to another. During these transformations, many GHG emissions (nitrous oxide, methane, and CO_2) are released. With processing, some parts of a particular form of energy may be removed to both reduce impurities and increase hydrocarbon content of pipeline quality. An example is natural gas when non-hydrocarbon gases are removed through processing and vented into the atmosphere. This process leads to CO_2 releases. In terms of pipeline transportation, GHG emissions depend on the particular fluid, pipeline dimensions, ambient conditions, and the degree of substitution between pipeline and rail.

Buildings

Buildings contribute GHG emissions to the atmosphere through their operational phase. The main source is the consumption of energy. Given the growth in new construction and the inefficiencies of existing structures worldwide, GHG emissions from buildings will increase. But the building sector has potential for delivering cost-effective reductions in GHG emissions. Buildings have relatively long lifespans. Actions taken today to reduce emissions will have benefits over the long term. Besides reducing emissions, a benefit of retrofitting existing buildings and creating sustainable designs for new buildings is energy efficiency. As a result, the building sector should exist at the forefront of nations' plans to reduce GHG emissions. Efficient oversight should help builders adopt international best practices. Investment should support improvements in energy efficiency and emission reduction programs. But opportunities for small reductions in emissions are spread across millions of buildings, which possess different stakeholders in various stages of building's lives. As a result of these barriers, emission reduction in the building sector often requires the establishment of national energy standards.

Decay Models

After GHG emissions are released from electricity generation, heat production, agriculture and forestry, industry, transportation, and buildings, they cycle through the atmosphere, oceans, and land surfaces. Eventually, each greenhouse gas finds a *natural sink*, which serves as a reservoir that takes up the gas from its natural cycle. Cycling may occur in a period of time from a few days to millions of years. Carbon from the combustion of fossil fuels, for example, may be cycled back into the atmosphere in a few hours. It may be absorbed by the oceans in a matter of days. It may also be stored within ocean sediments for millions of years. When GHG emissions come from an economic or energy process, a natural sink will absorb the gas.

In other contexts for GHG emissions, however, such as methane and CO_2 from solid waste disposal, *decay models* are relevant. These models demonstrate that the rate of decay of waste and the resulting GHG emissions depends on the waste mass decay rate per unit of time and the resulting potential emission generation capacity. For solid waste, these parameters are a function of waste characteristics, moisture content, nutrients in the landfill, climate conditions, and waste management practices. This estimation is important because solid waste disposal sites are a significant source of anthropogenic GHG emissions. Solid waste disposal sites emit more than 10 percent of global anthropogenic methane. These emissions are expected to increase in developing countries, remain stable in emerging economies, and decrease in developed countries. With methane, nitrous oxide, and CO_2 emissions from soil tillage in agriculture, decay models calculate emissions by considering soil layers in tilled plots, gas diffusion and convection, organic matter, soil temperature, and moisture.

Atmospheric Concentration of Greenhouse Gases

The *greenhouse effect* makes the Earth hospitable for living. About one-third of the energy that flows from the sun to the Earth reflects off clouds and the planet's surface, heading back into space. The rest is absorbed by oceans and land, which then emit it in the form of infrared radiation. The GHG in the atmosphere (CO_2, methane, ozone, nitrous oxide, halocarbons, and water vapor) absorb the long-wavelength, infrared radiation (figure 12.3), and then subsequently release it in all directions, including back to the Earth's surface. The greenhouse effect is this bouncing around of energy, essential to life.

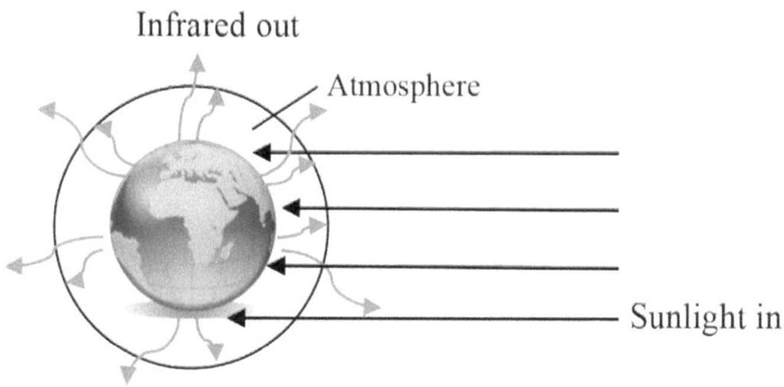

Figure 12.3 The Greenhouse Effect. *Source*: Author.

Without it, the average global temperature would be much colder, around –10°C at the Equator. (The atmosphere in figure 12.3 is not drawn to scale: at the size of the Earth, the atmosphere would be the width of a thin circle drawn outside the planet's surface.)

The process is analogous to the way glass keeps a greenhouse warm; however, GHG absorb but do not block infrared radiation:

> When the Earth's slow cyclic tilting and wobbling along it's eccentric orbital path once again leads to a major cooling period some 50,000 years from now, enough of our heat-trapping carbon emissions will still remain in the atmosphere to warm the planet just enough to weaken that chill. In other words, our impacts on global climate are so profound that we will have canceled the next ice age. (Stager, 2015)

GHG differ with respect to their ability to absorb infrared radiation, and therefore possess a different ability to trap heat radiated from the Earth's surface. Usually measured over a certain time interval, such as 100 years, the IPCC (2007) provides a Global Warming Potential, relative to carbon dioxide, set as the numeraire equal to one: methane = 21; nitrous oxide = 310; hydro fluorocarbons = 1,300; chlorofluorocarbons = 9,300. Per unit chlorofluorocarbons have a greater potential for global warming than carbon dioxide; however, carbon dioxide is much more plentiful.

Research starting in the nineteenth century identified water vapor and CO_2 as the most important GHG. Today, water vapor accounts for most of the greenhouse effect. Nitrous oxide results when oxygen and nitrogen combine during fossil fuel combustion. Methane exists in geological deposits such as natural gas fields, coal seams, landfills, rice fields, and livestock. Halocarbons are synthetic chemicals, including chlorofluorocarbons (CFCs), used in refrigerators and spray cans. Beginning in 1987, CFCs were phased out in most global industries. But unlike water vapor and clouds that respond to changes in air pressure and temperature by evaporating, condensing, and precipitating, CO_2 does not condense or precipitate.

A Rise in Atmospheric CO_2 Concentration

The concentration of CO_2 in the atmosphere increased from 277 parts per million (ppm) in 1750 at the beginning of industrialization to more than 415 in 2019, a concentration that last occurred 3 million years ago (U.S. Global Change Research Program, 2017a). At that time, the ocean level was more than 10 feet higher than it is today. In 1960, one metric ton of CO_2 emissions led to 400 kilograms of CO_2 remaining in the atmosphere. Today it is 450 kilograms. The natural process that absorbs CO_2 from the atmosphere has been compromised. But "Models project that unless forceful steps are taken to reduce fossil fuel use, concentrations of CO_2 will reach 700–900 ppm by 2100" (Nordhaus, 2019). This could lead to an atmospheric concentration of CO_2 that has not occurred in tens of millions of years. In this context, three trends are important. First, by 2100, humanity is on course to increase the atmospheric concentration of CO_2. Second, climate change is a lagged indicator: because of the slow uptake of heat by oceans, the world is at an early stage of anthropogenic climate change. Third, if humanity exhausts the carbon reserves currently buried in the ground, CO_2 concentration will continue to rise for centuries.

Global Carbon Project

The Global Carbon Project (www.globalcarbonproject.org) characterizes how anthropogenic CO_2 emissions impact the greenhouse effect. This project provides a framework to evaluate patterns, variability, and interactions with CO_2 emissions. It also offers a representation of the overall perturbation of the global carbon cycle caused by anthropogenic activities. In the global carbon project, CO_2 emissions flow from two sources: fossil fuels and industry (E_{FFI}) and deforestation and other land-use changes (E_{DLU}). These emissions are balanced by the growth rate in atmospheric CO_2 concentration (G_{AC}) and the uptake of carbon by sinks in the land (S_L) and ocean (S_O). As was explained earlier, a natural sink is a part of the atmosphere, land, or ocean that absorbs CO_2. Carbon dioxide emissions must either flow into the atmosphere or become absorbed by the land or global ocean. Carbon dioxide emissions and their partitioning among the atmosphere, land, and ocean are therefore in balance: $E_{FFI} + E_{DLU} = G_{AC} + S_L + S_O$. Since the beginning of this century, more than 90 percent of total CO_2 emissions come from E_{FFI} and less than 10 percent from E_{DLU}. Total emissions were partitioned ($G_{AC} + S_L + S_O$) among the atmosphere (44%), land (30%), and ocean (26%). According to the Global Carbon Project, since 1960, the values of all variables except land-use changes have increased.

Radiative Forcing

Radiative forcing, a method to assess past, present, and future climate perturbations, quantifies an imbalance in the Earth's atmosphere from either anthropogenic activities or natural changes. Earth's *energy balance* results from energy flows from the Sun to the Earth and from the Earth back into the atmosphere and space. A balance between absorbed and radiated energy determines average global temperature. When in equilibrium, this balance leads to stable surface temperatures. Without energy balance, average surface temperature may rise.

Radiative forcing determines the factors that alter energy balance, including GHG and aerosol emissions, cloud reflectivity, and *insolation*: the intensity of the Sun's solar energy. These forces, both natural and anthropogenic, may cause the atmosphere to absorb more GHG and warm the climate system. Radiative forcing of CO_2, important for this chapter, refers to the difference between incoming solar radiation and outgoing infrared radiation resulting from a higher concentration of CO_2. To understand this process, climate scientists study the energy balance between the lower atmosphere (troposphere) and the upper atmosphere (stratosphere). When the system is in equilibrium, as much energy flows upward across the troposphere-stratosphere boundary that flows downward, but any new forcing upsets the balance. A change in solar radiation may cause radiative forcing; however, since the beginning of the Industrial Revolution, the most important form of radiative forcing has been a higher concentration of CO_2 in the troposphere.

Rise in Temperature

Radiative forcing increases the atmospheric concentration of GHG, leading to greater absorption of infrared radiation. Higher temperatures result. In the last thirty years, the world has experienced the twenty hottest years ever recorded. For two days in June, 2018, cities in Iran and Pakistan experienced temperatures that exceeded 129°F, the highest ever recorded in those areas. The emission path the world is on today is likely to increase average global temperature by 1.5°C by 2040, 2°C a few decades after that, and 4°C by the end of the century (Wallace-Wells, 2019). IPCC (2018) provides a similar result, concluding that it is almost certain that global average temperature will rise in a range from 1.4°C (2.5°F) to 5.8°C (10.4°F) by 2100.

But even 1.5°C of warming is likely to destroy the world's coral reefs, displace millions of people because of sea-level rise, decrease global crop yields, create ice-free summers in the Artic, and decimate marine fisheries (IPCC, 2018). As temperatures rise, many of the biggest cities in South Asia and the Middle East could become lethally hot, as early as 2050. Because GHG persist in the atmosphere, the heat-trapping gases we release this century will warm the Earth for 100,000 years (Stager, 2015). To have a chance to even limit warming to 1.5°C, the world would have to cut global CO_2 emissions in half between 2020 and 2030 and then to zero by 2050, an unlikely scenario (IPCC, 2018).

To understand this process, radiative forcing (RF) alters surface temperature (ΔT): $\Delta T = \gamma RF$, where γ is a measure of climate sensitivity. This equation demonstrates a linear relationship of global mean climate change between two equilibrium states. The more significant is radiative forcing—such as a rapidly accelerating atmospheric concentration of CO_2—the greater the increase in average global temperature.

Nicholas Stern (2008) argues that *climate sensitivity* demonstrates the likelihood that a higher concentration of CO_2 will lead to an increase in average global temperature: with 78 percent likelihood, a CO_2 concentration of 450 ppm will increase average global temperature by 2°C relative to preindustrial levels. A CO_2 concentration of 650 ppm, however, will increase average global temperature by 2°C with 100 percent likelihood. Temperature increases at or above 5°C would most likely lead to the harshest possible damage effects.

Important in this context are *feedback effects*, which occur when one part of a system creates additional changes in other parts. *Negative feedback effects* reduce the magnitude of climate change. *Positive feedback effects* exacerbate initial changes in the climate system. The most important of these is the water vapor feedback. An increase in atmospheric CO_2 concentration raises surface temperature. More evaporation of surface water then occurs, increasing the atmosphere's capacity to absorb solar energy. This further enhances the greenhouse effect, and the process continues.

Climate models demonstrate that water vapor provides the most significant climate feedback. But even though water vapor accounts for half of the Earth's greenhouse effect, it is not the cause of the change in global climate. An alteration of the climate system is a function of the direct (no feedback response) of a change in the concentration of GHG in the atmosphere. The absorption of radiation and the concentration of GHG determine average surface temperature.

Climate models also show that ocean "pumps" water circulation. In winter, cold, dense water sinks beneath warmer water in the North Atlantic Ocean. Sinking water feeds the global system of currents. To replace the cold water, warm tropical water is pulled northward, transporting tropical heat to the North Atlantic region. Winters in the north are warmer than they would be otherwise. In addition, the global system of currents sinks CO_2 from the air first to water on the surface and then into the depths. This partially offsets atmospheric buildup of CO_2. The concern is that, if warmer air does not allow ice formation in northern latitudes, cold water may not be available to sink into the deepwater conveyor in the North Atlantic. As a result, warmer air may not follow to northern latitudes, and northern winters could experience the paradoxical reality of more severe coldness. Hundreds of thousands of years in the future, cultures and species that have grown accustomed to a warming planet will have to adapt to "strange new kinds of environmental change in reverse," such as a rising sea levels and a cooling planet (Stager, 2015).

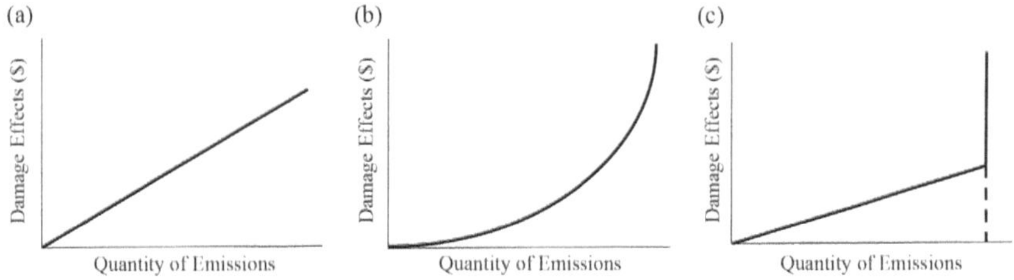

Figure 12.4 Damage Functions. *Source*: Author.

Damage Functions

A *damage function* demonstrates different possible relationships between GHG emissions and damage effects, including a linear relationship in figure 12.4 (a) or a cubic relationship in figure 12.4 (b), when damage effects are proportional to a change in emissions to the power of three. For example, higher global average temperatures will melt ice sheets at increasing rates. Figure 12.4 (c) incorporates a *threshold effect*: instead of gradual, continuous change, a higher global temperature may lead to sudden, more harmful impacts, such as the collapse of the Greenland ice sheet.

Embedded in the damage function is a probabilistic framework, related to the magnitude of damage effects. For example, the number of people experiencing hydroelectric power risks, habitat degradation, change in crop yields, water stress, heat waves, and more volatile storms will increase as the global mean temperature rises. But more frequent storms will have different durations, wind speeds, and locational effects. Over time, changes in these variables will determine specific damage effects.

In this framework, a damage function demonstrates the relationship between greater GHG emissions, a rise in temperature, and specific damage effects. But varying assumptions with respect to locational effects, population density, methods of adaptation, and others would lead to different results. An interesting aspect of the damage function framework, however, is that it does not demonstrate a reversible process. Once GHG emissions increase atmospheric concentrations, the process of climate change will lead to specific damage effects. Over time, lower emissions levels will not reverse the damage effects.

Social Cost of Carbon

From an economics perspective, what is the monetary value of emission damage? For policy applications, damage effects must be valued in economic terms. The research of Professor William Nordhaus provides context. Concerning the climate crisis, the most important concept, according to Nordhaus

(2017), is the *social cost of carbon* (SCC). The term SCC represents the economic cost that results from an additional ton of carbon dioxide or its equivalent. That is, SCC is the economic value of marginal damage from emissions. In more technical terms, SCC is the change in the discounted value of welfare that results from an additional unit of CO_2 or its equivalent. For climate change policy, SCC constitutes an important tool. For policies that regulate greenhouse gas emissions, the numerical value of SCC provides a method to estimate economic damages. In other words, the concept translates the effects of climate change into economic terms, thus helping policymakers assess the economic impacts of decisions that would decrease emissions. Currently, the SCC is used by governments at all levels to inform billions of dollars of investment and policy decisions in the United States and abroad with respect to the climate crisis. For example, if a policy intends to reduce emissions by 1,000,000 tons, and the SCC is valued at $50 per ton, then the benefit of policy implementation would equal $50,000,000, the value of damage avoided.

The DICE Model

The question becomes SCC estimation. What steps are involved? Specialized computer models, such as the DICE model—Dynamic Integrated Model of Climate and the Economy—developed by Professor Nordhaus, predict future emissions, model future climate responses, assess the economic impact of climate changes, and calculate the present value of future damages. Taken together, these steps provide a baseline value for the damages from emissions. When economists then alter model variables, such as the level of future emissions, it is possible to calculate the changes in the economic value of damages. In an article that applies the DICE model, Nordhaus (2017) determines a value of $31.20 per ton of CO_2, which is equal to SCC. This means that every ton of CO_2 emissions leads to more than thirty dollars of damage to humans and the environment. Interested readers may use this number to calculate the value of reducing CO_2 emissions by billions of tons, which is required to stabilize global temperature.

This value may also serve as the rate for a tax on carbon. The reason is that for any climate policy to be effective, it must increase the price of CO_2. Establishing a price for CO_2 corrects the underpricing of the climate externality. According to Nordhaus (2019), increasing the price of carbon would achieve four goals. First, it would signal to consumers which goods and services are carbon-intensive. Second, it would signal to producers which resource inputs are carbon-intensive. Third, it would incentivize the development of new low-carbon products and processes. Finally, a price for carbon would economize on the information necessary to achieve these goals.

Damage Effects

Global civilization is organized around the climate that has existed since the middle ages. But climate change could re-order this structure. The most extreme environmental and economic impacts will occur in equatorial and low-latitude areas, many in developing countries. The extent to which these areas become hotter and less-desirable, major damage effects will occur:

- Extreme weather
- Rising ocean levels
- Loss of biodiversity
- Climate conflict
- Food insecurity
- Impacts on land, income, and infrastructure

Extreme Weather

The IPCC (2018) forecasts more extreme weather conditions. A recent example is Hurricane Irene, which pounded the east coast of the United States during August of 2011, leading to flooding; damage to buildings, roads and power lines; and fatalities. But severe weather includes more than storms and floods. Heat waves, droughts, and wildfires—such as those in California—cause extensive economic damages. If weather trends continue, areas that exhibit specific weather patterns—droughts in the southwest of the United States, rain and flooding in the upper Midwest—will experience these same events but with greater severity. In latitudes that experience frequent storms, more water in the atmosphere makes rainfall heavier. In latitudes with drier conditions, higher temperatures increase evaporation, prolonging droughts. If the average global temperature reaches 2°C above preindustrial levels, for example, 5.99 billion people will experience more severe heat waves (Wallace-Wells, 2019). As aquifers are no longer able to support agriculture and growing populations, humans will migrate to areas with more stable water supplies.

Rising Sea Levels

Warmer temperatures melt glaciers and ice sheets on land, resulting in rising sea levels. For example, "global average sea level has risen by about 7–8 inches since 1900, with almost half of that rise occurring since 1993. . . . Global sea level rise has already affected the United States; the incidence of daily tidal flooding is accelerating in more than 25 Atlantic and Gulf Coast cities" (U.S. Global Change Research Program, 2017a). When sea ice retreats, the previously unexposed water absorbs more heat from the sun than white ice. As a result, global average sea levels will continue to rise "by one to four feet by 2100. A rise as much as eight feet by 2100 cannot be ruled out" (U.S. Global Change Research Program, 2017a). The problem is that, if the world does not stabilize GHG emissions, the damage caused by rising sea levels could equal trillions of dollars.

Loss of Biodiversity

Extreme weather conditions—particularly wildfires, droughts, and flooding—compromise the resilience of terrestrial ecosystems. The four primary terrestrial ecosystems—grassland, temperate forest, boreal forest and tundra—are vulnerable to climate change. Adaptation must occur to warmer temperatures, extreme weather, and prolonged droughts. Habitats will change, altering the geographic distribution of flora and fauna. In an article in *Science*, Chen et al. (2011) tracked the movement of 2,000 animal and plant species for a decade. They found that species shifted to higher elevations. Because of increasing heat, species move 13.3 yards higher in altitude and 11 miles higher in latitude, the equivalent of shifting away from the equator at 20 centimeters per hour. According to Macauley and Morris (2011), the growth of plants is a function of spring-like conditions. With a higher annual temperature, more rain in northern latitudes, and more droughts in many mid-latitude regions, ecosystems will struggle to adapt. If the average global temperature reaches 2°C above preindustrial levels, 680 million people will directly experience losses from habitat degradation (Wallace-Wells, 2019).

Climate Conflict

With climate change, security as traditionally understood to include political and military threats must expand to include potential conflict from climate variability. As people flee rising sea levels and resource scarcity, they will be forced to find fresh water and food supplies. If temperatures rise beyond 2°C, as much as a quarter of the world's population could experience desertification and drought. Climate conflict is a function of the proliferation of both violence and climate-related shocks. First, rising sea levels and more extreme weather conditions may create large-scale human dislocation. (Hundreds of millions of people live on or near the coast. Human settlements along the coast in Malaysia and Indonesia will be among the first to experience the impact of higher sea levels.) The Center for Climate Systems Research (CCSR) of the Earth Institute at Columbia University uses a map that considers long-range, aggregate projections of where people are likely to live in the future. The Center explains that, over time, fewer people will live in the Philippines, Turkey, Cambodia, and Myanmar, among others, as inhabitants seek more resources.

Second, a changing climate creates resource conflicts. Droughts, a reduction of arable land, water shortages, and competition over energy resources already exist. If the average global temperature reaches 2°C above preindustrial levels, 3.66 billion people will directly experience water stress (Wallace-Wells, 2019). Conflicts in the Middle East and Central Africa involve access to stable water sources. For many developing countries, a decrease in agricultural productivity may reduce food security.

Third, border disputes and the loss of territory—including entire island countries—will lead to environmentally induced migration. The need to accommodate climate refugees will tax the developed world. The fact that climate change poses security challenges is important for the Pentagon and State Department. The world's melting glaciers, rising temperatures, and human displacement pose direct threats to the security of nations.

Food Insecurity

Worldwide, climate change is altering growing patterns. In the United States, wheat and cotton production is slowly migrating northward. Developing countries such as Mexico and Guatemala, which rely on small-scale farming, are experiencing disruptions to historical practices. Climate change will also alter irrigation. As a result, regions that produce agricultural surpluses, such as the Mayo and Yaqui Valleys in northern Mexico, could experience steep declines. If the average global temperature reaches 2°C above preindustrial levels, more than 300 million people will experience losses from changes in crop yields (Wallace-Wells, 2019). Ultimately, the impact of climate change on agricultural productivity will depend on changes in temperature, precipitation, soil, energy prices, and networks of trade.

Impacts on Land, Income, and Infrastructure

Decreasing land values harm poor nations (Easterbrook, 2007). But historically privileged countries in northern latitudes may not decline geopolitically. Water rationing, de-population, foreclosures, and other forms of economic disruption could become commonplace in areas such as the southern United States, central China, southern Europe, Australia, and almost all of Africa. Conversely, over the next several decades, high-latitude areas could see an appreciation in land values, including the northern United States, Canada, and Scandinavia. Cities with technological and industrial bases in these regions, such as Chicago, Montreal, and Oslo, could benefit from an influx of workers. In addition, temperature and income are inversely related (Ng and Zhao, 2011): a global increase of 1°C leads to a 3 percent decrease in income and "significant infrastructure damage" to roads, bridges, telecommunications, and energy systems. While water-front property normally generates a premium, insurance companies are becoming less likely to offer insurance packages for structures that are likely to experience severe weather conditions.

ECONOMIC AND ENERGY ACTIVITY REDUX

The damage effects in the integrated assessment model impact economic and energy activity. The U.S. Global Change Research Program (2017b) raises the possibility that a warming climate could reduce GDP by 10 percent, impeding the rate of economic growth over this century. Economic losses will include damages to communities, social systems, infrastructure, ecosystems, regional economies and industries that depend on natural resources, and households through higher electricity costs. But most likely, the damage effects will not be evenly distributed, depending on the characteristics of employment and location of jobs. In addition, added risks occur with interconnected systems that are "already exposed to a range of stressors such as aging and deteriorating infrastructure, land-use changes, and population growth" (U.S. Global Change Research Program, 2017b). Extreme climate-related impacts on one system risk failures of other systems, including food production and distribution, energy, and national security.

However, for decades, GDP and CO_2 emissions have not moved in tandem (figure 12.5). This demonstrates that global *carbon intensity* (CO_2/GDP) is declining while CO_2 emissions are increasing. It may be that, if energy innovations and public polices first stabilize and eventually decrease CO_2 emissions, the warning of U.S. Global Change Research Program (2017b) that a warming climate will slow GDP growth will not come to fruition.

In an empirical investigation, Nathaniel Aden (2016), a research fellow at the World Resources Institute, discovered that, since the beginning of this century, more than twenty countries—including the United States and Belgium—have reduced their annual CO_2 emissions while growing their economies. In the United States, between 2000 and 2014, GDP increased by 28 percent while CO_2 emissions fell by 6 percent. In Belgium, GDP increased by 21 percent, but emissions decreased by 12 percent. Many other country examples exist.

MOVING FORWARD: THE WEDGE FRAMEWORK

In response to the climate crisis, economists, natural scientists, and policy makers have focused on three potential strategies: geoengineering, carbon removal, and abatement. Geoengineering, which means injecting

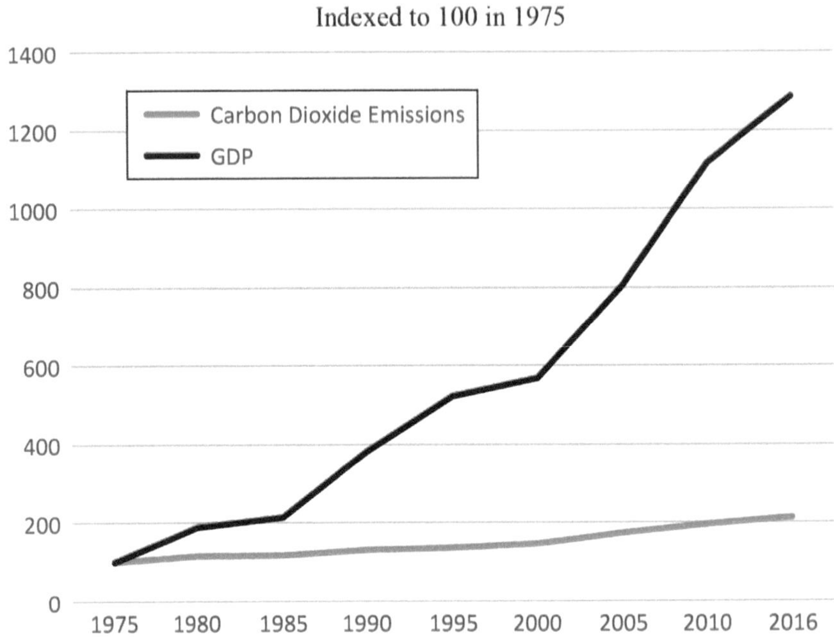

Figure 12.5 Decoupling of Global CO_2 Emissions and GDP. *Source*: Author using data from the Global Carbon Project and The World Bank, http://folk.uio.no/roberan/GCB 2018.shtml, http://www.multpl.com/world-gdp/table/by-year.

stratospheric aerosols to cool the planet, does not serve as a cost-effective option. A process of carbon removal, in the form of carbon capture and storage, while appealing, does not currently entail technology that can remove billions of tons of CO_2 from the atmosphere at a manageable cost. This leaves abatement. The IPCC (2018) report describes Nordhaus' (2018) ideas on carbon taxation as essential for slowing the CO_2 emissions that are heating the atmosphere. But Nordhaus (2018) argues that international targets of temperature changes outlined in IPCC (2018) appear to be "unrealistically ambitious." He argues for a more stringent carbon tax that would reduce fossil fuel consumption.

The size of the threat of the climate crisis means that every level of organization, from cities to states to nations to international agreements must implement coordinated responses. In this context, Pacala and Socolow (2004) argue, in an influential article published in *Science* magazine—cited more than two thousand times—that humanity possesses the technological and scientific know-how to solve the climate problem. A portfolio of technology "wedges" currently exists that could meet the world's demand for energy while limiting the trajectory of CO_2 emissions. Pacala and Socolow propose fifteen wedges, including vehicle efficiency, energy efficiency of power plants and buildings, the substitution of natural gas for coal, nuclear energy, and a greater consumption of renewables. The wedge approach assumes that, to avoid a CO_2 concentration in excess of 500 ppm, CO_2 emission growth must decrease to zero. Achieving this goal requires the choice of specific stabilization wedges: steps that would each prevent a billion metric tons of carbon per year from being emitted. Specifically, society must become more energy efficient, conserve resources, decarbonize, and strengthen natural sinks.

Efficiency and Conservation

Many opportunities exist to improve *energy efficiency*. A higher level of energy efficiency means the production or provision of a product or service with fewer energy resources. On the demand side, by installing insulation and new heating and cooling equipment, households may increase the efficiency of energy use. On the supply side, a higher level of energy efficiency means raising the performance of power plants, improving the process of transportation, and improving the extraction of energy resources. One caveat in this area, the *paradox of plenty*, occurs when higher levels of energy efficiency lead to monetary savings, which in turn, lead to a countering force: an increase in the consumption of energy. If the reduction of GHG emissions serves as the goal, public policy that complements methods to achieve energy efficiency—such as the establishment of a price for carbon, as advocated by William Nordhaus (2019)—provides incentive to reduce energy consumption.

Decarbonization

Because of the external costs from traditional energy sources and the ongoing depletion of fossil fuels, countries should implement a process of *decarbonization*: reliance on less carbon-intensive and even carbon-free energy. Along with efficiency and conservation, this option serves as a permanent path to the mitigation of CO_2 emissions. For decarbonization, a greater use of renewable energy and carbon capture and storage would accelerate the process: "If we started a broad decarbonization effort today—a gargantuan undertaking to overhaul our energy systems, building and transportation infrastructure and how we produce our food—the . . . rate of emissions reduction would (decline)" (Wallace-Wells, 2019).

Natural Sinks

Important wedge opportunities exist with natural sinks, which are reservoirs that accumulate and store carbon. In ecosystems, *carbon sequestration* occurs when the amount of CO_2 absorbed by organisms and soil exceeds the amount of the gas released by decomposition. Soil serves as a long-term reservoir, globally storing more carbon than terrestrial vegetation. Grasslands contribute to soil reservoirs: higher levels of CO_2 concentration in the atmosphere stimulate the growth of grassland plants. In the process, the plants draw nitrogen from the soil. In the areas of forest and agricultural management, if the current rate of deforestation decreases to zero, millions of acres are reforested in tropical and temperate zones and plantations are established on millions of acres of non-forested land the natural world would absorb a much higher amount of CO_2 from the atmosphere. In addition, during the process of industrial agriculture, when farmers convert forest or grassland to cropland, as much as one-half of the carbon in the soil is lost (Pacala and Socolow, 2004). The reason is that annual tilling increases the rate of decomposition of organic matter. The practices of cover crops, erosion control, and conservation tilling, however, reverse carbon losses. If these techniques expand in industrial agriculture, not only would wedge opportunities exist, but more sustainable food production would occur.

SUMMARY

The integrated assessment model of climate change demonstrates how economic and energy activity leads to both climate change and damage effects. Averting climate change will come with an economic cost. But the switch to a lower level of carbon intensity may eventually enrich the global economy. The problem is the atmospheric concentration of CO_2 is increasing. The accompanying rise in the average surface temperature leads to economic and environmental damages. Extreme weather, rising sea levels, a loss of biodiversity, conflict, food insecurity, and other damage effects serve as climate change problems. But the size of the threats necessitates organization at every level. National agreements, countries, states, and communities must implement greater energy efficiency and conservation, methods of decarbonization, and processes that strengthen natural sinks. This activity will determine whether the atmospheric concentration of CO_2 eventually stabilizes.

CONCEPTS

Carbon cycle
Carbon intensity
Carbon sequestration
Climate change

Climate sensitivity
Damage function
Decarbonization
Decay models
Energy balance
Energy efficiency
Feedback effects
Fuel efficiency
Global warming
Greenhouse effect
Greenhouse gases
Insolation
Natural sink
Negative feedback effects
Non-excludability
Non-rivalry
Paradox of plenty
Positive feedback effects
Radiative forcing
Social cost of carbon
Threshold effect

QUESTIONS

1. Explain each part of the integrated assessment model of climate change. Trace how an increase in the consumption of fossil fuels plays out in the model framework.
2. Explain the difference between the natural greenhouse effect and the anthropogenic impacts. What specific human activities contribute to the process of climate change?
3. The process of climate sensitivity refers to the likelihood that an increase in the atmospheric concentration of CO_2 will lead to a higher average temperature. The article by Stern (2008) discusses this process. Read the article and pay particular attention to discussion of this process. For global civilization, what are the risks of a higher average global temperature?
4. Review the scientific evidence that points to the contemporary role of humans in the process of climate change. According to the scientific evidence, discuss the extent to which human activity in the era of industrialization and globalization has altered the Earth's climate.
5. Many climate models show that severe weather and drought conditions will impact regions of the world differently. Research climate change

models such as the RICE and DICE models of Yale University and the GISS model of the Goddard Institute for Space Studies. Consider how changes in CO_2 concentration will impact global temperature and precipitation. How will these changes impact land values, especially in low-latitude and coastal regions? Which developed and developing countries will feel the greatest burden from climate change? How may a reduction in natural resources impact living standards and the potential for migration?

6. Read the influential article by Pacala and Socolow (2004), cited in the Bibliography. Describe the wedge framework, including the three categories of activities necessary to reduce CO_2 emissions and the fifteen wedges. Given the current state of the global economy, which activities are most viable?

Chapter 13

Energy Security

CLOSE ENCOUNTERS

On May 17, 2016, near the Chinese coast, two Chinese fighter jets flew dangerously close to an American surveillance aircraft. While the Pentagon raised concerns about the encounter, China rejected the U.S. account of the incident. Instead, by regularly sending flights near its territory, China accused the United States of threating its security. For both countries, the incident rekindled memories of a 2001 collision off the Chinese coast between a Chinese fighter jet and an American surveillance plane. A diplomatic crisis ensued.

In the South China Sea, China has transformed contested rocks and reefs into artificial islands. Many new islets exist. Airstrips and other military structures now lay claim to these small islands. But because of these actions, China is at odds with other countries in the region. The South China Sea is contested by the Philippines, Vietnam, Japan, and other Southeast Asian nations. These countries worry that China will use these bases to interfere with their rights to both fish and extract gas and oil.

During 2016, Asian countries pushed back. Vietnam seized a Chinese vessel for illegally entering its waters. Indonesia threatened to defend its territorial claims with fighter jets. Japan sent a submarine to make a port call in the Philippines, a sign of security cooperation between the two countries. The United States and the Philippines collaborated on their annual naval war games, military simulations in preparation for future conflict. The United States also carried out two patrols by aircraft and warships in disputed territory. But when a U.S. navy destroyer passed near the Fiery Cross Reef, currently being built into an island outpost, China sent fighter jets to patrol the area.

Why do countries focus on the South China Sea? Rich in natural resources, the sea serves as a vital waterway for $5 trillion in annual global trade. But along with long-standing maritime disputes, two strategic interests create a potentially dangerous environment. First, the South China Sea and the adjacent Straits of Malacca serve as crucial points of global transit (*choke points*). On its way to Asian markets, more than 30 percent of the world's shipped oil passes through the Strait of Malacca. Through the South China Sea, oil tankers move almost 80 percent of Chinese imports of crude oil and almost 70 percent of South Korean energy supplies. Second, the South China Sea possesses significant oil and gas deposits, equivalent to tens of billions of barrels. As a result, each country in the region has declared the South China Sea a national priority, investing in diplomatic and military resources to protect its interests. The South China Sea demonstrates that countries employ methods of international relations—diplomatic, military, and economic—to secure the global supply of energy. But these actions sometimes lead to conflict.

In the award-winning book, *The Quest: Energy, Security, and the Remaking of the Modern World* (2012)—required reading for students of energy economics—the Pulitzer Prize winning author Daniel Yergin explains why both the desire for energy security and examples like the South China Sea are important:

> Energy security needs to be thought of not just in terms of energy supply itself but also in terms of the protection of the entire chain through which supplies move from initial production down to the final consumer. It is an awesome task. For the infrastructure and supply chains were built over many decades without the same emphasis on security as would be the case today. The system is vast—electric power plants, refineries, off shore platforms, terminals, ports, pipelines, high-voltage transmission lines, distribution wires, gas storage fields, storage tanks, substations, etc.

This vast, global, and diverse energy network highlights why *energy security*—the ability to meet energy demand in the absence of conflict, high prices, or environmental degradation—is important: it determines the extent to which economic, diplomatic, and military resources must be allocated to maintain accessible and affordable energy flows for the world's inhabitants.

Energy possesses strategic value. Countries have a fundamental need for energy to power their economies. Disruption, turmoil, shortages, natural disasters, and volatile prices demonstrate how tangible and fundamental energy is to modern life. Threats to the supply of energy lead to conflicts in the Middle East, the South China Sea, and other parts of the world. In the last few decades, major disruptions in the oil market have created problems for energy systems. Examples include Hurricane Katrina in 2005, the war in Iraq in 2003, the Venezuelan strike in 2002, the Iraqi export suspension in 2001, and the Gulf Crisis in 1990–1991. The establishment of stable and reliable energy flows now constitutes, and will continue to constitute, a fundamental challenge during this century.

Daniel Yergin conceptualizes this important topic. In an essay published in 2006 in *Foreign Affairs*, Yergin argues that "energy security does not stand by itself but is lodged in the larger relations among nations and how they interact with one another." (Yergin's article, published before the "Arab Spring," in 2011—in which political turmoil and public demonstrations led to upheaval in some countries and the threat of an oil shock worldwide—is important. The article explains the global impact of political instability on energy markets in the Middle East.)

The interconnectedness that Yergin describes means that a nation may take steps to strengthen both its domestic energy infrastructure and connections to global energy networks. But these challenges are daunting, especially in a global perspective. Every day tens of millions of barrels of oil cross oceans on tankers. Hundreds of millions of tons of liquid natural gas cross borders. The point of this chapter is that these and other global resource flows increase the degree of integration of energy systems, but also make them more vulnerable to disruption. To address these challenges, the following sections develop a model of energy security, consider energy and geopolitics, and discuss methods to increase energy security.

MODEL OF ENERGY SECURITY

The concept of energy security has evolved. In the 1970s, it meant the stable flow of oil at reasonable prices. In the 1980s, energy security included secure nuclear facilities. In the 1990s, energy security incorporated stable and affordable flows of natural gas. Today, traditional energy markets, multiple cross-border pipelines, a growing renewable energy infrastructure, hundreds of refineries, thousands of offshore platforms, and millions of miles of global transmission lines are interconnected to parts of global energy networks. With the emergence of these long-distance networks, both centralized and distributed energy providers develop in parallel. Climate policy addresses fossil fuel consumption. These changes create unforeseen security challenges, as energy systems transition to cleaner technologies. Energy security has evolved to account for changing global conditions, including nations diversifying their energy supplies, the need for energy to fuel economic growth, threats of terrorism, instability in some energy exporting nations, and volatile energy prices.

The desire among nations to establish stable sources of energy depends on energy markets and a vast, global energy infrastructure described in Yergin's (2012) quote at the beginning of the chapter. But interdependencies exist between financial and energy markets, technology and power generation, refining, and distribution. These relationships heighten the risk of disruptions in energy supply through market disturbances, political turmoil, technical failures, natural disasters, or accidents.

In this volatile framework, the key to energy security is diversification. The existence of many energy sources hedges against disruption in individual markets. But diversification entails more than reliance on a number of technologies. An additional aspect of diversification is the degree of centralization of energy sources. Centralized power, for example, in the form of nuclear, coal, hydroelectric, or geothermal technologies is most prone to disruption from natural disasters, war, or terrorism. In contrast, distributed energy technologies such as solar, wind, or waves are least prone to disruption. As a result, energy systems that develop multiple technologies with different degrees of centralization provide safeguards against disruptions.

Another aspect of diversification is the ability to address intermittent supply. For example, an energy system may implement renewable technology in the form of wind or solar; however, these technologies lead to intermittency, because the wind does not always blow and the sun does not always shine. Energy systems that address this problem will employ geothermal and hydroelectric technologies, smart meters, and battery storage (Jacobson, 2009).

Today stable energy systems exemplify diversification. But a contemporary approach to energy security must include other goals, including the establishment of excess production capacity, plans to respond to high energy prices, access to information (such as that supplied by the International Energy Agency), recognition of global integration, and acknowledgment that disruptions have a temporal dimension.

We may therefore think of energy security in a multidimensional context, as the continuity of energy supply at affordable prices in the absence of both conflict and damage to the environment. In other words, energy security is the "low vulnerability of vital energy systems" (Cherp and Jewell, 2014). Vital energy systems, in this context, support critical functions (power, electricity, fuels, buildings, infrastructure, and transportation) with energy resources, technologies, and important uses linked together by resource flows.

Countries view energy security, however, through different lenses, depending on their unique characteristics. Examples include resource endowments and positions with respect to energy exports, imports, and cross transit. Energy exporting countries such as Saudi Arabia want to maintain the security of energy demand, higher prices, and stable markets. Importing countries such as South Korea look to diversity imports, lower prices, and substitute fuels. Cross-transit countries that rely on transportation networks focus on trade, competition, and the quantity of energy reaching domestic markets.

However, if countries become too absorbed with individual aspects of energy security such as stable supplies, other elements become more obscure.

Countries such as India with large rural populations and a growing energy system must not forget problems of indoor air pollution and energy poverty. Policymakers who enhance energy diversification to include nuclear power in countries like Japan increase their vulnerability to natural disasters. As it turns out, this cycle is common. A nation may solve one problem but create another. Therefore, energy security requires an understanding of energy interconnections and interdependencies.

Given these tradeoffs, secure energy systems meet energy demand while withstanding disturbances. They are flexible and adaptable. They do not impose undue burden on the environment. But local, regional, and global disruptions impact energy supply chains. When external threats come to fruition, resilient energy systems address the threats, secure energy supplies, and re-establish stable market conditions. The following model of energy security reflects these complexities by including multidimensional and integrated characterizations of risk and uncertainty, dimensions of security, and impacts (figure 13.1).

SOURCES OF DISRUPTION

Many potential disruptions exist. Disruptions characterized with risk refer to those with well-understood outcomes and probabilities. These are generated within energy systems and have technical and human origins. Technical risk includes blackouts, emissions infrastructure problems, mechanical failure, thermal failure, and waste. These sources of risk involve the technical aspects of providing power to electricity grids, buildings, manufacturing processes, and transportation. They are also important for fuel choices, greenhouse gas emissions, and global warming. Human risk includes employee errors and poor management. Uncertain disruptions or threats refer to those with well-understood outcomes but possess different probabilities of occurrence. These are external to energy systems, often uncontrollable, and have economic, geological, geopolitical, natural, societal, and technological origins (Kucharski and Unesaki, 2015).

Energy System

An energy system consists of the interconnected components of technology, infrastructure, and institutions that convert sources of energy into energy services. The energy system is thus the supply chain that entails the procurement of primary energy sources, the processes of transformation, and final energy demand. It is vulnerable to risks, threats, and systemic failures. The energy system interacts with other systems, including the economy, financial markets, international trade, politics and government, public and civil society, and telecommunications.

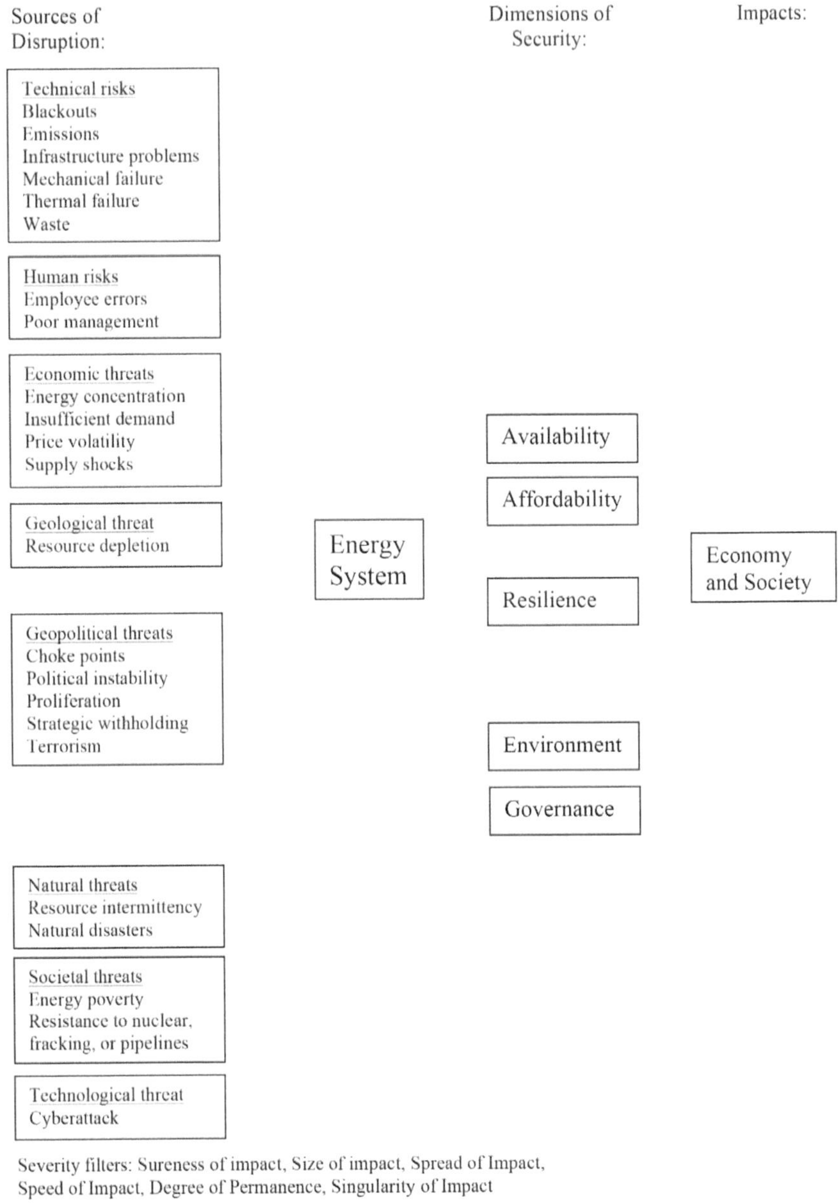

Figure 13.1 Model of Energy Security. *Sources*: Author using information from Kucharski and Unesaki (2015), Sovacool and Saunders (2014), Winzer (2012), and Loschel et al. (2010).

Dimensions of Security

Five dimensions encapsulate the challenges of energy security and provide a multidimensional view of the problem: availability, affordability, resilience, environment, and governance (Sovacool and Saunders, 2014).

Availability

In an energy system, a high degree of *availability* means an uninterrupted and sufficient energy supply. Because of energy integration, the following factors impact availability: domestic energy extraction and provision, diversification, and alliances. However, a disruption may or may not alter energy services. For example, hybrid cars possess dual charging units, with power sources that include both fossil fuels and electricity. An oil shock may increase the price at the pump, but not the price of charging. As another example, the Baltic Countries of Estonia, Latvia, and Lithuania import all of their natural gas from Russia. Energy supply disruptions from geopolitical conflict or political instability impact peak winter consumption. Households cannot replace gas with alternative fuels. Without paying higher prices, they are unable to heat their homes. As a third example, on August 14, 2003, a widespread power outage impacted 45 million people in eight U.S. states and 10 million people in Canada. The primary cause of the blackout was a software bug in the alarm system at a power station in Ohio. That evening, some power was restored, but for a week, many households did not have power. As a final example, the Hurricanes Katrina and Rita, in 2005, simultaneously disrupted electric power, natural gas, and oil markets in southern states in the United States. These natural disasters gave warning that future problems of availability may require multifaceted responses.

Affordability

In an energy system, a high degree of *affordability* occurs when consumers purchase energy with normal budget outlays and minimum price *volatility*—when prices differ from normal trends. In many energy markets, the price of natural gas is indexed to the price of oil. This scenario creates greater price security and less volatility; however, if a decrease in the supply of natural gas is accompanied by stable price, both excess demand and a reduction in the physical availability of the resource occur. Affordability also includes equity, which entails the extent to which higher energy prices impact lower-income households.

Resilience

The *resilience* of an energy system is its capacity to absorb disturbances and maintain its essential structure and functions. A resilient energy system is normally diversified with respect to its energy sources and includes an important component of decentralization. Even though different disturbances may push the energy system away from its usual state, a resilient system possesses the methods and capabilities that minimize the loss of energy services to end users.

Environment

Secure energy systems meet energy demand while preserving environmental quality. Secure energy systems must address the reality that flows of waste, pollution, and emissions impact water supplies, land use, air quality, wildlife, the availability of resources, ecosystems, the atmosphere, and other aspects of environmental systems.

Governance

For an energy system, *governance* includes both public accountability and energy efficiency. Public accountability is intended to reduce corruption, increase transparency, and deter the distorting influence of special interests. Energy efficiency—using less energy to provide the same service or providing more services with the same energy—involves improving the performance of the energy system, which includes the energy infrastructure, labor force, equipment, and dependence on unstable sources. Efficiency is a cost-effective way to increase energy security.

Impacts

Disruptions impact the dimensions of security and alter the continuity of energy services. But disruptions have multiple effects on regions, utilities, and consumers. We must therefore establish the context of energy security by addressing the following question, posed by Cherp and Jewell (2014): "Energy security for whom?" As an example, if the oil supply decreases because of strategic withholding, the impact depends on the actor or institution under consideration. A higher global price benefits producers. The change in oil revenue depends on price elasticity of demand. The higher price hurts consumers. On the other hand, consumers may adjust their behavior and become less dependent on oil for transportation. The overall impact, therefore, depends not only on the actors or institutions under consideration but also the degree of resilience of the actors or institutions. Moving forward, the model of energy security considers the economic and social impacts of disruptions on "typical" end users of energy, particularly households.

Severity Filters

Severity filters determine the extent to which the disruptions create deleterious outcomes. This depends on which severity filters are activated and how the filters interact. Severe impacts, such as the blackouts from Hurricane Katrina, in 2005, reduce energy security in the short term. A case such as this activates severity filters, triggering impacts on the economy and society. In other situations, such as when pirates attempt to block the movement of oil tankers in transit choke points, but do not succeed, a high degree of energy security remains.

Sureness of Impact

Sureness of impact entails the probability of a specific threat. The probability depends on both the specific energy system and disruption. What is the probability of a threat occurring? In advanced energy systems, local problems such as mechanical failure may possess small probabilities of creating specific threats. These systems have sufficient levels of oversight. Global sources of risk, however, such as resource depletion, may possess equal probabilities of occurring for energy systems in all countries. Four levels of risk probability exist:

- Unknown
- Stochastic
- Probabilistic
- Deterministic

First, the probability of a threat may be unknown. Second, the probability may be stochastic with a random probability distribution. Third, threats may be probabilistic: the time of occurrence is unknown but the probability is calculated with a degree of confidence. Fourth, threats may be deterministic: the time of occurrence and probability are calculated with degrees of confidence.

Size of Impact

The size of impact describes its magnitude:

- Phase changes
- Small changes
- Impending changes

Phase changes describe how disturbances such as ongoing greenhouse gas emissions could alter environmental and/or social conditions. Small changes such as resource intermittency impact individuals but do not alter energy systems. Impending changes increase the likelihood of harmful outcomes, but do not directly impact consumers.

Spread of Impact

The spread of impact describes the relevant geographical unit:

- Global
- National
- Local

Some threats, including geopolitical risk or strategic withholding, exist at the global level and impact all energy systems simultaneously. Other threats such as political instability that restrict energy exports exist at the national level. A final geographical unit, the local level, may experience the impact of mechanical failure or targeted terrorism. In addition to geography, the spread of impact is a function of government response, energy sub-markets, and bifurcated transmission networks. In the case of the Maldives, rising sea levels from global warming serve as a national threat. Energy submarkets may offer locational pricing, so a national supply disruption may impact regions in different ways. Because they establish subsystems for electricity transmission, bifurcated transmission networks reduce the spread of disruptions.

Speed of Impact

The speed of impact refers to the time frame in which the disturbance materializes:

- Very short term: a few hours or less
- Short term: less than two years
- Medium term: between two and fifteen years
- Long run: between fifteen and fifty years
- Very long run: greater than fifty years

Very short term or near real-time disturbances occur quickly, such as the termination of electricity service from blackouts, cyberattacks, natural disasters, and resource intermittency. Short-term disruptions may be transitory, including price volatility, supply shocks, and human error. Medium-term disruptions take longer to unfold, including political instability and proliferation. Long run disruptions involve infrastructure, energy substitution, and the diversification of technology. Disruptions over the very long run include fossil fuel depletion and emissions of greenhouse gases.

Degree of Permanence

The degree of permanence refers to whether the disturbance will be sustained over time. This severity filter determines how adaptable a system is to specific impacts:

- Transitory
- Sustained
- Permanent

Transitory impacts include disruptions like price volatility. But disturbances that occur quickly or slowly could be sustained, such as political instability or emission damage. Certain disruptions such as resource depletion create permanent impacts. In this case, energy systems must diversify, as scarcity increases.

Singularity of Impact

The singularity of impact describes the frequency of occurrence. It is important in preparing for responses to the sources of risk:

- Frequent
- Infrequent
- Singular

Frequent threats require continuous monitoring. Infrequent threats such as natural disasters require planning and forecasting. Singular threats such as resource depletion have not occurred.

APPLICATION OF THE MODEL

To apply the model of energy security, table 13.1 includes the sources of disruption, dimensions of security, and security filters. This information reveals that the sources of disruption, even when operating in isolation, have widespread impacts.

Interdependencies

The severity filters are interconnected. Christian Winzer (2012), an economist at the University of Cambridge, in his article on "Conceptualizing Energy Security," describes such interdependencies. First, the geographic spread of an impact increases its scope. A local impact of lower supply and higher

Table 13.1 Sources of Risk, Dimensions of Security, and Severity Filters

Source of Disruption	*Type*	*Dimension of Security*	*Sureness of Impact*	*Size of Impact*	*Spread of Impact*	*Speed of Impact*	*Degree of Permanence*	*Singularity of Impact*
Blackouts	Technical	Availability	Probabilistic	Small	Local	Very short	Transitory	Infrequent
Emissions	Technical	Environment	Probabilistic	Phase	Global	Very long	Sustained	Frequent
Infrastructure problems	Technical	Availability, Resilience	Probabilistic	Impending	Local	Long	Sustained	Infrequent
Mechanical failure	Technical	Availability, Resilience	Probabilistic	Small	Local	Very short	Transitory	Infrequent
Thermal failure	Technical	Availability, Resilience	Probabilistic	Small	Local	Very short	Transitory	Infrequent
Waste	Technical	Environment	Probabilistic	Small	Local	Medium	Sustained	Frequent
Employee errors	Human	Governance	Probabilistic	Small	Local	Short	Transitory	Infrequent
Poor management	Human	Governance	Probabilistic	Small	Local	Short	Transitory	Infrequent
Energy concentration	Economic	Affordability, Resilience	Stochastic	Impending	National	Long	Sustained	Frequent
Insufficient demand	Economic	Affordability, Environment	Stochastic	Impending	National	Short	Transitory	Infrequent
Price volatility	Economic	Affordability	Stochastic	Small	National	Short	Transitory	Frequent
Supply shocks	Economic	Availability	Stochastic	Small	National	Short	Transitory	Infrequent
Resource depletion	Geological	Availability	Unknown	Phase	Global	Very long	Permanent	Singular
Choke points	Geopolitical	Availability, Governance	Stochastic	Impending	Global	Short	Transitory	Frequent
Political instability	Geopolitical	Availability, Governance	Stochastic	Impending	National	Medium	Sustained	Frequent
Proliferation	Geopolitical	Governance	Probabilistic	Impending	Global	Medium	Sustained	Infrequent

Strategic withholding	Geopolitical	Availability, Affordability	Probabilistic	Small	Global	Short	Transitory	Infrequent
Terrorism	Geopolitical	Resilience, Governance	Unknown	Phase	National	Short	Transitory	Infrequent
Resource intermittency	Natural	Availability	Stochastic	Small	Global	Very short	Transitory	Frequent
Natural disasters	Natural	Availability, Resilience	Unknown	Phase	Local	Very short	Transitory	Infrequent
Energy poverty	Societal	Affordability	Deterministic	Small	National	Long	Sustained	Frequent
Resistance	Societal	Governance	Probabilistic	Small	Local	Medium	Sustained	Frequent
Cyberattack	Techno-logical	Resilience	Stochastic	Impending	National	Very short	Transitory	Frequent

Sources: Author using information from Kucharski and Unesaki (2015), Sovacool and Saunders (2014), Winzer (2012), and Loschel et al. (2010).

prices for a small number of consumers will not alter the production of output. But simultaneous increases in energy prices at the national level operate as a tax on all consumers, slowing spending at the macro level and impacting economic activity. Second, a connection exists between the singularity and the speed of a threat. Slow threats take time to materialize, so they do not occur at high frequencies. The depletion of fossil fuels will occur over decades or centuries and is thus a singular threat. Third, the degree of singularity of a threat is related to the sureness of impact. Frequently occurring events such as cyberattacks in an interconnected world are likely to create consistent probabilities from security analysts. Threats that are unique, however, are difficult subjects for probability estimation. Fourth, the speed and size of impact are related. Faster threats that impact energy availability, affordability, and resilience have the potential to increase the magnitude of the threat and impact the economy and society. Finally, other interdependencies, not mentioned in this paragraph, may materialize in different circumstances. The reader is encouraged to identify them.

RANKING THE SECURITY OF ENERGY SYSTEMS

Given the model of energy security, which nations perform well? To address this question, Brown and Sovacool (2010) first establish a number of indicators to measure the dimensions of energy security. For twenty-two Organization for Economic Cooperation and Development countries, the authors then quantify the indicators. Finally, they rank the countries according to empirical results. The findings are illuminating: the energy systems in the United Kingdom, New Zealand, Denmark, Austria, Australia, Greece, Turkey, and Switzerland all rank highly. The United States ranks last. What specific factors account for this result? Measured by sulfur dioxide and carbon dioxide emissions, the United States has the worst record for the environment of the countries in the study. The United States also has a high level of electricity consumption per capita, which reduces its rating. The countries that rank highly have relatively low levels of oil and natural gas import dependence (availability), electricity and gasoline prices (affordability), energy per unit of economic output (resilience), and emissions (environment).

ENERGY SECURITY AND INDEPENDENCE

Energy security does not imply energy independence. In the strictest sense, *energy independence* means satisfying demand with domestic energy sources. This self-sufficiency eliminates the need for imports, mitigates the influence of foreign instability, and offers symbolic power for politicians in election years. It is also both inadvisable and impossible. Self-sufficiency is inadvisable because isolationism in one economic sector is not consistent with openness in others. Self-sufficiency is impossible because energy markets are deeply integrated in a global web of relationships. For example, the United States exports coal to Canada, Mexico, Brazil, Belgium, Germany, Italy, the Netherlands, Ukraine, India, Japan, South Korea, and others. For well-functioning economies, these countries rely on coal imports. The United States imports oil from Saudi Arabia, Venezuela, Brazil, Ecuador, Iraq, Kuwait, Nigeria, and others. In terms of renewables, while the United States produces wind turbines, it imports equipment from companies like Vestas (Denmark) and Siemens Energy (Germany). U.S. imports for solar panels, valued in the billions of dollars, come from China, Taiwan, and elsewhere.

ENERGY SECURITY AND POLICY CHOICE

These complexities encourage policy makers to evaluate energy choices and their tradeoffs. The pursuit of individual policy packages may achieve certain dimensions of energy security, but not others. The goal of fighting global warming might entail carbon taxation, more renewable technology, the phasing out of coal-fired power plants, and ramping up nuclear energy. But a goal of reducing the reliance of energy systems on water might entail the removal of all subsidies for fossil fuels, more renewable energy, the phasing out of coal-fired power plants, and less nuclear energy. In addition, policy choices in specific energy systems are a function of existing technologies that nations use to pursue the dimensions of energy security. As a result, a nation that has already allocated a large amount of resources for renewables may be more open to the pursuit of more wind and solar. Energy security is therefore "intrinsically relative, not absolute," according to Sovacool and Saunders (2014). To achieve a greater level of energy security, a nation must prioritize the dimensions of energy security.

ENERGY SECURITY AND GEOPOLITICS

As the model of energy security demonstrates, energy security exists in a global context. Energy security depends as much on how countries manage their relationships as how prepared they are for energy disruptions. While globalization involves the flows of capital, information, technology, and trade, geopolitics addresses the entities—often governments and militaries—that attempt to influence or gain control over these flows. *Geopolitics*—the study of the relationship between power and space—examines the role of spatial factors (such as access to resources or the territorial location of supply and demand) that shape international relations. Energy security in a broad, geopolitical context entails the establishment of secure and resilient energy systems without contorting a country's diplomatic, political, or military arrangements.

In this context, what is the external cost of energy security? If a growing percentage of a country's government budget is necessary for military engagement in order to safeguard an energy system, the country is not energy secure. But if energy is to reach its destination, a country must establish secure transportation routes. To this end, countries may allocate diplomatic and military resources. As an example, fossil fuels from domestic sources are less vulnerable to disruption than fossil fuels flowing around the world. The reason is that choke points exist on sea routes where oil and liquid natural gas are transported. These routes, including the Suez Canal, the Strait of Hormuz, and the Strait of Malacca, are vulnerable to military conflict, accidents, or terrorist attacks. Another, the Bosporus Strait in Turkey, is 19 miles long and half a mile wide at its narrowest point. But every day 3 million barrels of Russian and Central Asian oil are transported on it, through the middle of Istanbul. In this area, a surge in piracy or regional instability disrupts the global oil market.

The consideration of geopolitics highlights energy security as a dynamic process. Energy security is a function of changing and interrelated domestic and global factors, including energy independence, diplomatic relations, and global markets.

ENERGY AND GEOPOLITICAL RISK

In October 1973, members of the Organization of Petroleum Exporting Countries (OPEC), plus Egypt and Syria, initiated an oil embargo. By restricting oil supplied in the global market, the "shock" increased the price of oil and disrupted the global economy. The embargo was a response to involvement of the United States and other countries in the 1973 Yom Kippur War between Arab states and Israel. Because the embargo occurred at a time of increasing oil consumption, many countries implemented actions to reduce future oil dependence, including efficiency and collaboration.

In 1974, a desire to mend the fractured spirit of the time led to the convening of thirteen industrial and oil-producing nations at the Washington Energy Conference. While a discussion of energy independence characterized the meeting, participating countries outlined a new energy security system for future crises and disruptions. From the conference emerged the International

Energy Treaty, which encouraged collaboration between industrialized countries during future supply shocks. The system—broadened and updated over time—serves as the foundation for the idea of energy security today. The treaty created the International Energy Agency (IEA), which works to ensure clean, affordable, and reliable energy for its twenty-nine members. Today the IEA serves as an excellent source of information on global energy markets.

The International Energy Treaty, however, did not prevent a subsequent shock. In 1979, the second oil embargo—stemming from the Iranian Revolution—decreased the global supply of oil, resulting in higher prices. In Iran, the production of oil fell by millions of barrels a day. During 1980, following the outbreak of the Iraq-Iran war, the production of oil in Iran nearly stopped. Iraq's production was severely curtailed. In much of the industrialized world, economic recession lingered. The price of oil did not return to its pre-crisis level until 1985.

ENERGY SECURITY AND GRAND STRATEGY

A *grand strategy* refers to the intersection of energy security and national security. Meghan L. O'Sullivan (2013), Professor of the Practice of International Affairs at the Harvard University Kennedy School, argues that this framework guides instruments of national power to advance economic, political, and diplomatic objectives. A grand strategy has three parts: goals, methods, and means. The goals include economic prosperity, political stability, and environmental quality. Securing stable energy flows at affordable prices constitutes another. This goal is so fundamental to the achievement of economic prosperity that countries employ many instrumental methods to achieve the goal. While energy exports and imports connect countries through exchange, the existence of energy resources in volatile areas creates conflict. The first Gulf War in 1991 serves as an example. In order to protect Kuwait, keep Iraqi forces away from the rich oil fields of Saudi Arabia, and maintain stability in the global oil market, military efforts by the United States and its allies pushed Iraqi forces out of Kuwait after they invaded. In this example, energy shaped and influenced military strategy. Countries may also use energy to cement alliances, advance their foreign policy interests, or project power. To achieve these objectives, a country may provide discounted energy exports. In the 1990s, after the collapse of the Soviet Union, Russia provided subsidized energy to the Commonwealth of Independent States. During the same decade, Iraq provided cheap oil to Jordan under the UN Oil-for-Food program. During the reign of Hugo Chavez (1999–2013), Venezuela provided inexpensive energy to Cuba and Bolivia, to maintain support for the country's political regime (O'Sullivan, 2013).

FUTURE TRENDS

Fossil fuels account for 80 percent of the world's primary energy. The IEA (2017b) forecasts this percentage to remain roughly the same for upcoming decades. Most discussions of energy security and geopolitics therefore focus on oil and natural gas; coal resources are more evenly distributed geographically. Six global trends serve as context for discussions of energy security (Bradshaw, 2009). First, the world is experiencing a global shift in energy demand. Changes in population, urbanization, and economic development are increasing the demand for energy in developing countries. Over time, most of the global growth in energy demand will occur in non-OECD countries. Second, a spatial mismatch exists between major oil consumers and reserve holders. Industrial countries have developed global oil and gas networks. Each day, millions of barrels of oil and billions of cubic meters of natural gas move through global networks. But the Middle East controls 50 percent of the world's oil. North American countries and Asian Pacific countries consume more than 55 percent of the daily total. Third, because of technological advances in fracking and horizontal drilling, natural gas serves as an important fuel for both electricity generation and industrial processes. Market competition contributes to the increase in demand for natural gas, but so does its lower carbon content. Compared to oil, natural gas is both cleaner and better positioned to satisfy the environmental criterion for energy security. Fourth, the United States is addicted to oil. It has 5 percent of the world's population, but consumes 20 percent of the world's oil. An increase in oil production and decrease in imports, however, will alter the country's geopolitical strategies. Fifth, the European Union imports the largest percentage of natural gas from Russia, about 25 percent of its total consumption. With rising natural gas import dependency, the EU could experience an even greater reliance on Russia. Sixth, China has the highest level of energy consumption in aggregate terms. China is the second largest consumer of oil and third largest importer after the United States and Japan. China's investments in the oil industries of many African countries, including Sudan and Niger, expand global networks, but risk establishing greater levels of geopolitical instability.

ENHANCING ENERGY SECURITY

This chapter argues that an important aspect of energy policy is to enhance energy security. A comprehensive assessment of risks and threats includes the type and source of disruption and vulnerabilities that exist in the energy system. Policy should match the source of risk or uncertainty with an appropriate response.

In general, countries increase energy security through diversification and domestic sourcing, but not all energy systems have the ability to implement multiple technologies or meet even small portions of demand with domestic sources. But a greater reliance on global markets increases the vulnerability of energy systems to price fluctuations, supply disruptions, and strategic withholding. Even more, geopolitical risk from the possibility of future disruptions in energy markets—similar to the oil shocks of the 1970s—permeates the foreign policy thinking of many countries. To enhance energy security in a world of global convergence and complexity, countries may implement countermeasures, including the diversification of supply, smart planning, market integration, access to information, pursuit of well-functioning markets, and public policy.

Diversification of Supply

Increasing the number of energy technologies and developing decentralized and renewable technologies reduces the impact of disruptions. In contrast, centralized technologies such as nuclear, coal, hydroelectric, and ethanol are at the greatest risk for disruptions from hurricanes, earthquakes, floods, or terrorist attacks. With centralized power sources, the larger the plant, the greater the risk for collateral damage. With coal and ethanol, collateral damage includes chemical releases. With hydroelectric power, flooding results. With nuclear power, collateral damage includes the release of radiation. Whereas nuclear plants are designed to withstand tornadoes, other power plants are not.

Smart Planning

Nations should plan for disruptions, so buffers exist. Smart planning facilitates flexible responses to external and internal disruptions. One example is strategic reserves, a safeguard against strategic withholding or geopolitical risk. In the United States, the strategic petroleum reserve, an emergency fuel storage of oil maintained by the U.S. Department of Energy, has the capacity to hold more than 700 million barrels of oil. This amount equals more than a month's supply. Other examples are spare production capacity, adequate storage, and the stockpiling of equipment along the energy supply chain. When natural disasters such as hurricanes, earthquakes, and tsunamis knock out power facilities and sections of the electricity grid, the availability of critical parts such as transformers for substations facilitates a faster recovery. When Hurricane Katrina pounded the United States in 2005, several refineries were damaged. They had to be partially or completely shut down for repairs, which took several months.

Market Integration

For most countries, market integration means the energy system relies on both domestic and foreign markets. In this context, security depends on the degree to which energy systems provide substitute fuels in the presence of market disruptions. An example is electricity. Interconnected electricity networks are preferred in the European Union. But the most important global example is oil. Daily, more than 90 million barrels are consumed. That translates into 35 billion barrels a year. This market demonstrates that security resides in global stability. Disruption in one part of the world leads to volatility everywhere. But secession from the global market is not an option. Energy systems must capitalize on global markets, but plan for global disruptions.

Access to Information

Energy security requires reliable information. When markets experience stable prices for fuel inputs and electricity output, producers and consumers benefit. In the presence of price volatility or other disruptions, however, reliable information helps policymakers formulate appropriate responses. The private and public sectors must collaborate to ensure that these statistics are available. At the global level, the IEA and the International Energy Forum provide useful information. In the United States, information and data are provided by the Energy Information Administration, an independent arm of the Department of Energy. Students of energy economics are encouraged to study the data and information of these important institutions.

Pursuit of Well-Functioning Markets

Well-functioning markets contribute to energy security by encouraging the forces of supply and demand to absorb shocks, resolve shortfalls, and address disruptions. A phase of resource intermittency that leads to higher prices will signal to consumers to adjust their spending patterns. Higher prices signal to producers to increase quantity supplied. Problem such as blackouts affect many consumers. The reliability of service depends on the robustness of the market.

Public Policy

Markets do not solve all security problems. Because energy systems are fundamental for strong economies, government guidance, regulation, and policies are necessary to enhance energy security. With the provision of electricity, for example, many countries have implemented independent transmission system operators responsible for both the short-term balancing of supply and demand and the provision of quality standards. Other policies may encourage a greater provision of renewables, increase vehicle standards, enhance energy conservation and efficiency, and enlighten the public on the importance of energy security. But regulatory failure, when it occurs, takes many forms. The regulation of electricity prices, for example, while important to protect consumers, may mask changes in the market. If a price change does not reflect a market imbalance, consumers do not have all the information necessary to make rational decisions. With these examples, policy makers must implement policy prescriptions for energy security that are equitable, robust, and politically feasible.

SUMMARY

Energy security means the stable flow of energy at affordable prices in the absence of both conflict and environmental degradation. While internal and external disruptions impact the dimensions of energy security, including availability, affordability, resilience, environment, and governance, countries may take countermeasures to prepare for disruptions. Countermeasures include the diversification of supply, smart planning, market integration, access to information, pursuit of well-functioning markets, and public policy. To enhance energy security, countries also need capable indicators that measure all of the following: risks to energy systems, dimensions of energy security, how disruptions impinge upon the most critical of these dimensions, and tradeoffs between energy choices. For example, a movement to diversify an energy system by increasing production from renewable technology may lead to more intermittency. As a result, corresponding data on technological adaptability and the provision of electricity helps to signify either progress or regress with respect to energy security. Overall, a multifaceted dataset for all dimensions of security demonstrates the complexity of assessment. Ultimately, however, the point of energy security is heterogeneity. Countries, energy operators, and consumers are not equally concerned about the dimensions of security. But over time energy security will increase in importance as energy systems become more integrated and susceptible to disruption.

CONCEPTS

Affordability
Availability
Choke points

Energy independence
Energy security
Geopolitics
Governance
Grand strategy
Resilience
Volatility

QUESTIONS

1. In table 13.1, do you agree with the labels for the severity filters? Which would you change? Why?
2. Figure 13.1 shows the dimensions of energy security. Pick a disruption such as mechanical failure, proliferation, or natural disaster. What is a real-world example? How could the disruption impact households?
3. Use the information from figure 13.1 on the dimensions of energy security plus the descriptions of severity filters to draw a diagram that determines the possible outcomes when a disruption impacts an energy system. Using your diagram, map two scenarios that include severity filters, one that has occurred and one that could occur.
4. In table 13.1, sources of disruption and severity filters describe how risks and threats impact energy systems. Many of the severity filters have interdependent impacts. As an application, pick a disruption such as supply shock or resource depletion. Determine how the severity filters unfold in interdependent ways.
5. Develop a set of numerical measures to evaluate each dimension of security. For example, data on primary energy supply, the fraction of primary energy as imports, and a diversification index (by fuel type or supplier) could measure the dimension of availability. When your method of evaluation is finished, use country data to evaluate how energy security changes over time. The chapter by Von Hippel et al. (2011), listed in the Bibliography, provides examples.

Chapter 14

Conclusion

Achieving a Clean Energy Transformation

DEFINING CHALLENGE

Solving the problem of climate change is this century's defining challenge. Global average temperatures are rising. Anthropogenic emissions of greenhouse gases are increasing. Without sustained action to reduce these emissions, the global temperature will continue to rise this century beyond the 2°C threshold set by the Paris Agreement of 2016. But meeting the world's growing appetite for energy while reducing greenhouse gas emissions will be impossible without major increases in energy efficiency and conservation, a massive deployment of wind, solar, geothermal, and other low-carbon technologies, advances in battery storage, and a major commitment to decentralized power systems. A failure to act will compromise the goal of climate stability. It will also undermine the objective of energy security. Solving the problem of climate change will require decarbonization of the global energy system, a massive reduction in the amount of gaseous carbon compounds released into the atmosphere per unit of energy output.

The road to decarbonization will be difficult. The analogy by Richard Lester (2016), Professor in the Nuclear Science and Engineering Department at the Massachusetts Institute of Technology, demonstrates why: if all the coal used in coal-fired power stations in one year were loaded onto a single train, the train would be 83,000 miles long. But replacing the coal with wind would require a train 135,000 miles long filled with wind turbines. Even more, to meet the goal of greenhouse gas emission reduction by mid-century, the deployment of the turbines would have to accelerate well beyond the current rate of turbine installation.

The decarbonization of energy systems will require a sustained effort over multiple generations. But private companies seem unlikely to spur the effort. Complementary actions by the private and public sectors are therefore necessary to create sustainable energy outcomes, including a stable long-term energy supply, reliable baseload power generation, limited atmospheric and environmental consequences, limited health effects, and strong economic contributions. The joint effort requires new policy initiatives, technology, and pricing regimes.

Decarbonization also requires *energy transformation*. As Lester and Hart (2012) explain in a book on energy innovation, "To avoid the most harmful effects of rising greenhouse gas concentrations while still meeting the growing demand for affordable and reliable energy services, nothing less than a fundamental transformation of current patterns of energy production, delivery, and use on a global scale will be required." More than a question of semantics, the focus should be on energy system "transformation." This transformation includes the speed in which the process of "transition" of specific aspects of the system takes place.

In this context, clean energy transformation would create new patterns of energy supply, demand, and market organization. It would necessitate new energy resources for the power, electricity, transportation, industrial, and commercial sectors. It would lead to new consumer behavior. Clean energy transformation would create greater degrees of energy availability, affordability, resilience, environmental quality, and governance, leading to more favorable economic and social outcomes. It would be large-scale and long-term in nature.

The IPCC (2018) report argues for immediate action to address the problem of climate change. Even though the world has locked in rising atmospheric greenhouse gas concentrations, actions taken to reduce future emissions will moderate the eventual impact on temperature. If little action occurs, average global temperature will continue to rise unabated throughout this century. As the IPCC (2018) report concludes, the climate impacts would be severe.

Transition to a cleaner energy system serves as the focus of this chapter. *Energy transition* is a "particularly significant set of changes to the patterns of energy use in a society, potentially affecting resources, carriers, converters, and services" (Sovacool, 2017). Energy transition is the time between the introduction of a new technology or resource and its growth to a significant portion of the market. To explore this concept, the chapter first discusses decarbonization and clean energy transformation. It then addresses the way forward, energy innovation, policies for energy transformation, visions of the future revisited, and the potential for a new energy paradigm.

THE ROAD TO DECARBONIZATION AND CLEAN ENERGY TRANSFORMATION

Transitions in technology or resources entail substitutions and conversions. Renewables replace fossil fuels. Electric cars replace vehicles with combustion engines. Centralized systems of power include decentralized contributions. As a result, this century's energy transition, not reducible to a single factor, is complex, multidimensional, and cumulative. If energy transition creates a clean energy system, it will require alterations at local, national, and global levels. For example, a clean energy system must establish new price signals, economies of scale for renewable resources, legal regulations, technologies, social values, and consumer behaviors.

In this context, the important question relates to time: how long do energy transitions take? In chapter 1, the book explained two visions of the future. The mainstream but pessimistic vision holds that energy transitions are long and protracted affairs. The alternative but optimistic vision holds that energy transitions occur quickly. Now that we have studied energy markets, fossil fuels, nuclear power, alternative technologies such as biofuels, geothermal, hydro, solar, and wind, and energy innovation, we may establish an informed position. But we must acknowledge that both protracted and quick energy transitions provide useful examples.

ENERGY TRANSITION AS A LONG AND PROTRACTED PROCESS

The establishment of new energy, economic, political, and social realities that lead to transformative change may take decades or centuries. No quick fixes are possible: both energy transitions (processes) and true transformations (outcomes) are slow affairs. According to Sovacool (2017), support for this protracted position stems from three areas: the historical record, change in a comparative context, and path dependency.

First, in history, energy transitions have taken time. Coal passed the 25 percent share of the global marketplace 500 years after the first commercial mines were developed in England. Oil took 90 years to surpass the same mark. Wind turbines, solar panels, hydroelectricity, and even nuclear power have yet to surpass the 25 percent mark. Steam engines, designed in the 1770s, did not take off until the 1800s. The internal combustion engine, developed in the mid-1880s, did not become widespread until the 1920s (Sovacool, 2017).

Second, new energy resources may gain market share but lag far behind market leaders. In the United States, hydroelectricity grew by threefold in the

15-year period culminating in 1964, but because other sources of energy grew faster, the national share fell from 32 percent to 16 percent. In the first ten years of this century, U.S. solar power grew by a factor of 16, investment in solar heating grew threefold, and investment in wind grew fourfold. But the overall contribution of these resources to final energy consumption increased from one-tenth of 1 percent to almost 1 percent, hardly a game changing increase (Sovacool, 2017).

Third, *path dependency* refers to the tendency that systems become committed to certain patterns of development, resulting from structural properties, institutions, behaviors, and values. Because these patterns are locked in place, energy transformation is difficult to achieve. Energy systems create their own positions of inertia. They undertake specific patterns of behavior for baseload electricity generation and the supply of fuels for the power, transportation, buildings, industry, and commercial sectors. Existing energy policies, resource capabilities, technological capacities, production possibilities, institutional legacies, tax codes, financial markets, and consumer behaviors support existing energy pathways (Sovacool, 2017).

Collectively, these institutions, patterns, and behaviors have locked us into the current era of carbon-dependent energy systems. This is why forecasts by the U.S. EIA (2018) predict that three-fourths of energy in 2040 will still come from fossil fuels.

ENERGY TRANSITION AS AN EXPEDITED AND QUICKER PROCESS

But expedited and quicker examples include transitions in energy end-use and successful transitions expediting future actions (Sovacool, 2017). At least five recent examples of rapid transition in energy end-use exist. In nine years, ending in the year 2000, Sweden phased in an almost complete shift to energy efficient lighting. In less than twenty years, the use of cookstoves in China reached half a billion people. To improve air quality, Indonesia implemented a three-year process of conversion of kerosene stoves to liquefied petroleum gas stoves, which served almost two-thirds of the country's households. In six years, Brazil successfully introduced flex-fuel vehicles that are capable of running on any blend of ethanol. This gives drivers the flexibility of switching between various blends of ethanol and gasoline and accounts for 90 percent of the country's vehicles. In the United States, in less than twenty years, air conditioning reached more than 50 million people.

The key for expedited energy transition is learning from previous success. Technological advance, for example, while integrated in markets, institutions, and policies, may be affordable, achievable, and transformative. Technological innovation and deployment may occur rapidly by creating new practices and behaviors that lead to decarbonization. Because we now have increasing knowledge of energy transition, we may apply it to future programs. Smart progression expedites energy transformation (Sovacool, 2017).

THE PATH DEPENDENCE OF ENERGY TRANSITION

As Sovacool (2017) explains, energy transitions are influenced by exogenous factors such as energy accidents (Fukushima), shortage conditions (the oil embargoes in the 1970s), or military conflict (the world wars stimulating the development of nuclear programs). Energy transitions are also influenced by endogenous factors such as aggressive policy implementation, stakeholder actions, political will, and economic circumstances. The implication is that most energy transitions result from a number of factors. They are complex, specific, and cumulative. As a result, they are explained by the process of path dependence: current decisions depend on past knowledge but are limited by the current competence base. Motorized vehicles, for example, are actually the amalgamation of a number of inventions, including the assembly line, the wheel, electric lighting, batteries, and combustion engines.

With path dependence, the world will continue to rely on fossil fuels and nuclear power, even when renewables become more cost-effective. (The world still uses steam engines and wood power.) Thus, "transitions often appear not as an exponential line . . . but as a punctuated equilibrium, which dips and rises" (Sovacool, 2017). These dips and rises are nonlinear pathways, drawing on synergistic advances in multiple areas. With clean energy technology, synergies include advances in computing, genetic engineering, energy transfer, storage capacity, and nanotechnology. Future energy transitions will therefore accelerate in ways that are different from past transitions and vary according to the path of technological advance.

Transition to More Solar Energy

Currently, solar energy accounts for a small percentage of electricity generation. But it deserves attention in the context of a clean energy transition because of its high sustainability rating. By mid-century, the requirements for limited environmental and atmospheric impacts from our energy choices will be valued higher than they are today. To reduce carbon dioxide emissions, renewable resources will move to the forefront. As a result, both photovoltaic and concentrated solar technologies will serve as important options in the process of decarbonization. Sunlight has the highest potential of the Earth's renewable energy sources. Solar energy could generate more than 15 terawatts of power with 10 percent efficiency conversion using technology that covers 2 percent of the Earth's land surface. In 2050, this would provide more than 50 percent of the electricity necessary to meet global demand. This would also contribute to the process of decarbonization.

But according to MIT (2015), even when solar power is more competitive, two things must happen for large-scale adoption. First, average cost must continue to decrease. Second, the solar supply chain must scale up. Emerging solar technologies and silicon-based panels must receive continued investment. Advances in energy storage technologies must address the problem of intermittency. Public policies must continue to provide incentives for both photovoltaic installation and the deployment of solar farms. To increase solar capacity, capital and labor constraints must not be binding. In the short term, technological gains will flow from incremental advances in efficiency, the streamlining of manufacturing, and consumer behavior. Over the longer term, the potential for a solar scale-up and massive transition will depend on the development of innovative technologies.

Transition to More Wind Energy

Wind is the world's fastest growing source of renewable energy. In the United States and Germany, wind accounts for sizable levels of renewable capacity added each year. But on a global scale, a small percentage of electricity generation comes from wind power. The U.S. Department of Energy established a goal to generate 20 percent of the country's electricity in a decade. Globally, wind could generate more than 20 percent of electricity. Are these realistic targets?

On one hand, the greater the wind capacity, the more challenging it is to integrate wind power. Also, like solar, the electricity sector does not rely on wind to generate baseload power. When the wind does not blow, the system must rely on other energy resources. Moreover, the supply of wind is dispersed, and not always near population centers.

On the other hand, with wind farms, the marginal cost of providing an additional kilowatt hour of electricity is low. Wind results from differences in atmospheric pressure, solar radiation, irregularities on the Earth's surface such as mountains and valleys, and the spinning of the planet itself. When air is heated by the sun, it becomes lighter and rises. This creates a vacuum. Cooler air then fills the vacuum. The flow of air may be as strong as hurricane winds or as gentle as a breeze. The point is the sun will continue to shine, and wind will continue to blow. This qualifies wind as a sustainable form of energy.

Today, innovation in wind power increases both the reliability and the efficiency of turbines. Wind power does not lead to greenhouse gas emissions. In Europe, Germany and Spain serve as leaders, with wind generating up to 20 percent of electricity supply. In these and other European countries, wind capacity continues to rise. Worldwide, sales of wind-generating equipment increase annually. A conventional turbine generates more than a hundred times as much electricity as a turbine from 1980.

A full transition to a mature wind industry, however, will require the development of large-scale wind farms all over the world. Developers must buy turbines, seek regulatory approval, negotiate purchase contracts with utilities, and provide grid connections. As these processes evolve, wind power could exceed nuclear power electricity generation. Wind power, like solar, could become a key component of clean energy transformation.

Transition to Smart Grids

Today's electric grids are often regional networks loosely connected with low-capacity lines. Commercial customers pay less for electricity than residential and industrial customers, because larger customers purchase power with both lower delivery costs and higher voltages. Many grids are older, suffer from energy inefficiencies, and require capital upgrades.

But the MIT (2011) study on the future of the electric grid discusses many opportunities. First, as electricity generation from renewable sources increases, transmission networks could become more flexible. Second, the electric power system could become more interconnected. Third, as new generators are built, the capacity of the transmission network could increase. Fourth, electric grids could enhance distribution by fully integrating advanced information technology, sensor capabilities, and new communications infrastructures. This could stimulate power flows in real time, help operators anticipate and respond to problems, and increase system agility and responsiveness. Finally, technological advance could establish decentralized networks. These smart systems could provide two-way methods of communication between power generation, homes, factories, commercial centers, buildings, and electric vehicles.

THE WAY FORWARD: ACHIEVING THE CLEAN ENERGY TRANSFORMATION

This book argues that clean energy transformation will fuel global prosperity. But an increase in the supply of energy, resulting from economic growth, currently leads to more greenhouse gas emissions. The challenge is to therefore decouple economic growth and greenhouse gases. As the climate change chapter in this book makes clear, this process is underway. But there are several pathways to lower emission levels. The IEA (2014b) identifies five.

Take Immediate Action

Actions taken today include the implementation of climate change adaptation and mitigation policies. According to IEA (2014b), the following four actions would deliver most of the emission reduction necessary: energy efficiency, the reduction of coal-fired power generation, the phasing down of fossil fuel subsidies, and the reduction of methane flaring and venting in gas and oil production. These actions have zero net cost: the costs of implementation would be offset by benefits. Europe should focus on inefficient coal production and energy efficiency. The Middle East should focus on the reduction of methane emissions and the phasing down of fossil fuel subsidies. North America should focus on the reduction of coal-fired power generation and energy efficiency. But these actions should address long-term consequences. For example, a switch to more gas-fired electricity generation and away from coal would provide short-term environmental gains; however, a longer term strategy of clean energy transformation, which emphasizes renewable technology, should influence investment decisions in natural gas.

Decarbonize the Electricity Sector

Electricity sectors generate 25 percent of the world's greenhouse gas emissions. To achieve the 2°C scenario of the Paris Agreement and contribute to the process of decarbonization, these emissions must decrease. One way is to decrease electricity demand from high-emission sources with energy efficiency and conservation. Another way is to develop a cleaner supply of electricity with the deployment of cleaner technologies. Equipment retirements and policy interventions are necessary to accelerate the process of decarbonization in the electricity sector (IEA, 2014b).

Reshape Investment and Accelerate Innovations

Clean energy transformation requires a shift in investment. Variable generation resources, such as wind and solar, necessitate the implementation of non-dispatchable technology, not controlled by utility operators. New energy health sensors reduce system failures and regulate the flow of electricity from clean energy sources. Power stations, transmission lines, transmission substations, and distribution lines must be reconfigured with clean technology options. As the cost of technologies such as photovoltaic modules, battery storage, and wind turbines decreases, achieving the 2°C scenario will become more likely (IEA, 2014b).

Mobilize Non-Climate Goals

Even though the problem of climate change serves as motivation for transformation in energy systems, non-climate goals are also important (IEA, 2014b):

- The desire for air quality and public health motivates efforts for energy efficiency.
- The goals of energy security, diversification, and lower energy dependence motivate efforts for fuel economy and renewable technologies.
- The preference for improvements in transportation networks motivates the development of alternative vehicles.
- The desire for sustainable development motivates efforts for clean energy production, greater efficiencies in power generation, and zero carbon buildings and homes.
- The goal of increasing living standards motivates the expansion of public transportation.
- The preference for stronger public budgets motivates fossil fuel subsidy phase-outs.

Strengthen the Resilience of Energy Systems

Climate change threatens the security of energy systems. Risks stem from the outcomes of a changing climate. These outcomes could lead to technical risks, including blackouts and infrastructure problems; geopolitical threats such as political instability; and natural threats, including natural disasters. To both hedge against these risks and provide a pathway to clean energy transformation, countries should increase the *resilience* of their energy systems, the extent to which systems may undergo change while maintaining structure, functions, and options to develop. The impact of climate change on an energy system depends on the degree of vulnerability of the system. At any scale, the degree of vulnerability is a function of the sensitivity and exposure of that system to hazardous conditions. It is also a function of the resilience of the system, the abilities to adapt, cope, recover, and transform. Resilience is determined by power asymmetries, whose needs are being met through strategic responses, and the relative strength of the institutions within which management practices are embedded. With the outcomes of climate change altering the structure and functions of energy systems, an increase in resilience will strengthen the ability of energy systems to transition to cleaner technology.

Unlocking Energy Innovation

The debate over climate change has focused on the idea that the price of fossil fuels must increase to the point where significant reductions in carbon dioxide emissions occur. This is certainly important. But Lester and Hart (2012) argue for a pathway of innovation that will build public support for energy transformation. The costs to workers, communities, and industries of higher energy prices should be balanced, according to Lester and Hart (2012), by safer, better, and more cost-effective energy services. These services—such as the provision of clean electricity—would be made possible by new energy institutions, business models, and technologies.

History provides reason for hope. In the United States, the private and public sectors working in tandem built systems of innovation that led to transformation in information technology, communications, social media, health, and national defense. But creating such an environment will accelerate the pace of energy innovation and the number of low-carbon options. Fortunately, "organizations and individuals are knit together by a set of beliefs, norms, incentives, and laws that give each a productive role to play. A lot of competition exists, but so does mutually beneficial cooperation" (Lester and Hart, 2012). The system of innovation does not always lead to an intended outcome. But it provides context, incentive for technological advance, and includes four stages, according to Lester and Hart (2012):

- Create options
- Demonstrate viability
- Establish conditions for early adoption
- Improve output and processes

Each stage involves the flow of knowledge. When creating options, innovation pathways encourage ideas and attract new entrants. The key is to expand technical expertise in a particular area. While most ideas originate in the private sector, public funding contributes. To demonstrate viability, business, technical, and regulatory risks must decrease to the point that innovation becomes attractive to investors, providers, and consumers. The key is to create a reasonable time horizon. In this stage, private investors and innovators share much of the cost and risk. By establishing conditions for early adoption, innovators and investors advance strategies for market development, create the necessary infrastructure, and implement early deployment of the energy good or service. Capabilities for manufacturing and distribution are then established. Early adopters provide feedback. Knowledge and learning about the innovation increase, but unit costs decrease. When improving output and processes, market share increases. Companies that sell new products or services refine designs, business models, production systems, and analysis of consumer behavior. More marketable and technological versions of the output advance. Evolutionary improvements exceed the value gained at first deployment (Lester and Hart, 2012).

When applying this framework, innovators acknowledge that consumers value the services that energy provides, not the energy itself. Consumers want a stable supply of electricity, reliable vehicles, dependable heating and cooling systems, and steady costs. But to achieve these outcomes, the markets, infrastructures, and policies that create these outcomes must evolve.

The time element creates a challenging environment for innovation. The innovator faces high expectations from consumers in terms of reliability, quality, and cost. But this context differs from recent innovations such as social media and the smart phone, which were new products or services. Consumers did not have preconceived expectations with respect to performance and outcomes. Preferences developed over time. The implication is the "energy sector is deeply embedded in the fourth stage of the innovation process" (Lester and Hart, 2012). To be effective, new energy innovations must be driven by both market forces and incentives from the public sector. Innovations that are not developed to scale, such carbon capture and storage, are not effective on a global or even national level.

Energy innovation will not occur quickly, because of the large number of features in the system. Lester and Hart (2012) envision energy transformation occurring in three waves, when different sectors are ready for transformation. The first wave, beginning immediately, should focus on energy efficiency in buildings, transportation, and power generation. The second wave, developing with the first and continuing to the middle of the century, should deploy low-carbon technologies for electricity generation, including advances with renewables and electric transportation. The third wave, occurring in the second half of the century, should entail dramatic advances in technology, including carbon-neutral biofuels, advanced solar capabilities, fusion, networked cities, and linkages between power generation and user inputs.

A number of advances demonstrate the existence of the first two waves. In the United States, energy efficiency is contributing to the stabilization of electricity consumption. A number of states offer incentives for energy efficiency. Many states also implement policies that decouple the revenue streams of utilities from sales. This offers a reward for a reliable supply of electricity and more renewables. Others, such as the Energy Independence and Security Act of 2007, provide incentives for more efficient light bulbs and tighter building codes (Massey, 2014).

With decarbonization, large-scale battery storage for power stations is preparing for unprecedented growth. Growing energy storage capacity enhances grid reliability, reduces the likelihood of power outages, and lowers peak demand charges. Such storage capability is coming into the market in the form of lithium-ion battery systems, now in place in some Southern California utilities (Cusick, 2017). A growing market for solar panels and wind turbines leads to fewer carbon dioxide emissions, job creation, and the saving of fresh water. With respect to jobs, expanding solar and wind creates more jobs than expanding fossil fuel and nuclear power stations. Some jobs are in the construction of infrastructure. Others are in installation, maintenance, and engineering. With respect to water, to produce 1 megawatt-hour of electricity, enough to power 164 homes, nuclear energy requires 13,000 gallons of water; coal requires 669 gallons; and natural gas requires 385. In contrast, solar and wind do not require any water (Castillo et al., 2018).

POLICIES FOR CLEAN ENERGY TRANSFORMATION

To achieve clean energy transformation, it is necessary to create an informed, consistent, and innovative policy framework. So far, this has been difficult to achieve. One reason has been the inability of the world to come together and develop a coherent energy policy in the face of climate change. Another reason is the influence of the fossil fuel industry. Nevertheless, optimal energy policy would alter the decision calculus affecting business investment, government spending, and household consumption, and therefore clean energy transformation. Optimal policy would decrease carbon intensity and provide more efficient energy generation.

According to Aldy and Stavins (2012), there are three ways to achieve this goal: price greenhouse gas emissions commensurate with their external costs; subsidize the process of energy innovation; and mandate changes in energy technology and emissions performance. While all three serve important roles in achieving energy transformation, externality pricing creates incentives for innovation, promotes cost-effective emission reduction, and improves the fiscal position of governments. When households and businesses face a common energy price that reflects the external cost of greenhouse gas emissions, informed responses favor clean energy alternatives. In addition, government defers to the private sector for innovative ideas.

As this book explains, different options are available. The carbon tax is the most straight-forward policy to price greenhouse gas emissions. It is administratively efficient and incorporates existing methods for reporting and fuel-supply monitoring. It also potentially yields a double dividend of a cleaner environment and tax system efficiency gains, if revenue recycling occurs and tax interaction effects are minimized. A cap-and-trade system, another policy option, regulates stationary pollution sources by requiring polluters to pay to pollute. Faced with a choice of abating emissions or purchasing an allowance, firms will choose the least-cost option. In this system, trading leads to the allowances being put to their most valued uses. Clean energy standards, a third option, establish a technology-oriented goal for the electricity sector. In a method similar to cap-and-trade, power plants using suitable technology may sell tradable credits to power plants that don't have such technology. This activity minimizes the costs of meeting the standard's goal. The difference between the two policies is that the clean energy standard establishes the policy goal in terms of technology, but cap-and-trade establishes the goal in terms of emissions.

But public policies create distributional consequences. Price changes vary across sectors of the economy, income groups, and regions. Higher energy prices impact poorer households the most. As a result, methods of redistribution, which may occur when revenue is raised through carbon taxes or cap-and-trade systems, may be necessary to mitigate harmful effects of new energy policies. Another issue is the process of legislation. Throughout much of the industrialized world, cap-and-trade systems have emerged as politically feasible, but carbon taxes remain a more direct way to price emissions. Finally, new energy policy benefits from previously successful experiences. One example is the 2008 carbon tax levied in British Columbia, which was implemented gradually and supplemented with government payments sent to households representing expected revenue. Another example is the sulfur dioxide cap-and-trade program in the United States, established under Title IV of the 1990 Clean Air Act Amendments. Under the program, emissions declined.

Another policy challenge is that, over the long-term, energy innovations must compete with conventional energy technologies. The reason is the *commercialization gap*, which means the gap between the number of clean energy technology initiatives the economy needs and the number of clean energy projects that actually occur. The number of projects that are implemented is lower than the optimal amount because they are too risky for private equity or too capital intensive for venture capital. Closing the commercialization gap requires both the allocation of public dollars and encouragement of private investment. Previous examples in the United States include the nuclear energy program in the 1950s and 1960s that led to the development of light water reactors and the reaction to the 1970s oil embargoes that led to the development of the solar industry (Yanosek, 2012).

Renewable energy policies in over 100 countries establish objectives and targets, create markets, reduce upfront costs, develop capacity, and remove barriers. They impact the availability, price, and growth of new technology. No one policy drives the process of clean energy transformation, so many are needed: renewable portfolio standards, feed-in-tariffs, building codes, tax credits, and subsidies establish national renewable energy capacity targets, incentives to develop renewable power generation technologies, network connections, purchase agreements for clean electricity production, and methods to develop and deploy more efficient and less expensive renewable technologies (El-Ashry, 2012).

VISIONS OF THE FUTURE REVISITED

In chapter 1, this book made the case that there is reason to be optimistic about a clean energy future. After reading this book, do you agree? That is, are recent trends any indication of future success? The author's answer is a guarded "yes." For reference, *The Political Economy of Clean Energy Transitions* (2017)—a book important for students of energy economics—provides three reasons for guarded optimism.

First, the Paris Climate Agreement (2016), signed by 195 countries within the United Nations Framework Convention on Climate Change, represents a shift in negotiation style. Instead of a centralized approach, the Paris Agreement valued decentralization. Individual countries negotiated fair and achievable greenhouse gas emission trajectories.

Second, the rapid pace of technological advance in renewable energy is influencing the political economy of clean energy transformation. Moving forward, politics will influence policies. Policies will impact technological advance. This advance influences politics. In a ten-year period, the global solar module price index—a measure of spot prices for dominant solar technologies—fell by a factor of four, exceeding many forecasts. While not as dramatic as solar, decreases in the cost of wind power have also been rapid. These changes have increased the consumption of renewable energy.

Third, countries now have a much greater understanding of the complex intersectionality of climate change problems, adaptation strategies, and mitigation options. The implication is that a clean energy transformation is becoming more fully integrated into the process of economic decision making.

A NEW ENERGY PARADIGM?

Whether or not the pessimistic or optimistic vision of the future seems more likely, we are entering a period of time in which some are calling a "new energy paradigm" (Petit, 2017; Bernstein and Collins, 2013; Helm, 2007).

Thomas Kuhn (1962), in his famous book, *The Structure of Scientific Revolutions*, defines *paradigm* as "universally recognized scientific achievements that for a time provide model problems and solutions to a community

Table 14.1 Characteristics of the Current Energy Paradigm

Scale	*Area*	*Characteristic*
World	Electricity generation	Global reliance on fossil fuels for electricity generation
	Carbon dioxide emissions	Global increase in carbon dioxide emissions
	Population and energy demand	Global increases in both population and energy demand, the latter with relatively high-carbon fuels
	Production	Oil accounts for the largest share of total energy production
	Growth in energy	Renewables are the fastest growing energy source
United States	Electricity generation	Reliance on natural gas, coal, and nuclear for electricity generation
	Carbon dioxide emissions	National leveling of carbon dioxide emissions: even though CO_2 emission increased during the first seven years of the current century, the country experienced a leveling of these emissions since
	Population and energy demand	National increases in both population and energy demand. The latter is dominated by oil, natural gas, coal, and nuclear power
	Production	Natural gas accounts for the largest share of total energy production
	Growth in energy	Natural gas production is increasing fastest; on a percentage basis, non-hydroelectric renewables are growing the most

Source: Author.

of practitioners." What is the prevailing set of problems and solutions with respect to energy? That is, what is the current paradigm? The current energy paradigm has man characteristics (table 14.1).

But a new energy paradigm would entail a movement away from fossil fuels, especially with respect to electricity generation; an increase in energy efficiency and conservation; and an increase in demand for renewable energy resources.

What do the forecasts show? The International Energy Agency's *World Energy Outlook 2017* forecasts the following trends to 2040:

- Rapid deployment and falling costs of clean energy technologies
- The growing electrification of energy
- Global energy needs rising more slowly than in the past but expanding by 30 percent, equivalent to adding another China and India to today's demand
- A rising trajectory for oil, although demand will slow starting in the mid-2020s due to greater efficiency and fuel switching in vehicles
- A growing global economy at an average rate that exceeds 3 percent annually

- A population that grows to more than 9 billion
- A process of urbanization that adds a city the size of Shanghai every 4 months
- A change in meeting global energy needs in favor of natural gas, renewables, and energy efficiency

In terms of the United States, the U.S. EIA (2018b) forecasts the following trends to 2050:

- High economic growth case: GDP growth of 2.6 percent and energy consumption of 0.7 percent annually
- A mix of energy consumption changing from oil and coal to natural gas and non-hydroelectric renewables and a flat contribution from nuclear power
- Fewer carbon dioxide emissions from oil and coal, but more from natural gas
- More energy exports
- Energy efficiency, fuel economy improvements, and structural changes in the economy that decrease energy intensity (units of energy consumed per unit of GDP)

A number of reasons would create a *paradigm shift* in energy, when it becomes increasingly hard to reconcile accepted wisdom with existing evidence. First, new renewable electricity generation technologies are commercially viable. Technological advancements have created performance improvements and cost reductions, particularly with solar photovoltaics and land-based wind turbines. These advances, complemented by new business models for renewables, innovative financing, and supportive policies, have created new market opportunities. As markets expand and technologies improve, therefore, cost reductions will continue. The implication is that the cost of electricity from renewable sources will become favorable for both utility and residential markets. As more renewable energy options for electricity generation emerge, less water intensive and cleaner processes will encourage rapid deployment in both decentralized and centralized markets.

Second, the sustainability criteria demonstrate a clear advantage for solar and wind. In the chapters on fossil fuels, nuclear power, and renewables, the six sustainability criteria were applied to each energy technology. Table 14.2 summarizes the results.

Third, clean energy technologies advance programs of energy security: countries rely less on fuel imports. Advances in battery storage are occurring. Net gains exist with the development of renewable energy generation. These developments point to the growth in regional energy trade as a complement to greater energy security at the national level (Arent et al., 2017).

Table 14.2 Energy Technology and the Sustainability Criteria

Sustainability Criteria	*Oil*	*Coal*	*Natural gas*	*Nuclear*	*Bioenergy*	*Geothermal*	*Hydro*	*Solar*	*Wind*
Long-term energy supply					√	√	√	√	√
Baseload power		√	√	√			√		
Environmental impacts								√	√
Atmospheric consequences				√				√	√
Human health				√		√	√	√	√
Economic performance	√		√	√		√		√	√

Source: Author.

Fourth, the challenge of climate change will become so encompassing for economies, policy makers, markets, and business models that a clean energy future will serve as an important organizing principle.

Fifth, the dispersion of solar, wind, and geothermal technologies present attractive pathways to decentralization. This approach provides an opportunity to leapfrog expensive investments in energy infrastructure. The dispersed nature of future expansion will appeal to both developed and urban environments and developing and rural environments without sophisticated grids. Advances in energy storage, methods of communications, and data analytics accelerate the process of decentralization (Arent et al., 2017).

Whether a new energy paradigm takes shape, however, depends on both deployment strategies and the availability of new technologies. The deployment of advancing technology into both markets and the repertoires of businesses and households hinges on nationally customized strategies, focused public policy and regulation, engagement in the private sector, market reforms, and analytical data and tools. Ongoing innovations in energy systems necessitate the adaptation of markets and policies when incremental change occurs. But with paradigm shifts, evolutionary change leads to the availability of new ways of providing required services and solving existing problems. With its new organizing principles and methods, a clean energy system could represent a paradigm shift, but only if innovative approaches to policy and regulation complement technological advance.

Contemporary conventional wisdom, or generally accepted belief, is that the global economy relies mostly on fossil fuels and nuclear power, with renewables making a small but growing contribution in sectors such as electric power, transportation, construction, and manufacturing. This is true. Given the aforementioned national and global energy forecasts from the U.S. Energy Information Administration and the International Energy Agency, respectively, it is difficult to argue that a paradigm shift is currently underway. In fact, the general trends that now exist should extend into the immediate future. But eventually, the price differentials between renewables, fossil fuels, and nuclear will cease to exist. The growing alarm about the effects of climatic changes will place greater value on decarbonization. In particular, clean energy, energy efficiency, and conservation will eventually rule the day. When this happens, a paradigm shift will occur.

SUMMARY

Whether or not the future ushers in a new energy paradigm, an appropriate price for carbon must accompany the process of energy transition. Prices make markets work. But a price for carbon, while necessary, is not sufficient to stimulate energy innovation and create a clean energy transformation. The other steps discussed in this chapter for energy transformation—take immediate action, decarbonize the electricity sector, reshape investment and accelerate innovations, mobilize non-climate goals, and strengthen the resilience of the energy system—will help market participants make informed decisions. But the way forward should focus on reducing barriers to energy innovation in the early stages of adoption. Developing clean energy sectors to scale; integrating them into overall energy systems; and adapting energy technology to consumer behavior—these activities are complex and slow. They are also expensive. They will require billions of dollars over multiple generations. Not only will public funds have to complement private investment, but examples of clean energy transitions will have to compete with fossil fuel based energy networks. The latter possess strong political relationships and powerful constituencies.

Energy transition will require upfront investments in the electricity grid, renewable technology, and policy recalibration. This resource allocation increases per unit cost of clean energy, which must compete with the incumbent fossil fuel networks. A modest carbon tax will not eliminate the gap. The 2018 co-Nobel Prize winner in economics, William Nordhaus, argues that uncertainties with respect to the impacts of climate change should dictate a stronger carbon tax policy. This policy is also necessary to help usher in a clean energy transition.

As learning occurs, the unit price of energy output will decrease. Over time, the gap between the unit price of the provision of clean energy and the unit price of dirty energy may be negligible. It is already the case that, in many parts of the world, including North America, the average cost of energy per kilowatt hour for wind and solar is competitive with gas and less than coal. For wind and solar, this is due to economies of scale, not improvements in performance. But the reality is that, on a global scale, renewables do not produce a significant amount of the world's electricity, excluding hydropower. A carbon price would make clean energy even more attractive. It would accelerate the movement to clean energy transformation. Overall, there is reason for optimism with respect to policy applications, business models, innovative energy technologies, human behavior, and methods of network organizations between now and the middle of the century that will both fight climate change and lead to clean energy transformation.

CONCEPTS

Commercialization gap
Energy transformation
Energy transition
Paradigm
Paradigm shift
Path dependency
Resilience

QUESTIONS

1. What technologies and policies should be at the center of energy transformation?
2. Do specific examples of fast energy transition in areas such as air conditioning lend credibility to the argument for the viability of overall energy system transformation?
3. Is it possible for the world to rely on renewable energy sources for electricity generation?
4. What technological solutions are available to solve the problem that solar and wind energy are not always available when they are needed?
5. What policies may create incentive for energy transformation while providing meaningful regulation for the electricity market?
6. Will energy transition drive innovation or vice versa?
7. The transition to renewables will cost billions of dollars over multiple generations. How will countries finance the process? How do the costs of transition compare to the benefits?
8. Identify the important characteristics of the current energy paradigm. What would a new energy paradigm entail? What factors would create a paradigm shift?

Bibliography

Aden, Nathaniel. 2016. *The Roads to Decoupling: 21 Countries Are Reducing Carbon Emissions While Growing GDP*. World Resources Institute, April 5. https://www.wri.org/blog/2016/04/roads-decoupling-21-countries-are-reducing-carbon-emissions-while-growing-gdp.

Aldy, Joseph, and Robert N. Stavins. 2012. "Using the Market to Address Climate Change: Insights from Theory & Experience." *Daedalus* 141, no. 2 (Spring): 45–60.

Alizamir, Saed, Francis de Vericourt, and Peng Sun. 2016. "Efficient Feed-In-Tariffs Policies for Renewable Energy Technologies." *Operations Research* 64, no. 1 (May): 52–66.

Allcott, Hunt. 2011. "Social Norms and Energy Conservation." *Journal of Public Economics* 95, nos. 9–10: 1082–1095.

Allcott, Hunt, and Michael Greenstone. 2012. "Is There an Energy Efficiency Gap?" *Journal of Economic Perspectives* 26, no. 1 (Winter): 3–28.

Allcott, Hunt, and T. Rogers. 2014. "The Short-Run and Long-Run Effects of Behavioral Interventions: Experimental Evidence from Energy Conservation." *American Economic Review* 104, no. 10 (October): 3003–3037.

Andor, Mark A., and Katja M. Fels. 2018. "Behavioral Economics and Energy Conservation—A Systematic Review of Non-price Interventions and Their Causal Effects." *Ecological Economics* 148: 178–210.

Arent, Douglas, Channing Arndt, Mackay Miller, Finn Tarp, and Owen Zinaman. 2017. "Introduction and Synthesis." In *The Political Economy of Clean Energy Transitions*, edited by Douglas Arent, 3–15. Oxford: Oxford University Press.

Asensio, Omar L., and Magali A. Delmas. 2016. "The Dynamics of Behavior Change: Evidence from Energy Conservation." *Journal of Economic Behavior & Organization* 126: 196–212.

Avery, John S. 2007. *Energy, Resources, and the Long-Term Future*. London: World Scientific.

Banks, Ferdinand E. 2007. *The Political Economy of World Energy*. London: World Scientific.

Bardi, Ugo. 2013. "The Grand Challenge of the Energy Transition." *Frontiers in Energy Research* 1, no. 2 (August): 1–4.

Baumeister, Christiane, and Lutz Kilian. 2016. "Forty Years of Oil Price Fluctuations: Why the Price of Oil May Still Surprise Us." *Journal of Economic Perspectives* 30, no. 1 (Winter): 139–160.

Bernstein, Mark, and Myles Collins. 2013. "Saving Energy Through Better Information: A New Energy Paradigm?" *Contemporary Economic Policy* 32, no. 1 (November): 219–229.

Biello, David. 2010. "The Start-Up Pains of a Smarter Electricity Grid." *Scientific American*, May 10, 2010. http://www.scientificamerican.com/article/start-up-pains-of-smart-grid/.

Black, Brian C. 2014. *Crude Reality: Petroleum in World History*. Lanham, MD: Rowman & Littlefield.

Blackwill, Robert D., and Meghan L. O'Sullivan. 2014. "America's Energy Edge: The Geopolitical Consequences of the Shale Revolution." *Foreign Affairs* 93, no. 2 (March/April): 102–114.

Bortolini, Marco, Maurizio Faccio, Mauro Gamberi, and Francesco Pilati. 2016. "Multi-Objective Design of Multi-Modal Fresh Food Distribution Networks." *International Journal of Logistics Systems and Management* 24, no. 2: 155–177.

Bradshaw, M. 2009. "The Geopolitics of Global Energy Security." *Geography Compass* 3, no. 5: 1920–1937.

Broder, John M. 2010. "Cap-and-Trade Loses Its Standing as Energy Policy of Choice." *New York Times*, March 25, 2010. https://www.nytimes.com/2010/03/26/science/earth/26climate.html.

Brown, Marilyn A., and Benjamin K. Sovacool. 2010. "Competing Dimensions of Energy Security: An International Perspective." *Annual Review of Environment and Resources* 35: 77–108.

Canning, Patrick, Ainsley Charles, Sonya Huang, Karen R. Polenske, and Arnold Waters. 2010. *Energy Use in the U.S. Food System*. Economic Research Report Number 94. Washington, DC: USDA.

Cardwell, Diane, and Clifford Krauss. 2017. "A Big Test for Big Batteries." *New York Times*, January 15, 2017.

Castillo, Luciano, Walter Gutierrez, and Jay Gore. 2018. "Renewable Energy Saves Water and Creates Jobs." *Scientific American*, August 7, 2018. https://www.scientificamerican.com/article/renewable-energy-saves-water-and-creates-jobs/.

Chen, I-Ching, Jane K. Hill, Ralf Ohlemuller, David B. Roy, and Chris D. Thomas. 2011. "Rapid Range Shifts of Species Associated with High Levels of Climate Warming." *Science* 333: 19.

Cherp, Aleh, and Jessica Jewell. 2014. "The Concept of Energy Security: Beyond the Four A's." *Energy Policy* 75: 415–421.

Clemente, Jude. 2015. "The Amazing Rise in U.S. Proven Natural Gas Reserves and Use." *Forbes*, June 2, 2015. https://www.forbes.com/sites/judeclemente/2015/06/02/the-amazing-rise-in-u-s-proven-natural-gas-reserves-and-use/#7ef2dadc2e16.

Clo, Alberto. 2000. *Oil Economics and Policy*. Boston: Kluwer Academic Publishers.

Coase, R. 1960. "The Problem of Social Cost." *The Journal of Law and Economics* 3 (October): 1–44.

Collier, Paul, and Anthony J. Venables. 2014. "Closing Coal: Economic and Moral Incentives." *Oxford Review of Economic Policy* 30, no. 3 (October): 492–512.

Cooper, Mark. 2014. "Small Modular Reactors and the Future of Nuclear Power in the United States." *Energy Research & Social Science* 3 (September): 161–177.

Covert, Thomas, Michael Greenstone, and Christopher R. Knittel. 2016. "Will We Ever Stop Using Fossil Fuels?" *Journal of Economic Perspectives* 30, no. 1 (Winter): 1–23.

Curry, Andrew. 2017. "What Lies Beneath." *The Atlantic*, October.

Cusick, Daniel. 2017. "Battery Storage Poised to Expand Rapidly." *Scientific American*, January 1, 2017. https://www.scientificamerican.com/article/battery-storage-poised-to-expand-rapidly/.

Dai, Shifeng, and Robert B. Finkelman. 2018. "Coal as a Promising Source of Critical Elements: Progress and Future Prospects." *International Journal of Coal Geology* 186 (February): 155–164.

Davis, Lucas W. 2012. "Prospects for Nuclear Power." *Journal of Economic Perspectives* 26, no. 1 (Winter): 49–66.

Delbeke, J., G. Klaassen, T. van Lerland, and P. Zapfel. 2010. "The Role of Environmental Economics in Recent Policy Making at the European Commission." *Review of Environmental Economics and Policy* 4, no. 1 (November): 24–43.

Dennis, Brady, and Chris Mooney. 2018. "'We are in Trouble.' Global Carbon Emissions Reached a Record High in 2018." *The Washington Post*, December 5, 2018.

Dennis, Keith. 2015. "Environmentally Beneficial Electrification: Electricity as the End-Use Option." *The Electricity Journal* 28, no. 9 (November): 100–112.

Dennis, Keith, Ken Colburn, and Jim Lazar. 2016. "Environmentally Beneficial Electrification: The Dawn of 'Emissions Efficiency.'" *The Electricity Journal* 29, no. 6: 52–58.

Deutch, John, and Ernest Moniz. 2003. *The Future of Nuclear Power: An Interdisciplinary MIT Study*. Cambridge, MA: Massachusetts Institute of Technology.

Easterbrook, Gregg. 2007. "Global Warming: Who Loses—and Who Wins?" *The Atlantic*, April. https://www.theatlantic.com/magazine/toc/2007/04/.

Eaton. 2015. *Blackout Tracker: United States Annual Report*. http://powerquality.eaton.com/blackouttracker/default.asp.

Edenhofer, Ottmar, Jan C. Steckel, Michael Jakob, and Christoph Bertram. 2018. "Reports of Coal's Terminal Decline May be Exaggerated." *Environmental Research Letters* 13, no. 2 (February): 1–9.

El-Ashry, Mohamed T. 2012. "National Policies to Promote Renewable Energy." *Daedalus* 141, no. 2 (Spring): 105–110.

Evans, Robert L. 2008. "Energy Conversion Chain Analysis of Sustainable Energy Systems: A Transportation Case Study." *Bulletin of Science, Technology & Society* 28, no. 2 (April): 128–137.

Evans, Robert L. 2007. *Fueling Our Future: An Introduction to Sustainable Energy*. Cambridge: Cambridge University Press.

Fan, Maureen. 2008. "China Keeps Car Rules Imposed for Olympics." *The Washington Post*, October 2, 2008. http://www.washingtonpost.com/wpdyn/content/article/2008/10/01/AR2008100102874.html.

Fell, Michael J. 2017. "Energy Services: A Conceptual Review." *Energy Research & Social Science* 27 (May): 129–140.

Ford, Michael J., Ahmed Abdulla, M. Granger Morgan, and David G. Victor. 2017. "Expert Assessments of the State of U.S. Advanced Fission Innovation." *Energy Policy* 108: 194–200.

Fowlie, Meredith, Michael Greenstone, and Catherine Wolfram. 2018. "Do Energy Efficiency Investments Deliver? Evidence from the Weatherization Assistance Program." *The Quarterly Journal of Economics* 133, no. 3 (August): 1597–1644.

Frederiks, Elisha, Karen Stenner, and Elizabeth V. Hobman. 2015. "Household Energy Use: Applying Behavioral Economics to Understand Consumer Decision-Making and Behavior." *Renewable and Sustainable Energy Reviews* 41 (January): 1385–1394.

Friedmann, S. Julio. 2011. "Carbon Capture and Green Technology." *Foreign Affairs*, September 11, 2011.

Gerarden, Todd, Richard G. Newell, and Robert N. Stavins. 2015. "Deconstructing the Energy-Efficiency Gap: Conceptual Frameworks and Evidence." *American Economic Review* 105, no. 5 (May): 183–186.

Gillingham, Kenneth, Amelia Keyes, and Karen Palmer. 2018. "Advances in Evaluating Energy Efficient Policies and Programs." *Annual Review of Resource Economics* 10 (October): 511–532.

Gillingham, Kenneth, Richard G. Newell, and Karen Palmer. 2009. "Energy Efficiency Economics and Policy." *Annual Review of Resource Economics* 1 (June): 597–620.

Goldberg, Stephen M., and Robert Rosner. 2011. *Nuclear Reactors: Generation to Generation*. Cambridge, MA: American Academy of Arts and Sciences.

Goldstone, Jack A. 2010. "The New Population Bomb: The Four Megatrends That Will Change the World." *Foreign Affairs* 89, no. 1 (January/February): 31–43.

Goodstein, David, and Michael Intriligator. 2012. *Climate Change and the Energy Problem: Physical Science and Economics Perspective*. Singapore: World Scientific Publishing Company.

Goulder, Lawrence H., and Ian Parry. 2008. "Instrument Choice in Environmental Policy." *Review of Environmental Economics and Policy* 2, no. 2 (July): 152–174.

Gunders, Dana. 2012. *Wasted: How America is Losing Up to 40 Percent of Its Food from Farm to Fork to Landfill*. Washington, DC: Natural Resources Defense Council.

Hamilton, James. 2009. "Causes and Consequences of the Oil Shock of 2007–2008." *Brookings Papers on Economic Activity* 1: 215–261.

Hansen, J., M. Sato, P. Khaecha, G. Russell, D. Lea, and M. Siddall. 2007. "Climate Change and Trace Gases." *Philosophical Transactions of The Royal Society A* 365: 1925–1954.

Haszeldine, R. Stuart. 2009. "Carbon Capture and Storage: How Green Can Black Be?" *Science* 325, no. 5948 (September): 1647–1652.

Hefner III, Robert A. 2014. "The United States of Gas: Why the Shale Revolution Could Have Happened Only in America." *Foreign Affairs* 93, no. 3 (May/June): 9–14.

Helm, Dieter. 2007. "The New Energy Paradigm." In *The New Energy Paradigm*, edited by Dieter Helm, 9–35. New York: Oxford University Press.

Herring, Horace. 2010. *Nuclear or Not? Does Nuclear Power Have a Place in a Sustainable Energy Future?* Basingstoke, UK: Palgrave Macmillan.

Howarth, Robert H., Renee Santoro, and Anthony Ingraffea. 2011. "Methane and the Greenhouse-Gas Footprint of Natural Gas from Shale Formations." *Climatic Change* 106 (June): 679–690.

Hubbert, M. King. 1956. "Nuclear Energy and the Fossil Fuels." Presentation to the American Petroleum Institute, Shell Development Company.

Hubbert, M. King. 1949. "Energy from Fossil Fuels." *Science* 109, no. 2823 (February): 103–109.

Ibrahim, H., A. Ilinca, and J. Perron. 2008. "Energy Storage Systems—Characteristics and Comparisons." *Renewable and Sustainable Energy Reviews* 12: 1221–1250.

Ingraham, Christopher. 2017. "The Entire Coal Industry Employs Fewer People than Arby's." *Washington Post*, March 31, 2017.

Intergovernmental Panel on Climate Change (IPCC). 2018. *Climate Change 2018.* United Nations/IPCC.

IPCC. 2014a. *Climate Change 2014: Impacts, Adaptation, and Vulnerability*. Working Group II Report. United Nations/IPCC.

IPCC. 2014b. *Climate Change 2014: Mitigation of Climate Change*. Working Group III Report. United Nations/IPCC.

IPCC. 2013. *Climate Change 2013: The Physical Science Basis*. Working Group I Report. United Nations/IPCC.

IPCC. 2007. *The Physical Science Basis*. Working Group I Report. United Nations/IPCC.

International Energy Agency (IEA). 2018. *Energy Efficiency 2018: Analysis and Outlooks to 2040*. Paris: OECD/IEA.

IEA. 2017a. *Key World Energy Statistics*. Paris: OECD/IEA.

IEA. 2017b. *World Energy Outlook 2017*. Paris: OECD/IEA.

IEA. 2016a. *Decoupling of Global Emissions and Economic Growth Confirmed.* Paris: OECD/IEA.

IEA. 2016b. *World Energy Outlook*. Paris: OECD/IEA.

IEA. 2015. *World Energy Outlook Special Report 2015: Energy and Climate Change.* Paris: OECD/IEA.

IEA. 2014a. *Capturing the Multiple Benefits of Energy Efficiency*. Paris: OECD/IEA.

IEA. 2014b. *The Way Forward: Five Key Actions to Achieve a Low-Carbon Energy Sector*. Paris: OECD/IEA.

IEA. 2013. *Medium-Term Oil Market Report*. Paris: OECD/IEA.

Jacobson, Mark Z. 2009. "Review of Solutions to Global Warming, Air Pollution, and Energy Security." *Energy and Environmental Science* 2: 148–173.

Jacobson, Mark Z. and Mark A. Delucchi. 2009. "A Plan to Power 100 Percent of the Planet with Renewables." *Scientific American*, November 16, 2009. https://www.scientificamerican.com/article/a-path-to-sustainable-energy-by-2030/.

Jaffe, Amy M. 2011. "A Reality Check on Renewables." *New York Times*, November 6, 2011.

Jaffe, Adam B., Richard G. Newell, and Robert N. Stavins. 2004. "Economics of Energy Efficiency." In *Encyclopedia of Energy*, Vol. 2, edited by Cutler J. Cleveland, 79–90. New York: Elsevier Inc.

Jaramillo, Paulina, W. Michael Griffin, and H. Scott Matthews. 2007. "Comparative Life-Cycle Air Emissions of Coal, Domestic Natural Gas, LNG, and SNG for Electricity Generation." *Environmental Science and Technology* 41, no. 17: 6290–6296.

Joskow, Paul L. 2013. "Natural Gas: From Shortages to Abundance in the United States." *American Economic Review: Papers and Proceedings* 103, no. 3 (May): 338–343.

Kallis, Giorgos, and Jalel Sager. 2017. "Oil and the Economy: A Systematic Review of the Literature for Ecological Economists." *Ecological Economics* 131: 561–571.

Kern, F., P. Kivimaa, and M. Martiskainen. 2017. "Policy Packaging or Policy Patching? The Development of Complex Energy Efficiency Policy Mixes." *Energy Research & Social Science* 23 (January): 11–25.

Kerr, Richard A. 2011. "Peak Oil Production May Already Be Here." *Science* 331 (March): 1510–1511.

Kerr, Richard A. 2010. "Natural Gas From Shale Bursts Onto the Scene." *Science* 328 (June): 1624–1626.

Kibert, Charles J. 2013. *Sustainable Construction: Green Building Design and Delivery*, 3rd Edition. Hoboken: John Wiley & Sons, Inc.

Kilian, Lutz. 2008. "The Economic Effects of Energy Price Shocks." *Journal of Economic Literature* 46, no. 4 (December): 871–909.

Kruger, Joseph. 2016. "Responding to the Clean Power Plan and the Utility of the Future: Recommendation for States." *Resources* 192: 20–26.

Krupnick, Alan, Daniel Shawhan, and Kristin Hayes. 2016. "Harmonizing North American Electricity Policy and Planning: An Action Agenda." *Resources* 192: 35–39.

Krupp, Fred. 2014. "Don't Just Drill, Baby—Drill Carefully: How to Make Fracking Safer for the Environment." *Foreign Affairs* 93, no. 3 (May/June): 15–20.

Kucharski, Jeffrey, and Hironobu Unesaki. 2015. "A Policy-Oriented Approach to Energy Security." *Procedia Environmental Sciences* 28: 27–36.

Kuhn, Thomas. 1962. *The Structure of Scientific Revolutions*. Chicago: University of Chicago Press.

Lappé, Anna. 2010. *Diet for a Hot Planet*. New York: Bloomsbury.

Lasky, Julie. 2011. "The Architect Jeanne Gang on Winning a MacArthur Fellowship." *New York Times*, September 28, 2011.

Leipprand, Anna, and Christian Flachsland. 2018. "Regime Destabilization in Energy Transitions: The German Debate on the Future of Coal." *Energy Research & Social Science* 40: 190–204.

Lester, Richard K. 2016. "A Roadmap for U.S. Nuclear Energy Innovation." *Issues in Science and Technology* 32, no. 2 (Winter): 45–54.

Lester, Richard K., and David M. Hart. 2012. *Unlocking Energy Innovation: How America Can Build A Low-Cost, Low-Carbon Energy System*. Cambridge, MA: The MIT Press.

Lovering, Jessica R., Arthur Yip, and Ted Nordhaus. 2016. "Historical Construction Costs of Global Nuclear Power Reactors." *Energy Policy* 91 (April): 371–382.

Macauley, Molly, and Daniel F. Morris. 2011. "Climate Change in the United States: Expected Environmental Impacts and Necessary Federal Action." *Resources* 178 (Summer): 20–26.

Malthus, Thomas. 1798. *An Essay on the Principle of Population*. London: J. Johnson.

Massachusetts Institute of Technology (MIT). 2015. *The Future of Solar Energy: An Interdisciplinary MIT Study*. Cambridge, MA: Energy Initiative of the Massachusetts Institute of Technology.

Massey, Nathanael. 2014. "Is Energy Efficiency Finally Reducing the Use of Electricity?" *Scientific American*, February 26, 2014. https://www.scientificamerican.com/article/is-energy-efficiency-finally-reducing-the-use-of-electricity/.

Matisoff, Daniel C., Douglas S. Noonan, and Anna M. Mazzolini. 2014. "Performance of Marketing Benefits? The Case of LEED Certification." *Environmental Science & Technology* 48, no. 3 (January): 2001–2007.

McKinsey & Company. 2009. *Unlocking Energy Efficiency in the U.S. Economy*. Technical Report, McKinsey Global Energy and Materials.

Miller, Nicholas. 2017. "Why Nuclear Energy Programs Rarely Lead to Proliferation." *International Security* 42, no. 2: 40–77.

Minkel, J. R. 2008. "The 2003 Northeast Blackout—Five Years Later." *Scientific American*, August 13, 2008. http://www.scientificamerican.com/article/2003-blackout-five-years-later/.

MIT. 2011. *The Future of the Electric Grid: An Interdisciplinary MIT Study*. Cambridge, MA: Energy Initiative of the Massachusetts Institute of Technology.

Monteiro, C., J. Moubarac, G. Cannon, S. Ng, and B. Popkin. 2013. "Ultra-Processed Products are Becoming Dominant in the Global Food System." *Obesity Reviews* 14, no. S2 (November): 21–28.

Montgomery, Scott L. 2010. *The Powers that Be*. Chicago: University of Chicago Press.

Narang, Vipin. 2017. "Strategies of Nuclear Proliferation." *International Security* 41, no. 3: 110–150.

Ng, Pin T., and Xiaobing Zhao. 2011. "No Matter How it is Measured, Income Declines with Global Warming." *Ecological Economics* 70, no. 5: 963–970.

Nordhaus, William. 2019. "Climate Change: The Ultimate Challenge for Economics." *American Economic Review* 109, no. 6 (June): 1991–2014.

Nordhaus, William. 2018. "Projections and Uncertainties about Climate Change in an Era of Minimal Climate Policies." *American Economic Journal: Economic Policy* 10, no. 3 (August): 333–360.

Nordhaus, William. 2017. "Revisiting the Social Cost of Carbon." *PNAS* 114, no. 7 (January): 1518–1523.

Nordhaus, William. 2013. *The Climate Casino*. New Haven: Yale University Press.

O'Sullivan, Meghan. 2013. "The Entanglement of Energy, Grand Strategy, and International Security." In *The Handbook of Global Energy Policy*, edited by Andreas Goldthau, 30–47. New York: Wiley-Blackwell.

Pacala, Stephen, and Robert Socolow. 2004. "Stabilization Wedges: Solving the Climate Problem for the Next 50 Years with Current Technologies." *Science* 305: 968–972.

Petit, Vincent. 2017. *The Energy Transition: An Overview of the True Challenge of the 21st Century*. New York: Springer International Publishing.

Pigou, Arthur C. 1920. *The Economics of Welfare*. London: Macmillan.

Poumanyvong, Phetkeo, and Shinji Kaneko. 2010. "Does Urbanization Lead to Less Energy Use and Lower CO_2 Emissions? A Cross-Country Analysis." *Ecological Economics* 70, no. 2 (December): 434–444.

Ramana, M. V. 2016. "Second Life or Half-Life? The Contested Future of Nuclear Power and Its Potential Role in a Sustainable Energy Transition." In *The Palgrave Handbook of the International Political Economy of Energy*, edited by Thijs Van de Graaf, Benjamin K. Sovacool, Arunabha Ghosh, Florian Kern, and Michael T. Klare, 363–396. London: Palgrave Macmillan.

Resources for the Future (RFF) and the National Energy Policy Institute (NEPI). 2010. *Toward a New National Energy Policy: Assessing the Options*. Washington, DC: Resources for the Future.

Rios-Marcado, Roger Z., and Conrado Borraz-Sanchez. 2015. "Optimization Problems in Natural Gas Transportation Systems: A State-of-the-art Review." *Applied Energy* 147, no. 1: 536–555.

Sadorsky, Perry. 2013. "Do Urbanization and Industrialization Affect Energy Intensity in Developing Countries?" *Energy Economics* 37: 52–59.

Simon, Christopher A. 2007. *Alternative Energy: Political, Economic, and Social Feasibility*. Lanham: Rowman & Littlefield Publishers, Inc.

Socolow, Robert, and Alexander Glaser. 2009. "Balancing Risks: Nuclear Energy and Climate Change." *Daedalus* 138, no. 4: 31–44.

Sorrell, Steve. 2015. "Reducing Energy Demand: A Review of Issues, Challenges and Approaches." *Renewable and Sustainable Energy Reviews* 47 (July): 74–82.

Sovacool, Benjamin. 2017. "The History and Politics of Energy Transitions: Comparing Contested Views and Finding Common Ground." In *The Political Economy of Clean Energy Transitions*, edited by Douglas Arent, 16–38. Oxford: Oxford University Press.

Sovacool, Benjamin. 2016. "How Long Will It Take? Conceptualizing the Temporal Dynamics of Energy Transitions." *Energy Research & Social Science* 13 (March): 202–215.

Sovacool, Benjamin. 2009. "The Importance of Comprehensiveness in Renewable Electricity and Energy-Efficient Policy." *Energy Policy* 37 (April): 1529–1541.

Sovacool, Benjamin, and Harry Saunders. 2014. "Competing Policy Packages and the Complexity of Energy Security." *Energy* 67: 641–651.

Sovacool, Benjamin, and Gotz Walter. 2018. "Major Hydropower States, Sustainable Development, and Energy Security: Insights from a Preliminary Cross-Comparative Assessment." *Energy* 142, no. 1: 1074–1082.

Sovacool, Benjamin, and Charmaine Watts. 2009. "Going Completely Renewable: Is It Possible (Let Alone Desirable)?" *The Electricity Journal* 22, no. 4 (May): 95–111.

Stager, Curt. 2015. "Tales of a Warmer Planet." *New York Times*, November 29, 2015. https://www.nytimes.com/2015/11/29/opinion/sunday/tales-of-a-warmer-planet.html.

Stavins, Robert. 2008. "A Meaningful U.S. Cap-and-Trade System to Address Climate Change." *Harvard Environmental Law Review* 32: 293–371.

Steg, Linda. 2008. "Promoting Household Energy Conservation." *Energy Policy* 36, no. 12 (December): 4449–4453.

Stern, Nicholas. 2008. "The Economics of Climate Change." *American Economic Review* 98, no. 2 (May): 1–37.

Stern, Nicholas. 2007. *The Economics of Climate Change: The Stern Review*. Cambridge University Press.

Sternberg, Andre, and Andre Bardow. 2015. "Power-to-What? Environmental Assessment of Energy Storage Systems." *Energy & Environmental Science* 8: 389–400.

Stronberg, Joel B. 2016. "Natural Gas: Bridge or Barrier to a Clean Energy Future?" *Renewable Energy World*, June 24, 2016. https://www.renewableenergyworld.com/articles/2016/06/natural-gas-bridge-or-barrier-to-a-clean-energy-future.html.

Swanson, Sandra A. 2010. "Securing the Smart Grid." *Scientific American*, May 13, 2010. http://www.scientificamerican.com/article/securing-the-smart-grid/.

Taylor, James. 2017. "Natural Gas is the Future of Energy, and it's not Even Close." *Forbes*, January 10, 2017. https://www.forbes.com/sites/jamestaylor/2017/01/10/natural-gas-is-the-future-of-energy-and-its-not-even-close/#625ae50364ae.

The World Bank. 2014. "Database World Development Indicators: Electricity Production, Sources, and Access." http://wdi.worldbank.org/table/3.7.

Tietenberg, Tom. 2006. *Emissions Trading: Principles and Practice*, 2nd Edition. Washington, DC: RFF Press.

Tietenberg, Tom, and Lynne Lewis. 2018. *Environmental and Natural Resource Economics*, 11th Edition. New York: Pearson.

Tomczak, Jay. 2006. *Implications of Fossil Fuel Dependence for the Food System.* Michigan State University, Tompkins Country Relocalization Project, California: Post Carbon Institute.

United Nations Environmental Program. 2016. *Global Trends in Renewable Energy Investment 2016*. New York: United Nations.

United Nations Population Division. 2017. *World Population Prospects: The 2017 Revision*. New York: United Nations.

U.S. Department of Energy (DOE). 2015a. *Quadrennial Technology Review: Energy Transmission, Storage, and Distribution Infrastructure*. Washington, DC: DOE.

U.S. DOE. 2015b. *Quadrennial Technology Review: An Assessment of Energy Technologies and Research Opportunities*. Washington, DC: DOE.

U.S. Energy Information Administration (EIA). 2018a. *Electric Power Annual.* Washington, DC: Department of Energy.

U.S. EIA. 2018b. *Annual Energy Outlook*. Washington, DC: Department of Energy.

U.S. EIA. 2018c. *Monthly Energy Review, April*. Washington, DC: Department of Energy.

U.S. EIA. 2017. *Annual Energy Outlook 2017: With Projections to 2040*. Washington, DC: Department of Energy.

U.S. EIA. 2016. *Capital Cost Estimates for Utility Scale Electricity Generating Plants*. Washington, DC: Department of Energy.

U.S. EIA. 2015. *Annual Energy Outlook*. Washington, DC: Department of Energy.

U.S. EIA. 2013. *Annual Energy Outlook*. Washington, DC: Department of Energy.

U.S. Global Change Research Program. 2017a. *Climate Science Special Report: Fourth National Climate Assessment, Volume I*. Washington, DC: U.S. Global Change Research Program.

U.S. Global Change Research Program. 2017b. *Climate Science Special Report: Fourth National Climate Assessment, Volume II: Impacts, Risks, and Adaptation in the United States*. Washington, DC: U.S. Global Change Research Program.

Vegel, Benjamin, and Jason C. Quinn. 2017. "Economic Evaluation of Small Modular Nuclear Reactors and the Complications of Regulatory Fee Structure." *Energy Policy* 104 (May): 395–403.

Von Hippel, D., T. Suzuki, J. Williams, T. Savage, and P. Hayes. 2011. "Evaluating the Energy Security Impacts of Energy Policies." In *The Routledge Handbook of Energy Security*, edited by Benjuamin K. Sovacool, 74–95. New York: Routledge.

Wagner, Gernot. 2011. "Going Green but Getting Nowhere." *New York Times*, September 7, 2011. https://www.nytimes.com/2011/09/08/opinion/going-green-but-getting-nowhere.html.

Wallace-Wells, David. 2019. "Time to Panic." *New York Times*, February 17, 2019. https://www.nytimes.com/2019/02/16/opinion/sunday/fear-panic-climate-change-warming.html.

Wang, Qiang, Xi Chen, Awadhesh N. Jha, and Howard Rogers. 2014. "Natural Gas from Shale Formation – The Evolution, Evidences and Challenges of Shale Gas Revolution in United States." *Renewable and Sustainable Energy Reviews* 30 (February): 1–28.

Wang, Yue. 2013. "More People Have Cell Phones Than Toilets, U.N. Study Shows." *Time*, March 25, 2013. http://newsfeed.time.com/2013/03/25/more-people-have-cell-phones-than-toilets-u-n-study-shows/.

Webber, Michael E. 2012. "How to Make the Food System More Energy Efficient." *Scientific American*, January. https://www.scientificamerican.com/article/more-food-less-energy/.

Weeks, Jennifer. 2010. "U.S. Electrical Grid Undergoes Massive Transition to Connect to Renewables." *Scientific American*, April 28, 2010. https://www.scientificamerican.com/article/what-is-the-smart-grid.

Wheatley, Spencer, Benjamin K. Sovacool, and Didier Sornette. 2016. "Reassessing the Safety of Nuclear Power." *Energy Research & Social Science* 15: 96–100.

Wilson, Charlie, Tom Hargreaves, and Richard Hauxwell-Baldwin. 2017. "Benefits and Risks of Smart Home Technologies." *Energy Policy* 103 (April): 72–83.

Winzer, Christian. 2012. "Conceptualizing Energy Security." *Energy Policy* 46: 36–48.

World Energy Council. 2016a. *World Energy Resources: Bioenergy*. London: WEC.

World Energy Council. 2016b. *World Energy Resources: Geothermal.* London: WEC.

World Energy Council. 2016c. *World Energy Resources: Hydropower.* London: WEC.

Yanosek, Kassia. 2012. "Policies for Financing the Energy Transition." *Daedalus* 141, no. 2 (April): 94–104.

Yergin, Daniel. 2012. *The Quest: Energy, Security, and the Remaking of the Modern World.* Revised and Updated. New York: Penguin Press.

Yergin, Daniel. 2006. "Ensuring Energy Security." *Foreign Affairs* 85, no. 2 (March/April): 69–82. http://www.un.org/ga/61/second/daniel_yergin_energysecurity.pdf.

Zarfl, C., A. Lumsdon, J. Berlekamp, L. Tydecks, and K. Tockner. 2015. "A Global Boom in Hydropower Dam Construction." *Aquatic Sciences* 77, no. 1: 161–170.

Zeller, Jr., Tom. 2010. "A Battle in Mining Country Pits Coal Against Wind." *New York Times*, August 14, 2010. https://www.nytimes.com/2010/08/15/business/energy-environment/15coal.html.

Index

About the Author

Thomas R. Sadler, PhD, is professor of economics at Western Illinois University. He teaches courses in energy economics, environmental economics, globalization, and many other areas. His research and writing focus on the economics of energy and the environment, with emphasis on contemporary policy applications. In his free time, he runs, reads, kayaks, hikes, and camps.

www.ingramcontent.com/pod-product-compliance
Ingram Content Group UK Ltd.
Pitfield, Milton Keynes, MK11 3LW, UK
UKHW040233290926
15471UKWH00002B/172